THE BOOK OF ROADS & KINGDOMS

Also by Richard Fidler

Ghost Empire

'A brilliant reconstruction of the saga of power, glory, invasion and decay that is the one-thousand year story of Constantinople. A truly marvellous book.' – Simon Winchester

Saga Land

(co-authored with Kári Gíslason)

'I adored this book – a wondrous compendium of Iceland's best sagas.' – Hannah Kent

The Golden Maze

'The times, the places and the people are vibrant, arresting and breathing … This is the magic and power of this work.'
– Favel Parrett

THE BOOK OF ROADS & KINGDOMS

RICHARD FIDLER

ABC BOOKS

The ABC 'Wave' device is a trademark of the Australian Broadcasting Corporation and is used under licence by HarperCollins*Publishers* Australia.

HarperCollins*Publishers*
Australia • Brazil • Canada • France • Germany • Holland • India
Italy • Japan • Mexico • New Zealand • Poland • Spain • Sweden
Switzerland • United Kingdom • United States of America

HarperCollins acknowledges the Traditional Custodians of the land upon which we live and work, and pays respect to Elders past and present.

First published in Australia in 2022
by HarperCollins*Publishers* Australia Pty Limited
Gadigal Country
Level 13, 201 Elizabeth Street, Sydney NSW 2000
ABN 36 009 913 517
harpercollins.com.au

ISBN 978 0 7333 4259 2 (hardback)
ISBN 978 1 4607 1527 7 (ebook)

Cover design by Mark Campbell, HarperCollins Design Studio
Cover illustration © Yehrin Tong
Author photo by Sally Flegg
Maps by Alex Hotchin
Index by Garry Cousins
Typeset in Minion Pro by Kelli Lonergan
Printed and bound in Australia by McPherson's Printing Group

MIX
Paper | Supporting responsible forestry
FSC® C001695
FSC www.fsc.org

To my father and his wall of history books in the living room.

CONTENTS

TIMELINE

323 B.C.E. Alexander the Great dies in Babylon.

140–87 B.C.E Emperor Wudi constructs the Han Great Wall of China and the Jade Gate near Dunhuang.

226 C.E. Ctesiphon becomes the capital of Sassanid Persia.

330 C.E. Constantine the Great inaugurates Constantinople as the Second Rome.

366 The first of the Thousand Buddha Caves is excavated at Dunhuang.

476 The Western Roman Empire expires with the abdication of Romulus Augustulus in Italy.

541–549 Plague courses through the Eastern Roman and Persian Empires.

c.570 The Prophet MUHAMMAD is born.

602 Persia invades the Roman Empire.

610 Muhammad receives the first of his Quranic revelations in the Cave of Hira.

Heraclius becomes emperor in Constantinople.

618 The Tang Dynasty is founded in China by Li Yuan.

622 The Hijra: Muhammad and his followers migrate to Medina.

Muhammad draws up the constitution of the first Islamic State.

624 Muhammad changes the direction of Muslim prayer from Jerusalem to Mecca.

Muhammad's believers win a stunning victory over the Quraysh at the Battle of Badr.

628 Sassanid ruler Khusrau II is deposed and executed in Ctesiphon.

629 The Syriac translation of *The Alexander Romance* appears in northern Mesopotamia.

The Chinese monk Xuanzang begins a pilgrimage from China to India.

630 Muhammad and his followers enter Mecca.

632 Muhammad dies. **ABU BAKR** becomes the first of the Rashidun caliphs.

Yazdegerd III, the last of the Sassanid rulers, takes the throne.

634 Abu Bakr dies. **UMAR** becomes caliph.

The Arabs are defeated by the Persians at the Battle of the Bridge.

635 Arab forces capture Damascus.

636 The Arabs defeat the Roman Army at the Battle of Yarmouk.

637 Arabs forces defeat the Persians at the Battle of al-Qadisiyya in Iraq, then seize the Sassanid capital Ctesiphon.

638 Patriarch Sophronius surrenders Jerusalem to Caliph Umar.

641 Alexandria surrenders to Arab forces.

Roman Emperor Heraclius dies.

642 The Sassanid Empire collapses.

Alexandria surrenders.

The Romans completely withdraw from Egypt.

644 Umar is assassinated by a slave. **UTHMAN** becomes caliph.

645 Xuanzang returns to the Tang capital, Chang An, with Buddhist scriptures.

651 Caliph Uthman summons a commission to prepare the canonical version of the Quran.

Yazdegerd III is killed in Merv, ending the Sassanid Dynasty.

649–55 The Arab navy wins control of the Eastern Mediterranean at the Battle of the Masts.

656 Uthman is assassinated by mutinous Muslim soldiers. **ALI** becomes caliph.

Muawiya, Governor of Syria, revolts. The First Fitna (Muslim civil war) begins.

661 Ali is assassinated at Kufa, ending the civil war and the era of the Rashidun caliphs. **MUAWIYA** becomes the first Umayyad caliph and moves his capital from Medina to Damascus.

674–78 The First Arab siege of Constantinople. takes place.

'Greek fire' is deployed by the Romans against the Arab fleet.

680 Muawiya dies. **YAZID** becomes the second Umayyad caliph.

The second Muslim civil war begins.

Arab-led forces reach the Atlantic shore of North Africa.

683–92 The Second Arab Civil War erupts. Caliph Yazid puts the holy city of Mecca under siege.

685 After years of chaos, **ABD AL-MALIK** emerges as the caliph.

691 The Dome of the Rock is founded in Jerusalem.

697 Berber queen Kahina dies.

700 Abd al-Malik issues new currency and makes Arabic the official language of the caliphate.

711 Arab raiders invade Spain.

712 Arabs capture Samarkand.

715 The second Arab siege of Constantinople takes place.

The Abbasid conspiracy against the Umayyads begins in Khorasan.

717 The Arab siege of Constantinople ends.

732 The Muslims are defeated in France at the Battle of Poitiers, ending Muslim penetration of Western Europe.

747 Abu Muslim leads the Abbasid insurrection in Khorasan.

749 Marwan II, the last Umayyad caliph, is beheaded. **SAFFAH** becomes the first Abbasid caliph.

751 The Chinese army is defeated by the Muslims at the Battle of Talas.

Paper-making begins to spread from Central Asia into the Muslim world.

754 Saffah dies. **MANSUR** becomes the second Abbasid caliph.

755 Mansur orders the execution of Abu Muslim.

The An Lushan Rebellion breaks out in China.

756 In Spain, Abd al-Rahman I becomes the Emir of Cordoba.

762 BAGHDAD IS FOUNDED.

766 Future caliph Harun al-Rashid is born.

771 Charlemagne becomes King of the Franks.

775 Mansur dies while leading a pilgrimage to Mecca. **MAHDI** becomes caliph.

782 Alcuin of York becomes Master of the Palace School in Aachen.

785 Mahdi dies. **HADI** begins his brief reign as caliph.

786 Hadi dies. **HARUN AL-RASHID** becomes caliph.

787 Irene becomes empress regent in Constantinople.

789 Harun al-Rashid's mother Khayzuran dies.

793 Norse raiders attack a monastery on Lindisfarne Island, off the English coast, signalling the start of the Viking invasions.

794 Construction begins on Charlemagne's palace complex at Aachen.

796 Harun al-Rashid moves his court from Baghdad to Raqqa.

Charlemagne's army seizes the Avar's Ring Fortress in modern-day Hungary.

797 Harun al-Rashid marches against the Romans.

Irene deposes her son and proclaims herself 'emperor' in Constantinople.

Charlemagne sends envoys to Harun al-Rashid.

800 Charlemagne is crowned Holy Roman Emperor in Rome.

802 Harun al-Rashid draws up his succession plans with his sons in Mecca.

Irene is ousted in Constantinople. Nicephorus becomes emperor in her place.

Charlemagne's envoys return to Aachen from Baghdad with the gift of an elephant from Harun al-Rashid.

803 Harun al-Rashid's administrators, the Barmakids, fall from favour.

809 Harun al-Rashid dies. **AMIN** becomes caliph.

809–13 The Fourth Fitna, Muslim civil war, breaks out between Mamun and his brother Amin.

813 Baghdad is besieged and Amin is killed. **MAMUN** becomes caliph.

814 Charlemagne dies.

822 Ziryab the musician, composer, and gourmand, arrives in Cordoba.

828 The Shammasiyah Observatory, the first in the Islamic world, is established in Baghdad.

830s The House of Wisdom is founded in Baghdad.

The Banu Musa brothers measure the circumference of the Earth.

831 Harun al-Rashid's wife Zubaydah dies.

The Arabic emirate of Sicily is established.

833 Mamun dies. **MUTASIM** becomes caliph and brings Turkish slave-soldiers into Baghdad, causing disruption.

835 The Huang Chao Rebellion breaks out in China

836 Mutasim moves with his Turkish troops to a new capital, Samarra.

840 Cordoban diplomat and poet Ghazal arrives in Constantinople.

842 Mutasim dies. **WATHIQ** becomes caliph.

Wathiq orders a guide and interpreter named Sallam to lead an expedition in search of the wall of Gog and Magog.

844 Sallam the Interpreter returns to Baghdad.

Viking raiders are defeated by the Emirate of Cordoba.

845 Ghazal allegedly is sent on a diplomatic mission to 'the King of the Vikings'.

847–48 Wathiq dies from dropsy. **MUTAWAKKIL** becomes caliph.

Mutawakkil commissions the construction of Samarra's Great Mosque and Spiral Minaret.

850 Mutawakkil decrees new restrictions on Christians and Jews, bans theological debate.

851–52 Book 1 of *Accounts of China and India* is compiled by an unknown author.

858–63 China is devastated by severe drought and famine.

861 Mutawakkil is killed in Samarra. **MUNTASIR** becomes caliph, but real power now lies with his Turkish military commanders.

862 Muntasir dies and is replaced by **MUSTAIN**, triggering the 'Anarchy in Samarra'.

865 Supporters of Mustain's brother Mutazz besiege Baghdad.

866 Mustain abdicates in favour of **MUTAZZ**.

868 *The Diamond Sutra*, the world's oldest printed book, is produced in Sichuan Province.

869 Mutazz is deposed and replaced by his cousin **MUHTADI**.

The Zanj Rebellion begins in Basra.

870 Muhtadi is murdered and replaced by his cousin **MUTAMID**.

Ibn Khordadbeh compiles *The Book of Roads and Kingdoms* in Baghdad.

871 Basra is sacked by Zanj rebels.

Arab aristocrat Ibn Wahb boards a ship for China.

878 Huang Chao's bandit army sacks Guangzhou.

The Muslim conquest of Sicily is complete.

883 The Zanj Rebellion is crushed by Mutamid's brother Muwaffaq.

Huang Chao dies in Henan Province.

892 Mutamid dies, allegedly from too much drink and food.

MUTADID takes power.

c. **896** Historian and geographer Masudi is born in Baghdad.

902 Mutadid dies. **MUKTAFI** becomes caliph.

906 The Chinese Tang Dynasty collapses.

908 Muktafi dies. At thirteen, **MUQTADIR** becomes the youngest ever Abbasid caliph.

909 The rival Fatimid Caliphate is established in North Africa.

915 Historian Tabari completes his sweeping world chronicle, *The History of the Prophets and King*, in Baghdad.

917 Roman ambassadors visit Baghdad.

Masudi sails to Africa.

920s Abu Zayd compiles Book 2 of *Accounts of India and China* in Siraf.

921 Muqtadir sends Ibn Fadlan and company on a mission to the Volga.

929 Qarmatian raiders attack Baghdad.

932 Muqtadir is deposed and killed at the Baghdad city gates. **QAHIR** becomes caliph.

934 Qahir is deposed, blinded and imprisoned.

943 Geographer Ibn Hawqal begins his global travels.

946 Mustakfi is deposed. **MUTI** is made puppet caliph.

947 Masudi writes *Meadows of Gold and Mines of Gems.*

956 Masudi dies.

c. **960** According to legend, the Sultanate of Kilwa is founded in East Africa.

968 The Fatimids enter Egypt.

972 Ibn Hawqal visits Sicily.

1029 Polymath Biruni writes *The Book of India.*

1071 The Normans conquer Palermo, Sicily.

1086 Ibn Hawqal writes *Configurations of the Earth.*

1095 Pope Urban II initiates the Crusades against Muslims in the Holy Land.

1099 Jerusalem is captured by the Crusaders.

1154 Geographer Idrisi completes his world map in Sicily.

1171 The great Muslim general Saladin abolishes the Fatimid Caliphate and realigns Egypt's allegiance to the Abbasid Caliphate.

1180 NASIR becomes caliph and attempts a revival of the Abbasid Caliphate, which now occupies only a sliver of land in Iraq.

1184 Andalusian traveller Ibn Jubayr visits Baghdad.

1204 The Venetian navy and the armies of the Fourth Crusade sack Constantinople.

1206 Genghis Khan becomes the ruler of the Mongol Empire.

1211 Mongols conquer Northern China.

1219 The Khwarezmian Shah Muhammad II clashes with Genghis Khan. Mongol armies enter the Muslim lands.

1220–21 Bukhara, Samarkand and Merv fall to the Mongols.

1227 Genghis Khan dies. The Mongol conquests are suspended until a new Great Khan can be elected.

1229 Genghis Khan's son Ogodei is elected Great Khan of the Mongols.

1236 Cordoba falls to the Christian *reconquista* of Spain.

1242 **MUSTASIM**, the last of the Abbasid caliphs, assumes the throne in Baghdad.

1258 Mongols, led by Hulagu Khan, take Baghdad.

Mustasim is trampled to death, bringing the Abbasid Caliphate to an end.

1271 Venetian merchant Marco Polo and his father set out for China.

1302 Amir Khusrau writes 'The Three Princes of Sarandib'.

1375 Philosopher and historian Ibn Khaldun begins work on his *Muqaddimah* while in exile in North Africa.

1453 Constantinople falls to the Ottoman Turks.

1895 Explorer Sven Hedin launches an expedition to find the lost cities of the Taklamakan Desert.

1900 Chinese monk Wang Yuanlu discovers the Library Cave at Dunhuang.

British-Hungarian archaeologist Aurel Stein leads his first expedition into Chinese Turkestan.

The Boxer Rebellion begins in China.

1907 Aurel Stein locates the ruins of the Jade Gate and identifies the Han Great Wall in the Taklamakan Desert. Stein also gleans a trove of ancient documents from the Library Cave.

1924 American archaeologist Langdon Warner removes Buddhist frescoes from the Thousand Buddha Caves.

the
ABBASID CALIPHATE
c. 800 C.E.

Aral Sea
Caspian Sea
Caucasus Mountains
Samarkand
Bukhara
Merv
Baghdad
Kufa
Basra
Zagros Mountains
Hindu Kush
Persian Gulf
Abbasid Caliphate
Medina
Mecca
Arabian Sea
Red Sea
0
500
1000
1500
2000 km
SCALE

INTRODUCTION

THIS IS HOW you become invisible (anyone can do this).

First, you must find a dead cat. The animal must have already died from old age or from some misadventure (you must not slaughter one for this purpose). Carefully remove the dead cat's head and hollow out its eyes. Then take it to a patch of ground in a place where no one is likely to visit.

Dig a hole. The hole should be as deep as the distance from your elbow to your fingertips. Put some dung at the bottom. Then place the cat's head inside the pit, so it faces up to the sky.

Now you must do this: in both eye sockets, place a castor oil seed. Then fill the rest of the hole with dung and pat it down. Sprinkle a handful of fine dirt around the edges in a circle, and then place a round stone on top. No one must see you do this.

Every day, for the next thirty days, you must irrigate the site with blood (this should be procured from a blood-letter; again, no creature should be harmed). If, after forty days, there is a shoot from the soil – good. If not, continue watering it with blood for sixty days. If it sprouts – good. If not, then continue watering it in this manner for seventy days. If not, then for ninety days. Tell no one of this.

After a time, one or two plants may grow. When they begin to bear fruit (and this is crucial), you must not let it fall from the tree to the ground. Instead, carefully harvest some seeds from the pods. This should be done while the moon is waxing, not waning.

Then you must climb up to a high place, like a rooftop, and sit there with the seeds in your lap. To your left, there must be a fourteen-year-old boy on the cusp of puberty. To your right there must be another fourteen-year-old boy who is also not yet a man. Put one of the seeds in your mouth. Then turn to the boy on your left and ask, 'Do you see me?'

If the boy says, 'Yes', then turn to the boy on your right (taking care not to lose your balance on the rooftop) and ask, 'Do you see me?'

If he also says, 'Yes', then throw away the seed and place another in your mouth.

Repeat this process with each of the other seeds, until you find the one seed that, when placed in your mouth, will make both boys answer 'No' (they will likely say this with some astonishment).

Carefully place this special seed inside a signet ring, concealed under a jewel, and wear it on your finger. Then, whenever you wish to avoid someone in the marketplace, put the ring in your mouth and disappear.

Many people have done this and succeeded.

THIS FORMULA FOR INVISIBILITY, written more than a thousand years ago, is attributed to a medieval Arab scholar and traveller named Masudi (more correctly: ʾAbū al-Ḥasan ʿAlī ibn al-Husayn ibn ʿAlī al-Masʿūdī).[1] His dead-cat recipe appears in a tenth-century book on the medical and magical uses of animals. Only a fragment of the book survives. The blending of magic and medicine was common enough in the early medieval world, but I suspect Masudi's cat's-head potion was a kind of practical joke, designed to lure a credulous fool onto a rooftop and have him ask silly questions to a couple of bewildered kids. The clue, I think, is that he insists on an already-dead cat: he wants no animals harmed in the making of this prank.

MASUDI WAS A HISTORIAN and geographer living in Baghdad, in the sunset of a golden age of science and literature. Raised in a city of people obsessed with books, foreign lands, and books *about* foreign lands, Masudi became one of the best-travelled people on the planet. In Persia, he wandered through Zoroastrian fire temples; in Jerusalem, he explored the labyrinthine passages of the Church of the Holy Sepulchre; in India, he observed Hindu ceremonies. Journeying by camel, horse and boat, he travelled to the shores of the Caspian Sea, to Sri Lanka and to Zanzibar on the East African coast. In an age when Europeans hardly ventured beyond the villages they were born in, Masudi traversed the known world, roving 'from one quarter of the earth to the other as the sun makes his revolutions'.[2]

Masudi poured his observations and experiences into some twenty books, most of them lost to us. His greatest surviving work, *Meadows of Gold and Mines of Gems*, is itself a jewel of a book, a compendium of gossipy sketches of the feats and failures of the caliphs and accounts of distant foreign lands. Worldly, good-humoured and interested in everything, Masudi was one of the most brilliant conversationalists of his time. I've returned to him again and again in the writing of this book.

MASUDI LIVED IN THE capital of the largest realm the world had ever known: the empire of the Abbasid Caliphs. At the height of its glory in the eighth and ninth centuries, the Abbasid Caliphate ruled over a dominion extending from North Africa, through Arabia, Mesopotamia, Iran, Central Asia to the Indus Valley, an imperium vaster than that of any Roman emperor. Its great metropolis Baghdad was, for a time, the biggest city in the world, rivalled only by Constantinople and the Chinese capital Chang An in size and majesty.

It was an empire fuelled by travel and trade, with Baghdad at the centre of a nexus of silk roads that branched out to China, India and Europe. Fabrics traded on these routes took their names from the regions in the caliphate where they were manufactured: gauze originated from Gaza, muslin came from Mosul, and heavy-woven Fustian cloth came from Fustat, the predecessor of modern-day Cairo.[3]

Masudi had seen much of that empire and the lands that lay beyond its borders. For him, to range across the surface of the Earth was to act in obedience to the wisdom of his nomadic Bedouin ancestors. 'The Arab wise men would state,' he wrote, 'that houses and a life confined between four walls constitute an impediment to freedom in this world. They remove man's independence and inhibit his noblest ambitions.' The dangers and discomforts of travel were far preferable to being stuck at home. He needed travel, he said, 'to satisfy my thirst for knowledge, and to learn the peculiarities of the various nations and parts of the world, by witnessing them, and the state of foreign countries, by seeing them'.[4]

I BEGAN THIS BOOK at the start of the COVID-19 pandemic, after my travel plans – along with those of just about everyone else on the planet – had to be cancelled. With everyone confined to quarters, and city centres eerily empty, the world seemed both enveloped in crisis and strangely becalmed. Stuck at home for months on end, I began dreaming of the medieval world. I remembered a Norse woman from a thousand years ago named Gudrid the Far-Traveller who joined a Viking voyage to North America, returned to Iceland, and then went on a pilgrimage to Rome, where she told the pope of her adventures.[5]

Gudrid's story sent me searching for more reports of Viking encounters with distant peoples, which led me to Ibn Fadlan: a tenth-century Arab diplomat who travelled all the way from Baghdad to the river-lands of modern-day Russia, where he witnessed a harrowing Viking funeral on the Volga. The educated and urbane Ibn Fadlan was so distressed and horrified by the ordeal of his journey that he suffered something like a mental breakdown. As I read his report of his journey to the Volga, I thought his voice sounded strangely modern; he seemed like a twenty-first-century time-traveller dropped into a medieval wilderness, forced to rely on the hospitality of strangers in a dark, cold land.

Ibn Fadlan's report of his journey to the north, I discovered, was just one of thousands of accounts by Arab and Persian merchants, diplomats and writers of their adventures in medieval China, India,

Africa and Europe. Scholars working in Baghdad's great library, the House of Wisdom, compiled these travellers' reports into massive geographic tomes. One of these works, *The Book of Roads and Kingdoms*, lends its name to the title of this book.

The Muslims living in this golden age were particularly primed for travel by two of the pillars of their faith. The first was the *hajj*, the pilgrimage to the Holy City of Mecca, which elevated the act of travel to a holy rite, intensifying its spiritual and emotional power. The second was *salat*, the practice of praying five times a day towards Mecca, which habituated Muslims to locating their geographical position in relation to the Holy City. As they passed along the roads, rivers and oceans of the world, they took comfort from the daily rituals of their faith, and took courage from a commandment attributed to Muhammad: *seek knowledge, even as far as China*.[6]

The Prophet's injunction was not a cheerful encouragement to trip around the globe, but a heroic call to expose oneself to the wonder and weirdness of the world, in the face of all its dangers and discomforts. 'My adventurous soul finds peace in alien things,' wrote the poet and traveller Abu Dular, 'not in the comfort of the known world.'[7]

The Muslim travellers of the Abbasid Caliphate were also fortified by an intellectual confidence, a profound certainty that they lived in the greatest city in the centre of the world, and that they belonged to an enlightened community that possessed God's truth and accepted God's law. In the golden age of Islam, it was claimed, even the Emperor of China was obliged to admit that the ruler of Baghdad was to be ranked above all other kings, 'for he is at the centre of the world and all other kings are ranged around him'.[8]

The titles of the Abbasid-era geographies reflect their authors' joyful enthusiasm for the outside world: *Meadows of Gold and Mines of Gems*, *The Marvels of India*, *Wonders of the Created World*, *The Book of Curious and Entertaining Information*, *The Book of Gifts and Rarities*. Pieced together, they form a crazy-quilt atlas of a lost world, an era when the fabulous civilisations of the silk roads reached out and touched each other. The stories contained within these books, written in an age before every single inch of the planet was mapped and surveilled by Google Earth, are full of wonder and terror. Theirs was a culture that prized practical geography but also relished storytelling – this is the world that gave us *The Thousand and One Nights* after all – and so their accounts sometimes shift between the precise and plausible, and the bizarre and fantastical. As these merchants, sailors, soldiers and diplomats pushed out towards a distant horizon, they remembered a commandment constantly repeated in the Quran: *go about the Earth and look*.

Occidentalists in the House of Islam

THE TRANSLITERATION OF ARABIC names into English is a clumsy process that almost always fails to capture the poetic nuances of the Arabic language. This is why I have chosen to avoid using the diacritical markings used in academic translations, which are only likely to confuse readers who have no familiarity with the Arabic, Persian and Turkic languages.

Likewise, I have omitted the Arabic definite article 'al-' from personal names, unless the historical figure is best known by a name that includes it. The scholar al-Masudi, therefore, becomes simply Masudi; the founder of Baghdad, al-Mansur, is named as Mansur; whereas the historical caliph made famous by his fictional portrayal in *The Thousand and One Nights* remains Harun al-Rashid.

I have, in some places, relied on translations from European Orientalist scholars from the nineteenth and twentieth centuries.

Today, the work of these academics is considered, in some places, controversial. In the 1970s, the Palestinian-American intellectual Edward Said famously attacked the whole tradition of European 'Orientalism'. Orientalist scholars, he argued, were performing the work of Western imperialism by infantilising the people of the Near and Middle East (a zone better described in any case as Western Asia). Orientalism, it was said, dehumanised its subjects by exaggerating differences and imposing crude stereotypes like those embedded in Kipling's poem, 'The White Man's Burden':

> Take up the White Man's burden
> Send forth the best ye breed
> Go send your sons to exile
> To serve your captives' need
> To wait in heavy harness
> On fluttered folk and wild
> Your new-caught, sullen peoples,
> Half devil and half child.[9]

As an Arab migrant educated in the Western canon, Edward Said was well placed to recognise the gaps in understanding between the West and the East. Like other migrants from the Arab world to America, Said had grown up with the crude racist clichés embedded in twentieth-century pop culture: the sinister snake charmer; the wobbling belly-dancer; the impetuous Saracen warrior waving his scimitar; the emir leering over a harem of kohl-eyed female slaves. These grotesque tropes have proven hard to kill, and have even resurfaced as pastiche in the *Star Wars* films, in the form of a hook-nosed alien merchant in *The Phantom Menace*, and the slug monster Jabba the Hut (Jabar meaning 'mighty one' or 'tyrant' in Arabic) who appears in *The Return of the Jedi* with an enchained Princess Leia in a cartoon harem outfit.

Said's book *Orientalism* provoked angry responses from European academics, who pointed at its flaws and apparent fabrications; they countered that many of the Orientalists under attack were, if anything, chauvinists *against* the West. In any case, it is fascinating, though hardly surprising, to see similar imperialist assumptions surfacing here and there in the medieval Arab and Persian accounts of foreign peoples. While these men accorded the civilisations of China, India and Constantinople some respect, the kingdoms of western Europe were often too backward and poor to attract much interest from them.

I REFER TO 'IRAQ' and 'Iran' frequently in these pages, not as political entities but as geographic zones. Iraq – bordered by the Arabian Desert, the Zagros Mountains and the Persian Gulf – encompasses the rich alluvial lands of ancient Mesopotamia. On the far side of the Zagros Mountains lies the Iranian plateau, the homeland of the Persians, surrounded by mountain ranges, salt deserts, the Gulf and the Caspian Sea.

Throughout the Middle Ages, the great rival of the Muslim Abbasid Caliphate was the Eastern, or Later Roman, Empire, centred around the city of Constantinople – the subject of my earlier book *Ghost Empire*. Today this glittering civilisation is more commonly known as the 'Byzantine' Empire, or more simply 'Byzantium', but these are terms coined by historians long after it had ceased to exist to distinguish it from the ancient Roman Empire of Augustus, Nero and Trajan. By the time of Muhammad's birth in the sixth century, the Later Roman Empire had evolved into a very different creature: its rulers spoke Greek, not Latin; they were Christians, not pagans;

and the city of Rome itself lay outside its borders. For all that, the Romans of Constantinople were more conscious of the continuities with their ancient forebears than the disruptions. As was the case with *Ghost Empire*, I have chosen to call them Romans instead of Byzantines, because that's what they called themselves. The Arabs knew them as the *Rum*.*

FROM THE START, Muslims were encouraged to expose themselves to the wonder and strangeness of the world. The words of the Quran reminded them that 'God has made the earth for you as a carpet spread out, so that you may roam its broad roads'.[10] It was a commandment for the Arabs to transform themselves, to see themselves not as a marginal collection of feuding tribes, but as a people who held the fate of the world in their hands. At the time when Muhammad received the words of the Quran, the inhabitants of the Hijaz in western Arabia had been a desert-bound people, living on the fringes of two colossal and ancient empires. But within the space of a century, they had torn off the better part of one of those empires and completely overrun the other. Their sudden emergence as a great and enduring power constitutes one of the most dramatic upheavals in the history of the world.

* Even today, the tiny remnant community of Greek Orthodox Christians living in Istanbul are known as the *Rum*, or 'Romans'.

BOOK ONE

The Crossroads of the Universe

KHUSRAU II
Sassanid King of Kings

HERACLIUS
Emperor of the Romans

MUHAMMAD
Prophet and founder of Islam

ABU BAKR, UMAR and UTHMAN
First, second and third of the Rashidun ('Rightly Guided') caliphs

ALI
Son-in-law and nephew of the Prophet,
and fourth of the Rashidun caliphs

AISHA
Wife of the Prophet

MUAWIYA
First of the Umayyad caliphs

YAZDEGERD III
Last of the Sassanid rulers

ABD al MALIK
Fifth of the Umayyad caliphs, builder of the Dome of the Rock

SAFFAH ('the Blood-Shedder')
First of the Abbasid caliphs

MANSUR ('the Victorious One')
Second of the Abbasid caliphs and founder of the City of Peace

the PRE-ISLAMIC WORLD c. 600 C.E.

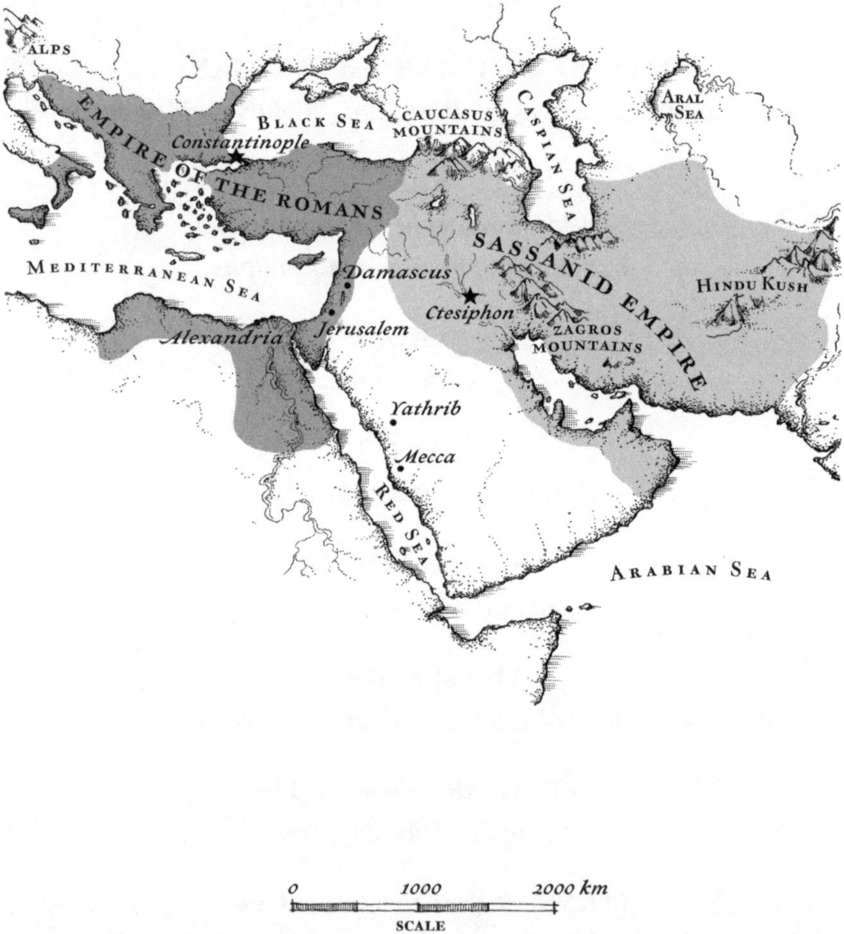

The Two Eyes of the World

THE WATERS OF THE Tigris River originate from a lake in the snow-capped Taurus Mountains of Anatolia. From there they rush through the centre of Iraq until they join the Tigris's cousin, the Euphrates, and then empty into the Persian Gulf. In the lower part of Iraq, both rivers irrigate a fertile floodplain, criss-crossed by a network of ancient canals that were built by the world's earliest civilisations. The empires of Sumer, Babylon and Assyria sprang up in this rich, alluvial zone that became known as Mesopotamia, 'the Land Between the Rivers'.

There are several ancient documents that refer in passing to a settlement on the Tigris named 'Bagdadu' or 'Bagdatha' that existed centuries before the arrival of Islam. The town's name might be of Persian origin, meaning 'Founded by God', or could be drawn from a humbler Aramaic phrase meaning 'Enclosure of Sheep'.[1]

In the seventh century, the little village was dwarfed by the nearby city of Ctesiphon, which lay thirty-five kilometres downstream along the Tigris. Ctesiphon, the royal capital of the Sassanid kings of Persia, was crowded with monuments that awed and intimidated all who approached it. Foreign envoys entered Ctesiphon's royal palace through the colossal Arch of Khusrau, the biggest unsupported brick arch in the world, which still stands today. In the palace's royal reception hall, visitors prostrated themselves before the shahanshah, the king of kings, who sat beneath a crown so weighted with gold and precious stones it had to be suspended by a chain from the ceiling.[2] Three empty chairs were kept in place below the king's throne – one for the Emperor of the Romans, one for the Khan of the Khazars, and one for the Emperor of China – reserved for the day when these rulers came to Ctesiphon as the shahanshah's humble vassals.[3]

The Sassanid elite of Ctesiphon regarded themselves as the rightful rulers of the world. Even so, they lived there like expatriates in a foreign land; their traditional heartlands lay to the east, on the Iranian plateau, where they retreated to escape the stifling heat of the Iraqi summer. While in Ctesiphon, they held themselves at a distance from the rest of the city's inhabitants, dwelling in their own separate quarter, in mansions stocked with storerooms of ice brought down from the mountains as a defence against the constant humidity.[4]

The Arch of Khusrau, Iraq
Photographed by Henri Cartier Bresson, 1950

THE RELIGION OF the Persian elite held it at an even greater distance from the local Iraqis. In 600 C.E., Ctesiphon's population was largely Christian, while the Persian aristocracy held to their Zoroastrian faith. Their religion spoke of a universal struggle between Ohrmazd, the God of Light and Truth, and Ahriman, the God of the Lie. Fire, they believed, was a force of purification that burnt through everything false and unclean. The most sacred centres of Zoroastrianism were three fire temples that sat far away atop remote mountain locations in Iran – the Fire of the Stallion, the Fire of the Farr ('Spirit') and the Fire of Mihr-is-Great – where priests tended the sacred flames that kept darkness and chaos at bay. But within Iraq, Zoroastrianism lacked popular appeal; there were no major fire temples in Ctesiphon, no great buildings of public Zoroastrian worship.

THE PERSIANS' WESTWARD THRUST from Iran into the richer and more populous lands of Mesopotamia had pressed them hard against the eastern borders of their ancient rivals the Romans. The bristling Roman behemoth reacted by invading Mesopotamia repeatedly, seizing Ctesiphon five times, only to relinquish it later. In 116 C.E., the Emperor Trajan had led his legions all the way down to the mouth of the Persian Gulf. Looking out at the merchant ships setting out for India, the emperor, an ageing veteran, said wistfully that if he'd been a younger man, as Alexander the Great had been when he conquered Persia, then he too would have crossed over into India.[5]

In the third century, the mounting problems of imperial overstretch had driven the Roman Empire into a protracted crisis. Between 235 and 285, at least thirty emperors had come and gone in a murderous cycle of assassinations and coups. In 260, a Roman counterattack against a Persian invasion ended in an unthinkable disaster when the Emperor Valerian was captured by the enemy. After his death, the exultant Persian king Shapur I reportedly ordered the emperor's corpse to be flayed; his skin was then stuffed with straw and preserved as a trophy.[6]

The empire had appeared to be doomed until a general named Diocletian had taken the throne in 284 and pulled it out of its death spiral. Realising the empire was too big for any one man to run effectively, Diocletian partitioned it: he would rule the richer eastern provinces from his capital of Nicomedia in Asia Minor, while his loyal friend Maximian would administer the western provinces from Milan. The city of Rome had by then become strategically irrelevant. Roman emperors were too preoccupied fighting off the Persians to the east, and fending off the influx of barbarian tribes across the Danube and the Rhine, to pay much attention to the ancient capital, stranded halfway down the Italian peninsula. The centre of imperial gravity had shifted; the capital was now wherever the emperor and his court happened to be. 'Roman-ness' had long since come to signify an overarching civilisational identity rather than allegiance to a single city; one could be Roman in Africa, Armenia or Britain without ever having set foot in Rome.

To solve the nagging problem of imperial succession, Diocletian appointed a deputy emperor for himself and Maximian, creating a college of four imperial 'brothers' known as the Tetrarchy. But after Diocletian's abdication in 305, the imperial 'brothers' and several of their sons plunged the empire again into a long series of exhausting civil wars that ended in 324 with the triumph of Constantine the Great, who emerged as sole ruler of a reunited empire.

CONSTANTINE IS REMEMBERED today as a world-transformative figure: firstly, for transforming Christianity from a minority eastern cult into the official religion of the Roman Empire; and secondly, for his decision to found a new imperial capital in the East on the site of the ancient Greek city of Byzantium. In 330 C.E., the Emperor inaugurated his new capital with lavish public ceremonies, naming it Nova Roma,

'New Rome', but the city soon became known as Constantinople, the city of Constantine.

The Old Rome had grown up as a cramped hodgepodge of narrow streets and rickety tenements; the New Rome, well-planned and surrounded by water on three sides, swiftly became the most breathtakingly beautiful city in the world.

After Constantine's death in 337, the Roman Empire was again partitioned, but over time, the relentless incursions of the Germanic tribes on the empire's doorstep bashed and battered the western half down to a nub. The Visigoths crossed the Alps and in 410 they sacked the city of Rome. In 429, another Germanic tribe, the Vandals, seized the province of North Africa; in 445 they invaded Italy, and Rome was sacked again; this time even the gilt bronze tiles on the temple of Jupiter were torn away and carried off by the invaders, giving rise to the term 'vandalism'.

Finally, in 476 C.E., the last Western Roman Emperor, a fourteen-year-old boy named Romulus Augustulus, was sent on his way by a barbarian chieftain named Odoacer, who named himself King of Italy. Odoacer offered to rule in the name of Zeno, the Eastern Roman Emperor, but in reality, he ruled his new domain free of interference from distant Constantinople.

The sad abdication of the boy emperor is often said to mark the end of the Roman Empire, but its richer sibling, the Eastern Roman Empire, survived the fall of the West. Ruling from the Great Palace of the Caesars in Constantinople, the Eastern Roman emperors kept their grip on their provinces in Greece, the Balkans, Asia Minor, Syria, Palestine and Egypt. This later Roman Empire would endure for another thousand years, with Constantinople as the world's pre-eminent Christian city for most of that time.

CONSTANTINE'S DECISION TO found his new capital on the threshold of Europe and Asia had brought the epicentre of Roman power much closer to Ctesiphon. The two empires were coming together and growing apart. Roman emperors became Persianised, remote and mysterious, adorning themselves with eye makeup, jewel-encrusted garments and glittering diadems. The successors of Augustus, who had once styled themselves as first among equals, now required all who approached them to prostrate themselves and kiss the hem of the ruler's purple robe. As Christians, Roman emperors could no longer claim to be gods or demi-gods. But they could and did swathe themselves in mystique, and assert their status as God's intimate confidantes, just as their Persian counterparts upheld themselves as defenders of the Zoroastrian faith and the nexus between this world and the next.

Religious opinion was hardening in both empires: just as the Roman world became more thoroughly Christianised, the Sassanid elites were moving towards a more militant form of Zoroastrianism, which stressed constant struggle and renewal through cleansing fire.[7]

RELATIONS BETWEEN THE PERSIANS and Romans had come to operate on a shared assumption that they were the only two powers in the world that really mattered. 'God effected that the whole world should be illumined from the very beginning by two eyes,' a Persian shahanshah had boasted in a letter to Constantinople, 'namely by the most powerful kingdom of the Romans and by the most prudent sceptre of the Persian State.'[8]

From their respective monumental capitals, Constantinople and Ctesiphon, the Two Eyes of the World peered down at the subjugated lands around them. Yet their imperial gazes struggled to penetrate the triangular wedge of land to the south: the Arabian

Peninsula. From the Roman and Persian points of view, Arabia was a hostile and undesirable place: its interior was barely habitable; it had no forests, lakes or grasslands, and no permanent rivers; the peninsula was barricaded on three sides by the sea and had few natural harbours.

Roman geographers divided Arabia into three broad zones. At the top was Arabia Petraea, 'Rocky Arabia', an area once inhabited by the Nabateans, an Arabic people who created their capital, Petra, by carving monumental buildings from the rock face. At the bottom, in the southwest corner of the peninsula, was Arabia Felix, 'Happy Arabia', the relatively fertile coastal strip that makes up modern-day Yemen, populated by fishermen, farmers and artisans. Between those two zones lay Arabia Deserta, 'Abandoned Arabia', the hot, arid centre, where fresh water could only be gathered from wells or from the occasional stormwater flash flood.

The desert-dwelling Bedouins of Arabia scratched a living from these arid lands as herders and traders, moving from oasis to oasis. In lean times, they would muster parties of men on camel and horseback to raid farms and townships on the Roman and Persian frontiers, but in Constantinople and Ctesiphon they were regarded as a nuisance rather than a serious threat. The Bedouin were, according to the Roman general Belisarius, 'unable to storm a wall, but the cleverest of all men at plundering'.[9]

Rather than build and maintain a series of expensive fortresses to protect their frontiers from these raiders, both the Romans and the Persians hired tribes of Arab mercenaries, the Ghassanids and the Lakhmids, to occupy a protective buffer zone in the desert borderlands, and to fight proxy wars on their behalf.

THE BARRENNESS OF THE landscape made large cities and central governments almost impossible in Arabia, forcing the inhabitants to rely on bonds of extended kinship for protection. The scarcity of food and water made them fiercely egalitarian: tribal leaders were expected to care for the welfare of their followers and display personal courage in battle. The raiding of a caravan or a town was considered morally acceptable, as long as such raids were conducted under the rules laid down by tradition. Wherever possible, goods were to be seized without taking life; murder and manslaughter were seen as severe crimes, to be paid for with blood.

There was also no religious unity among the Arabs, prior to Islam. In the early seventh century, there were groups of Jewish and Christian Arabs in the settled areas, but the Bedouin continued to worship an assortment of pagan deities. Bedouin herders setting up camp at dusk would typically select four stones from their surroundings: three to prop up their cooking pot and a fourth to worship as their little god for the night, which they honoured by walking around the stone in a circle, just as Muslims later would circumambulate around the Kaaba in Mecca.[10]

AS A PEOPLE inured to a hard life in a majestic but unforgiving land, Bedouin nomads prized poets and poetry with an intensity that modern people might find hard to grasp. Seated under the stars at a caravan site or campfire, the Bedouin poet acted as troubadour, historian and shaman for a circle of enraptured listeners. Later, after the Arabs had won an empire and become city-dwellers, the romance of Bedouin life still flickered in their collective imagination. Mutanabbi, an urbane tenth-century Arab poet, could feel his Bedouin heritage surging in his blood when he wrote:

I am known to night and horses and the desert,
to sword and lance,
to parchment and pen.[11]

IN THE 530s, the Two Eyes of the World were commanded by autocrats of towering self-confidence. In Ctesiphon, Khusrau I assumed the title of 'Immortal Soul'; while in Constantinople, the Emperor Justinian ruthlessly crushed a mass uprising in the Hippodrome, and to make amends to his god and his people, sponsored the construction of the world's greatest church, the Hagia Sophia, a stupendous building project that was completed in just five years and ten months. In his public proclamations, Justinian gave thanks to the Christian god for endowing him with such surpassing genius: 'Those things which seemed to many former emperors to require correction, but which none of them ventured to carry to effect, we have decided to accomplish at the present time, with the assistance of almighty God.'[12]

But just when both Justinian and Khusrau imagined themselves to be reaching up to the veil of Heaven, the natural world pulled them down to Earth. In 537, Justinian's court historian Procopius noticed a strange dimming in the skies over Constantinople: 'During this year,' he wrote, 'a most dread portent took place. For the sun gave forth its light without brightness … and it seemed exceedingly like the sun in eclipse.'[13] The culprit was a volcanic eruption in Iceland that had ejected more than 100 megatons of sulphur dioxide into the atmosphere. The atmospheric cloak brought on the coldest decade in recorded history, resulting in crop failures and famine all over the world. A second, larger eruption in 540 sent global temperatures plunging lower still.[14]

The cooling of the Earth made the northern reaches of the Nile River suddenly more congenial for plague rats that carried fleas in their fur infected with the lethal bacterium *Yersinia pestis*. The rats migrated on barges to the port city of Alexandria, and from there to all points around the Mediterranean. The resulting plague pandemic, the world's first, scythed through both great empires, bringing 'famine, pestilence, madness and fury'.[15] The devastating plague waves would recede, only to wash over the two empires again and again in 558, 573 and 599, leaving corpse-strewn streets, half-emptied cities, fields untended and frontier fortresses abandoned. Confronted by this spectacle of desolation, one Roman mourned that 'nations have been wiped out, cities enslaved, populations uprooted and displaced, so that all mankind has been involved in the upheaval'.[16]

But in the hot deserts of Arabia, where there were no large population centres, no grain silos and no rats to speak of, *Yersinia pestis* kept its distance.

HAGGARD AND HOLLOWED OUT by decades of plague and famine, the Romans and Persians resumed their border skirmishes spasmodically and inconclusively until their ancient rivalry entered its terminal phase after a brutal assassination in Constantinople. In 602, the Roman emperor Maurice was overthrown and murdered by his general Phocas, an outrage that gave the Sassanid ruler Khusrau II a pretext to go to war against the treacherous usurper. The Persians, to their surprise, easily overran the sparsely defended frontier fortresses, and kept marching deeper into Roman territory, taking Syria, and then large swathes of Asia Minor. By 607, the Sassanid army was camped on the eastern shores of the Bosphorus, their watch-fires clearly visible from Constantinople's sea walls.

Emperor Phocas, now widely detested as a failure and a moral reprobate, was himself overthrown in 610 by the son of the governor of Carthage, a charismatic leader named Heraclius. Hemmed in within his walled city, Emperor Heraclius could do nothing as Khusrau's troops seized Egypt and Palestine. Then in 614, the Persians seized Jerusalem and carried off the holiest relic in Christendom, the fragments of the True Cross of Christ, as a war trophy.

A defiant Heraclius now recast the struggle as a holy war. Over the course of a decade, the emperor slowly husbanded the forces within his walled city, going so far as to melt the treasures of the Hagia Sophia to make gold and silver coins to pay for more arms and mercenaries.

By 624, Heraclius had marshalled enough resources to take the fight back to the Persians, leading his army on a long march through the mountains of Armenia into the Sassanid heartlands. To avenge the theft of the True Cross, Heraclius ordered a lightning raid on the Zoroastrian Fire Temple of the Stallion where his men killed the guardian priests and extinguished the eternal flame. In 627, the Romans invaded Khusrau's summer palace, where the exotic animals of his royal zoo were slaughtered, roasted and served up to Heraclius's hungry troops.

Feeling cursed by God, the Persians deposed Khusrau II in 628. The shahanshah, stricken with dysentery, was locked in a room without food for a week, until his guards entered his room and shot him to death with arrows.

KHUSRAU'S SON AND SUCCESSOR Kavad II agreed to surrender all the conquered lands to the Romans and to hand back the True Cross, which a solemn Heraclius personally returned to Jerusalem, entering the city as a humble pilgrim. After an absence of twenty years, Roman bureaucrats re-entered Syria, Palestine and Egypt, expecting to pick up where they'd left off. But the aura of greatness was gone. The people of the provinces had seen the exalted Romans take a beating, and they resented the high taxes extracted from them by Constantinople to repair the broken empire.

In Ctesiphon, the situation continued to deteriorate. Military defeat and the destruction of the fire temple had left the Sassanid elite staring at a gaping spiritual void. Six months into his reign, Kavad II died of plague and was replaced by Ardashir, his eight-year-old son. Then, with the connivance of Roman troops, Ardashir was murdered and replaced by his senior general, Shahrbaraz. A month later, Shahrbaraz too was assassinated. In 632, the last of the Sassanids, Yazdegerd III, was placed on the throne. Like Ardashir before him, he was still only a boy. For a dizzying moment it looked like Persia might fall so low as to become a Roman vassal state, but the cash-strapped Romans were barely coping themselves. When they took back control of Palestine, they could no longer afford to subsidise the Arab border tribes. A Roman paymaster told a group of Arab mercenaries, 'The emperor can barely pay his soldiers their wages, much less you dogs.'[17]

Wracked with exhaustion, pestilence and self-doubt, the Two Eyes of the World were turned inwards, unable to see the revolution unfolding on the Arabian Peninsula.

Desert Lightning

WE KNOW EVERYTHING and at the same time very little of the life of Muhammad, the founder and prophet of Islam. Unlike other religions, whose origins are enshrouded in myth and mystery, Islam has long been said to have been born 'in the full light of history'.[18]

The non-Muslim documentary record of Muhammad's life is scant, but there's enough to attest to his existence as a revolutionary Arab leader. A tract written in 634 by a Greek Christian in Palestine refers to him in passing:

> A false prophet has appeared among the Saracens ... He is an impostor. Do the prophets come with sword and chariot? ... There is no truth to be found in the so-called prophet, only bloodshed; for he says he has the keys to paradise, which is incredible.[19]

Another, later document from an Armenian bishop mentions an Arab cult leader named 'Mahmet' who united the Arabs 'under the authority of a single man, under a single law'.[20]

Far greater detail can be found in the traditional sources: the holy book of Islam, the Quran, the canonical biographies and the *hadiths*, the collection of anecdotes of Muhammad's life as remembered by his companions. The *hadiths* in particular offer a huge amount of colour and detail. 'For the life of Muhammad,' wrote novelist Salman Rushdie, 'we know everything more or less. We know where he lived, what his economic situation was, who he fell in love with.'

The official biographies, compiled more than a century after his death, rely on oral tradition: a medium of transmission that cannot be discounted, yet one that secular historians must regard as frustratingly unstable. The *hadiths* seem more promising, insofar as Muslim scholars subsequently devoted enormous attention to establishing reliable chains of transmission connecting the stories to people who lived and walked alongside the Prophet. But these too were collated long after everyone who knew Muhammad was dead, and were open to distortion by those wanting to insert words into the Prophet's mouth during the feuds of the post-Muhammad era. But while the traditional sources should not be uncritically accepted, neither should they be rejected out of hand. 'Minimalism', as one historian reminds us, 'is not the way to throw light on a dark age.'[21]

ACCORDING TO MUSLIM TRADITION, Muhammad was born sometime around 570 C.E. in Mecca, then a trading post on the north–south overland trade route running though the Arabian Peninsula. Muhammad belonged to Mecca's dominant tribe, the Quraysh, who worshipped a desert god named Allah, along with hundreds of lesser pagan deities. Their stone effigies sat within Mecca's cubic shrine, the Kaaba, which was believed to have been built in the time of Abraham.

Trade had made the Qurayshi merchants of Mecca rich, and in Muhammad's time, disparities in wealth had become glaringly visible. The spectacle of prosperous Quraysh luxuriating in silk, scented oils and fine food was an affront to the ancient Bedouin ideals of manliness and austerity. Islam was founded in this unsettled environment of social dislocation and anxiety.

As a young man, Muhammad rode with the trading caravans that passed between Mecca and Syria, where he may have picked up Jewish and Christian teachings. He was charismatic and earnt a reputation for his ability to settle disputes. According to one *hadith*, Muhammad once came upon a group of tribal leaders gathered around the Kaaba, which had just been renovated after a destructive flash flood. The men were arguing over who should have the honour of reinstating the shrine's most sacred relic, a meteorite known as the Black Stone. Muhammad solved the dispute by coming forward, laying down his cloak and asking them to gently place the Black

Stone at its centre. Then he invited all the clan leaders to hold the edge of the cloak and carry the relic to its correct position, where Muhammad lifted it up and installed it in its place, thus satisfying the honour of everyone present.[22]

As he entered his late thirties, Muhammad began to wander through the mountains overlooking Mecca. In 610, while meditating in a cave, he received an electrifying vision of the archangel Gabriel, who seemed to fill up the entirety of the sky.

'Recite!' the angel said.

'What shall I recite?' Muhammad asked.

'Recite in the name of your Lord who created, created man from clots of blood! O Muhammad, you are the prophet of God and I am Gabriel.'[23]

And from Muhammad's mouth came words and verses. The language coursed through him like an electric shock. Afterwards, it was said, the words seemed to be 'inscribed upon his heart.'

At first, he told only his family and close friends of this, but then he received another revelation, urging him to preach to his tribe, the Quraysh, and he began to gather followers. More recitations would follow over the next twenty-two years. His most wrenching vision came to him one night in 620, when, according to Muslim tradition, he fell asleep beside the Kaaba in Mecca and was carried off by the archangel Gabriel to a place identified as 'the furthest mosque', which was understood to be the Temple Mount in Jerusalem. On this miraculous Night Journey, Muhammad met Adam, Abraham, Jesus and Moses, then was given a tour of Heaven, where he witnessed God enthroned and surrounded by angels.

MUHAMMAD'S REVELATIONS WERE memorised by his growing body of companions and later written down on parchment, stones and palm leaves, and carved into the shoulder bone of a camel. Together, the recitations would form the body of the Quran, the first work of Arabic literature.

Muslim writers often attribute the power of the Quran to the sublime beauty of its language. Unlike the text of the Bible, which Christians understood to be divinely inspired but mediated by mortals, the Quran presents itself as the pristine, unadulterated word of God:

> I swear by all that you can see, and all that is hidden from your view, that this is the utterance of a noble messenger. It is no poet's speech: scant is your faith! It is no soothsayer's divination: how little you reflect! It is a revelation from the Lord of the Universe.[24]

MUHAMMAD IS PLACED in the ancient line of biblical prophets going back to Abraham, but after him, he said, there would be no more: the words of the Quran superseded all previous revelations and were to be accepted as God's *final* message to his people.[25] The message was given added urgency by its warning that time was running out. Humanity and the world were said to be racing towards an apocalypse, a day when all souls would be judged by God. 'The Hour of Doom is drawing near,' warns the Quran, 'and the moon is cleft in two.'[26]

THE NEW FAITH, which was to be called Islam, meaning 'Submission', drew heavily on the traditions of the Jews and the Christians. Both groups are honoured in the Quran as 'the People of the Book', but also castigated in some places as rebels and transgressors.[27] Like Judaism, Islam preached that God was one, undivided and indivisible, the sole creator of the universe. Its central message contained a ringing declaration of faith: there is no god but God and Muhammad is his messenger. All the little stone idols in the Kaaba were to be smashed; they were nothing more than petty demons sent to lure the weak-minded away from the One True God, Allah. Islam had the benefit of simplicity: unlike the Christians, who had been quarrelling for centuries over how it was that Christ could be both divine and human at the same time, Muhammad preached that Jesus was to be regarded as fully human – divinely inspired, but mortal. To Muhammad, the Christians' distinction between God the Father and God the Son smacked of polytheism, and their veneration of the holy images in their churches was nothing short of idolatry.

Islam, for its followers, was both cosmic in scope and practical in application. It was a very 'do-able' religion, less interested in the mortification of the flesh and the subtle inward search for sin than in adhering to a set list of simple duties in a timely manner to promote upright behaviour and group solidarity. Muhammad's followers were expected to give over a portion of their income to the destitute, and to abstain from food and drink within daylight hours during the month of Ramadan in order to acquaint themselves with the hardships of the poor and hungry. The new faith's obligations were sometimes onerous, but not unreasonable. Believers were expected to undergo a pilgrimage to Mecca at least once in their lives, unless they were too poor or disabled to be able to travel. Pregnant women, children and sick people were exempt from fasting during Ramadan.

MUHAMMAD'S REVOLUTIONARY MESSAGE won him powerful enemies among the wealthy Qurayshi merchants in Mecca, and in 622, he was forced to escape the city to foil a murder plot against him. He and some 200 followers migrated north through the desert to another oasis, Yathrib, later named Medina ('the city'), where he was welcomed by his many supporters.

In Medina, a constitution was drawn up that brought the Muslim emigrants and local tribes together in a single, distinctive community of 'Believers', an *ummah*, with Muhammad acting as the supreme mediator. The constitution of this Islamic State set the template for the caliphate that would emerge after the Prophet's death: each group was assigned specific rights and duties; non-Muslims were guaranteed peace, security and freedom of worship, provided they accepted Muhammad's political authority. For the Arabs, Muhammad's most radical idea was that belief superseded blood. Ties of kinship mattered less than the higher bonds formed among believers.

Muhammad and his followers now prepared for war against Mecca, launching a series of raids on Qurayshi merchant caravans passing through the desert. In 624, a large caravan set out from Gaza to Mecca, protected by a force of 950 men. Muhammad and his much smaller force pounced on them at the wells of Badr and won a stunning victory. The substantial booty was shared equitably among his supporters.

The success of Muhammad's campaigns won the pagans of Medina over to Islam; the Jewish tribes whom Muhammad suspected of disloyalty were killed or expelled from the city. After several failed attempts by the Meccans to seize Medina, a truce was signed, and in 630 Muhammad and 10,000 of his followers entered Mecca unharmed. According to Muslim tradition, the Prophet came directly to the Kaaba, smashed its pagan idols with his staff, and reconsecrated the shrine to the One True God, Allah.

Rightly Guided

THE MUSLIM HISTORIES record that in 632, having united the Arab tribes under his personal command, Muhammad succumbed to a fever and died in Medina, in the lap of his favourite wife Aisha. At that moment, his embryonic Islamic State was in serious danger of disintegration; his absence left his followers grief-stricken and lost. One of his companions later recalled, 'We were like sheep on a rainy night.'[28] But the Prophet's revolution had brought forth a generation of exceptionally talented Qurayshi leaders, loyal to each other, who resolved to continue Muhammad's work and resist backsliding into tribal feuding. They named the Prophet's close friend Abu Bakr as *khalifah* or caliph, meaning 'steward' or 'successor'.[29] But Abu Bakr's appointment was resented by those who insisted that in his last days, Muhammad had named his son-in-law Ali (who was also his nephew) as his successor, and that in any case, it was essential to keep the leadership within the Prophet's family. Over time, Ali's supporters formed a coalition that became known as the Shiat Ali, the 'Party of Ali', the antecedents of the Shia today, who form the largest minority within Islam. For now, though, Ali's disgruntled supporters swallowed their misgivings.

Abu Bakr, the first of the four Rashidun, or 'Rightly Guided', caliphs, shrewdly diverted the war-like energies of the Arab tribes away from internal feuding and turned them outwards, setting in train a cascading series of events that remade the map of the world.

Firstly, Abu Bakr suppressed a wave of tribal revolts known as the *riddah*, bringing central Arabia once again under Muslim control. Then, to keep the fractious tribal leaders pacified, he ordered a series of lightning raids on the Persian and Roman frontier settlements along the northern borders of Arabia. In 633, Muslim warriors, mounted on camels and horses, stormed into the garrison villages, seizing loot then slipping back into the desert before any defence could be mounted. The Arabs were shocked by how easy it all was and how poorly defended these towns were, and suddenly plunder turned into conquest.

AFTER HIS DEATH in 634, Abu Bakr was succeeded by Umar, another of the Prophet's close companions. Umar, the second of the Rightly Guided caliphs, reorganised the Arab forces into a fast-moving, disciplined army, and the tempo of conquest picked up dramatically.

In 634, an army led by Khalid ibn Walid, the Muslims' most gifted general, marched into Syria and took the ancient city of Damascus from the Romans. Khalid promised the city's leaders he would protect the lives, property and churches of the city's largely Christian population, as long as they acknowledged the authority of the caliph and paid a special poll tax levied on unbelievers known as the *jizya*.

TWO YEARS LATER, Arab warriors invaded Palestine and confronted a Roman coalition army of Slav, Frankish, Georgian, Christian Arab and Armenian soldiers at the Yarmouk River near the Sea of Galilee. After a gruelling six-day battle, the Muslims led by Khalid defeated and destroyed the numerically superior Roman forces. After 700 years as imperial provinces, Syria and Palestine were lost to the Romans forever. Emperor Heraclius, sick at heart and weary beyond belief, boarded a ship that set sail for Constantinople. On his departure, he was said to have cried out: 'Peace be upon you, Syria. What an excellent country this is for the enemy.'[30]

The departure of the Romans left the Orthodox patriarch Sophronius as the most senior figure in Jerusalem. For some months Sophronius had been observing the relentless advance of the 'Saracens' with dread and dismay.* In an anguished letter to the pope, he had expressed his desperate hope that Christ would 'deliver these vile creatures, as before, to be the footstool of our God-given emperors'.[31]

As Umar's army of believers amassed at the gates of the Holy City, Sophronius concluded that something had gone badly wrong. He came to believe that in their sinfulness, he and his community of Christians had somehow brought this calamity down upon themselves. 'We are ourselves, in truth, responsible for all these things,' he wrote sadly, 'and no word will be found for our defence.' Realising that no help from Rome or Constantinople would be forthcoming, Sophronius offered to surrender the city to the Arabs, but only after he'd received a personal promise of toleration and protection for his people from Caliph Umar himself.

Such was the importance of the prize of Jerusalem, the site of Muhammad's miraculous Night Journey, that Umar duly rode up from Medina on a white camel to the Holy City. Sophronius received him on the Mount of Olives with icy courtesy, and agreed to give him a tour. Umar asked Sophronius to take him to the Church of the Holy Sepulchre, built on the site where Christians believe Christ was entombed and resurrected. The caliph's visit to the church coincided with the time of prayer, so Sophronius invited him to pray where he stood, but the caliph generously demurred, saying that if he did, it would instantly transform the church into a Muslim house of worship.[32]

Umar then asked to be taken to the site where the Temple of Solomon had stood centuries earlier, and saw that the Romans had been using the site as a rubbish dump. Umar was appalled by the desecration and ordered the refuse to be cleared away. As the caliph

* 'Saracen', at this time, referred to desert-dwellers in general. It was later, during the Crusades, when Christian writers came to deploy it more commonly as a term for Muslims in general.

wandered through the ruins, Sophronius was said to have muttered helplessly, 'Behold, the Abomination of Desolation, spoken of by the Prophet Daniel, that standeth in the Holy Place.'[33]

IN 641, SEVEN YEARS after the conquest of Palestine and Syria, another Arab army crossed the Sinai and surged into Egypt, the most important source of grain for the empire since ancient times. But Roman authority in Egypt, only recently re-established after the Persian invasions, was shaky. Christians were bitterly divided between the Orthodox establishment and the local Coptic monks who were persecuted as heretics. The Copts, who preferred to be ruled by tolerant infidels than by oppressive co-religionists, offered little resistance to the invaders as they seized fort after fort along the Nile, and within a few months, the Arabs arrived at the gates of Alexandria on the shores of the Mediterranean.

The Roman authorities were frozen with indecision as to whether to fight or to arrive at an accommodation with the invaders. Cyrus, the Orthodox patriarch of Alexandria, approached the Arab commander Amr to negotiate a peaceful surrender on behalf of the Roman authorities. 'God has delivered this land into your hands,' Cyrus told Amr. 'Let there be no more enmity between you and Rome.' In return for annual tribute to the caliphate, the Arabs vowed to protect the possessions and churches of the Christians. The Roman garrison sailed away to Constantinople, never to return, bringing a thousand years of Greco-Roman control of Egypt to an end.

THE SUDDEN LOSS of half their empire felt to the Romans like a fall from grace, a demotion from superpower status. The Arab invasions cancelled their pretensions to mastery of the Mediterranean world and forced the empire to re-invent itself as a smaller, more compact entity with a harder shell. The Roman Empire of Constantinople would one day revive and re-emerge into greatness, but for now, the loss of so much territory and treasure left it traumatised and defensive. Concluding that their sins had driven God to turn his face from them, the chastened Romans entered a dark age.

THE ARABS, ON THE other hand, could only draw the opposite conclusion: that everything was unfolding just as it should, and that God had sanctioned and smoothed the path for *jihad*, the struggle against unbelievers.

Jihad is spoken of in the Quran as a sombre religious duty. 'Fighting is obligatory for you,' it warns the believers, 'as much as you dislike it.'[34] The invasions of Christian-dominated lands by the early Islamic State were often cruel and brutal, but they were not the totalising campaigns of religious extermination associated with the modern Islamist army of the same name. Although inspired by Islam, the *jihadi*s of the early Arab conquests fought to impose political rather than religious supremacy over subject populations. They did this in the knowledge that Muslims still represented only a tiny minority in the newly conquered lands, living among much larger populations of Christians, Jews and Zoroastrians. Attempting to forcibly convert their new subjects through murderous persecution was neither practical nor desirable. Conquered peoples were of course welcome to adopt Islam, but from the start, the caliph's men promised not to interfere with those wanting to stick with their old religion, as long as they followed the established formula of acknowledging the authority of their new Muslim governor and paying their taxes. The special poll tax, the *jizya*, would no doubt have been unwelcome, but it was likely no more onerous than the taxes previously demanded of them by the Romans or Persians. Moreover, the revenue from the poll tax gave caliphs a powerful incentive to encourage loyal Christians and Jews *not* to convert.

It was not coercion but the absence of coercion that eventually won over the vanquished lands to the new faith; the moral energy and simplicity of Islam helped it take root in the ruined temples of the old empires. 'The Muslims', it was said, 'talked their way into the Middle East quite as much as they fought their way across it.'[35]

The Last Shahanshah

THE ROMAN EMPIRE of Constantinople would survive the Arab onslaught, albeit in a radically truncated form. The 400-year-old Sassanid Empire, however, would not, but in its death throes it presented an awesome spectacle, and even succeeded in handing the rampaging Arab forces their first major defeat.

In 634, Caliph Umar sent a Bedouin army into neighbouring Mesopotamia, where it was confronted by a far larger Persian force, waiting for it on the opposite side of an irrigation canal straddled by a single rickety bridge. The assembled Persian army, led by Rostam Farrokhzad, an Iranian nobleman whom the Arabs nicknamed 'the Eye-Browed One', formed an awesome spectacle: thousands of Persian archers stood in rows, flanked on both sides by heavy cavalry with horses draped in chain mail. At the rear stood a line of war elephants, a creature unknown to most of the desert warriors. A single warrior held aloft a long banner made of tiger pelts.[36]

The impetuous Arab commander Abu Ubayd made the first move, leading a party of men across the canal through a shower of Persian arrows, into the path of the war elephants. The Arabs' horses, terrified by the massive, trumpeting creatures, reared up and threw off their riders. Abu Ubayd and several warriors tried to attack one of the elephants by hacking at its leg; the elephant retaliated by stomping Abu Ubayd to death.

The loss of their commander sent the Arab troops into a panicked retreat, but the bridge had been cut, and many were driven into the canal, where they drowned. The survivors scattered and fled into the safety of the desert. Slowly and steadily, the Persian army pushed the Arabs back to the borders of their desert enclave.

UMAR RESPONDED TO the debacle of the Battle of the Bridge, as it became known, by treating it as a setback rather than as a defeat. On 6 January 637, he sent a fresh Arab army to attack the Persians at the town of Qadisiyyah on the banks of the Euphrates. This time, the disciplined Arab archers were able to bring superior fire power against the enemy. When the Persians deployed their war elephants, the Arab warriors kept their nerve. Dismounting from their horses, they used their swords to cut the straps of the howdahs secured on the elephants' backs, sending their riders crashing to the ground.

The battle raged for days, until a night offensive by the Arabs took the Persians by surprise and routed them from their camp. Rostam Farrokhzad was killed in the fighting. The Arab cavalry chased the fleeing Persians and caught them in the ruins of nearby Babylon, where they were put to the sword.

Back on the offensive, the Arab forces steadily regained control of southern Iraq, and in 638 they encircled Ctesiphon, set up their catapults on the western banks of the Tigris, and began to pound the city's walls.

INSIDE CTESIPHON, THE twelve-year-old Yazdegerd III, the last of the Sassanid rulers, was holed up in the royal palace. All his immediate predecessors had been murdered or carried off by the plague, his court was disintegrating, and now Rostam, his mentor and chief defender, was dead.

Six months into the relentless siege, Yazdegerd conceded that the situation was hopeless and agreed to evacuate the capital. After packing up the most precious and portable of the Sassanid treasures, the shahanshah led his people on a procession out of the city's eastern gates. Yazdegerd had been told they were safe from the invaders, who were massed on the other side of the swollen Tigris, but a party of Arab horsemen found a fording point in the river and chased after them. Yazdegerd and his men were forced to dump most of their treasures and raced east to the safety of the Zagros Mountains.

WITH THE SHAHANSHAH and his followers gone, the ragged Arab warriors entered the silent streets of Ctesiphon without further resistance. Wrapped in their camel blankets, they wandered through the royal palace in amazement, finding abandoned baskets of gold and silver trinkets. A jar of aromatic camphor was mistaken for salt and sprinkled onto bread.[37]

The raiders gathered up the royal treasures into a mountainous heap and divided them, keeping a fifth of the goods aside for Caliph Umar in Medina. The single largest prize was a 900-square-metre golden carpet known as the King's Spring. The Sassanid court had reclined on it during their parties to recreate a sense of being in a magical garden. Precious stones resembling luscious fruits were woven into the fabric; the springwaters were depicted with streams of golden thread. Not knowing how to split the King's Spring, the warriors cut it into equal pieces.[38]

IN THEIR HEADLONG ESCAPE from Ctesiphon, Yazdegerd and his bodyguards crossed the Zagros Mountains and regrouped in Media, on the Iranian plateau. Yazdegerd spent the next two decades trying to raise an army to take back his lost lands, but in 642, his forces were again defeated by the Arabs at Nahavand in western Iran, leaving him no choice but to run further east, to the city of Merv in modern-day Turkmenistan.

Yazdegerd was murdered in 651 while hiding in a watermill on the outskirts of Merv. The miller who stabbed him to steal his jewellery was said to have been unaware he'd killed the last of the Sassanid kings.

Fitna

IN THE TWENTY YEARS since Muhammad's death, the world had been turned upside down. In later centuries, Muslims would look back at this era of conquests as a period when God smiled on the endeavours of the Rightly Guided caliphs and smoothed their path to victory, fulfilling the promise of the Quran: God has made the earth for you as a carpet spread out, so that you may roam its broad roads.

A Muslim pamphleteer would write nostalgically of this time:

> We set out, barefoot and naked, lacking in every kind of equipment, utterly powerless, deprived in every sort of armament and devoid of all the necessary provisions, to fight the peoples with the most widely extended empires, the peoples that were most manifestly mighty, possessing the most numerous troops … namely the Persians and the Romans. We went to meet them

> with small abilities and weak forces, and God made us triumph and gave us possession of their territories.[39]

HAVING COME OUT of desert wilderness, the Arabs were now masters of some of the lushest, most productive lands in the world. Their conquest of Syria, Palestine, Egypt, Iraq and Iran had restored the natural unity of the Fertile Crescent, the great arc of arable lands lying between Egypt and Mesopotamia. This rich agricultural zone, divided for centuries between two ancient empires, now formed the heartland of the new one. Tax and tribute from these lands now flowed not to Constantinople or Ctesiphon, but to the Arab capital of Medina.

To administer the spoils of victory, Umar created the caliphate's first bureaucratic apparatus: a *diwan*, a register of those entitled to military pensions and to a share of the loot from the conquests. Umar's *diwan* was the prototype for the great bureaucratic departments of the caliphate's civil service that were to be run by secretaries and overseen by a chief minister, the vizier. As these institutions grew in size and professionalism, the term *diwan* evolved to mean 'customs house' and 'council chamber'. In Europe, the word 'divan' would eventually come to denote the kind of low cushioned bench that was to be found in such chambers of assembly.

UMAR'S SPECTACULARLY SUCCESSFUL reign came to an abrupt halt in October 644. While visiting the marketplace in Medina, the caliph was approached for advice by a Persian slave apprentice named Abu Luluah, who complained that his master was taking too much money from him.

'You say you have skills as a carpenter and stonemason,' the caliph said. 'Perhaps you should build a windmill and make money from that.'

'Thank you for your wisdom, O Commander of the Faithful!' Abu Luluah replied. 'If you survive, I will make you a windmill that everyone will talk about.'[40]

Umar walked away thinking that was an odd thing to say. Three days later, while leading morning prayers in the mosque, he saw the apprentice coming through the crowd with a dagger. Abu Luluah stabbed Umar six times, fatally wounding him.

As the caliph lay dying, a committee of senior men convened to choose his successor. Again, the claim of the Prophet's son-in-law Ali was overlooked in favour of Uthman, another of Muhammad's early converts. Within the divided leadership group, Uthman seems to have been everyone's second-favourite candidate.

UTHMAN CUT A VERY different figure from that of the charismatic Umar, who had lived in pious simplicity. The new caliph was a wealthy merchant, and had been the first of the Umayyads, a sub-clan within the Quraysh, to defect from the Meccan elite to join Muhammad's revolution. The traditional accounts describe Uthman as elegant and 'overgroomed',[41] qualities that kept him at an awkward remove from the flinty desert warriors in his charge. Umar had been able to smother any squabbling between the tribes through the force of his personality, but Uthman, who was more a manager than a warrior-king, had to rely on his friendly, easy-going nature to win people over.

Despite the growing tensions in Medina, the first half of Uthman's twelve-year reign passed successfully. In the east, Muslim armies subdued the last of the Sassanid provinces; in the west, they pushed further across the Maghreb – the coastal lands between Morocco and Egypt; and in the north they ranged into the mountainous realm of Armenia. On the Syrian coast, Uthman's nephew Muawiya had built the first Muslim navy and was ready to challenge Roman domination of the eastern Mediterranean.

But the dramatic transformation of the Arabs from desert nomads to imperial masters posed questions that cut to the core of their identity. Should they hold fast to their Bedouin traditions, or should they accept the challenge of settled life and build an empire for the ages? The Prophet had urged them to triumph over the infidel kingdoms, while at the same time living together simply as brothers and sisters; but the acquisition of an empire brought with it the inevitable problems of hierarchy and preferential treatment.

In a move that provoked deep resentment, Uthman insisted that he and he alone had the power to appoint and dismiss provincial governors, and to ensure their loyalty, he had handed out these lucrative posts almost exclusively to members of his own clan, the Umayyads. Uthman's appointment of relatives to plum positions left many old warriors seething. Successful governors were replaced by mediocre and incompetent place-holders who had nothing to recommend them other than their loyalty to Uthman. Muhammad's revolutionaries thought they'd overturned the social order, only to see the born-to-rule Qurayshi aristocracy slip comfortably back into power.

The old egalitarianism was slipping away. Under Umar, the spoils of conquest had been distributed among the warriors, with a fifth held in reserve for the caliph in Medina. Uthman now kept aside another portion of the loot for his Umayyad governors. When challenged, he replied that it was his prerogative to distribute money as he saw fit for the greater good; 'otherwise,' he asked, 'why am I a caliph?'[42] But such statements meant little to the Bedouin warriors, who traditionally gave their obedience to a leader, not to an institution.

Uthman became more and more isolated. Both the Prophet's wife

Aisha and nephew Ali began to distance themselves from him. In Medina, disgruntled warriors heckled him in the street. Rocks were thrown at him while he led prayers in the mosque.

With his enemies closing in, a badly rattled Uthman wrote to his cousin Muawiya, the Governor of Syria, to beg for help: 'The people of Medina have become unbelievers,' he wrote, 'they have abandoned obedience and renounced their oath of allegiance. Therefore send to me the Syrian soldiers who are at your disposal, on every camel you have, whether docile or stubborn.'[43]

But Muawiya dragged his feet, not wanting at this stage to alienate the senior men in Medina. No one, it seemed, was rushing to Uthman's aid, but equally no one wanted to be complicit in his violent overthrow – that was, until 656, when bands of mutinous soldiers in Egypt and Iraq rode down to Medina to confront him. Aisha may well have known what was coming, because she chose this moment to leave Medina on a pilgrimage.

The rebel soldiers put the caliph's house to siege and cut off supplies of food and water. When they heard that a relief force was on its way from the provinces to rescue Uthman, several rioters broke into his house. Finding the caliph alone and at prayer, they pulled him up by his beard and stabbed him in the head with a broad, iron-headed arrow.

AFTER UTHMAN'S ASSASSINATION, a coalition of mutineers and prominent figures in Medina quickly gathered to proclaim Ali as the fourth caliph. Ali had kept his distance from the plotters, but as the chief beneficiary of a murderous coup, a cloud of illegitimacy hung over his reign from the start.

Umar's murder had been horrific, but he had died at the hand of a foreign slave. Uthman, however, had been murdered by his fellow believers, an act that scandalised the Muslim world and plunged it into *fitna* – civil war.

Ali accelerated the descent into war by dismissing Uthman's appointees, but in Syria, the wily Muawiya refused to leave his post, and said he would not declare his allegiance to Ali until his uncle's killers, now part of the ruling clique in Medina, had been handed over to him for retributive justice. Muawiya ordered Uthman's blood-soaked robe to be brought to Damascus and had it draped over the *minbar* in the main mosque.

AISHA WAS ALSO AT odds with Ali. The personal animosity between the Prophet's wife and his son-in-law went back to an incident decades earlier, when Aisha, still a teenager, had accompanied Muhammad on a desert journey to Medina. When the caravan had paused for a short break, Aisha had slipped away from the camp to relieve herself, and had been accidentally left behind. The next morning, a soldier named Safwan ibn Muattal found her and escorted her back to Medina, but rumours spread that something improper had happened between her and the handsome Safwan in the desert. As the scandal grew, Ali advised Muhammad to abandon Aisha. 'Women are plentiful,' he had said, 'and you can easily change one for another.'[44]

Disturbed by the gossip, Muhammad came to Aisha's house to see her. She furiously denied the rumours, but as she did so, a vision came upon the Prophet. When he awoke, Muhammad joyfully said that God had told him of her innocence. He then went outside to recite the divine message, and to order her accusers to be flogged.[45]

Although vindicated, Aisha had nursed a grudge against Ali for advising her husband to abandon her. After Uthman's murder, two former companions of the Prophet came to her to plot an uprising.

The three travelled together to the Muslim garrison city of Basra in southern Iraq where they raised a thousand-strong rebel army.

Ali pursued them into Iraq and set up his court in the nearby city of Kufa, which he made his new capital. From Kufa, he led a loyal army south to Basra to confront Aisha's rebels.

This was the first time a caliph had led an army against his fellow Muslims. Both sides were anguished and reluctant to fight, but after three days of fruitless negotiations, Ali lost patience and gave the order to attack. Aisha watched the fighting from a distance, seated on the back of her red camel. The clash, which accordingly became known as the Battle of the Camel, ended in victory for Ali's forces. Aisha was captured and sent back to Medina, where she was given a pension and left unharmed on the understanding that she would live quietly and no longer engage in political activity.

ALI HAD SHORED UP his position in Iraq, but in Syria, a furious Muawiya continued to defy him. When accused of disloyalty, Muawiya shot back with a sharp reminder of the bad faith Ali had displayed to his predecessors as caliph: 'Each one you envied,' he wrote, 'and against each one you revolted. We knew that from your looking askance, your offensive speech, your heavy sighing, and your holding back from the caliphs. To each one of them you had to be led, as the male camel is led by the wood stick through its nose, in order to give your pledge of allegiance.'[46]

This insolence could no longer be ignored, and in the summer of 657, Ali's Iraqi army marched north to confront Muawiya's Syrians on the banks of the Euphrates. But again, Muslim soldiers on both sides were sick at heart to be fighting brothers, friends and cousins, and were anxious to avoid bloodshed. After a brief and unsatisfactory skirmish, the two sides agreed to negotiate. Muawiya offered to recognise Ali's authority as caliph, if in return he were given control of Syria and Egypt. This offer was rejected out of hand, as was Ali's challenge to fight a one-on-one duel with Muawiya.

Fighting resumed on 26 July, and after three days Ali's forces had the advantage. Then, in a desperate move to forestall defeat, Muawiya's men called for an armistice by raising up pages of the Quran on their lances and chanting, 'Let the book of God be the judge between us!'[47]

The invoking of the Quran generated intense moral anguish within Ali's army, and the most pious of his commanders told him he had no choice but to accept the call to arbitration. Ali reluctantly agreed, and the armies, incredibly, withdrew from the battlefield to await the verdict of the two arbiters chosen by both camps. Ali felt he had to consent to the truce to hold his army together, but the fact remains that on the cusp of total victory, he failed to finish off his most lethal enemy.

AS THE ARBITRATION PROCESS dragged on and on, Ali's prestige disintegrated among the fiercest of his Bedouin warriors, who thought legalistic discussion, under the circumstances, was madness. After two months, the arbiters ruled that Uthman had indeed been killed wrongfully, and that his cousin Muawiya was within his rights to seek revenge against the assassins. Ali denounced the verdict as contrary to the Quran, but his position was now fatally weakened. More and more senior men pledged their allegiance to Muawiya as the true caliph.

The messy situation was further complicated by a group of fanatical dissidents in Ali's party, who now insisted that Ali should never have accepted arbitration in the first place; the right to judge, they insisted, belonged to God alone. These hardliners, who became known as the Kharijites – 'Those Who Go Out'[48] – marched off and occupied the town of Nahrawan on the Tigris, where they murdered every inhabitant who did not accept their militant views.[49] For the fundamentalist Kharijites, a Muslim who had committed a grievous sin was no longer a Muslim at all, but a heathen, a *kafir*, who should rightfully be hunted down and killed. They were to be the first in a long line of militant sects that would torment the caliphate in the centuries to come.

MUAWIYA, NOW IN firm control of both Egypt and Syria, could afford to sit back and wait while Ali's authority seeped away from him. On Friday 26 January 661, while entering the mosque in Kufa, Ali was attacked and killed by a Kharijite assassin wielding a poisoned sword. He was the third successive caliph to be murdered.

Ali's followers rallied around his son Hasan, but rather than risk further bloodshed, Hasan agreed to abdicate and make peace with Muawiya, bringing the first Muslim civil war to an end, and with it the era that would later be remembered by Sunni Muslims as the time of the Rashidun, or 'Rightly Guided', caliphs.

The Rise of the Umayyads

'I TRIUMPHED OVER ALI', Muawiya claimed, 'because I held my secrets close while he revealed his.'[50] As the first of the Umayyad caliphs, Muawiya was seen as a controversial figure by Abbasid historians, but all sides admitted his capacity for shrewdness and an inner quality identified as *hilm* – the ability to conceal emotions and withstand provocation.

Muawiya continued Uthman's work of refashioning the ramshackle, improvised structure of the Islamic State into a smoothly-run empire with an efficient tax-collection system, a speedy postal network known as the *barid*, and a well-paid standing army operating from fixed bases in Syria, Iraq and Egypt. He moved the capital from Medina to Damascus where he had lived for decades and felt most at home. No longer an eastern outpost of the Roman world, Damascus was now the Islamic world's window on the West.

The Arabs were now masters of a wildly diverse range of provinces inhabited by peoples of different backgrounds and religious beliefs, in which Muslims still formed only a tiny minority. The caliphs took care to minimise conflict between their occupying armies and the newly vanquished peoples by sequestering their soldiers in new, purpose-built garrison cities such as Basra and Kufa in Iraq, and Fustat in Egypt. Segregating the troops kept them from being absorbed into local populations where they might lose their distinctive identity, and averted any tensions that might arise from the sight of swaggering conquerors walking the streets of foreign cities.

The pace of conquest, which had halted momentarily during the civil war, now picked up speed again. To the east, Arab troops invaded eastern Iran and occupied the silk-road city of Merv, which subsequently became the caliphate's easternmost stronghold.

In North Africa, Arab forces raced from one end of the Maghreb to the other. In 680, striking out from the newly founded garrison city of Kairouan, the Arab commander Uqba led his men on a daring raid through the High Atlas Mountains in modern-day Morocco, down to the Atlantic coast. On reaching the beach, Uqba was said to have galloped into the surf, crying out to the open sky: 'O Lord, if the sea did not stop me, I would go through the lands like Alexander the Great, defending your faith and fighting the unbelievers!'[51] It was a moment that curiously echoed Trajan's melancholy comment about Alexander at the mouth of the Persian Gulf five centuries earlier.

IN THE MEDITERRANEAN, Muawiya's forces were slowly closing in on Constantinople. Muslim leaders had long dreamt of taking the Roman capital, and with it the claim of the caesars to a universal empire. The conquest of Constantinople would open the door to Christian Europe. 'Tighten the noose around the Romans,' Muawiya predicted, 'and the other nations will follow.'[52]

But Constantinople, the best defended city in the world, was too hard a nut for Muawiya to crack. Situated on a peninsula, the city was protected from naval attack on three sides by high sea walls. A land army could only approach it from the west, but there it would run into the legendary Theodosian Walls, a triple-layered defence network of parallel ditches and battlements that no army had ever penetrated. Even Atilla the Hun had balked at the challenge of the Theodosian Walls.

And yet the presence of such a mighty Christian city, far bigger than any the Muslims had built, was an intolerable affront to Muawiya. Recognising the scale of the challenge, Muawiya proceeded slowly and methodically, setting up his forces for a long siege and blockade.

A chain of forward supply bases was set up between Damascus and the Aegean Sea, and in 670, a fleet of 400 Muslim ships sailed up through the Dardanelles to secure a naval base on the southern shore of the Sea of Marmara. In 672, three more fleets arrived, giving the Arabs a stranglehold on the sea lanes coming in and out of Constantinople. In 674, Muawiya tightened the noose, despatching his armies by ship to a captured harbour just below the Theodosian Walls. It was the first time Muslim troops had set foot in Europe.

For five long years Muawiya's forces blockaded Constantinople, skirmishing with the Roman fleet in the summer, then retiring in the winter months to their makeshift port on the Sea of Marmara to repair their war galleys. Protected by their towering, encompassing walls, the

Romans withstood the repeated assaults, living off their grain stores and fish harvested from the city's harbour, the Golden Horn.

Then in 678, the Roman navy counterattacked. A fleet of fast-moving *dromons* – swift, lightweight galleys – bore down on the caliph's ships and barges, shooting streams of flaming black liquid. The jets of liquid fire exploded on the Muslim decks and hulls, incinerating ship after ship and enveloping the fleet in choking black smoke. To their horror, the Muslim sailors who leapt into the sea found themselves engulfed by the oily inferno, which could somehow blaze on the water's surface.

The fluid, which came to be known as 'Greek fire', was a devastating and terrifying new weapon of war. Not a single Arab ship was said to have escaped the inferno.

With the Muslim navy in ruins, the remnant of Muawiya's land forces, who could 'no longer bear the pain of hunger and pestilence', trudged back to Syria.[53]

MUAWIYA DIED TWO YEARS later in Damascus and was succeeded by his son Yazid, a move that affirmed the Umayyad clan as the ruling dynasty of the caliphate. Yazid's appointment was unpopular, a symptom, in the eyes of some, of the degeneration of the caliphate. The exalted role of 'successor to the Prophet' had descended into mere kingship, the inheritance of worthless, soft-handed princelings. Rumours of Yazid's luxurious lifestyle and his love of animals led him to be denounced from the pulpit in Mecca as 'Yazid of liquors, Yazid of whoring! Yazid of panthers, Yazid of apes!'[54]

Festering dissatisfaction with Caliph Yazid encouraged Husayn, the second son of Ali, to launch an insurrection, but Husayn was defeated and beheaded at the Battle of Karbala in 680. A separate rebellion then flared up in Mecca, led by Ibn Zubayr, the son of another of Muhammad's companions, who declared himself a rival caliph.

This second *fitna* was longer, bloodier and even more dispiriting than the first. When Yazid sent an army from Syria to put Mecca under siege in 683, the unthinkable happened: an ember from a burning spear set alight the curtains of the Kaaba, leaving the walls 'cracked and black'.[55] When Yazid died unexpectedly later that year, the siege collapsed ignominiously.

He was succeeded by his sickly teenage son, Muawiya II, who lasted a month before succumbing to the plague. The caliphate fell into disarray until Abd al-Malik, a distant cousin of Muawiya, emerged as caliph in April 685.

ABD AL-MALIK, SUPREMELY capable and ambitious, was described as being of medium build with long hair and large eyes. He had gold bridge work on his teeth and was known as 'the Fly-Killer' for his particularly evil halitosis, which was said to cause flies to drop dead when they passed his mouth.[56]

Abd al-Malik was no stranger to violence: as a child he had witnessed the gruesome murder of Caliph Uthman, as the assassins broke into his house in Medina. At sixteen, he had led an army on campaign against the Romans. His harsh early life had made him immune to blandishments: he was said to have dismissed the prattling of a sycophant with 'Don't flatter me; I know myself better than you.'[57]

After putting down Ibn Zubayr's revolt, Abd al-Malik embarked on a series of far-reaching reforms. In 693, he issued a new Muslim currency, replacing the Roman denarius with the Muslim gold dinar and the silver dirham, which carried the simple Arabic inscription 'There is no God but God and Muhammad is His Messenger'. The imperial postal service, the *barid*, was strengthened and streamlined, enabling efficient communication from the centre of the empire to the periphery. Roads connecting Damascus with Palestine were built or repaired. The conscript army was transformed into a professional force led by salaried officers.

Most significantly, Abd al-Malik decreed that the caliphate would no longer govern in Greek or Persian; from now on its officials would speak and write in Arabic only. The caliph, it was said, had been driven to make the change after a Greek scribe was caught urinating in his inkstand.[58] Henceforth, bureaucratic documents would be written in Arabic, and anyone wanting to join the ruling elite had to learn it. Scribes and bookkeepers proficient in Arabic were suddenly in high demand. Greek, which had been spoken since the time of Alexander the Great, disappeared almost entirely as a spoken language in Syria, Palestine and Iraq.

Abd al-Malik's reign was the moment when the caliphate took stock of itself; it was longer a mere insurgency, nor a brief flash of lightning across the sky, but a distinctive great power in its own right. Islam too was evolving, from a conqueror's cult into a state religion. Seven decades had passed since the death of Muhammad, and first-hand knowledge of him was fading from living memory. Abd al-Malik could now invoke his name to justify his decisions by pointing to things the Prophet was believed to have said and done, without fear of contradiction from those who had known him personally, and he exalted Muhammad's name in official documents, on coins, and on the walls of mosques.

The second caliph, Umar, had left the Jews and Christians of Jerusalem guessing and hoping that the faith of the conquering Arabs might be an offshoot of their own. As late as the 680s, a Christian monk in northern Iraq could refer to Muhammad as a 'guide' who had instructed the Arabs in the Jewish Torah.[59] But Abd al-Malik ensured there could no longer be any such confusion. The new faith now came into its own as a distinctive, stand-alone religion. No longer content to camp out on the site where Solomon's Temple once stood, he ordered the rough wooden mosque on Jerusalem's Temple Mount to be taken down and replaced by a magnificent octagonal shrine, the Dome of the Rock, an Islamic successor to the Temple of Solomon and a rival to the Church of the Holy Sepulchre.

The Dome of the Rock still dominates the Jerusalem skyline today, standing dramatically aloof from the closely packed buildings surrounding it. Although architecturally influenced by nearby churches, the Dome of the Rock is regarded as perhaps the first conscious work of art created by Islamic civilisation.[60] An inscription inside its octagonal base goes as far as to rebuke Christians for their belief in the Holy Trinity: *So believe in God and his apostles, and do not say that God is three. Stop! It is better for you. Surely God is one God. He is exalted beyond having a son.*[61]

The Dome of the Rock, Jerusalem
Photographed in the 1920s, before the dome was gilded

By the time of his death in 705, Abd al-Malik had transformed the empire of the Arabs from a fractious collection of conquered lands into a more coherent Islamic State, consecrated in the faith and administered in the language of the Prophet.

Islam legitimised the caliphate, just as the caliphate supported and glorified Islam. Caliphs began to carry themselves like Persian kings. A wall mosaic created in Jordan at this time depicts six infidel kings – the Caesar of the Romans, the Visigoth king of Spain, Khusrau II of Persia, the Negus of Ethiopia and two other obscure rulers – gathered around the throne in Damascus to pay homage to the Commander of the Faithful, the most powerful man in the world.

Wider Still and Wider

MEANWHILE, THE WARRIORS of Islam pushed the borders of their empire out to its furthest limits in the east and in the west. In North Africa and Central Asia, the Muslim armies stormed into new territories, were rolled back, then surged forward again. Victories would be followed by setbacks, devastating defeats and then renewed assaults against the infidels.

In 706, a Muslim army arrived at the banks of the Amu Darya, known in ancient times as the Oxus River. Behind them lay the conquered Iranian province of Khorasan – 'the Land Where the Sun Arrives From' – and its capital Merv, which now served as the army's base of operations. To the east, beyond the Amu Darya, lay the rich Central Asian cities of Bukhara and Samarkand. So far the princes in these provinces had offered fierce resistance to the invaders, and the Arab general Qutaybah warned his soldiers to steel themselves for 'the greatest of distances and the sharpest of pains'.[62]

Their first target, the city of Paykand, quickly surrendered, but when the troops moved on, the inhabitants of Paykand rose up and killed their new Muslim governor. In retaliation, Qutaybah's men re-invaded and killed every man of fighting age they could find, then took the women and children into slavery. The plundering troops helped themselves to the city's treasures – bolts of Chinese silk, gold and silver goblets, ceremonial weapons and two gigantic pearls, 'each the size of a pigeon's egg'. The Buddhist statues they discovered were melted down into coins.[63] The Muslims next rode on to Bukhara, which surrendered after a fierce and bloody battle, then doubled back to quash a Buddhist rebellion in Bactria.

The long-drawn-out cycle of attack, surrender, rebellion and reconquest played out over decades and would never be quite complete. After fifty years, the city of Samarkand became the only enduring stronghold of the caliphate beyond the Amu Darya.

In the southeast, the Arabs entered the lower Indus Valley and conquered Sind in modern-day Pakistan, a land celebrated by the victorious Muslims as 'the land of gold and of commerce, of medicaments and simples, of sweetmeats and resources, of rice, bananas and wondrous things'.[64] The Buddhists and Hindus of these lands were regarded by Muslims as idolators, and not included as People of the Book. But the Muslim conqueror of Sind wisely decided on a live-and-let-live policy, telling Buddhist priests they would be allowed to attend and maintain their temples, as long as they paid their taxes.

NORTH AFRICA PROVED as difficult to nail down as Central Asia. The conquest of the Maghreb was a decades-long project that was never fully accomplished. Even after the area became predominantly Muslim, independent dynasties continued to spring up to defy the caliph's authority.

The key outpost for the caliph's armies in the Maghreb was the garrison city of Kairouan, in modern-day Tunisia. But the Berber tribes dwelling in the lands outside Kairouan's walls refused to be subjugated. In the late seventh century, the Berbers united under the leadership of a charismatic queen known as Kahina – 'the Sorceress' – a wild-haired, visionary resistance fighter in the mould of Joan of Arc. Kahina kept her followers spellbound by uttering prophecies in an ecstatic trance while pounding at her breast. Descending from their stronghold in the Aures Mountains, Kahina's Berber warriors took Carthage in 688 and destroyed an Arab army at the Meskiana River.

On hearing of the defeat, the caliph had sent reinforcements to Kairouan, but rather than surrender, Kahina decided to make the Maghreb a prize not worth having. In an incendiary speech, she reminded her Berber warriors:

> The Arabs only want Africa for its cities, and gold and silver, while we only want agriculture and flocks. The only solution is the destruction of the whole of Africa so that the Arabs lose interest in it and they never return again![65]

It was a losing gambit. Kahina's scorched-earth policy alienated too many of her Berber subjects. Those who did not flee the area sided with the invaders against her. In 698, the Arabs retook Carthage and obliterated the city, as the Romans had done nine centuries earlier – pulling down its walls, smashing the aqueducts and laying waste to its fields.

As the Muslim army moved into Kahina's mountain stronghold, the prophetess was struck with a vision of her own doom, and she told her sons to escape by defecting to the Arab side. She made a last stand in a mountain pass, where she was killed by the Arabs. A local legend grew up around her, which claimed that she was 127 years old when she fell.[66]

WITH THE NORTH AFRICAN coast subdued, Arab raiders began hearing stories of the riches that awaited them across the narrow strait of water between Tangier and Spain. In April 711, a raiding army sailed out and disembarked onto a strip of land dominated by a mountain shaped like a gigantic tooth. They named it Jabal Tariq, 'Tariq's Mountain', after their commander; later the rock's name would be anglicised as Gibraltar.

Tariq's cavalry raced north into the Spanish interior until it ran into a massed army of Christian Visigoths clad in armour and chain mail, led by their king, Roderic. Seeing the weight of numbers was against him, Tariq told his men their only choices were to fight or die.

Accounts of the subsequent Arab victory are confused and entangled with legend. One part of the Visigoth forces was said to have defected to the Muslims, while another, whose commander hoped to take the throne in the event of the king's death, stood back from the fighting. In the end, the Christian army was destroyed, and the rival nobles were killed along with Roderic.

The larger part of Spain was given over to the victorious Muslims, who named the country al-Andalus, 'the Land of the Vandals', after the previous inhabitants. From al-Andalus sprang the Emirate of Cordoba, whose capital would one day rival Baghdad.

BY THE EARLY eighth century, the Umayyad Caliphate had become the dominant power in the Mediterranean. And yet, the Christian citadel of Constantinople stood defiantly intact behind its high stone walls, an insufferable stumbling block for the Muslims on the threshold of Europe. And so when reports of internal tensions within the city reached the ears of Caliph Sulayman, Abd al-Malik's son and successor, he made plans for another coordinated siege. Sulayman's ambitions had been enflamed by an enigmatic Islamic prophecy foretelling that the Roman capital would one day fall to a great Muslim leader with the name of a prophet, and Sulayman (Solomon) believed he might be that man.

In 715, Sulayman sent a massive invasion force to envelop and overwhelm Constantinople by land and sea. The hundred-thousand-strong Muslim army marched across Asia Minor to the shores of the Hellespont to meet their transport ships, which ferried them over to the European side of the strait. On 15 August, the Arab general Maslama positioned his men in fortified camps along the entire five-kilometre length of the Theodosian Walls.

But this second great Muslim siege of Constantinople also failed, spectacularly and catastrophically. Both the Muslim and Roman sources attest to the scale of the disaster. The naval blockade of the city collapsed when the Muslim fleet was again blasted with Greek fire. When Sulayman sent in a fresh fleet, the Christian galley slaves on his ships joyfully defected to the Romans. At the same time, the Muslim army at the Theodosian Walls was hit by an exceptionally cold winter that turned its campsites into a barren, frozen hell: 'The Muslim army suffered what no army had suffered previously,' recorded the Muslim chronicler Tabari. 'They ate animals, skins, tree roots, leaves – indeed, everything except dirt,'[67]

Sulayman died in 717 of the plague, and the order was given for the Muslim forces to withdraw from Constantinople and return to Damascus, but the transport fleet was hammered by a gale at sea, and then engulfed by a volcanic eruption from the island of Thera, which sent flaming gobs of ash onto the decks of their ships. 'Only ten survived', a Roman chronicler gloated, 'to tell us and the Arabs the magnitude of what God had done to them.'[68]

The failure of the second Arab siege of Constantinople stymied the Muslim advance into eastern Europe. Then in 732, an Umayyad army from al-Andalus was defeated at Poitiers in France by a Frankish army led by Charlemagne's grandfather, Charles Martel, checking the Muslim advance into western Europe as well. The dream of a universal House of Islam would have to be postponed indefinitely.

The Abbasid Conspiracy

IF THE ARABS were not to be granted dominion over the entirety of the known world, there was no question they had conquered the better part of it. A Muslim could now ride a horse all the way from the mountains of the Hindu Kush to the Atlantic Coast without ever stepping outside the borders of the caliphate. Persians, Egyptians, Berbers, Sindis and Turks in the conquered lands, either through conviction, ambition or simple convenience, were being won over to Islam, and expecting to be accorded the same status as the conquering Arabs. 'Whoever speaks Arabic is an Arab',[69] Muhammad had declared emphatically, and gradually, the distinction between an ethnic Arab and a cultural Arab began to blur. Non-Arabs wanting to enter the House of Islam could become *mawali*, 'clients' of an Arab sponsor.

But as masses of non-Arabs adopted the faith, the tension between 'Arab exclusiveness and Muslim inclusiveness'[70] became more tightly strung. Despite Muhammad's proclamation of universal brotherhood among Muslims, the newcomers remained locked outside the ruling Umayyad elite, which was still dominated by high-born Arabs of Qurayshi origin.

But while the *mawali* were tugging at the door, the Umayyad edifice was collapsing from within. With the frontier no longer expanding, opportunities for foreign plunder dried up. Tribal antagonisms resurfaced, the army became factionalised, and the empire descended into a third harrowing civil war. A new Kharijite rebellion broke out in Iraq. By 743, rumours of degeneracy in the caliphal palace again swirled through the empire; the Caliph Walid II, it was said, had become deranged by sex and alcohol, and was openly caressing his servants and slaves in the palace.

Beset by multiple crises, the centre lost touch with the periphery. The Arab elites living in the faraway province of Khorasan, twenty days ride from Damascus, had come to lead distinctively different lives from their cousins in the capital. Just as the ancient Romans had adopted the culture and fashions of the sophisticated Greeks, the Arabs dwelling in the rich silk-road cities of Samarkand and Merv had begun to shed their coarse-cloth desert robes and adorn themselves in the more refined Persian modes of dress. Intermarriage between Arab soldiers and Persian women was widespread and their children were often fluent in both Arabic and Persian dialects.

The Umayyad obsession with the conquest of Constantinople had little relevance to Khorasanis rubbing up against the Tang Empire of China, and a settled view took hold, among Arabs and *mawali* alike, that the Umayyad clan was confiscating far too much revenue from the provinces. Qutaybah, the conqueror of Central Asia and Governor of Khorasan, fired off a letter to Damascus, threatening to cast off his allegiance to the caliph, 'like a pair of sandals'.[71]

THE RUN OF MUSLIM defeats in Europe and elsewhere had deepened the conviction in these outlying provinces that God had turned his face from the sinful Umayyads. In Khorasan, revolutionary Shia groups preached against the Umayyads in hushed voices, arguing that only a return to rule by caliphs drawn from the Prophet's bloodline could redeem the Islamic State and bring justice and peace to its people. This would of course include the family of Ali, but also, and less obviously, the living descendants of the Prophet's paternal uncle, Abbas – less obvious because although Abbas had been supportive of Muhammad in his early years, he had fought on the wrong side in the Battle of Badr and had only become a Muslim after the defeat of the Meccans. Nonetheless, his blood connection to the Prophet lent his descendants a certain mystique.

In June 747, a charismatic former slave operating under the pseudonym Abu Muslim ('Father of a Muslim') openly called for insurrection outside the gates of the Khorasani capital Merv. Abu Muslim was an uncompromising revolutionary from an obscure background; once, when pressed about his ancestry, he snapped, 'The knowledge of my deeds is better for you than the knowledge of my pedigree.'[72] Soon enough, almost the whole of the Khorasani army joined the revolt. Although the Shia groups hoped and expected the figurehead of the revolution would be one of the Alids, the family of Ali, Abu Muslim and his co-conspirators revealed their caliph-in-waiting was Abu al-Abbas, a member of the Abbasid clan. The revolutionaries dyed their robes and banners black to signify their allegiance to their chosen dynasty.

THE ABBASID REVOLUTION was as much a moral crusade as it was a social uprising, a call to recover the utopian, communitarian spirit of early Islam. After seizing control of Merv, the Abbasid army marched westward into Iraq, where they proclaimed Abu al-Abbas as caliph. In the Great Mosque of Kufa, the bright rebirth of Islam was declared:

> Now are the dark nights of the world put to flight, its covering lifted, now light breaks in the earth and the heavens, and the sun rises from the springs of day while the moon ascends from its appointed place. He who fashioned the bow takes it up, and the arrow returns to him who shot it. The right to rule has come back to where it originated, among the people of the house of your Prophet.[73]

The dwindling, demoralised Umayyads made their last stand against the Abbasid army in northern Iraq, at the Battle of the Zab River. It was said that as the armies prepared to fight, Marwan II, the last of the Umayyad caliphs, noticed that several crows had lit on the fluttering black banners of the Abbasids. 'Do you not see how black is joined to black?' he asked his lieutenants. 'You are a fine force indeed, but what use is a force, when time has run its course?'[74]

The Umayyad cavalry charged towards the Abbasid lines, but the Abbasid soldiers had fixed their lances in the ground with their tips angled up towards the enemy. The tactic turned the velocity of the cavalry attack against itself, as the horses and riders impaled themselves on the wall of spears. Umayyad military power was shattered. Marwan fled to Egypt, where he was found and beheaded. Damascus fell to the Abbasids in April 750, bringing the Umayyad era to a close.

ABU AL-ABBAS, THE first caliph of the new Abbasid Dynasty, was awarded a regnal name, Saffah, which means 'Giver of Gifts' but can also mean 'Shedder of Blood'.[75] It was an appropriate title, because once in power, Saffah attempted to annihilate every trace of the Umayyads, both living and dead. The depth of his vindictiveness was not apparent until, in an apparent gesture of reconciliation, he invited the remaining eighty members of the clan to a banquet in Kufa. As the guests took their seats, assassins charged into the room and bludgeoned them to death. Afterwards, leather cloaks were thrown over the dead and dying so that Saffah and his generals could resume their meal.

Saffah then travelled to Syria, where he ordered the tombs of the Umayyads to be desecrated. The dead caliphs were exhumed and burnt and their ashes scattered to the winds.

The only Umayyad to escape the net of Saffah's persecution was a prince named Abd al-Rahman, who had wisely skipped the banquet and fled to Spain. There he became the emir of the rival Emirate of Cordoba, in defiance of the Abbasid Caliphate.

Rizma

THE CHINESE HAD been keeping a close eye on the rise of the Arabs, whom they called *Ta-shih*. A Tang Dynasty annal from 801 records their potted version of how the Arabs had risen to the status of a great power:

> Some say that in the beginning there was a Persian who supposedly had the help of a spirit in obtaining edged weapons [with which] he killed people, subsequently calling for all the Persians to become his followers … After this the masses gradually gave their allegiance, and subsequently Persia was extinguished and Byzantium was crushed, as were also Indian cities.

The Chinese account notes with approval the dignified bearing of the Muslims:

> Their men and women are handsome and tall, their clothing is bright and clean, and their manners are elegant. When a woman goes out in public, she must cover her face irrespective of her lofty or lowly social position. They perform ritual prayers five times a day.[76]

In 713, an Arab envoy arrived at the Chinese capital Chang An, and presented the emperor with 'beautiful horses and a magnificent girdle', but refused to kowtow to him. 'In my country,' the Muslim said, 'we only bow to God, never to a prince.' The envoy's life was spared by the intercession of a Chinese official, who diplomatically observed that differences in court etiquette between countries should not be considered a crime.[77]

Just as the caliphate was extending to its easternmost limits, China was pushing further out to its west. Between the two great powers lay a scattering of silk-road kingdoms and principalities in Central Asia that survived by playing one side off against the other.

The over-extended Chinese and Muslim empires would likely have kept their distance from each other had they not been drawn into a local conflict between Tashkent and Fergana (both in modern-day Uzbekistan). The Tang Chinese, called in to assist Fergana, found themselves up against an Abbasid army led by Abu Muslim, summoned to help defend his client king in Tashkent.

The two imperial armies clashed for the first and last time in July 751 in the valley of the Talas River, some 500 kilometres northeast of Samarkand. According to the Tang account, after five days of fighting, their Turkish allies, the Karluks, switched sides and attacked the Chinese from the rear, resulting in the total defeat of the Tang army in Central Asia.

KHORASAN
c. 770 C.E.

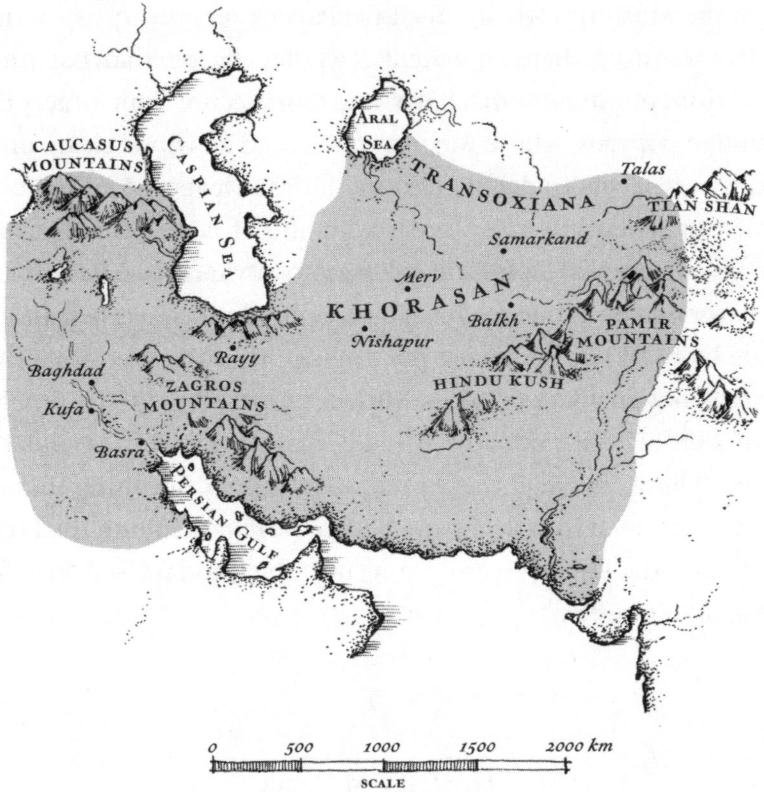

IN THE AFTERMATH of the Battle of Talas, the captured Chinese prisoners of war were put to work in the caliphate. Among these prisoners were said to be several skilled papermakers, who introduced that technology to the city of Samarkand. After that, the Arab historian Thalibi recorded, 'paper was manufactured on a wide scale and passed into general use, until it became an important export commodity for the people of Samarkand. Its value was universally recognized and people everywhere used it.'[78]

Today the story of the captured Chinese papermakers is widely considered a myth, but it is certainly true that the use of paper took off in the Muslim world at this time. Paper's superiority as a writing surface was immediately apparent. It was far cheaper than parchment made from precious animal hides, and more secure from forgery than Egyptian papyrus, whose waxy surface could be wiped clean, unlike ink, which seeped indelibly into the fibres of paper. And there was something about the crisp, pristine nature of new paper that made it a pleasure to trail an ink-tipped brush or stylus across its surface.

Paper had been invented in China eight centuries earlier, and was made by mashing up woody plant fibres in water, then smoothing the pulp out on a screen to dry. Muslims now carried the technology from Central Asia into the Middle East, North Africa and then Spain. Along the way, the Arabic word *rizma*, meaning 'bundle', was transformed into the Spanish word *resma*, then into the French *rayme* and the English word 'ream', now the standardised term for a sheaf of 500 sheets.[79]

The City of Peace

IN 754, SAFFAH succumbed to smallpox and was replaced by his younger brother, who took the regnal name of Mansur – 'the Victorious One'. In the course of his twenty-one-year reign, Mansur transformed the Islamic State, and with it the entire world.

Tall and thin, with weather-beaten skin and a long wispy beard, the second of the Abbasid caliphs was a man of sober habits: he piously avoided wine and hated music, which disrupted his long bouts of silent reflection. Mansur worked long hours, performed his prayers diligently and delivered sermons in the mosque on a Friday.

He often wept while preaching. When his hair turned grey, he dyed it with saffron. He was said to be a notorious penny-pincher in his household, going so far as to strike a deal permitting his cook to keep the head, feet and skins of the game animals in the kitchen, but only if the cook provided his own firewood and seasonings.[80]

Conscious of his dignity, Mansur took care to avoid being drawn into disputes with lesser men. When challenged to a duel by a rival, the caliph sent the upstart a message in the form of a fable:

> The pig challenged the lion to a fight, but the lion said, 'You are only a pig, and no match for me. When I kill you, it will be said of me that I killed a mere pig, and it will hurt my reputation.' The pig then said that if the lion didn't fight, then he would tell all the other lions that he was a coward. The lion replied, 'Bearing the dishonour of your lies is easier for me than the shame of staining my moustache with your blood.'[81]

It would have been unwise for Mansur's enemies to mistake his restraint for squeamishness. The most consequential of the Abbasid caliphs was determined to construct a new order on the rubble of the old, and was prepared to push every enemy, real or potential, into an open grave.

Among them was Abu Muslim, the uncompromising general who had led the overthrow of the Umayyads. After the Abbasid revolution, Abu Muslim had remained in Khorasan as governor, but the warrior had little respect for those who had never led forces in battle, and from the outset his relations with Mansur had been strained. When Mansur succeeded his brother as caliph, Abu Muslim had waited several days before sending him an oath of allegiance, which Mansur interpreted as a subtle act of intimidation. The message, when it did arrive, fulsomely insisted that there was no one among Mansur's lieutenants 'who asserts your claim more vigorously, who counsels you with a purer heart, and who is more desirous of what would please you than I'. But Mansur knew from his spies that Abu Muslim had often spoken of him privately with contempt.

Tensions between the two men increased when Mansur attempted to reconcile the Arab and Persian wings of his empire by reaching out to relatives of the defeated Umayyads, a gesture that infuriated the hardline general. Concerned that Abu Muslim might instigate another rebellion out of Khorasan, Mansur decided to kill him. He sent a friendly note to Abu Muslim, praising his accomplishments and inviting him to come to Kufa to resolve any misunderstandings between them. The caliph's messenger was instructed to hint to Abu Muslim that the caliph was ready to promote him and even make him his right-hand man.

Abu Muslim agonised over whether to obey the caliph's command, suspecting he was being summoned to his death yet knowing that to refuse would constitute an act of rebellion. He received a worrying note from his deputy in Khorasan, urging him not to disobey his caliph, which indicated that his loyalists were slipping away from him. Then another messenger came with more praise from the caliph, and an invitation to meet him in Iraq.

An obedient Abu Muslim made the long journey west to the caliph's camp on the Tigris outside Ctesiphon, but when he entered Mansur's tent, he found the warm welcome he had been promised was not forthcoming. 'Go away,' Mansur told him irritably, 'go and bathe, for travel is a dirty business.'

When Abu Muslim returned the next morning, Mansur clapped his hands and four assassins emerged from behind the tent flaps and cut him to pieces. His mutilated remains were thrown into the Tigris.[82]

THE ELIMINATION OF Abu Muslim angered his allies in Khorasan, but it succeeded in its larger objective, which was to reassure the Arab aristocracy, who had long feared and hated the radical general as a threat to their power and privileges.

Having crushed the threat of rebellion in the east, Mansur could now turn his attention to the creation of a new capital for his empire. Saffah's capital Kufa was still a rough garrison town, and Medina, stranded in the Arabian Desert, was too isolated; Damascus, with its great mosque, was certainly impressive, but it was a city made great by the Romans, and tainted by its Umayyad past.

Mansur resolved instead to create a new, purpose-built capital in Mesopotamia, at the centre of the known world, rooted in the *sawad*, the black-soil farming lands between the Tigris and Euphrates.

In 762, the caliph and his entourage rode up to the Tigris River and stopped at the little village of Baghdad. It was high summer. Mansur crossed the river, performed his late-afternoon prayers, then spent the night in a nearby Christian monastery. He slept well, and the next morning he looked around and found nothing that did not please him.

Baghdad, he was delighted to see, lay on the road to Khorasan, and was adjacent to Mesopotamia's ancient canal system. The rich agricultural lands nearby could support both his army and a large metropolitan population. Its proximity to Ctesiphon and the ruins of Babylon would bathe the capital in the intoxicating aura of those Mesopotamian civilisations. And its location would shift the whole focus of the Islamic State away from Europe and the Mediterranean towards the flourishing cosmopolitan empires of Asia.

'This is the site on which I shall build,' he told his companions. Baghdad, he predicted, would become 'the crossroads of the universe'. 'By God,' he declared, 'I will build this capital and live in it all my life. It will be the residence of my descendants. It will certainly be the most prosperous city in the world.'[83]

Mansur, an admirer of the mathematician Euclid, picked up a reed and traced the outline of the new capital as a perfect circle. The Round City was to be enclosed by two defensive outer walls and beyond them a deep moat. An army of architects, builders, engineers, carpenters, bricklayers and labourers was duly recruited and brought to the Tigris to begin construction. There were no stone quarries anywhere near the site, so the walls and buildings had to be constructed from bricks baked in the sun or fired in a kiln. Other bricks were scavenged from the ruins of the palace in Ctesiphon.

Mansur laid down the city's first brick with his own hands, and said, 'Build, then, with God's blessing.'[84]

In the centre of the Round City, an inner wall enclosed a royal zone that contained the caliphal residence, the Palace of the Golden Gate, as well as the offices of the *diwans*, the Great Mosque, the mansions of the caliph's sons, and homes for the caliph's staff and servants. The space between the outer and inner walls was filled with houses, canals and streets named after the trades of their inhabitants – 'Water-Carrier Street', 'Prayer-Crier Street', 'Horse-Guards Street'.[85] Three pontoon bridges crossed the fast-flowing Tigris, and the canals filled up with small boats and barges. Avenues lined with arcades radiated from the centre to the periphery like spokes on a wheel.

Mansur moved into his new palace in 763, and by 766, construction of the city was more or less complete. Baghdad grew very swiftly as migrants flooded in from across the empire. New districts sprang up outside the Round City on the eastern side of the river, where nobles, judges, merchants and courtiers built mansions, fountains and gardens. The district of Karkh hosted the city's riotous bazaars, crammed with fruit sellers, oil merchants, metalsmiths, soapmakers, fowlers, clothiers, drapers and weavers. To the east of the city, a slave market sold captives from Africa and Europe.

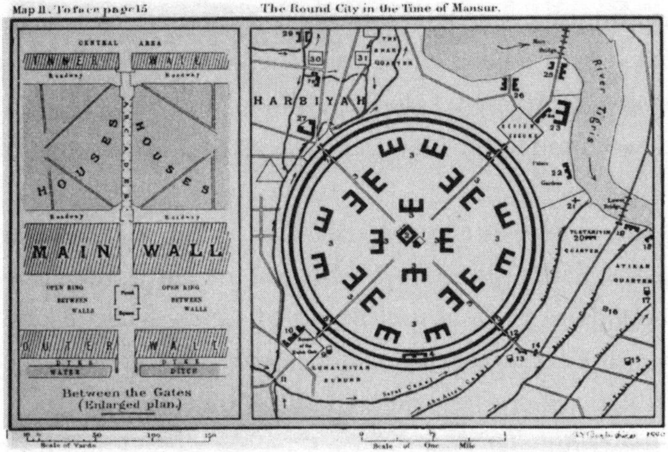

The Round City of Baghdad in the time of Caliph Mansur

MANSUR NAMED HIS gleaming new capital Madinat al-Salam, 'the City of Peace'. The Arab writer Jahiz would later marvel at the Round City's circular perfection: 'It is as though it is poured into a mould and cast.'[86]

Overland traffic passed in and out of the Round City through four ceremonial gates, placed equidistantly at cardinal points on the compass, leading to the four corners of the empire. The Kufa Gate led to the southwest, the Basra Gate to the southeast, the Damascus Gate to the northwest, and the Khorasan Gate to the northeast. Perched above each gate was a domed pavilion from which Mansur could survey the city, the river, the markets and the rich farmlands beyond its walls. 'Here is the Tigris,' he said one day, gesturing to the busy river, 'and nothing stands between it and China!'[87]

IN 775, FEELING his age and aware that death was drawing near, Mansur announced he would perform a final pilgrimage to Mecca, but he died before he could reach the Holy City. He was succeeded by his son Mahdi, an act that established the Abbasid caliphate as a hereditary monarchy, with Baghdad as the theatre for their royal pageantry.

Mansur would forever be regarded as the visionary who had founded the City of Peace and rebooted the entire imperial project. In his *Meadows of Gold and Mines of Gems*, Masudi praises 'his prudence, the rectitude of his judgement and the excellence of his policies,' which were 'beyond all description'.[88]

But the chronicler Tabari relates a story passed on by a member of Mansur's household that casts a shadow on his memory. It was said that as Mansur was preparing to leave Baghdad for his final pilgrimage, he handed the keys to the palace dungeons to Rita, his daughter-in-law, for safekeeping. Under no circumstances, he said, was she to unlock those doors while he was still alive.

When news came of Mansur's death, she and her husband Mahdi rushed down to unlock the cellar doors, hoping to find a hidden trove of treasures. Instead they found themselves in a long chamber filled with corpses. They saw dead children, young men and old men laid out in rows, each one with a scrap of paper stuffed in one ear detailing his name and family background. The dead were all members of the family of Ali who had instigated a failed uprising against Mansur a decade earlier.

The horrified Mahdi ordered a grave to be dug for their bodies and a tombstone to be placed over it.[89]

AS MANSUR HAD HOPED, the shift from Damascus to Baghdad moved the empire's centre of gravity eastward and recalibrated its outlook. The caliphate became more Persian, less Mediterranean; less obsessed with the challenge of Christian Constantinople and more open to the opportunities of Asia. Travellers, traders, soldiers and pilgrims came to the City of Peace from the furthest reaches of the empire and beyond. Baghdad, the first true Arab metropolis, quickly came to approach Constantinople in size and splendour. Within decades of its founding, it became the largest and richest city in the world.

Baghdad in the early medieval era was experiencing the very opposite of a Dark Age; it was instead a moment of expansive confidence, of science, poetry, music and money. Having been granted a vast empire by God, Muslim travellers set out from the four gates of the City of Peace to see it for themselves, driven by the search for money, power or enlightenment. Travelling by boat, horse or camel, they carried their lanterns into far-off lands only dimly known to them, and then further still into the perfect darkness of *terra incognita*.

BOOK TWO

West

HARUN al-RASHID ('Aaron the Rightly Guided')
Fifth of the Abbasid caliphs

CALIPH MAHDI and KHAYZURAN
Parents of Harun al-Rashid

ZUBAYDAH
First wife and cousin of Harun al-Rashid

YAHYA the BARMAKID
Persian vizier to Harun al-Rashid

AMIN and MAMUN
Sons of Harun al-Rashid, sixth and seventh of the Abbasid caliphs

CHARLEMAGNE ('Charles the Great')
King of the Franks and Holy Roman Emperor

ALCUIN of YORK
Scholar and tutor to Charlemagne

IRENE of ATHENS
Empress of Constantinople

ZIRYAB ('the Blackbird')
Musician, inventor and gourmand

GHAZAL ('the Gazelle')
Poet and diplomat

KINDI
Arab philosopher and astronomer

Ibn HAWQAL and ISTAKHRI
Travellers, geographers and mapmakers

IDRISI
Arab mapmaker at the court of Roger II, Norman king of Sicily

the KINGDOMS TO THE WEST
c. 800 C.E.

Karolus Magnus

FOUR THOUSAND KILOMETRES to the northwest of Baghdad lies the little German city of Aachen. Aachen was founded as a spa town by the Romans, who channelled its hot sulphuric waters into a complex of colonnaded bathhouses. When the empire in the West collapsed in 476 and the legions withdrew, barbarian tribes ransacked Aachen's villas and marbled open-air pools. The site was left in ruins until the late eighth century, when Charlemagne, the King of the Franks, began to winter there, lured by Aachen's hot springs and the plentiful game in its forests and pastures. Although he dressed as a Frank, the king enjoyed bathing like a Roman, often inviting his sons, friends and servants to join him in the warm, fizzing waters of the open-air baths.[1]

Since becoming sole ruler of a unified Frankish kingdom in 771, Charlemagne – 'Charles the Great' – had sent his conquering armies out in all directions from their base in northwestern Europe, until his empire encompassed most of modern-day France, Germany, the Netherlands, Switzerland, Austria and northern Italy. Having been at war for most of his reign, Charlemagne had kept his court constantly on the move. Now, having won an empire, he decided it was time to settle down in a purpose-built capital. He chose Aachen, which had become a kind of resort for him and his extended family.

In 794, construction began on a palace complex to serve as a residence, an administrative centre and a place of worship. Charlemagne's royal hall no longer exists, but the handsome octagonal chapel attached to it still stands. The Palatine Chapel, although modest in size compared with the great cathedrals of Europe, is a finely cut gem, clad in marble sheets that had to be hauled up from Rome and Ravenna, and crowned with a golden mosaic.

According to a local legend, when the funds to complete the chapel ran out, the local people cut a deal with the Devil, who agreed to give them the money in exchange for the first soul to enter the building when it was done. The Prince of Hell was expecting the bishop to lead the inaugural procession, but the cunning villagers captured a wolf and let it loose in the nave instead. The Devil instantly swooped down and tore out the creature's soul. When he realised he'd been tricked, he angrily slammed the chapel doors shut, but his thumb caught in the doorlatch and was sheared off. Howling in rage and agony, the Devil scuttled back to Hell, clutching his mutilated hand.*

BEHIND THE ALTAR of the Palatine Chapel lies a gaudy sarcophagus that holds Charlemagne's bones. A DNA study of the remains has revealed that he stood at six foot three, which chimes with the accounts of his contemporaries, who described him as large-framed with a slight pot-belly. He was said to have had a round head, with fair hair, a long nose and unusually large and piercing eyes.[2] His imposing physical presence was matched by an unshakeable sense of mission, tempered by a calm disposition and an affectionate nature that inspired deep loyalty among his subjects and soldiers. They saw him as a lightbringer, the redeemer of Christian Roman authority after centuries of darkness.

Even in Roman times, the province of Gaul had been a raw frontier land, open to waves of assault from the painted, bearded 'barbarians' who dwelt in the dense forests of Germany. When the Roman legions withdrew in the fifth century, living conditions fell drastically. Towns and cities shrank within their walls, roads fell into disrepair, the luxurious countryside villas of the Roman aristocracy

* Today tourists reach inside the mouth of the door knocker to feel the Devil's bronze thumb protruding from the door panel.

were abandoned or occupied by squatters. Literacy declined; art and handicrafts became cruder; economic activity became localised as trade links with the wider world dried up. Most people lived on farms or in timber-built villages linked by narrow, unpaved roads unsuited to wheeled vehicles, so travellers moved from place to place on foot or on horseback. At night, wolf packs came in from the forests to prowl through the deserted lanes of the towns and settlements.

A series of unstable petty kingdoms emerged, until a Germanic people, the Franks, came to dominate Gaul. The Franks, from whom we get the word 'frank', meaning free-speaking or candid, were ruled by a dynasty of kings, the Merovingians, who made the Roman city of Parisius – Paris – their capital. Over time, as the Franks adopted Christianity and absorbed elements of the vulgar Latin spoken in the former Roman settlements, the area became known as Francia, the Kingdom of the Franks.

The Merovingians maintained a shaky grip on Francia until they were superseded in 751 by a new dynasty, the Carolingians, named for its many kings called Charles. It was Charlemagne's grandfather, Charles Martel, who had led the Frankish armies to thwart the Muslim advance over the Pyrenees into France at the Battle of Poitiers in 732. The thought that the Muslim armies might have broken through at Poitiers and continued their northward march famously led historian Edward Gibbon to wonder in the eighteenth century:

> Perhaps the interpretation of the Koran would now be taught in the schools of Oxford, and her pulpits might demonstrate to a circumcised people the sanctity and truth of the revelation of Mahomet.[3]

IN HIS LIFETIME, Charlemagne was lionised as the ideal Christian king. An inscription running around the interior of the Palatine Chapel speaks of 'living stones joined in a bond of peace', but it was a peace imposed with fire and steel on the heathen lands that bordered his kingdom. The conquest of these pagan tribes not only brought him land and treasure, but also honoured a Heaven-mandated duty to scour these dark lands of their wickedness and unbelief. Unlike the warriors of Islam, who were more or less content to let conquered peoples come to the faith of their own accord, Charlemagne preached to the pagans with a 'tongue of iron'.[4]

The most incorrigible of his infidel neighbours were the Saxons, a tribe dwelling in the forests and marshes to the east. Despite the best efforts of Anglo-Saxon missionaries, the Saxons had held fast to their pantheon of Germanic gods, ruled by Wotan, the King of Valhalla, and Thor, the bringer of lightning and rain. Every church or monastery built on the Saxon lands had been pulled down.

As the ever-expanding Frankish frontier pushed up against the Saxon lands, border skirmishes escalated into pitched battles. Afterwards, the Franks would extract oaths of loyalty from the defeated Saxons and promises to accept baptism, only to later find out they'd torn down their crosses and broken out in revolt once more.

The Saxons' stubborn determination to preserve their ancient way of life was seen by the Franks as perverse and diabolical. In the summer of 772, an affronted Charlemagne led his army on a punitive mission into Saxon territory. Moving through dense forests that had once terrified Caesar's legions, the Franks came to a clearing, where they found the Saxons' great totem, the Irminsul, a gigantic oak tree the Saxons believed to be the central pillar of the universe. At the foot of the sacred tree lay a heap of Roman coins, precious gems and plundered items piled up as offerings to their gods. Charlemagne ordered the world-tree to be hacked down and its wood to be thrown onto a roaring bonfire. Returning to his kingdom, he doled out the Saxons' captured treasure to his allies, strengthening the bonds of loyalty to him.

In retaliation for this act of sacrilege, the Saxon tribes regrouped and assaulted the Frankish borderlands, razing churches and monasteries to the ground. There was by now, it was noted, 'immense hatred on both sides'.[5]

An infuriated Charlemagne now embarked on a methodical genocide of the Saxons, declaring his intent to wage war against the infidels until they had either been 'subjugated to Christianity, or completely annihilated'.[6] Steadily and relentlessly, the Frankish army invaded and colonised the Saxon lands piece by piece. Saxon families were systematically captured, deported and scattered to other parts of Charlemagne's realm. Those who remained were forced to accept either baptism or death.

In October 782, the Franks cornered the remaining Saxon rebels on the Aller River. Deciding to make an example of them, Charlemagne ordered his men to slaughter more than 4000 prisoners of war for violating their oaths of loyalty to him. Even his admirers were horrified by the massacres and forced conversions. 'How can a man be compelled to believe what he does not believe?' wrote his closest advisor, Alcuin of York. 'You may force a man to the font, but not to the faith.'[7]

WITH THE OBLITERATION of the Saxons accomplished, Charlemagne was now ready to turn his attention to the pagan Avars, a nomadic people originally from Central Asia who had settled centuries earlier on the Great Hungarian Plain. The Avars had once been a near-unstoppable force, rampaging through eastern Europe and extorting wagonloads of gold from Roman emperors who preferred to pay them off than to take on their lethal horseback archers. In 636, they had joined the Persians in a siege of Constantinople, but the Avars had since become more sedentary and preoccupied with internal struggles. In 791, an epidemic of horse flu destroyed most of what remained of their cavalry. The final blow came in 796, when a force led by Charlemagne's son Pepin and the Duke of Friuli invaded the Avar lands, meeting with little or no resistance.

Storming through the Hungarian Plain, the Frankish army seized the Avar citadel, a fortress known as the Ring that was protected by concentric circles of earthworks. Inside the Ring they found a vast storehouse of gold and silver accumulated from centuries of extortion and plunder. Fifteen ox-drawn wagons were required to haul the treasure back to Aachen.

The mountain of Avar treasure made Charlemagne stupefyingly rich. Einhard, his court historian, recorded breathlessly: 'The memory of man cannot recall any war against the Franks by which they were so enriched and their material possessions so increased.'[8]

Einhard's choice of phrase 'against the Franks' implied that the Avars, not they, were the aggressors, and that the Avars' resistance to Christianity was the offence that justified an invasion that left their fortress a ruin and the Hungarian Plain a sparsely inhabited wasteland. 'All their nobility died in this war, all their glory departed,' noted Einhard elegiacally.[9] The survivors were Christianised, and within a few decades, the Avars and their distinctive culture had completely vanished.

SUCH APOCALYPTIC SCENES were a world away from the busy, bucolic life enjoyed by Charlemagne's family and staff at Aachen. With his treasury now filled with Avar gold, he could build up his estate into a fitting royal residence, where he could hunt, swim and feast.

We know that Charlemagne kept a fine table at Aachen. He drafted a charter of instructions to his stewards, listing the items to be provided to the royal household from his estates: fish, game, cheese, butter, mustard, vinegar, honey, cucumbers, melons, artichokes, peas, carrots, onions, leeks, radishes, wine and beer. He demanded fresh herbs and spices to flavour his food: sage, cumin, rosemary, caraway, fenugreek, dill, sweet fennel, coriander and parsley. There are guidelines for the keeping of bees, the collecting of eggs and the killing of game birds. Swans, peacocks, pheasants, ducks, pigeons, partridges and turtle doves were to be kept on the estates for the sake of ornament. Food brought to the king's table was to be 'made or prepared with the greatest attention to cleanliness'. The stewards were therefore to ensure that the king's wine-presses were kept in good order, and that no one dared to crush the grapes with their bare feet.[10]

Charlemagne's travels had made him something of a gourmand. On campaign in 774, he had stopped at the Abbaye de Jouarre in Brie, where the monks made a particular kind of soft cheese with a thin white crust and a creamy, straw-coloured interior. Charlemagne declared it to be one of the most sublime things he'd ever tasted, and had two wheels of Brie de Meaux delivered to Aachen every year.[11] He was likewise delighted when he discovered the tangy blue-veined cheese aged in the limestone caves of Roquefort.

The sprawling palace complex at Aachen had to be large enough to accommodate the extended royal family. Charlemagne had at least eighteen children by his successive wives and concubines, and they in turn produced countless grandchildren. His unhappy first marriage to a Lombard princess named Desiderata lasted a year before it was annulled. His second wife Hildegard died after giving birth to the ninth of their children; the infant daughter, herself named Hildegard, lived for little more than a month. The epitaph of the baby girl speaks of the grief that both deaths brought down upon the king:

> Hildegard you did not live for even a year.
> You never had a first birthday.
> Little girl, little maiden, you left behind grief that was not little.
> You pierce as with a spear the royal heart of your father,
> And bearing your mother's name, you renew the sorrow of
> her death
> After you scarcely lived forty days.[12]

Charlemagne's third wife, Fastrada, died at twenty-nine. His fourth, Luitgard, died childless in 800. He forbade his daughters from marrying, perhaps to forestall their offspring from challenging the line of succession, but he was untroubled by their love affairs and supported their common-law husbands by finding positions for them at court. After the death of his last wife, his daughters collectively took on the duties of the royal consort in order to manage his estates.

ALTHOUGH BARELY LITERATE, Charlemagne surrounded himself with scholars who were devoted, as he was, to salvaging something from the wreckage of Roman civilisation. This was all of a piece with his obligation, as he saw it, to retrieve the lost wisdom of the ancient world in order to decode the mysteries of the Bible. Unlike the Quran, which was received by Muslims as the pristine word of God, the Bible was understood by Christians to be mysterious and prophetic, and required knowledge of grammar, logic, mathematics and astronomy to fully understand.

Charlemagne was painfully aware of the gaps in his own education, and he struggled to learn to read and write as an adult. To practise his Latin and Greek letters, he kept a tablet by his pillow that he occasionally threw across the room in frustration. His willingness to expose himself to such moments of painful embarrassment says something of his drive for self-improvement. In Charlemagne's time there still lingered the Roman ideal of *sapientia et fortitudo*, the model of the great man who is strong in thought, word and deed. Determined to be remembered as something more than a conqueror, he issued an edict decreeing that every monastery and abbey in his realm should establish a school to teach boys from every social class (no one, it seems, thought to include girls). He declared his resolve to restore 'the workshops of knowledge, which, through the negligence of our ancestors, have been well-nigh deserted'. Leading by example, he invited his subjects to practise the seven liberal arts: grammar, rhetoric, logic, arithmetic, geometry, music and astronomy.[13]

To foster a culture of learning, Charlemagne brought the cream of Europe's scholars to Aachen and rewarded them handsomely with gold and grants of land. He encouraged them to vie for his attention through both jocular and serious debate, and even permitted his pre-eminent scholar, Alcuin of York, to contradict him, a privilege available to no one else in his court. Alcuin affectionately nicknamed him 'David', after the biblical king who was both a warrior and a poet, the slayer of Goliath who played the lyre and composed the Psalms in his downtime.

Alcuin had been raised and educated at York's famous cathedral school, renowned in the eighth century as the foremost centre of learning in western Europe. At York he was taught that God had created the world as a beautiful, intricate puzzle, but had also endowed humans with the tool of reason to figure out how it worked. For Alcuin, decoding the motion of the planets, the rising and setting of the moon and the tremors of land and sea was a joyful process that allowed him to glimpse the hand of God in everything.

In 781, he was in Italy on diplomatic business for the Bishop of York when he ran into Charlemagne and his retinue, who were on their way to Rome. Fully aware of Alcuin's reputation as the most learned man of his time, Charlemagne took the opportunity to invite the man of letters to join his elite coterie of scholars and philosophers.

In France, Alcuin served as Charlemagne's personal tutor and his director of public education. 'Nothing', he wrote to Charlemagne, 'is more essential to government, nothing more helpful in leading a moral life, than the beauty of wisdom.'[14] It was Alcuin, acting with Charlemagne's blessing, who instituted a universal calendar system for Western Christendom. The Muslim world had long since set its calendar to begin with Muhammad's flight to Medina; now Alcuin marked the birth of Christ as year 1 A.D., *anno Domini*, 'in the year of the Lord'.

The Italian intellectuals in Charlemagne's court had been a somewhat earnest and morose bunch, but Alcuin soon lightened the tone at Aachen, using his teacher's tools of jokes, puns and riddles to make learning pleasurable. He compiled a booklet of logic puzzles for his students and the king titled *Problems to Sharpen the Young*, which included the following variation of the classic river-crossing conundrum:

A man arrives at a river bank with a wolf, a goat and a cabbage.

*But his boat can only take one of them at a time. The goat will eat the cabbage if left alone with it, just as the wolf will eat the goat if the two are unsupervised. The wolf doesn't like cabbage. How many trips would it take to bring them all over intact?**

With his considerable wit, warmth and personal charm, Alcuin fostered a cult of friendship within Charlemagne's court. He gave people nicknames, which created a kind of jocular familiarity and deepened their affection for each other. He possessed, as one historian has noted, 'the inestimable gift, for any newly formed elite, of the ability to communicate to his colleagues the sense of belonging to a charmed circle'.[15] Unusually for his time, he included women in that circle: he became close to Charlemagne's daughters, and wrote a flurry of letters to leading women in Mercia and Northumbria, using his intimacy with them to influence the kings and nobles of those courts.

Alcuin was also able to cultivate a growing sense in Western Europe that Charlemagne had brought about a restoration of Christian Roman glory after a long night of barbarian darkness. 'Although the whole of Europe was once denuded with fire and sword by Goths and Huns,' Alcuin proclaimed to a friend, 'now, by God's mercy, Europe is as bright with churches as is the sky with stars.'[16] Alcuin told Charlemagne he was a greater figure than the pope in Rome or the emperor in Constantinople. 'You are more noble in your wisdom,' he wrote in a letter. 'You are more awe-inspiring in the dignity of your kingdom. The well-being of the churches of Christ rests on you alone.'[17] This was more than just flattery; the sentiment

* Alcuin's answer was seven. First, the man should take the goat across and leave it there. Then he should ferry the wolf over, but then bring the goat back with him to the starting point. Then, leaving the goat, he should bring the cabbage over and leave it safely with the wolf. Finally, he should row back to collect the goat again. 'By this procedure,' Alcuin wrote cheerfully, 'there would be some healthy rowing, but no lacerating catastrophe.' (Hadley & Singmaster, p. 111)

was commonly held among the king's court intellectuals. Einhard, his biographer, emotionally declared his desire to record the 'remarkable deeds of a man who was so kind to me', a king who was 'by far the most able and noble-spirited of all those who ruled over the nations in his time'.[18]

FOR THE RULER of so large a domain, a figure of such towering personal majesty, 'king' now seemed too paltry a title; at least, it did to the embattled Pope Leo III. Leo, who was under attack from supporters of a rival pope, had been badly beaten up in the street months earlier and was hoping to gain Charlemagne's support and protection. So when Charlemagne and his family came to Rome for an extended stay in 800, Leo made his move. On Christmas Day that year, as the king knelt at St Peter's tomb, Leo placed a crown on his head and proclaimed him *Imperator Romanorum*, Emperor of the Romans. The congregation duly hailed Charlemagne as Augustus and Leo threw himself at his feet. Charlemagne always claimed unconvincingly that the pope had taken him by surprise, but he was pleased enough by the honour to have coins minted showing him in classical profile crowned by a laurel wreath. The message was clear: the Roman Empire was back, and Aachen was to be its new capital.

A coin of Charlemagne, 'Karolus Magnus Imperator'

The Elephant and the Water-Clock

THE IMPERIAL CORONATION of Charlemagne was a dizzying moment for his subjects, but in the eyes of the wider world it took more than a crown and a cloak to transmute a barbarian king into a Roman emperor. Charlemagne, for all his accomplishments, presided over an empire that was technologically backward, culturally narrow and economically primitive, compared with the bigger, richer and more vibrant civilisations of the East. On the map his realm looked like an impressive restoration of the Western Roman Empire – minus Spain and North Africa, which were now under Muslim control, and Britain, which was ruled by a collection of petty monarchs. Yet the kingdom's vast spaces were thinly populated and Charlemagne was dependent on foreign plunder to bind them together. Outside of Italy, his empire lacked any commercial cities; it had no great metropolitan capital like Constantinople or Baghdad, furnished with palaces, grand libraries, sporting arenas and gargantuan houses of worship. There was no state taxation system, and his administration lacked permanent bureaucratic institutions like the *diwan*s of Baghdad. He was forced to rely on his army and personal bonds of loyalty to implement his edicts. While China, India and the Muslim world bought and sold sophisticated luxury goods, western Europe's principal export commodities were iron, timber and slaves captured from Central Europe and sold through the markets of Prague, Lyon and Venice.[19]

CHARLEMAGNE'S CLAIM TO the imperial purple was always going to be met with scorn and outrage by the Romans of Constantinople, who considered themselves the true heirs to the Roman name. Their capital on the Bosphorus, the incomparable queen of cities, was by far the biggest metropolis in Europe. Among such haughty sophisticates, Charlemagne could only be seen as a pretentious barbarian who had as much right to the title 'Roman Emperor' as a cat or a dog.

But at the time of his coronation, the ruler in Constantinople was the formidable Irene of Athens, the only woman ever to rule the empire in her own right, and with the audacity to style herself as emperor instead of empress. Charlemagne's supporters could argue that a woman could not possibly be emperor, and that their man, in accepting the crown from the pope, was simply occupying a vacant throne. The fact that the city of Rome itself lay within Charlemagne's realm, and not within Irene's, gave some credence to his claim to the title 'Emperor of the Romans'. Charlemagne nonetheless proposed marriage to Irene in 802, a union that would reunite the Eastern and Western Roman Empires under a single crown. But a cabal of horrified bureaucrats and military officers in Constantinople acted pre-emptively against the alliance and deposed their female emperor in October that year. Irene was sent into exile on the tiny island of Principo in the Sea of Marmara, and within a year she was dead.

STUNG BY CONSTANTINOPLE'S disdain, Charlemagne decided to reach over their heads to establish friendly relations with the Abbasid Caliphate. His ambassadors were evidently well received in Baghdad, and in the summer of 802 they returned to Aachen with an array of gifts for him from the great caliph of the Muslims, Harun al-Rashid.

Charlemagne had seen a great many things over his long reign, but even he must have been astonished and amused by the largest and noisiest of Harun's presents: a full-grown elephant named Abul-Abbas. The arrival of Abul-Abbas created a sensation in Europe: realistic images of elephants began to appear in carvings and manuscripts, suggesting that people had come from far and wide to catch a glimpse of the fabulous beast. Charlemagne's scribes boasted that the exotic gift was manifest proof of the caliph's high esteem for their king and an acknowledgement of their empire's elevation to great power status.

In 807, another caravan arrived from Baghdad laden with silken robes, perfumes and an enormous multi-coloured linen tent. The court was most impressed, however, by an ingenious mechanical water-clock. On the hour the device would drop a bronze ball into a metal bowl, where it rang a cymbal. A clockwork horseman would then pop out of one of twelve little doors to indicate the hour, while the rider representing the previous hour slipped back inside.[20] The Franks, who had been reckoning time with sundials, hourglasses and candle-clocks, were staggered by this demonstration of Abbasid technological prowess, as they were surely intended to be.

A ninth-century manuscript from the Abbey of St Denis, with an elephant's head incorporated into the text

The Golden Prime

THE BREATHLESS ACCOUNTS of the elephant and the water-clock are all one-sided. The Abbasid chroniclers, who routinely recorded diplomatic exchanges with Constantinople, India and China, made no mention of the embassies to Charlemagne: an omission implying that such exchanges with a damp and distant infidel kingdom were of little or no interest to them.

Travellers from Muslim Spain, however, showed a more lively interest in their Christian and pagan neighbours in northern Europe. In 965, a Jewish merchant and spy named Ibraham ibn Yaqub passed through Prague and produced a wonderfully lucid account of the Bohemian capital for the Emir of Cordoba. Writing in the polite, inquisitive style of an anthropologist on safari, he describes a city made of 'stone and lime', with a market selling slaves, tin and furs, a place where pagan men and women practised free love until they got married.[21] He respectfully describes a recently converted Christian Slavic king in the German city of Magdeburg as knowledgeable and powerful.

Yet in Baghdad, the kings of Christendom were harshly dismissed as *mukluk kuffar* – 'kings of unbelief'[22] – ruling over people too stupid or obtuse to accept Islam. Masudi wrote of the Franks as the Romans once had of the Arabs, as a pitiable people scratching a living from a harsh land:

> The power of the sun is weakened among the Franks because of its distance from them; cold and damp prevail in their regions, and snow and ice follow one another in endless succession. The warm humour is lacking among them; their bodies are large, their natures gross, their manners harsh, their understanding dull, and their tongues heavy. Their colour is so excessively white that they look blue; their skin is

> fine and their flesh coarse. Their eyes, too, are blue, matching their colouring; their hair is lank and reddish because of the damp mists. Their religious beliefs lack solidity, and this is because of the nature of cold and the lack of warmth.[23]

Masudi, like most other Abbasid geographers, was impressed by the theories of the Greek astronomer Ptolemy, whose work *Almagest* was translated several times into Arabic. Ptolemy had divided the known world into seven distinct bands of longitude he called 'climes', starting at the equator and concluding at the Arctic Circle. The nature of these climes, he believed, stamped the character of the people who lived in them. It apparently explained why those unfortunate enough to be living in the excessively cold or hot zones lived as wretchedly as they did. 'If the country is cold,' wrote the ninth-century essayist Jahiz, 'they are under cooked in the womb; if the country is hot, they are burnt in the womb.'

By the standards of this cooked-just-right theory, it was the people of Iraq who made the best humans, according to the tenth-century geographer Ibn al-Faqih:

> The people of Iraq have sound minds, commendable passions, balanced natures and high proficiency in every art, together with well-proportioned limbs, well-compounded humours, and a pale brown colour which is the most apt and proper colour. They are the ones done to a turn in the womb. They do not come out with something between blond, buff, blanded and leprous colouring, such as the infants dropped from the wombs of the women of the Slavs and others of similar light complexion; nor are they over done in the womb until they are burnt, so that the child comes out something between black and murky, malodorous, stinking,

> wholly-haired, with uneven limbs, deficient mind and depraved passions, such as the Zanj, the Ethiopians, and other blacks who resemble them. The Iraqis are neither half-baked dough nor burnt crust, but between the two.[24]

It was surely no coincidence, then, that the most brilliant cities, Baghdad and Constantinople, were located in the happiest and most temperate clime. Such theories could only redouble a conviction among the people of eighth-century Baghdad that they lived in the best of all places in the best of all times: in the City of Peace, during the reign of Harun al-Rashid.

HARUN AL-RASHID, TALL, good-looking and slim, with wavy hair and olive skin,[25] presided over an empire that stretched from North Africa to India. The English poet Tennyson would later fantasise about 'the golden prime, Of good Haroun Alraschid', and even in Harun's own time, Muslims could feel the sunshine of God's good will on their faces. 'Did you not see how the sun came out of hiding on Harun's accession and flooded the world with light?'[26] asked one giddy poet.

Harun was in all likelihood the wealthiest man who ever lived, and spent his riches freely. On his wedding day, he handed out fistfuls of gold and silver coins to people from all over his realm, while his servants distributed brocaded gowns, and scented oils from large glass bowls. To his wife Zubaydah he gave an ornate sleeveless jacket, a *badanah*, studded with oversized rubies and pearls.[27] 'So great were the splendours and riches of his reign,' wrote Masudi, 'such was its prosperity, that this period has been called "the honeymoon".'[28]

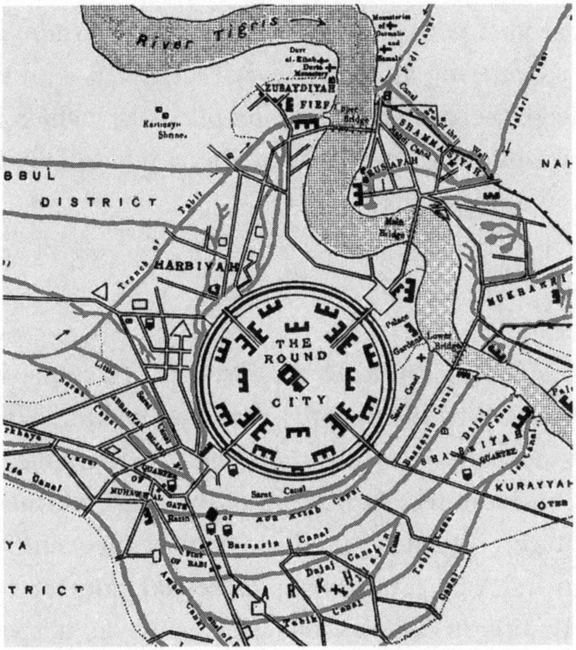

Baghdad, c. 800 C.E., during the reign of Harun al-Rashid

When Harun came to the throne, Baghdad had become the first medieval city to pass the population threshold of a million people.[29] In the new districts of Rusafa, Shammasiya and Mukharrim on the east bank of the Tigris, princes, courtiers and merchants built palaces and mansions that outshone the grandeur of the Golden Gate Palace in the Round City. While in Baghdad, Harun preferred to dwell in the Qasr al-Khuld, the Palace of Eternity, overlooking the Tigris, so named for its gardens, which were said to rival those in Paradise. Here the caliph could find some respite from the heat of the day and the pressures of court life, sitting in the shaded pavilions of an immense flowered pleasure garden, surrounded by waterfalls, and trees with precious gems studded into their trunks. The palace interiors facing the gardens had been decorated to subtly correspond with the colours blooming outside; one visitor later recalled entering an audience hall carpeted with pink fabric and attended by servants in matching pink silks, which looked out over the treetops of a garden that had 'burst into leaf with roses and peach and apple blossoms'.[30]

IN THE WESTERN WORLD, the historical Harun al-Rashid has long been eclipsed by his fictional persona: the king of an Arabian fantasia who appears repeatedly in *The Thousand and One Nights*. This fabulous compendium of stories, one of the greatest achievements in world literature, originated in India and was subsequently translated into Persian and Arabic, picking up more and more tales over many centuries. Its title in Arabic, *Alf Layla wa-Layla*, is spoken like a whisper, an enchantment.

The *Nights* were introduced to the West in 1704, when the French orientalist Antoine Galland published them in Paris as *Les Mille et Une Nuits*, with the addition of the tales of Ali Baba and the forty thieves and Aladdin that he'd picked up from a Syrian storyteller named Hanna Diyab, as well as the tales of Sinbad the Sailor that he'd found in a Constantinople marketplace.

The Argentine author Jorge Luis Borges thought the title *The Thousand and One Nights* was one of the most beautiful in the world. Its beauty, he thought, lay in that magic number: 'To say a *thousand nights* is to say infinite nights, countless nights. To say *a thousand and one nights* is to add one to infinity.'[31]

The tales are all told by the character Shahrazad (or Scheherazade), a woman who must forestall her execution at the hands of her husband, a murderous Persian king. She does this by spinning tales night after night, forcing the cruel king to postpone her death the next day so he can hear the end of the tale.

The stories are impregnated with the atmosphere of a restless midsummer night when it's too hot to sleep, shifting unpredictably from mystery to horror to bawdy comedy. One tale flows effortlessly into the next; some are nested inside other stories like Russian dolls. Reading them feels like swimming down to the bottom of a well and then coming back up for air. 'It is a book so vast', wrote Borges, 'that it is not necessary to have read it, for it is part of our memory – and also, now, part of tonight.'[32]

In these tales, Harun al-Rashid is typically found in his palace, bored out of his mind, so he orders Jafar the vizier and Masrur the executioner to accompany him on a nighttime expedition into the world's biggest city. Their wanderings inevitably lead them into a mystery or an adventure.

Like his fictional counterpart, the real Harun longed to escape the pressures and tedium of court life, and would slip into the palace gardens in the calm of the night, where 'amid the warm air, sweetened with the scent of the flowers, the caliph could expand his chest, in the city of Baghdad'.[33] Harun was among the best travelled of all the Abbasid caliphs, but he was a far more melancholic figure than the merry nocturnal adventurer in *The Thousand and One Nights* and, as time went on, a more temperamental one.

HARUN AL-RASHID, WHOSE name can be translated as 'Aaron the Rightly Guided', was born in 766 during the reign of his grandfather Mansur, in the Persian city of Rayy. He was the second son of Mansur's successor Mahdi and his wife Khayzuran, a former slave whose name means 'Bamboo' – a reference to her slender, supple figure. Harun was Khayzuran's favourite son, and she appears to have strongly favoured him over his older brother Musa. Mahdi placed Musa first in the line of succession, but in the event of Musa's death, he specified that Harun would come next.

Harun received an excellent education in history, geography, music and poetry, and was trained in the martial arts of swordplay and archery. He was said to be the only caliph other than Uthman who could recite the entire Quran from memory. At fourteen, his father Caliph Mahdi appointed him as nominal commander of an Abbasid army in a low-key campaign against some Roman fortresses in southern Anatolia. The young Harun, puffed up with pride and military zeal, was mocked by his older relatives for his teenage posturing,[34] but the expedition was modestly successful: a Roman castle was taken, and Christian prisoners of war were brought back to Baghdad.

Two years later, he was made the nominal head of another, more ambitious campaign, and this time his army cut a path right across Anatolia, all the way to the Bosphorus coast. Although they could not hope to penetrate Constantinople's formidable Theodosian Walls, the army spent weeks plundering the suburbs and towns beyond them. Eventually the Romans sued for peace and agreed to hand over tribute. There were no lasting territorial gains, but in Baghdad the campaign was trumpeted as a shattering success.

His father then appointed Harun governor of the western provinces, but again he served as a figurehead. It was Harun's tutor and mentor, a supremely capable Persian bureaucrat known as Yahya the Barmakid, who administered the province on his behalf.

Yahya was the scion of a clan of highly skilled Persian administrators from Balkh, in modern-day Afghanistan, who had served for generations as high priests of a great Buddhist monastery. After the Arab conquest of Balkh, the Barmakids converted to Islam, joined the Abbasid Revolution, and were swiftly appointed to senior bureaucratic positions in Baghdad. It was men like Yahya who Persianised the Abbasid state and professionalised its institutions.

Yahya became a second father-figure to the young Harun, and his family were exceptionally close to Queen Khayzuran. As an infant, Harun had been suckled by Yahya's wife, while Khayzuran had done the same for Yahya's son Fadl, essentially making the two boys foster-brothers. Both Yahya and Khayzuran conspired to press the caliph to flip the order of succession, and push Harun to the front of the line ahead of his older brother Musa.

Mahdi seemed willing to make the change, but in 785, before it could be made official, the caliph died in a freak accident.

MAHDI, WHO LOVED hunting and falconry, had travelled to the Zagros Mountains, north of Baghdad, accompanied by Harun, Yahya and a company of troops. But while chasing after a gazelle on the grounds of an old estate, his horse had bolted through the door of a ruined house, bashing his head into the lintel, killing him at once.[35]

Harun, distressed and confused, turned to Yahya, who told him the unfortunate timing of Mahdi's death meant that the throne must now legally pass to Musa, who was at that moment far away on campaign near the Caspian Sea. Yahya advised Harun to act quickly: he should at once inform his older brother of their father's death and offer his allegiance. In the meantime they would conceal Mahdi's death from the army. The death of a caliph was an ideal moment for troops to exploit the uncertainty by demanding a donative to smooth the transition to the new one.

Taking Yahya's advice, Harun quietly buried his father in the shade of a walnut tree. That night, his messenger slipped out of camp and rode off to the Caspian Sea, where he handed Musa his father's sceptre and seal ring. The caliph's senior men acknowledged him as caliph and he was given the regnal name of Hadi.

Meanwhile, in the Zagros Mountains, Harun told his father's still-unknowing troops they would soon be going back to Baghdad, and that they were all to receive a bonus of 200 dirhams. As Yahya predicted, the soldiers bolted for home at once to spend their money. But once in Baghdad, hearing that power had changed hands without their knowledge, the troops rioted in the streets, and only returned to their barracks after the chamberlain bowed to their demands and offered them a further two years' pay in advance.

CALIPH HADI WAS, like his brother, tall, but he had a florid complexion and a 'contracted upper lip', a description that may denote a cleft palate. In his youth he was mocked with the nickname 'Musa Shut Your Mouth'.[36]

Hadi inherited a court already split between a military faction and a clique of bureaucrats led by Yahya. The new caliph came down hard on the side of the generals and militarised the palace; he and his advisors swished about from room to room, accompanied by a cohort of bodyguards bearing unsheathed swords and arrow-strung bows. Hadi abandoned his father's conciliatory policy towards the Alids, the descendants of Ali, and stripped them of their privileges, igniting an Alid rebellion in 786 that he brutally suppressed. The leader of the revolt, Ali ibn Husayn, was killed and the remaining Alids scattered to the periphery of the Muslim world. Idris bin Abdallah, a cousin of Husayn, escaped to Morocco, where he would found the breakaway Idrisid monarchy in 788.

Hadi's relationship with his powerful mother had never been strong and he was determined to keep Khayzuran from engaging in politics. When she came to ask a favour on behalf of some courtier, Hadi bluntly told her to stop meddling in affairs of state and to amuse herself with a spindle instead.

'God knows, then,' she said, 'that I shall never ask you for anything again.'

'God knows,' replied Hadi, 'I won't be sorry about that.'

With that, Khayzuran walked out of the room. On Hadi's orders, officials and generals were forbidden to go to her, and for a while she became a powerless recluse in the harem. One account records that Hadi sent her a dish of poisoned rice with the message 'I found this tasty so you should have some of it too.' Khayzuran fed it to a dog, which subsequently dropped dead. She then sent a message to her son saying she had enjoyed the rice very much. Hadi replied: 'You can't have eaten it, because if you had, I would have been rid of you. What caliph was ever happy with his mother still alive?'[37]

Hadi soon soured on his younger brother as well. Customarily, a qualified brother would be placed next in line to the throne, ahead of a son. But although their father had specified that Harun was to become caliph in the event of Hadi's death, Hadi let it be known he intended to name his little boy Jafar as his successor instead. Hadi's men began to badmouth Harun in public forums, blaming Yahya as a bad influence.

Hadi summoned Yahya one night and, after extracting oaths of loyalty, demanded to know what Harun had been up to.

'He hasn't been up to anything,' Yahya sputtered, 'and it is not in his character or capability to do anything untoward.'[38]

Hadi seemed satisfied by this, but when Yahya told Harun of this exchange, the prince said he now had no wish to become caliph;

he wanted a quiet life with his wife Zubaydah, with whom he was deeply in love, and was ready to renounce his succession rights in favour of his nephew Jafar. Yahya, whose fate was now closely tied to Harun's, upbraided his protégé: a quiet life, he said, was nothing compared with the dignity of the caliphate. And in any case, Hadi's intentions now meant the door on this quiet life had closed, and if he didn't act, life might elude him altogether.

THE CRISIS CAME to a head on 14 September 786, when several things happened all at once. Hadi had become seriously ill and the question of succession had become critical. Hadi had set out for the town of Haditha, but had felt too sick to continue and returned home.

Hours later, he was found dead in his bed.

There were conflicting reports on the cause of death. One report suggests Hadi died of an abdominal ulcer; another alleges he was poisoned; yet another claims he was murdered by Khayzuran's slave girls, who had entered his room and smothered him in his sickbed by sitting on his face.[39]

On hearing of Hadi's death, Yahya and Hadi's chief advisor hurried into Harun's bedchamber. Yahya woke the sleeping prince by intoning, 'Arise, O Commander of the Faithful!'

Harun sat up, wrapped himself in his sheet and told Yahya not to say such dangerous things out loud. Then the advisor informed him of his brother's death and handed him the caliphal ring. Harun thought for a moment and said, 'Give me advice on what to do.'

Yahya was about to reply when a messenger rushed into the room and announced to Harun that his concubine Marajil had just given birth to his first child, a son: the boy who would later become the Caliph Mamun.

Harun told the messenger, 'I hereby name him Abdallah.' Then he said again to Yahya, 'Give me advice on what to do.'

He was not quite twenty-one.[40]

A Woman Aflame in Water

CALIPH HARUN AL-RASHID shied away from the burdens of high office and was happy to hand over the administration of his empire to Yahya, whom he appointed as vizier, a role that was something between a chief advisor and a prime minister, but one that could be deposed, arrested or executed at the whim of the caliph. 'My dear little father,' he told the older man, 'it was you who placed me on this throne by your happy influence and wise advice. And now I invest you with absolute power.'[41] Yahya in turn appointed his two sons, Fadl and Jafar, as his deputies.

Khayzuran, who once more had the ear of the caliph and his vizier, resumed her role as an influential palace figure. When she passed away in 789, Harun led her funeral procession, placing a tattered shawl on his head and walking barefoot through the mud to the cemetery. Khayzuran's estate on her death amounted to a staggering 160 million dirhams.[42]

Harun would periodically lead military campaigns against the Romans, and would make five pilgrimages to Mecca in the course of his life; but in Baghdad, he often felt enervated and would slip into the delirious distractions of palace life. Women were emboldened to flirt with him and used poetry to compete for his attention.

One night, while drinking wine with the Barmakids, a particularly talented slave singer beguiled him with a beautiful song. She sang to him:

I have lain sleepless so long
Insomnia is my lover.
My body is so worn away
It would seem created so.
My heart is drowned in my tears.
Who can say he has seen
A woman aflame in water?

Harun insisted she sing it again, and when she finished, a serving girl entered the room and presented him with a love letter from another woman in the form of an apple, with the following inscribed on it in ink that was scented with musk and ambergris:

Happiness has made you forget your promise;
I send you this apple to remind you.

Harun took another apple and wrote upon it:

You command me to fulfil my promise.
I did not forget; this apple is my excuse.

Then he asked someone to compose some lines of poetry on this theme, and his secretary said:

An apple marked by the pearls of her teeth
Is dearer to me than the world and all that's in it;
White marks on the red, inscribed with scented ink
As if plucked from the cheeks of she who gave it.[43]

IN BAGHDAD, WHERE highborn women were increasingly concealed and confined to the harem, singing girls became highly prized after-dinner companions and entertainers, performing a role not unlike Japanese geishas. The most talented and beautiful became courtesans of the rich and powerful. Most were slaves who had been singled out at an early age and sent to a special school for singing girls, where they would be given lessons in poetry and music, and trained to accompany themselves on the lute. When their education was complete, they would be sold on to a wealthy master, sometimes fetching thousands of gold dinars.

It's difficult to get a true sense of their lives, as the accounts of them were written by men who had become infatuated or enraged by their beauty and song. Their mastery of poetry made them skilled at flirting or deploying witty put-downs to deal with boorish drunks, but for all that, they were still slaves who were expected to be sexually available to their masters. The prolific Abbasid essayist Jahiz – 'the Bug-Eyed One' – wrote an *Epistle on Singing Girls*, in which he joked that women are a 'tillage ground' for men, in the same way that 'herbage is a provision for grazing animals'. And yet, he warns, a man pursuing a singing girl might find himself in dangerous territory:

> As soon as the observer notices her, she exchanges provocative glances with him, gives him playful smiles, dallies with him in verses set to music, falls in with his suggestions, is eager to drink when he drinks, expresses her fervent desire for him to stay a long while, her yearning for his prompt return, and her sorrow at his departure … bestows on him a lock of her hair, a piece of her robe, or a splinter from her plectrum … Yet for the most part singing girls are insincere, and given to deceit and

> treachery in squeezing out the property of the deluded victim and then abandoning him.[44]

In his *Epistle*, Jahiz likens the passion of love to medical illness, 'a malady which cannot be controlled … due to the position of the heart in relation to the limbs'.* But such cynicism was rare among Abbasid scholars and poets, who frequently pondered the mystery of romantic love, and its ability to crack open the soul and expose it to the most furious and sublime emotional weather.

Yahya the Barmakid held a symposium in his mansion one evening on the subject of love. All the participants were well-known free-thinkers.

'Describe love,' Yahya requested. 'Just give me a brief definition, as it comes to you.'

The first to speak was a Shia, who said:

> Love is the fruit of similarity and the index of the fusion of two souls. It issues forth from the sea of beauty, from the pure and subtle principle of its essence. Its extent is without bounds. Too much of it destroys the body.

The second man, a Kharijite, spoke of its occult energy:

> Love is a magic emission. It is more hidden and more glowing than a burning coal. It exists only through the union of two souls and two forms. It penetrates the heart like water from a rain cloud seeping through desert sands.

* In the end, Jahiz was killed not by a broken heart, but by his own library: he was reportedly crushed to death when a tower of books toppled onto him.

Another saw love as both a permanent wound and a poison:

> Love sets its seal upon the eyes and impresses its signet upon the heart. Its pasture is the body; it drinks from the liver, seat of passion … Love is a draught from death's cup, a drink from the cisterns of bereavement.

But then another likened love to a star whose radiance transfigures the soul:

> It darts rays of brilliant light which illuminate the sense of understanding and touch the very sources of life with their refulgence. From this ray, or glance, emanates a pure light which strikes the soul and becomes an essential part of it.

Then another man spoke up, a Zoroastrian from Persia, who considered the subject in medical terms. He wondered: how exactly does love enter the body? Does it come in through the eye or the ear? Does love originate from the will, or from sheer necessity? Ultimately, he concluded, who we fall in love with is beyond our control, determined before we are born:

> God, in his great wisdom and goodness, gives every soul at its creation a rounded form like a sphere. Then he splits it in two and places each half in a different body. Then, when one of these bodies meets that which encloses the other half of its own soul, love is of necessity born between them, owing to the fact that they were once one.[45]

AFTER THE DEATH of the queen mother, Harun's first wife and cousin Zubaydah became the most powerful woman in the harem and the empire. Her formal name was Amat al-Aziz, 'Handmaiden of the Almighty', but she was better known by her nickname Zubaydah, 'Little Butter Ball', which had been given to her by her affectionate grandfather, the Caliph Mansur. Harun was another of Mansur's many grandchildren, which made him his wife's first cousin.

Zubaydah, like Harun, was well educated and preposterously rich. As an Abbasid princess, she had known no other life. Her father had endowed her with her own palace, and an entire quarter of the city, the Zubaydiyah, which was populated by her retinue of followers and servants.[46] She travelled through the city streets in a litter made of silver, sandalwood and ebony. But her wealth was sometimes a literal, physical burden: during court ceremonies, her gowns were said to be so weighted down with gold and precious gems that two servants were required to help her stand up.

Zubaydah is well remembered today for her acts of charity and philanthropy. She sponsored and oversaw the construction of an underground aqueduct that brought water to Mecca, but her most enduring legacy is Zubaydah's Way, a 1400-kilometre pilgrimage road running from Kufa to Mecca that she equipped with cisterns, reservoirs for the relief of exhausted pilgrims.[47]

Harun would take several other wives and concubines, but he would remain closest to Zubaydah, who he said knew him best and gave him good advice. Nonetheless, she remained wary of his serial infatuations with singing girls. At one point, he became besotted with the wit and beauty of a singing girl named Inan, who enjoyed jousting verbally with his favourite poet Abu Nuwas, improvising verses back and forth. When the smitten Abu Nuwas also tried to seduce her, she batted him away. Harun approached her owner to purchase her, but he demanded an insanely high price of 100,000 dinars.

Harun then became obsessed with another famous slave singer named Dananir. When he presented her with a jewelled necklace worth 30,000 dinars, Zubaydah became alarmed. She complained to her uncles, who carefully broached the subject with Harun. He protested unconvincingly that he was fascinated by Dananir merely as an artist, not as a woman. Zubaydah then apologised to her husband for her jealousy, and presented him with ten slave girls to distract him; three of them would later give birth to sons.[48]

The Travels of Ziryab the Musician

EVEN IN MEDIEVAL BAGHDAD, the Devil was said to have the best tunes. Masudi relates a story from Harun's court composer Ishaq al-Mawsili, who once sat up late with the caliph, singing a song that seemed to enchant his master. 'Don't stop,' Harun said drowsily, so Ishaq repeated the song until the caliph had fallen asleep.

At that moment, Ishaq realised a stranger was in the room, standing behind him, and he turned to see a handsome young man in a robe of painted silk. The stranger rudely snatched Ishaq's lute from him and began to play with astonishing virtuosity. 'He made harmonies I never would have believed,' recalled Ishaq, as the stranger sang:

> Drink a few more cups with me, my friends,
> Before you go! Cupbearer, bring us some more
> Of this excellent, pure wine!
> Already the first light of morning has stripped
> Away the darkness and torn the chemise from the night.

When he had finished, the stranger put down the lute and said, 'Son of a whore, *that* is how you should sing.' And then he walked out of the room.

Ishaq went to find him, but no one had seen him enter or leave.

When Ishaq returned to his lute, the caliph woke up and asked what was going on. Ishaq told him the story and Harun said, 'Beyond any shadow of a doubt, you have received a visit from Satan.'

At Harun's request, Ishaq played the stranger's song, which had lodged itself in his memory. 'He listened with great pleasure,' Ishaq recalled, 'and then gave me a handsome present. After which I withdrew.'[49]

AS THE COURT'S pre-eminent musician, Ishaq ran a music conservatorium in Baghdad where he taught music theory, history and practice. His most gifted student was a singer-songwriter named Ali ibn Nafi, who was nicknamed Ziryab, 'the Blackbird', thanks to his beguiling singing voice and dark skin.

The circumstances of Ziryab's birth are obscure; it seems he entered Ishaq's family home as a slave, but was given his freedom once his aptitude as a composer and musician became apparent. Ziryab's chosen instrument was the *oud*, the almond-shaped Arabic lute, which had four strings, each one said to resonate emotionally with the four classical temperaments of the human body – melancholic, choleric, sanguine and phlegmatic. Frustrated by its limitations, Ziryab added a fifth string that he dyed red to represent the soul. Instead of strumming the instrument with a wooden plectrum, he picked the strings with a quill made from an eagle's feather.

When Ishaq introduced his talented apprentice to the caliph, Harun invited Ziryab to perform one of his own compositions. The Blackbird took up his customised lute and sang a song he'd written especially for the caliph, and Harun was deeply moved and impressed.

But Ziryab had performed too well. Afterwards, Ishaq reportedly told him he had no intention of being displaced as the caliph's favourite court musician, and that Ziryab should leave Baghdad at once, or risk becoming Ishaq's mortal enemy. Ziryab knew Ishaq had powerful friends in the military, and so the Blackbird flew away from Baghdad and never returned.

ZIRYAB AND HIS FAMILY travelled west, to the North African city of Kairouan in modern-day Tunisia, where he stayed for some years, establishing his reputation as a performer and composer, until he unintentionally offended the local emir and was expelled from the city. He crossed the Mediterranean and entered Muslim Spain – the Emirate of Cordoba – where he hoped to be welcomed by the new emir, Abd al-Rahman II, who was known to be a lover of music, and aware of Ziryab's stellar reputation.

The city of Cordoba was now the largest and richest European city outside Constantinople, endowed with running water, paved streets, gardens, libraries, bathhouses, fountains, churches and synagogues. Its centre was dominated by a dazzling great mosque that was supported internally by a forest of multi-coloured, double-arched pillars.

For once, Ziryab was in the right place at the right time: Abd al-Rahman was an ambitious ruler who wanted Cordoba to rival Baghdad as a centre of science, poetry and music, and so the brilliant Ziryab was a most welcome presence. The city's elite, conscious of their distance from Baghdad and anxious not to be seen as provincial hicks, recognised Ziryab as a man of consummate taste and refinement, and embraced him with open arms. Ziryab introduced the court to the latest Baghdadi styles of music, which drew on Persian, Greek and Indian traditions, and he set up an academy to teach these new forms to students from Andalusia and North Africa. It was said that every night, a *jinn* would teach Ziryab a new song in a dream; then, once he had it, he would call for two slave singers, Ghizlan and Hunayda, who would bring their lutes to his bed so he could teach it to them. Afterwards he would return to sleep and in the morning the women would play the song back to him.[50]

Ziryab quickly became not only Cordoba's pre-eminent musician, but also its arbiter of style. Both men and women adopted his mullet-like hairstyle, short at the sides and long at the back. He introduced the custom of seasonal changes in fashion, wearing loose white garments in the summer, then shifting into thicker layers of richly coloured clothes during the cooler months. He encouraged the use of toothpaste, and was said to have invented a form of anti-perspirant based on lead monoxide that would not stain clothes.[51] Ziryab is also credited with revolutionising Andalusian cuisine, introducing new items such as asparagus, coriander, tamarind and saffron to the cooking pot. He established the custom for dinner to be brought to the table not all at once but as a series of courses. He served food on fine ceramic plates instead of gold and silver platters, and poured wine into crystal glasses instead of metal goblets, allowing the contents of the glass to be seen and admired. The Blackbird's lovely voice, his easy familiarity with poetry, history and the cultures of foreign lands made him a perfect dinner companion.

The Travels of Ghazal the Poet

ZIRYAB'S ONLY RIVAL in Cordoba was the poet and diplomat Yahya ibn Hakam al-Bakri, nicknamed al-Ghazal, 'the Gazelle', for his lean, handsome figure and nimble wit. The Gazelle composed poetry for ceremonial occasions, but also enjoyed taking part in literary tournaments, and became feared for his sarcastic wit. He had the gift of knowing when to suddenly shift the tone of his conversation from exquisite refinement to crude vulgarity, making people explode with laughter.

There was not, it seems, room enough in Cordoba for two such gargantuan cultural entities, and so the Gazelle and the Blackbird came to loathe each other. When Ziryab introduced the game of chess to the city, Ghazal mocked it in verse as an invention of the devil. But in 832, he overstepped the mark when he penned a satirical put-down of Ziryab the court favourite, and the emir banished him temporarily from Cordoba. The Gazelle galloped all the way over to Baghdad, where he picked up the new, earthy style of modern urban poets like Abu Nuwas, who sat in taverns writing about love, longing and sexual desire.

After a year in exile, Ghazal was forgiven by the emir and permitted to return to Cordoba, where he experimented with this new, more intimate style, making him more popular than ever, but the emir had greater need of his abilities as a diplomat. The geopolitics of the era had led rulers to seek alliances that cut across the grain of their faiths. Just as Charlemagne had reached out to Harun al-Rashid, the Christians of Constantinople and the Muslims of Cordoba sent diplomatic feelers out towards each other. When, in 840, an ambassador from Constantinople arrived in Cordoba he was welcomed warmly by Abd al-Rahman II. The meeting went so well that the emir summoned Ghazal and told him he was sending him to accompany the ambassador back to Constantinople with a letter proposing an alliance against their mutual enemies in Baghdad. Ghazal tried to beg off, claiming that at fifty, he was too old for such a mission. But the emir insisted, and so in 840 C.E., the poet sailed off for the city of the Romans.

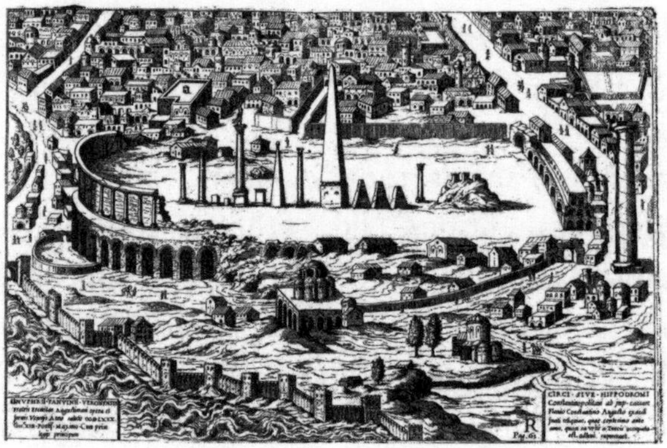

A seventeenth-century engraving of Constantinople, with the Hippodrome in the centre, the Column of Constantine to the right and the sea walls in the foreground

CONSTANTINOPLE, THE SECOND ROME, would always hold a certain mystique for medieval Muslims. The geographer al-Qazwini was moved to concede, 'Nothing like it was ever built, neither before nor after.'[52] The Queen of Cities was the unobtainable prize, Baghdad's only true rival as an imperial centre. The Prophet was said to have predicted that the proud city would one day fall to the warriors of Islam, but Constantinople had withstood two massive sieges by the caliphate and Islamic conquest of the city now seemed a distant hope.

Constantinople was as lovely as a dream. Visitors to the city responded emotionally to its size and majesty. It held the transcendently beautiful Hagia Sophia; its Hippodrome was the world's biggest sports stadium. Its colonnaded plazas were dominated by colossal statues from antiquity. 'We knew not whether we were in heaven, or on earth,' one foreign envoy reported breathlessly from Constantinople. 'For on earth there is no such splendour or such beauty, and we are at a loss how to describe it to you.'[53] In the ninth century, Roman emperors and their families dwelt in the Great Palace of the Caesars, a complex of pavilions and terraces that stepped down to the sparkling waters of the Sea of Marmara. They held court in a marble-panelled octagonal throne room and dined like ancient Romans in the Banquet Hall of the Nineteen Couches, where golden trays of food and wine were mechanically lowered from the ceiling.

The Gazelle, however, was unintimidated by the splendour of the Great Palace and the hauteur of the Roman courtiers. He refused to kiss the ground in front of the emperor, a practice that was regarded as idolatrous in the Islamic world. 'A Muslim only prostrates himself before the Creator,' he explained to his hosts.

Despite this uncomfortable opening move, Emperor Theophilus and his empress, Theodora, were soon amused by Ghazal's sly wit and outrageous charm. The emperor, who was fascinated by Islam, invited Ghazal to converse with him, but when the empress entered the throne room, 'wearing jewels and dressed like the rising sun', the Gazelle's eyes swivelled her way. He explained to the irritated emperor: 'I am so dazzled by the beauty of this queen and her extraordinary form that I am unaware of the reason you have called me here – and this is fair, for I have never seen a more beautiful image. Her black eyes have captivated me.' The Gazelle then improvised a few lines of florid verse:

> … daughter of Caesars
> Upon seeing the colour of her face
> One would think
> It was of silver or gold artfully polished.[54]

Although the Gazelle succeeded in charming Theodora and her son Michael, it's not clear whether he succeeded in establishing a formal alliance between the emir and the emperor. But Abd al-Rahman must have been pleased with his work, because when Ghazal returned to Cordoba in 845, it seems, the emir was ready to entrust him to lead another diplomatic mission that would take him all the way to Scandinavia, to parley with the King of the Vikings.*

THE VIKINGS HAD SURGED out of their rugged homelands decades earlier, first raiding then forming farming and trading settlements throughout Europe. To the Muslims, the Norse invaders were known as *majus*, pagan fire worshippers, who arrived without warning, raided coastal cities, then sailed home with heavy loads of plundered gold and silver. Troves of Muslim coins have been unearthed in Sweden, bearing inscriptions from faraway Baghdad, Isfahan, Cairo and Tashkent, some with the hammer of Thor etched onto their faces.[55]

In 844, just after Ghazal's mission to Constantinople, a fleet of Viking ships had sailed from northern France down to the western seaboard of Muslim Spain. The raiders sacked Lisbon on 20 August, then cruised into the Straits of Gibraltar, burning down the cities of Cadiz, Medina, Sidonia and Algeciras along the way. They sailed

* The word 'Viking', used here in its broadest sense to denote the seagoing Norse pagans of the medieval world, is drawn from the Norse word *vík* meaning 'inlet' or 'little bay'. A *vikinger* was one who inhabited such places.

up the Guadalquivir River to Seville, pillaging the city and the surrounding countryside.

With the unholy *majus* now only 140 kilometres away from Cordoba, Abd al-Rahman sent a large force to confront them south of Seville. The Vikings were no match for the emir's well-trained soldiers, who inflicted a devastating defeat on the raiders. The Vikings suffered the loss of more than a thousand men and thirty of their longships. The Vikings, shocked by the scale of their defeat, agreed to hand over their plundered gold and captured slaves in exchange for being allowed to depart safely from Andalusia.

Some time afterwards, according to an account from the Arab chronicler Ibn Dihya, an envoy from the King of the Vikings arrived in Cordoba to ask for a negotiated peace. The emir accepted the request and since he knew that the Gazelle 'knew his way in and out of every door', he sent the poet to lead the mission to the Viking lands.

WESTERN AND ARABIC scholars still debate whether this second mission ever took place. Ibn Dihya's account was written long after the event, and was drawn from another report, since lost, written by one of Ghazal's contemporaries. It's possible the story was muddled with Ghazal's visit to Constantinople. Whether true or not, it tells us something of how the Muslims saw the *majus* of Scandinavia, and it is at least culturally consistent with what we know of the Norse from the medieval sagas.

According to Ibn Dihya, Ghazal boarded a well-equipped ship on the southern coast of Andalusia and sailed north. Once it passed Cape Finisterre, the seas turned dark, the waves pitched up and the ship entered a mighty storm. Throughout the crisis, Ghazal's companions from Cordoba cringed in terror, while he stood on the deck in the howling wind and rain, addressing the storm with lines of poetry.

After the ship emerged from the storm, it continued on to an archipelago of islands: the homeland of 'the King of the Vikings', most likely King Horik of Denmark. Ghazal was then brought to the royal residence, which sat on 'a great island in the ocean, with flowing streams and gardens' – a description that fits the Danish island of Zealand.

The visitors were given a fine dwelling and after two days were summoned to appear before the king. As he had in Constantinople, Ghazal had made it clear that he would not bend the knee, nor would he do anything else that might contradict his religion. The king had apparently agreed to this, but when Ghazal came to meet with Horik, he saw that the king's men had built the doorway so low that he would be forced to crawl through it on his knees. The Gazelle was unperturbed; when he came to the entrance, he simply sat down, stretched his legs and slid his way in, feet first.

The king and the court were amused and impressed.

'We sought to humiliate him,' laughed Horik, 'and he greeted us with the soles of his shoes.'[56]

THE VIKING QUEEN, whose name was Nud, was anxious to see the visitor for herself and so she sent for him. Again, as with the empress in Constantinople, the Gazelle disconcerted her by gazing at her in wonderment.

'Ask him why he stares at me so,' Nud told her translator. 'Is it because he finds me very beautiful, or the opposite?'

'It is indeed because I have never seen anything more beautiful in all the world,' Ghazal replied. 'I have seen many women from among all the nations in the palaces of our emir, but never have I seen beauty such as this.'

She turned to her interpreter and said, 'Ask him: is he serious, or is he joking?'

'I am serious indeed,' he replied.

'Are there no beautiful women in your country?'

'They have beauty, but it is not like the beauty of the Queen. Her beauty can only be captured by poets.'

When he told her he would write such a poem that would make her famous in his country, the queen was pleased and offered him a gift, but he refused to accept it. He explained to the translator, 'It is gift enough for me to see her and to be received by her.' She sent the gift to his room anyway, and ordered that her door should never be closed to him.

After that, the queen and the poet met every day, and with each visit she sent another expensive gift to his room: either a fine robe, a delicacy, or some perfume. 'In this way,' he later confessed to his friend, 'I won her good graces and obtained from her more than I desired.' Ghazal's companions were scandalised and warned him to be more discreet. When he mentioned this to her, she laughed and said, 'We do not have such things in our religion, nor do we have jealousy. Our women are with our men only of their own choice. A woman stays with her husband as long as it pleases her to do so, and leaves him if it no longer pleases her.'

The Gazelle, although still handsome and upright, was now in his mid-fifties and his hair was turning grey. One day, the queen asked him his age and he said, 'Twenty!' She laughed and said, 'And how is it that a youth of twenty has so much grey hair?' The Gazelle grinned and shot back, 'Have you never seen a foal with grey hair?'

The queen asked him to dye his hair. He did as he was bid, and when he came to her the next morning she praised his newly-blackened coiffure. He said:

> In the morning she complimented me on the blackness of my dye,
> It was as though it had brought me back to my youth.
> But I see grey hair and the dye upon it
> As a sun that is swathed in mist.
> It is hidden for a while, and then the wind uncovers it,
> And the covering begins to fade away.[57]

Again, there is no mention of whether his diplomatic negotiations were successful or not, only that after twenty months in the Viking court, the Gazelle took his leave and returned home safely to the Muslim world.

Map of Denmark, from Olaus Magnus's Historia de Gentibus Septentrionalibus, *c. 1555.*

Enemy of Himself

AS THE GLORIOUS REIGN of Harun al-Rashid came to a close, Muslims were coming to accept that the expansion of the caliphate into the Christian West had reached its natural limits. The campaigns into Roman territory had become a perfunctory affair, an annual ritual. Occasionally a border fortress would change hands, but otherwise the lines of defence in Anatolia had become more or less fixed.

Harun's last great struggle against the Romans had been instigated by the abrasive emperor Nicephorus, who had refused to pay the annual tribute to Baghdad negotiated by his predecessor Irene. Determined to show his court he was made of sterner stuff than Irene, Nicephorus fired off an obnoxious letter to the caliph:

> The queen who was my predecessor set you up in the position of a rook, and herself as merely a pawn … but that arose from the weakness and deficient sense of women. Now, when you have read my letter, send back what you received of the money she sent … if not, then the sword will inevitably be set between us.

Harun wrote back in a fury:

> In the name of God, the Merciful, the Compassionate, from Harun the Commander of the Faithful to Nicephorus the dog of the Romans: O son of an infidel woman, you will not hear my reply but shall see it with your own eyes.[58]

On 11 June 806, Harun marched out from Iraq at the head of the largest Muslim army in history, wearing a cap emblazoned with

Warrior for the Faith and Pilgrim. The expedition met with easy success, running right over the fortress cities of Heraclea and Tyana. The Muslims confiscated the Roman gold they found there and enslaved their populations. Nicephorus, badly outnumbered, sued for peace. Harun inflicted a steep penalty for his impertinence: Nicephorus was now required to hand over an even bigger annual tribute to the caliphate. Nicephorus and his son were also obliged to pay an ignominious personal poll tax to Harun, levied at three gold coins each, to acknowledge their status as subjects of the caliph.

But although the campaign was a profound symbolic triumph, it had actually achieved very little for the Islamic State. No permanent territorial gains were made. Peace had been concluded on humiliating terms for the enemy, but from this point, the caliphate would no longer present such an existential threat to the Christians of Constantinople. The Queen of Cities had absorbed a century of hammer blows from the insurgent Muslims and survived. The advance of the Muslims into Europe had been checked. The Christian kingdoms to the West would have time to catch their breath. Meanwhile, the caliphate directed its energies and enthusiasm to the richer and more dynamic societies of the East.

IN 800, AS CHARLEMAGNE was being crowned in Rome, Harun al-Rashid recognised it was time to draw up plans for the succession. His eldest son, Mamun, was regarded as astute and capable; but Amin, the second-born, had the higher claim. Amin was the son of Zubaydah and was therefore descended from Abbasid royalty on both sides. Harun tried to circumvent any conflicts that might emerge after his death by drawing up a watertight legal agreement naming Amin as his first successor and Mamun as his second, and in December 802, he brought his two sons to the Holy City of Mecca to formalise the compact.

Although Amin was to inherit the throne from his father, the agreement stipulated that Mamun was to be placed next in line after him, and given independent control of the eastern provinces, ruling from Khorasan. Lengthy contracts were produced for both brothers, outlining their legal obligations to each other. The signed documents were posted on a wall inside the Kaaba, but then fell at once to the ground. An observer thought to himself: *Just as this document has fallen before being raised, so will this agreement be broken before reaching its term.*[59]

IN NAMING AMIN as his direct successor, Harun had bowed to pressure from Zubaydah, the most energetic supporter of her son's claim. But Masudi relates a tale, drawing on the mythological Three Fates, to suggest that Zubaydah was troubled by secret doubts about her son.

He wrote that the very night Zubaydah had conceived Amin, she dreamt that three women came into her room and sat around her bed. One of them drew near, placed her hand on Zubaydah's pregnant belly and said:

> A magnificent king,
> open-handed in his generosity,
> his yoke will be heavy,
> his life misfortune.

The second also touched her belly and said:

A weak-willed king,
blunt-edged, insincere in friendship;
he will rule as a despot
and by fortune be betrayed.

The third did the same and said:

A sensual king,
wasteful of blood,
surrounded by revolt
and sparing of justice.

Zubaydah woke up, deeply worried.

Then, after Amin's birth, the three weird sisters appeared to her again in the night, sitting by her bed, staring fixedly at her.

The first said:

A verdant tree,
a fair flower,
a lovely garden.

The second went on:

A copious spring,
but swift to run dry
and swiftly gone.

And the third:

Enemy of himself,
weak in power
and fast in rage – he will lose his throne.

The queen woke and told her servant of the dream, but the servant assured Zubaydah this was known to be a game played by the female demons who attend women in childbirth.

Then, when the boy was weaned, the three women appeared in the chamber once more, hovering over his cradle.

The first said:

A tyrant, a wastrel,
a babbling fool,
his way lost,
riding for a fall.

The second added:

His speeches contradictory,
his battles lost,
his desires baffled,
sad and with troubles overwhelmed.

The third ended:

Dig his grave, open his coffin,
bring out his winding sheet,
prepare the procession.
His death is better than his life.

ZUBAYDAH, FILLED WITH dread, consulted astrologers and dream-interpreters, who assured her that her son would live out long years of happiness. But her heart would not believe their promises.

'At last,' she later confessed, 'I began to reproach myself for my weakness and I said to myself: *Can love, care and forethought cheat destiny? Can anyone drive fate back from the one they love?*'[60]

Death Has Come for You at Night

THE LEGEND OF Harun al-Rashid is inextricably bound to the city of Baghdad, but it seems he came to hate the place. He called Baghdad 'the steam room', and tried several times to relocate to a cooler location, first in the foothills of the Zagros Mountains, then to the garrison city of Raqqa in Syria, where he ordered the construction of several palaces, though the administration of the empire remained in Baghdad.

He was also becoming weary of his chief advisors, the Barmakids, and resentful of their greed. Yahya and his sons Jafar and Fadl had come to monopolise the administration, and it was rumoured that their family fortune even outstripped the caliph's. Harun tried to push back against his dependence on them by using his chamberlain as an alternative source of advice. Then in 802, it seems Harun decided the Barmakids must die.

On his return from Mecca, Harun ordered the arrest of Yahya and his son Fadl. Then he sent his executioner Masrur to locate Yahya's other son, Jafar, who had once been Harun's closest companion and drinking partner, and ordered him to bring back Jafar's head.

Masrur led a contingent of soldiers to Jafar's house, where Jafar was entertaining some guests.

'Death has come for you at night,' said Masrur, dragging him into the yard.

'Oh God,' Jafar pleaded, 'the Commander of the Faithful wouldn't order you to do that unless he was drunk.'

He begged Masrur to check that his old friend really did want him dead. Masrur, who had spent many evenings with both Harun and Jafar, went back to the palace and appealed to him on Jafar's behalf.

The furious caliph snarled out an ugly obscenity: 'O you who suck your mother's clitoris, bring me Jafar's head!'[61]

The miserable Masrur did as he was bidden.

Jafar was decapitated and his head was brought to the palace. Harun ordered the body to be cut up and the pieces hung from the three main bridges of Baghdad.

Yahya and Fadl died in prison three years later. Their wealth and property were confiscated by the state.

HARUN WAS OFTEN TORN between his religious duty to act with justice and compassion, and his political duty, as he saw it, to destroy his enemies. He now began to dread his death and the punishments that might await him in the afterlife.

One afternoon, he summoned the famous preacher Ibn Sammak for spiritual advice. Sammak wasted no time with small talk and bluntly warned that before long, Harun would be standing in judgement before God. From there he would either be consigned to Paradise or to hellfire. 'There is no third place,' Sammak concluded darkly.

Harun, aware of his many sins, wept until his beard was wet with tears.

This was too much for his new vizier, Fadl ibn Rabi, who scolded Ibn Sammak: 'God forbid,' he said, 'how could anyone possibly doubt the Commander of the Faithful will instantly enter Paradise?'

The preacher, not deigning to glance at Rabi, looked hard at Harun and said, 'This man will not be at your side on that day.'[62]

IN LATE 808, HARUN rode out to Khorasan with his army to quell a local rebellion. It was a miserable journey: he was suffering from stomach cramps that were intensified by the jolting gait of his donkey. As the expedition rode on, he was appalled to realise that his eldest sons, Amin and Mamun, had placed spies within his entourage to keep tabs on the failing state of his health.

When he could ride no more, Harun called his senior men to his tent. He urged them to help keep the peace between his sons, then selected a silk winding sheet for himself.

Harun al-Rashid, fifth of the Abbasid caliphs, lingered for several months then died in March 809 in the Persian city of Tus. He had reigned as caliph for twenty-three years.

Compared with his illustrious predecessors, Harun al-Rashid's achievements were modest, but those who lived through the civil wars and disasters to come would look back with nostalgia on 'the honeymoon', a time when the caliphate still held sway over its provinces, when its battles against the Romans were easily won, when its palaces were filled with music and poetry and taxes flowed obediently into its treasury.

Wild Lions with Cruel Teeth

IN ACCORDANCE WITH Harun's wishes, Amin took the throne as caliph in Baghdad and Mamun was installed as governor of the east, ruling from the Khorasani city of Merv. But in the end, Harun's efforts to ensure a stable peace between his sons came to nothing. The separation ruptured the easy intimacy between the brothers, and their rival courts prodded them towards confrontation. An increasingly edgy Amin chose to flout the provisions of the agreement and curtail Mamun's independent control of Khorasan.

All attempts to find a settlement broke down amid rancorous accusations. Mamun, protected by the loyal Army of the East, simply ignored Amin's demands, and denigrated his brother's authority by removing the caliph's name from his coins and from the Friday prayers. Amin retaliated by ordering the succession documents to be brought from Mecca to Baghdad, and tearing them up. He then declared he was placing his own son in the immediate line of succession, making the breach between the brothers irreparable and tipping the empire back into a bitter, bloody civil war, remembered as the Fourth Fitna, or the Great Abbasid Civil War.

In March 811, Amin sent a 40,000-strong army marching towards Khorasan, bearing silver chains intended to bind Mamun and to drag him back to Baghdad as a common prisoner. Mamun in turn sent out a smaller but more experienced army, which defeated and scattered Amin's forces outside the city of Rayy. Mamun was declared caliph in Merv, while his general, Tahir, advanced into Iraq.

By the summer of 812, Mamun's loyalists had begun to close in on Baghdad. Amin frantically tried to rally the city's civilians, giving them money and arms, while Tahir's men settled outside the city walls and prepared for a long siege.

For more than a year, Tahir's siege engines pounded at the City of Peace. The bombardments of heavy stones and fiery projectiles forced Amin and his mother Zubaydah to abandon the Palace of Eternity and retreat to the inner fortress of Mansur's Round City. Life in Baghdad became unspeakably grim as a tight blockade choked off food supplies. Incursions into the city by Tahir's soldiers were met with hand-to-hand fighting by workers, beggars and shopkeepers loyal to Amin and to their city. These urban guerrillas, described by Masudi as 'naked warriors' for their lack of battle armour, fought fiercely in the streets with bricks and stones. 'The war', said one grim observer, 'has made the rabble give birth to wild lions with cruel teeth.'[63]

By September 813, the city was buckling under the pressure of mass starvation. A desperate Amin had his gold and silver vessels melted into coins, then issued them to his soldiers to keep them loyal. The grinding siege reached its endgame when Tahir's men cut down the pontoon bridges over the Tigris, isolating the Round City. Tahir's forces then entered the eastern suburbs and put them to the torch. A witness later described the chaos and horror:

> A black-eyed girl calls for a brother who is no more; he is fallen beside his friend, a stranger from afar, a headless cadaver in the middle of the street. The massacre reaches into every corner. The son defends his father no longer, the friend abandons his friend. All that we cherished has gone, and I weep.[64]

Amin tried to flee what was left of his city, but his boat was intercepted and overturned by Tahir's men, who then pulled him out of the water. He was held in custody for some days, before a group of Persian soldiers entered his room close to midnight, swords unsheathed. They stood in the doorway, hesitating, each unwilling to be the first to strike the Commander of the Faithful.

Amin tried to forestall them by crying out, 'I am the cousin of the Prophet of God! May God avenge my blood.' One of them stepped forward and hit him with a sword. Amin tried to fight him off with a cushion, but then the others piled on, pinning Amin down and cutting his jugular vein. His head was removed and brought to Tahir; the trunk of his body was wrapped in a horse blanket and carried away.[65]

WHEN ZUBAYDAH WAS INFORMED of Amin's death, she accepted the news stoically. One of her eunuchs asked her how she could just sit quietly and tolerate the outrage of her son's murder.

'Well, what can I do?' she replied.

'Go out,' he said, 'and demand vengeance for the blood which has been shed!'

'Go away, you bastard,' she said. 'Is it right that women should demand the price of blood and take the place of warriors?'

Instead, Zubaydah put on a hairshirt and a robe of mourning and wrote a letter to her victorious stepson. While she could not forgive Tahir for the murder of her son, she told Mamun she was willing to recognise him as caliph and to submit 'to the will of an all-powerful sovereign'.[66]

THE FOURTH FITNA was over. Mamun was now the undisputed supreme leader of the caliphate, but he began his reign with a series of missteps. Fearful of alienating his Khorasani power base, he chose to continue ruling from Merv rather than Baghdad. To impart a sense of a fresh beginning, he cast aside the traditional Abbasid black and donned green robes instead. In a gesture of reconciliation towards the Shia, he nominated an Alid prince, Ali al-Rida, as his successor. But he had tipped the balance too far away from the Abbasids, his own family, in Baghdad, and they began to rally around Mamun's uncle Ibrahim as a rival caliph.

Having no desire to resume the civil war, Mamun backed down and in 819 he returned to the City of Peace. On the long journey to Baghdad, Ali al-Rida died in suspicious circumstances, ending the controversy over the succession, but adding another ugly incident to the Alids' long list of grievances.

With the support of his loyal general Tahir, Mamun was able to reassert control over Baghdad, and an uneasy stability settled on the empire. The Palace of the Golden Gate and the Palace of Eternity had been damaged beyond repair during the long siege, so Mamun moved into a new palace on the river. He gave up wearing green and reinstated the traditional black robes and banners. He had become, like his father and grandfather, a traditional Abbasid caliph, ruling from the City of Peace.

And yet, the caliphate that re-emerged after the civil war had moved a long way from the empire of Harun al-Rashid. The old Arabic aristocracy had been largely displaced by a new military elite made up of eastern Persians and Turkic slave soldiers who had followed Mamun into Baghdad and assumed the senior positions. The army, garrisoned in the northeast of the city, now policed the streets of Baghdad. Soldiers regularly brawled in public with embittered members of the radicalised militias, the former 'naked warriors' who had fought so ferociously on Amin's behalf during the siege.

Although Amin was officially denounced as an oath-breaker, the murder of a caliph and the desolation of Baghdad had inflicted a traumatic wound on the city and left a cloud over Mamun's legitimacy. Mamun's propagandists tried to justify the overthrow of Amin by painting him as a frivolous drunkard, but overhanging everything was a terrible sense of grief and desecration. A boatman on the Tigris was heard to shout while passing Mamun's palace, 'How can I respect a man who kills his own brother?'[67]

Mamun recognised that he needed to reconcile with his own family, the Abbasids, and so he visited the grieving Zubaydah to assure her that the order to kill her son had not come from him. Zubaydah, choosing her words carefully, replied, 'There is a day on which you two will meet again, and I pray to God he will forgive you both.'[68]

Zubaydah the great survivor then agreed to Mamun's request to manage a set-piece spectacle that would lift the mood and quell some of the bitterness of the civil war: the royal wedding of Mamun to the daughter of his vizier, a young woman named Buran.

The nuptials took place in December 825 on the riverside country estate of Buran's family. After the ceremony, as the newlyweds were seated together, a thousand pearls were scattered from a dish all over Buran's body, then picked up and heaped on her lap and between her breasts.

'This is your wedding present,' said Mamun. Then he asked if there was anything else he could give her.

Buran said nothing until her grandmother prodded her to speak up. She begged Mamun to forgive and be reconciled with his uncle Ibrahim, who had allowed himself to become the figurehead of the Baghdad rebellion. Her second request was that Zubaydah be permitted to leave Baghdad to make a pilgrimage to Mecca. Mamun happily agreed to both requests, which would give him the opening he was looking for to completely mend his relationship with his family.

The next morning, his terrified uncle Ibrahim came out of hiding and was brought into Mamun's presence. Ibrahim threw himself on the ground, but Mamun said warmly, 'Oh uncle, do not worry any more.' Ibrahim kissed his hand and recited some lines of poetry. Mamun presented him with a sword and a robe of honour, and Ibrahim happily joined the throng of wedding guests outside.

The House of Wisdom

MAMUN WAS THE most intellectually curious of all the caliphs, and now that peace had come, he could direct his energy and patronage to the grand project of recovering the wisdom of the ancient Greeks and Egyptians. In 832, Mamun came to the Giza plateau in Egypt, intent on breaking into the Great Pyramid of Khufu.

The pyramids were the tallest and most enigmatic buildings in the Muslim lands. Hieroglyphs were unintelligible to Muslim scholars, and the purpose of the pyramids was unknown to them. When Mamun came to Egypt to see them for himself, he was accompanied by a crew of sappers, engineers, stonemasons and scholars, as well as Dionysius, the Christian archbishop of Antioch. Mamun had been told that the pyramids had most likely been grain storehouses for the pharaohs, but when he ordered catapults to hurl heavy stones at the slanting walls they refused to crumble, suggesting they were not hollow, but solidly built.

Then, according to one account, the archbishop Dionysius climbed into a tunnel entrance he'd spotted on the pyramid's north face. The archbishop crawled deep into the pyramid's interior, accompanied by the caliph and the workmen, who cleared a path through the blockages. They followed the tunnel deeper into the pyramid until they emerged into an inner chamber, only four metres by four metres in size. At the centre of this claustrophobic space, they discovered a marble sarcophagus with decayed human remains inside. The party was now seriously spooked. 'At that point,' according to the account, 'the caliph put an end to the expedition.'[69]

THERE WAS AN ANECDOTE told by a Baghdad bookseller to explain why philosophy and science flourished during Mamun's reign. It was said that the caliph had a peculiar dream one night: he was wandering through his palace when he found a strange man sitting on his throne. He asked the man who he was.

'I am Aristotle,' he said.

Mamun, who admired Aristotle above all other philosophers, was overjoyed. He asked if he could put a question to him and the Greek sage said that he could.

'What is goodness?' Mamun asked.

'Goodness is that which reason deems to be good,' he replied.

'And then what?'

He replied, 'That which *the law* deems to be good.'

'And then what?'

'That which *the mass of the people* deems to be good.'

'And then what?'

And Aristotle replied, 'And then there is no more "then".'[70]

SUCH ATTEMPTS TO DELINEATE philosophical distinctions between the contingently good and the eternally good were typical of Mamun's era, which was, in many ways, the true apogee of Islam's golden age. When Caliph Mansur, his great-grandfather, had founded

Baghdad, he had established a royal library that became known as the Bayt-al-Hikma, the 'House of Wisdom', but it was Mamun who expanded it and transformed it into a hyperactive enterprise, a place where scholars gathered and translated documents from ancient Persia, Greece and India, then added their own commentaries and ideas. A culture developed where students would sit on the floor gathered at the feet of a master scholar who was given the distinction of sitting on a chair, which is how the word 'chair' later came to signify a university professorship.[71]

This intellectual ferment was catalysed by several developments that came together during Mamun's reign. The first was the continued spread of Chinese paper-making technology that made books relatively inexpensive and easy to produce and digest. The flimsiness and tensile strength of paper allowed the pages of a book to be stacked and bound along one edge, forming it into a codex, a format that was more compact, robust and easier to flip through than a scroll.

The second innovation was the creation of a new, fluid style of Arabic calligraphy that could be 'written with a swiftness that is impossible in other scripts'.[72]

Thirdly, just as the new script sped up written communication, the adoption of Indian numerals by the Arabs radically accelerated computation. This elegant set of numbers (1,2,3,4,5 and so on), used almost universally today, would become known as 'Arabic' numerals because they were introduced to Europe from Muslim Spain, but the system originated in India, entering the Muslim world via Persia. The adoption of Indian numbers freed the act of calculation from the dead weight of Roman numerals, which had made arithmetic such an evil chore, as anyone who attempts to divide MDXXXVI into equal portions of XLVIII might appreciate.

Growing Arabic literacy and numeracy generated a large book-reading public, hungry for knowledge of the wider world, and so the volume of Arabic literature increased exponentially. Abbasid scholars pursued astronomy, medicine and geography, hoping to unlock the mysterious architecture of the Heavens, the Earth, and the human body. Scholars could make a living in Baghdad by composing and transcribing books and selling them in Sharkiya, a suburb between the river and the walls of the Round City that was given over to booksellers and papermakers. Translators of the ancient classics became among the most highly remunerated professionals in the empire; paid, it was said, the weight of their books in gold.[73] In the great houses of Baghdad, Medina, Kufa, Basra, Merv, Bukhara and Samarkand, intellectuals were paid to read their works at social gatherings and debate them afterwards.

Just as the Umayyads had radically enlarged the terrestrial borders of the caliphate, under the Abbasids, the frontiers of the mind were broadened and extended. The caliphate became an empire powered by Muslim theology, Greek science and Indian numbers.

The Stellar Rays

ISLAM WAS MATURING from its origins as a sublime but pragmatic faith that was primarily a religion of action. Being a good Muslim had traditionally been defined largely by what you did: praying, fasting, making a pilgrimage to Mecca, giving alms to the poor, and cleaving to virtues that conferred dignity, such as justice and compassion. But Muslims were now encountering Christian, Jewish and Buddhist philosophers in their conquered realms who challenged them with sophisticated questions about the nature of God and the architecture of the universe. How does something come from nothing? Do animals have souls? Why does plague kill the wicked man and the innocent infant alike? Muslim intellectuals recognised a growing need for ideas and answers that could unite Islamic thought with the wisdom of the ancient sages they admired the most: Aristotle, Plato, Euclid, Ptolemy and Hippocrates.

The man who laid the foundations of this new syncretic philosophy was a brilliant polymath named Abu Yusuf Yaqub al-Kindi. From his perch in the House of Wisdom, Kindi supervised the translation of countless Greek works into Arabic, and produced 260 books of his own on an astonishing range of subjects, including the movement of the planets, the workings of the human eye, and the making of perfumes, drugs and metal swords. Occasionally, Kindi even turned his hand to verses of love poetry:

In four of mine four of yours are sweet,
But I do not know which one causes me agony.
Is it your face in my eye, your taste in my mouth,
Your words in my ear, or the love in my heart?[74]

Kindi had been born into an Arab family with Bedouin origins that traced its lineage to pre-Islamic times. As a high-born Arab, he was often at odds with the sophisticated Persian intellectual elites of Baghdad, who had come to the City of Peace to take advantage of its wealth and opportunities for patronage.

As he contemplated the stars in Baghdad's night sky, Kindi wondered how it was that light from a distant star reached his eye. This led him to ponder the mysterious phenomenon of action-at-a-distance, the forces that invisibly connect objects across a void. How does a magnet invisibly pull iron filings to it? How does the Moon reach down to pull up and release the tides on Earth?

Kindi produced a treatise, *On the Stellar Rays*, in which he proposed that the stars were like lanterns with souls, bombarding the Earth with heavenly radiation. Like Plato, he thought the stars projected simple essential forms such as beauty, goodness and justice. But once they reached Earth, he said, these rays refracted and blended into each other, endowing material objects with more specific qualities like redness or coldness or tallness.

On the Stellar Rays was written at a moment when Islamic design was developing new decorative forms that beautifully illustrate Kindi's principle of interwoven stellar rays. Muslim architects and artists, forbidden to depict the human form, used cosmology and mathematics to generate abstract patterns with complex symmetries that could be as sublime in their own way as the Christian icons of Constantinople. These elegant forms of sacred geometry are imprinted throughout the Muslim world, singing the praises of the created universe and the glory of the night sky. You can still see these mesmerising patterns everywhere in the medieval medinas of Fez, Marrakech or Tangiers – sculpted in relief on the wall of a house, tiled inside the dome of a mosque, latticed on a heavy timber gate or stencilled on the pedestal of a drinking fountain, blending the wizardry of mathematics with magic, and the sacred with the everyday.

A fifteenth-century Islamic wall panel with geometric interlace

THE TRANSLATION MOVEMENT proceeded apace under Caliph Mamun's patronage, and as more of the ancient wisdom of the Greek sages was revealed, he sometimes prodded the scholars of Baghdad to test their claims. In 828, he funded the construction of an observatory in the Baghdad suburb of Shammasiyah to track the movement of the celestial bodies and to put the claims of the ancient astronomer Ptolemy under close scrutiny. It was the first observatory in the Islamic world.

When Mamun read that Ptolemy had calculated the circumference of the Earth and arrived at a figure of 24,000 miles, he became intrigued: how could anyone measure such a thing without circumnavigating the planet with a tape measure? Not content to passively accept this figure, he hired the services of the Banu Musa ('the sons of Moses') to test it.

The three Banu Musa brothers, Muhammad, Ahmed and Hassan, were wealthy scientists, mathematicians and inventors. The brothers were less interested in the abstract mysteries of stellar rays than they were in solving concrete problems, and had developed a strong antipathy to Kindi; according to one report, the brothers had vindictively stolen all the books in Kindi's library, presumably when he was out of town, before being forced to return them.[75] In 850, they wrote a how-to manual, *The Book of Ingenious Devices*, which included an automatic flute-player, 'the Instrument that Plays by Itself'. The device was an elaborate contraption of wheels, valves and pulleys that blew discrete puffs of air from a hydraulic drum into a nine-holed pipe.

When Mamun commissioned the Banu Musa to test Ptolemy's measurement of the circumference of the Earth, the brothers began scouting around for the flattest location they could find, settling on a desert plain in Sinjar, in northern Iraq. Using the Pole Star as a fixed point in the night sky, they calculated its elevation, then travelled due north, measuring the distance with pegs and rope, until they reached a point where the elevation had risen by exactly one degree. Then they set out due south from the original starting point until the elevation of the Pole Star had dropped by a degree. They found the distance was the same in either direction: 66.666 miles. Then, to be sure, they repeated the experiment in another location and recorded the same number. Multiplying the distance by 360 degrees, they arrived at precisely the same figure for the girth of the globe as Ptolemy: 24,000 miles, a number that was less than four per cent off the true figure of 24,900 miles. 'This is certain,' the brothers reported to Mamun confidently, 'and there is no doubt about it.'[76]

The Travels of Ibn Hawqal the Mapmaker

THE ACT OF MEASURING the globe's circumference induced a subtle but profound conceptual shift. It was one thing to observe, as a Bedouin warrior might, the Earth as a gigantic disc, spread out all around him; it was something else to imagine it from a distance as an entire spherical planet. To conceive such an image is to put the mind's eye in space, somewhere between the Earth and the Moon. Peering down from this imaginary perch, Muslim scholars created the most comprehensive maps of the Middle Ages. Their observations of the world enabled them to refute some fundamental axioms of the ancient Greeks.

More than a century after the Banu Musa brothers confirmed Ptolemy's measurement of the Earth, a geographer and mapmaker named Ibn Hawqal sailed down the coast of East Africa, going as far as twenty degrees below the equator. Contrary to Ptolemy's belief that such 'climes' should be uninhabitable, Ibn Hawqal found communities there with great numbers of people.

Ibn Hawqal spent thirty years of his life roaming the known world, passing though Khorasan, Turkestan, Egypt, North Africa and Andalusia. He explored the western edge of the Sahara, and visited Mozambique, Cordoba and Bukhara. After thirty years of travelling, he came to the city of Palermo in Sicily. Palermo, which had been conquered by the Arabs in 831, was to be the last stop on this epic expedition; afterwards he could claim to have seen the whole of the Islamic world. He later recorded his impressions in his book *The Face of the Earth*.

PALERMO, AT THE TIME of Ibn Hawqal's arrival, had never been so prosperous and stable. The city's gardens were lush and its orchards offered every kind of fruit. The Muslim administration had brought new and advanced agricultural techniques with them, introducing oranges, lemons, pistachios, melons and sugarcane to the island. Palermo's massive mosque, formerly its cathedral, regularly attracted 7000 worshippers on a Friday.

But perhaps the humidity got to Ibn Hawqal, because he hated just about everything he saw. As a geographer, he took care to record the layout of the city, its various quarters, the palace district with its mansions and baths, the waterfront with its naval arsenal and prison. Looking out from his high balcony, he saw the streets were crowded with hundreds of private mosques built by wealthy locals, which struck him as pretentious. The judges of Palermo, Ibn Hawqal found, were ignorant of the law; the schoolteachers were cowards trying to shirk military service.[77] On the waterfront, he observed the comings and goings of the city's low-life: 'freeloaders, scoundrels and renegades', he sniffed. Most of them, he thought, 'were pimps and perverts'. This was all of a piece with an air of general uncleanliness that seemed to hang over Palermo. The water, he noted, was 'thick and unhealthy', and although the gardens produced succulent vegetables, he was appalled to see the locals eating raw onions. This unseemly habit, he opined, 'has thwarted their imaginations, impaired their minds, numbed their senses, altered their thinking, clouded their understanding and even ruined their facial features … I have written a book with a full account of them', he concludes darkly. Unfortunately the book is lost to us.

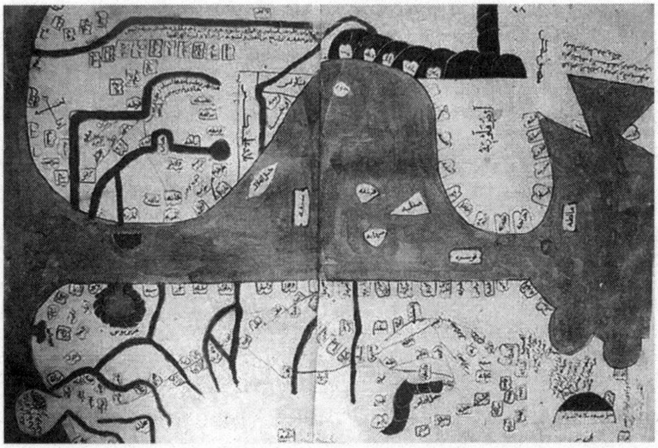

Ibn Hawqal's map of the Mediterranean

To accompany the text in *The Face of the Earth*, Ibn Hawqal created a beautiful three-page map of the Mediterranean Sea and the surrounding lands, which are easily recognisable to modern eyes.

Earlier Muslim scholars had created maps that look distinctly odd. Ibn Hawqal's friend and fellow geographer Istakhri had depicted the island of Sicily not as a familiar jagged triangle, but as a smooth circle. He created a whole compendium of navigation maps like this, drawn in simple geometric shapes. The Maghreb is presented as a smooth hump; bodies of water like the Persian Gulf are delineated with perfect curls and hooks. His map of Egypt shows the Nile as a straight blue rod running up from the African interior, before forking into the Mediterranean.

At first glance these maps might seem absurd, even child-like, but they were designed as schematic diagrams to be quickly absorbed and memorised by travellers, not unlike modern subway maps.[78] Ibn Hawqal, however, could draw on his travel experience to depict the Mediterranean coastline realistically with all its irregular bumps and inlets. And unlike Istakhri, his maps included some of the infidel kingdoms beyond the Muslim world.

WHILE IBN HAWQAL placed north in its conventional position at the top of his map, Istakhri followed the traditions of the Balkh school of geography, putting south at the top. Flipping the world like this is unsettling to modern eyes, but it is convention, not science, that places north at the apex of the world. The Earth rotates at an angle of 23.45 degrees relative to the plane of its orbit around the sun, but from the perspective of space, north and south, east and west are relative concepts that can be turned on their heads by any mapmaker.

The publication in 1569 of Gerardus Mercator's world map, with its reassuringly stable lines of longitude and latitude, was a defining [illegible]. A global consensus began to gather around the 'up-ness' of north, and the world came to accept a common geographical language. In 1973, when the Apollo 17 crew took their famous 'blue marble' photo of the Earth from space, NASA felt obliged to quietly invert the image, putting North Africa at the top of the picture and Antarctica at the bottom so as not to cause confusion or distress.[79]

To flip the map is to invert perceptions of power too. When I was a child, someone published an upside-down 'Australian Map of the World' on a poster as a joke, with the Great Southern Land centred at the top, and with Europe and North America ranged below it like vassal states. Australians, who sometimes felt like forgotten denizens of 'down under', could look up at such a map and imagine themselves as the inhabitants of the crown of the world.

The Disc of the World

A CENTURY AFTER Ibn Hawqal's unhappy sojourn, Palermo fell to an army of Norman invaders, who completed their conquest of the island in 1086, bringing two centuries of Muslim rule in Sicily to an end. Although they belonged to the Latin-speaking Church of Rome, the new Norman rulers were as tolerant as their Muslim predecessors; they retained Arabic and Greek as languages of government, and made use of Muslim artisans and architects.

In 1130, Sicily entered its own golden age of science when King Roger II took the throne. Roger, broad-minded and intellectually ambitious, enjoyed the company of his learned Muslim subjects and soon became known as 'the Baptised Sultan'.[80] In 1139, he invited a scholar from Cordoba named Muhammad al-Idrisi to join his court in Palermo; initially, he wanted Idrisi to draft a map that would encompass his lands in Calabria and North Africa, but at some point,

Roger radically widened the scope of the project and commissioned Idrisi to draw up a map of the entire world.

The creation of the map and its adjoining commentary was a colossal undertaking that absorbed both the Muslim scholar and the Christian king for fifteen years, and bound them together in friendship. Idrisi wrote warmly of Roger's constant pursuit of accurate data: travellers, merchants and scholars passing through Sicily were brought into the palace to be grilled by Roger on the places they'd been to, and what they knew of the lands, coastlines and cities they'd visited, as well as the customs and beliefs of the people within them. When two accounts differed, the king sent envoys to the disputed region to find out the truth and report back to him. Idrisi, for his part, drew on classical, European and Islamic sources, mining information from earlier works, such as Ibn Hawqal's *The Face of the Earth* and *The Book of Roads and Kingdoms.*

Having amassed a mountain of data, Idrisi set to work laying it out on a drawing board using Roger's cartographic instruments. Once Roger was satisfied with the draft, he ordered the map to be etched on an immense disc of pure silver. The disc was lost, but a copy of the circular map appeared in Idrisi's treatise *The Book of Pleasant Journeys into Faraway Lands*, which was completed in January 1154, a month before Roger's death.

Idrisi's world map was the most advanced the world had yet seen. The Mediterranean world is easily recognisable, as is the Arabian Peninsula and the Indian coast. Europe is rendered more precisely than ever before. Idrisi has followed Ptolemy's work in placing the source of the Nile deep in the heart of Africa, at a snowy peak called the Mountain of the Moon, and he correctly connects the Indian Ocean to the Pacific.

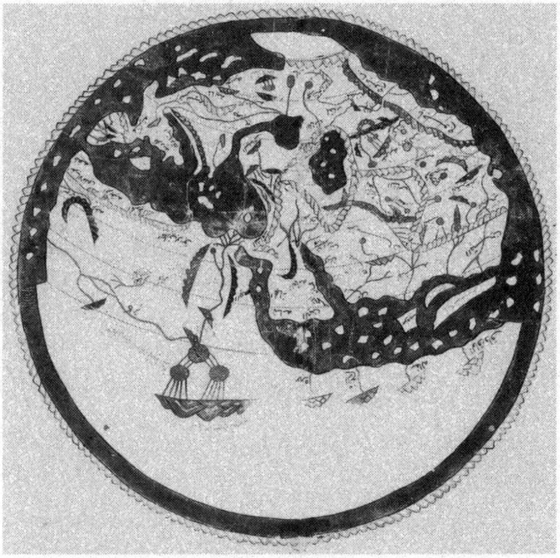

The world map of Idrisi (rotated 180 degrees)

IDRISI'S DISC OF THE world was accompanied by a set of seventy detailed regional maps, which, when patched together, form a sprawling rectangular composite known as the Tabula Rogeriana. In its northwest corner lie Ireland and England (identified as 'Anklitara'). In the southeast are the scattered Spice Islands of Malaya.

Towards the northeastern edge of the map, Idrisi sketched in a long barrier, resembling a necklace or a length of rope. Medieval Muslims, Jews and Christians alike would have recognised it at once as the famous wall of Gog and Magog – a barrier of iron bricks said to have been built in ancient times by Alexander the Great himself. Beyond the wall, they knew, lay the worst place in the world, a dark realm filled with apocalyptic monsters that were said to be 'as uncountable as the sands of the sea'.[81]

BOOK THREE

East

WATHIQ ('He Who Trusts in God')
Ninth of the Abbasid caliphs

ALEXANDER the GREAT ('the Two-Horned One')
World conqueror and builder of the Wall of Gog and Magog

SALLAM the INTERPRETER
Emissary of the caliph

XUANZANG
Buddhist pilgrim and translator

SVEN HEDIN
Swedish explorer of the Taklamakan Desert

Sir MARC AUREL STEIN
British-Hungarian archaeologist

WANG YUANLU
Guardian of the Thousand Buddha Caves

LANGDON WARNER
American archaeologist

the
KINGDOMS TO THE EAST
c. 850 C.E.

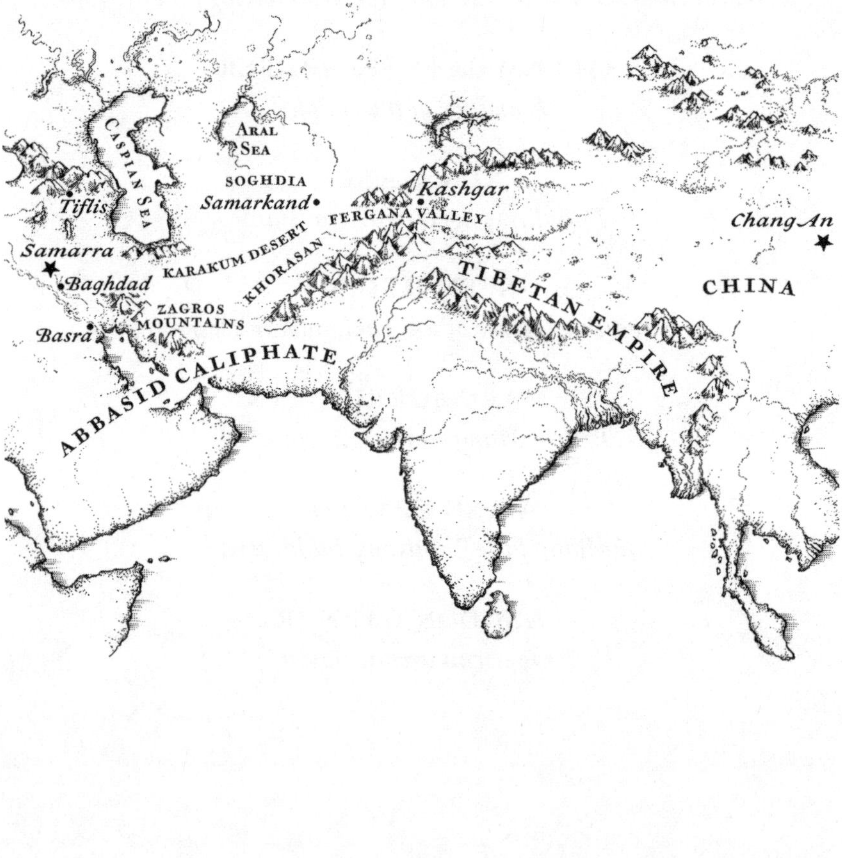

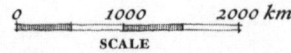

Nightmare in Samarra

ONE NIGHT IN 842, the Caliph Wathiq awoke in his bed seized with a dread that what he'd just seen in his sleep was no fantasy, but a vision of a terrible true thing.

Wathiq, ninth of the Abbasid rulers and grandson of Harun al-Rashid, lived in a palace located some 130 kilometres north of Baghdad, in the new Abbasid capital of Samarra. His father, Caliph Mutasim, had moved his court there from Baghdad to find room for his unruly slave soldiers whose presence had been widely resented in the City of Peace. If Baghdad had been conceived around a circle, Samarra was more like a Roman city: a grid set inside a rectangle, with avenues broad enough for the military to pass through. Samarra would remain the capital for another five decades, until 892, when the caliphs returned to Baghdad.

Wathiq ('He Who Trusts in God') was said to be well built, with a pale, ruddy complexion, but of a nervous and melancholic disposition. His most distinctive feature was a paralysed left eye, which had a little white fleck in it.[1]

That night in Samarra, Wathiq had been given a vision of the wall of Gog and Magog, the famous iron barrier that was said to be located somewhere in the northeastern corner of the world. The wall, which was mentioned in the Quran, was known to have been built in ancient times to pen in a race of hideous creatures that dwelt in the badlands behind it. But in his dream, Wathiq had been shown a breach in the barrier, and now he feared the worst: that the seething hordes of Gog and Magog would swarm across the face of the Earth, setting in train the end of the world and unleashing those final agonies prophesied in the Quran: *On that day the sky shall become like molten brass, and the mountains like tufts of wool scattered in the wind.*[2]

IN THE MUSLIM MAPS and geographies of the medieval world, the realm of Gog and Magog is represented as a Mordor-like zone of fire and ice enclosed by a steep mountain range. Mapmakers like Idrisi placed it in the darkened lands beyond Ptolemy's seventh clime.

But knowledge of Gog and Magog was by no means confined to Islamic tradition; apocalyptic prophecies concerning this realm appear in the scriptures of the Hebrews and Christians as well.[3] The meaning of Gog and Magog is a little slippery: in some traditions it was the name of one or two evil nations; in others it was the name of the creatures of those lands. In some reports the creatures of Gog and Magog were said to be a race of giants; in others they were no bigger than one foot tall. One particularly vivid account gave them dog-like teeth and long, elephantine ears: one to serve as a mattress to sleep on, the other to pull over themselves as a blanket. They were said to coo to one another like pigeons, and howl like dogs while copulating.[4] Sometimes the beasts of Gog and Magog were counted among the races of human beings; elsewhere they were classed as inhuman, foetus-eating abominations; but their existence was never seriously doubted. Nor was the strength of their numbers: the chronicler Tabari reckoned their population to be nine times that of human beings, which was hardly surprising, given that 'no male dies before having fathered a thousand children, nor any female before having given birth to the same number'.[5]

Muslims were warned in the pages of the Quran that a day would come when the hordes of Gog and Magog (Yajuj and Majuj) would break out of their mountain fastnesses and swarm across the cities of the world, signalling the End of Days, the time of tribulations and the Last Judgement. On that day, the unbelievers and idolators would become fuel for Hell, while Heaven would open for the righteous like the unfolding of a book.[6]

Until that day, however, the realm of Gog and Magog would remain sealed off from the outside world by an encircling mountain range and a great iron wall. The builder of this wall is named in the Quran as a great warrior, 'the Two-Horned One': a man better known to history as Alexander of Macedon, or Alexander the Great.

ALEXANDER HAD BEEN much on Wathiq's mind since he had become caliph. Although Alexander had been dead for a thousand years, stories still rang out across the medieval world of the young military genius whose armies had conquered every land between Greece and India. Wathiq reigned over an empire that was larger and more enduring than Alexander's, but the caliph had not built it, only inherited it. In Wathiq's imagination, Alexander's life shimmered like a golden tapestry. Every thread, it seemed, shone with a brilliant lustre.

Alexander had been born in 356 B.C.E. into the royal house of Macedon in Northern Greece. He was educated by Aristotle, the sage revered by Muslim scholars as the greatest of the Greek philosophers. At twenty, Alexander succeeded his father to the throne, and within two years had conquered all of Greece and was ready to lead his armies across the Hellespont.

In 333 B.C.E., he paused at the city of Gordium in Asia Minor to test himself against an ancient puzzle, the Gordian Knot: an oxen rope knotted too tightly to be unravelled. It was prophesied that whoever unwound it would conquer all of Asia. Alexander simply sliced through it with his sword: an act that has ever since served as a model of a creative solution to a seemingly intractable problem.

By 331 B.C.E., Alexander had conquered Syria and Egypt, and founded the city of Alexandria. A year later, he defeated the Persian king Darius III and entered the city of Babylon on a road strewn with flowers, filled with clouds of perfume and frankincense.[7] At twenty-nine, he led his armies still further east, into modern-day Afghanistan, and then crossed the Hindu Kush to defeat King Porus of India and his war elephants in the Punjab.

Alexander was now the master of a sprawling Eurasian empire and by far the richest Greek who had ever lived. He made plans to invade Arabia, but never lived to realise them, dying in Babylon of a fever on 10 June 323 B.C.E. He was thirty-two years old and had never known a military defeat.

After Alexander's death, the conquered lands were divided between his commanders. More Hellenistic cities bearing his name were established in Asia; Alexandria-at-World's-End, Alexandria Arachosia and Alexandria-in-the-Caucasus endure to this day as the cities of Khujand, Kandahar and Bagram respectively, and in the centuries following his death, the 'magic breath' of Greek images, ideas and mythologies blew into Central Asia, where they encountered similar divine winds coming in from India and China.[8]

THE EXAMPLE OF ALEXANDER'S brief, thrilling life inspired dreams of glory in the souls of kings and would-be conquerors, but ultimately left them restless and dissatisfied: Alexander had burnt so very brightly that every one of them would have to live in his shadow. Julius Caesar was said to have wept when he realised his hero had conquered much of the known world at thirty-two, while he, at thirty-three, was stuck in Spain with thinning hair, serving time as a mere provincial Roman governor.[9]

As the centuries rolled on, and the classical world that had given birth to Alexander fell into ruins, his legend endured and evolved. Folk tales of lesser kings and chieftains broke away from their origins and attached themselves to his name. Around the third century C.E., these legends, both real and fantastical, were bundled together into an enormously popular collection of tales known as *The Alexander Romance*, which was subsequently translated and disseminated throughout the medieval world. Each culture had their own version of Alexander: the Egyptians made him the son of an exiled pharaoh; the Hebrews portrayed him as a magic rabbi; for the Franks he was a knight in shining armour; the Romans portrayed him as a mysterious harbinger of Christ, the Saviour to come; and in the Muslim world, Alexander became a freewheeling adventurer, a hero to the downtrodden and a solver of problems.

The Arabic translation of *The Alexander Romance* tells of how he saved Alexandria from rampaging sea monsters. In the tale, Alexander seats himself inside a glass diving bell, which is lowered from a boat to the sea bed. He spends all day on the floor of the Mediterranean drawing sketches of the creatures. On his return to the surface, he hands the sketches to his men and directs them to build giant metal replicas of the monsters on the shoreline of Alexandria, which scares them away. Thus, Alexander saves his city, and in the process invents the bathysphere.

TO THE MEDIEVALS, such genius seemed to transcend mortal flesh, and so the anonymous authors of *The Alexander Romance* promoted him to semi-divine status; they insinuated that he was sired not by Philip of Macedon, but by the ram-headed Egyptian god Ammon. And it was this connection that identified Alexander to Muslims as Dhu al Qarnain, 'the Two-Horned One', named in the Quran as the builder of the barrier of Gog and Magog.

A sixteenth-century Islamic painting of Alexander the Great, lowered into the sea within a glass diving bell

Chapter 18 of the Quran relates that Alexander rode out one day to the lands of the rising sun. There he came across a village of people living by a muddy pool who begged for his protection from the hordes of Gog and Magog, dwelling nearby behind a mountain pass. The people offered to pay Alexander for his help, but the hero honourably refused their money. Instead he ordered them to build a wall to stop up the mountain pass.

'Bring me lumps of iron!' he demanded, and it was done.

Iron bricks were forged and put down in layers that rose up as high as the mountains on either side of the pass.

'Build a fire!' he commanded, and it was done.

Molten tar was boiled up in a cauldron and poured over the wall, adhering it seamlessly to the mountainside.

And with that, the creatures of Gog and Magog were trapped; they could neither climb over the mighty barrier, nor break through it.

His heroic task complete, Alexander took his leave from the rejoicing villagers, but not before delivering a solemn prophecy: 'This wall is proof of the mercy of my Lord. But when the promise of my Lord one day comes true, He will pull it down into rubble. And the promise of my Lord is always true.'[10]

IN WATHIQ'S MIND, THEREFORE, the implications of his vision of a broken barrier, should it be true, could hardly be more grave, or more urgent. The caliph wasted no time in summoning his advisors and commissioning an expedition that would travel to the eastern end of the known world to inspect the wall and report back on its condition. To lead the expedition, Wathiq's military commander recommended a man known as Sallam the Interpreter, who was said to be able to speak thirty languages. 'There is no one better for this task than him,' the general said.

'So Wathiq summoned me,' Sallam later recalled in his report, 'and assigned fifty strong young men to me.' The caliph also gave him 5000 dinars, a year's provisions, and arranged for every man in the party to be kitted out with a heavy felt-lined leather coat and boots for the cold weather. Two hundred mules were requisitioned to carry supplies and water. Whether these provisions would sustain them for a journey to the very edge of the map, no one could say.

Sallam and his entourage set out for the barrier of Gog and Magog in that year of 842, not knowing when or if they would return. The report of their journey to the east is recorded in Ibn Khordadbeh's classic Arabic geographical work *The Book of Roads and Kingdoms.**

The Travels of Sallam the Interpreter

SALLAM'S PARTY RODE NORTH out of Iraq into the Caucasus region, where they passed through the city of Tiflis. From there they reached the northern shores of the Caspian Sea and entered the lands of the Khazars, a Turkic people who had built a multi-ethnic commercial empire spanning modern-day Ukraine and southern Russia. Caught between the influence of Roman Christianity and Abbasid Islam, the Khazars had chosen instead to adopt Judaism as their religion, drafting their court documents in Hebrew and minting coins similar to the Muslim dinar, inscribed with the legend *Moses is the Messenger of God.*[11] Sallam's account says nothing of this, only that he and his entourage spent a day and a night as guests of the Khazar King, before moving on.

At this point, Sallam's expedition entered a land he describes as 'black and putrid'. They traversed this unpleasant landscape for ten days, covering their noses with vinegar-soaked rags to fend off the stench. From there they moved into another bleak zone of ruined cities they were told had been long ago 'invaded and devastated by the people of Gog and Magog'.

Sallam's party were now well beyond the borders of the caliphate, which made it all the more confusing when they came to a number

* The following account of Sallam the Interpreter's journey is drawn from several recensions and translations, published respectively in Travis Zadeh, *Mapping Frontiers Across Medieval Islam;* Paul Lunde and Caroline Stone's *Ibn Fadlan and the Land of Darkness*; and Emeri van Donzel and Andrea Schmidt's *Gog and Magog in Early Eastern Christian and Islamic Sources.*

of mountain fortresses garrisoned with troops who spoke Arabic and Persian and who knew the Quran. When Sallam told them that he and his men were emissaries of the caliph, they were stunned.

'The Commander of the Faithful?' they asked.

'Yes.'

'Is he old or young?'

'He is young.'

This too amazed them. 'Where does he live?' they asked.

'In Iraq, in a city named Samarra.'

'We have never heard of it,' they replied.

BEYOND THESE GARRISON Towns, Sallam and his men came to a walled city named 'Igu'. He noted:

> Igu is ten farsakhs in circumference and has gates of iron which are closed by lowering them. Within the confines of this city there are fields and windmills. It is in this city that the Two-Horned One camped with his army.

Three days later, following a line of fortresses and villages, Sallam records that they arrived at last at Alexander's great barrier.

THE WALL SALLAM DESCRIBES is just as it is in the Quran: a high barrier of iron bricks wedged between two mountains and crowned by a row of zigzag battlements. Scattered at its base were rusting cauldrons and ironmonger's tools left behind long ago by Alexander's workers. Two colossal iron gates stood at its centre, locked with a heavy bolt and key. Inscribed on the gates in iron letters was Alexander's ominous prediction: *When the promise of my Lord one day comes true, He will pull it down into rubble. And the promise of my Lord is always true.*

At the foot of the gate were two fortresses, garrisoned with soldiers. The captain of the guards was pleased to inform Sallam that the caliph's fears had been groundless: the wall was still as sound as it had been on the day Alexander's men completed its construction. Every Monday and Thursday, the captain said, he and his men would ride out at daybreak to inspect the wall. Three times a day they would clang a hammer on the iron gates and listen for a buzzing and rumbling on the other side. This assured them that Gog and Magog were safely penned in behind the wall.

Satisfied with everything he'd seen, Sallam pulled out a knife from his leggings and scratched away some iron dust from the iron gate, which he wrapped in a square of cloth to give to the caliph as proof that he had seen the wall.

SALLAM'S ACCOUNT OF HIS journey home is briskly described. The expedition came back through Samarkand, crossed the Oxus River (known to them as the Amu Darya), then passed through the Persian cities of Nishapur and Rayy, before returning to Samarra.

They'd been gone for more than two years. Only fourteen of the fifty men who had set out on the mission had returned from the long, perilous journey.

Sallam presented Wathiq with the iron filings he'd scratched from the wall, reassuring him that it was still intact and that his dream had been a mere phantasm. Wathiq gave thanks to God and rewarded Sallam and his men with a thousand gold coins each. Sallam then dictated the story of his adventure to Ibn Khordadbeh, who later inserted the report in his *Book of Roads and Kingdoms*, a compendium of maps, trade routes, and descriptions of foreign lands lying north, south, east and west of Baghdad.

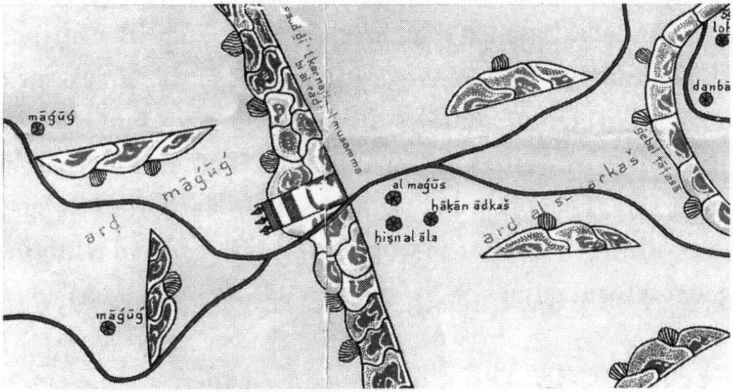

The gated wall of Gog and Magog (Yajuj and Majuj)

Desert Ghosts

THE STRANGE TALE of Sallam the Interpreter's expedition to the land of Gog and Magog – the distant location, the high metallic wall and the horde of rumbling monsters behind it – all sat quite neatly within Islamic tradition. Copies of *The Book of Roads and Kingdoms* circulated throughout the Arabic-speaking world, cementing a conviction that the Quran had spoken truly, that a mighty metal wall built at the command of Alexander the Great did indeed stand somewhere at the far edge of the world. Idrisi in Sicily, like many other geographers, readily accepted Sallam's account: 'As for the rampart of Gog and Magog,' Idrisi writes assuredly, 'it is mentioned in books and is successively confirmed by histories. Part of that is what Sallam the Interpreter has related.'[12]

But of course, we now know the historical Alexander never marched into East Asia, no such iron-and-copper wall was ever constructed, and the monsters of Gog and Magog do not exist. The geography of Sallam's journey is obscure in many places, and it's certainly possible that the tale was partially or entirely fabricated. The Abbasid world, which was probably more familiar at the time with the culture of classical Greece than that of the Greek-speaking Romans, loved Homeric tales of marvels and fantastic beings encountered by travellers in far-off lands. Some modern scholars have found it easy enough to discount Sallam's report as a charming fable, as nothing more than 'a wonder tale interspersed with three or four geographical names'.[13]

AND YET, IT COULD not be denied that there were elements of Sallam's account that tethered it to historical and geographical reality. Like any good explorer, Sallam was careful to enumerate distances and dates, and it is possible to pin out a plausible route eastward from Iraq that works well enough with Sallam's stated itinerary.

Identifying specific locations on the map is admittedly tricky. Tiflis in the Caucasus can be recognised readily enough as the Georgian capital Tbilisi; the Khazar capital Itil can be located on the delta of the Volga River where it flows into the Caspian Sea. But from there, tracking Sallam's journey requires some informed guesswork. His mention of a 'black putrid land' has led one translator to suggest the expedition might have passed around the Aral Sea into the lands near Lake Balkhash, north of the Tian Shan Mountains.[14] A more likely route, it seems to me, would have Sallam's party emerging from the Khazar lands into the adjacent Karakum Desert in modern-day Turkmenistan. The Karakum, a baking-hot expanse whose name means 'Black Sands', is known for its dark, shale-rich sand and its plentiful deposits of noxious methane gas. A 'black and putrid land' indeed.*

After that, Sallam claimed his party trekked for twenty days though a zone of 'ruined cities'. At the time of his journey, traders and pilgrims moving east from the Karakum Desert would make their way through the high passes of the Pamir Mountains, which funnelled them into the city of Kashgar in China's Xinjiang Province.

Kashgar was a garrison town and a key trading post on the silk roads connecting the Chinese capital Chang An with India, the Muslim world and Europe. Travellers coming down from the harsh mountain passes would be relieved to find themselves in a well-irrigated oasis town with paved streets and canals shaded by willows, poplars and mulberry trees.[15]

The comforts of Kashgar stood in stark contrast to the unforgiving landscapes that lay beyond its walls. For travellers going on to China, the city was a final stepping-off point before entering one of the most inhospitable environments on Earth: the Taklamakan Desert.

THE TAKLAMAKAN IS A wasteland roughly the size of Germany. In Turkic, its name means 'Once You Enter, You Cannot Leave'.[16] Unlike the central deserts of Australia and Africa, the Taklamakan experiences wild seasonal variations: the searing heat of summer plummets to sub-zero temperatures in the winter months. The terrain varies from steep sand dunes, rising as high as ninety metres, to the flat salt plains of Lop on the desert's eastern fringe.

---

* Extracting resources from the Karakum's honeycombed subterranean bed is still a hazardous business. In 1971, an entire Russian gas rig collapsed into one of the Karakum's gas-filled underground caves. Soviet engineers ignited the methane in the now-open crater, hoping to burn it off. More than five decades later, the gaping fire pit, nicknamed 'the Gate to Hell', is still blazing away.

from the

KARAKUM TO THE TAKLAMAKAN

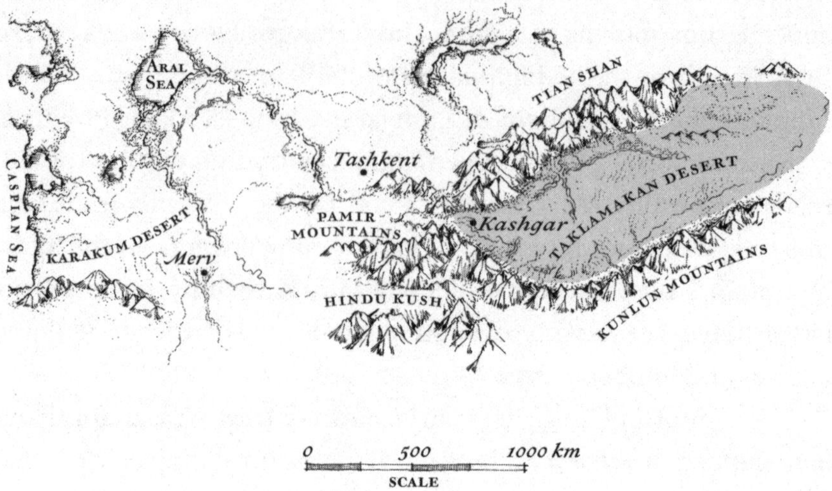

In Sallam's day, those who attempted a desert crossing risked exposing themselves to the full fury of the *kara buran*, the black hurricane, a phenomenon described by a modern German explorer as follows:

> Quite suddenly the sky grows dark. The sun becomes a dark-red ball of fire seen through the fast-thickening veil of dust, a muffled howl is followed by a piercing whistle, and a moment after, the storm bursts with appalling violence upon the caravan. Enormous masses of sand, mixed with pebbles, are forcibly lifted up, whirled round, and dashed down on man and beast; the darkness increases and strange, clashing noises mingle with the roar and howl of the storm, caused by the violent contact of great stones as they are whirled up through the air. The whole

> happening is like hell let loose … Any traveller overwhelmed by such a storm must, in spite of the heat, entirely envelop himself in felts to escape injury from the stones dashing round with such mad force; man and horse must lie down and endure the rage of the hurricane, which often lasts for hours together … The beasts, too, lose their reason from terror of the sandstorm, and rush off to a lingering death in the desert solitudes.[17]

EVEN WHEN QUIET and still, the Taklamakan seemed to exert its malice on medieval trespassers. It was said to be haunted by phantoms that deranged the mind, particularly in the Desert of Lop on the Taklamakan's eastern fringes, a desiccated saltpan waste that had once been the bed of a lake.

In 630 C.E., a Chinese monk named Xuanzang* passed through the Taklamakan on a heroic pilgrimage to India to retrieve copies of the Buddhist sutras in the original Sanskrit. For a while, he found a path by following a trail of bleached bones and horse dung. Then, in the distance, he saw a group of soldiers dressed in fur and felt, their lances and banners glittering under the blazing sun. As they came closer, new figures emerged and flew towards him, changing shape, then dissipating into nothingness. In the void, he heard alluring voices calling, 'Do not fear! Do not fear!'[18]

The Venetian merchant Marco Polo, who passed through the Desert of Lop some six centuries later, also spoke of its power to lure travellers to their deaths:

> The truth is this: when a man is riding by night through this desert and something happens to make him loiter and lose

---

* Known as 'Hsuan Tsang' or 'Hiuen Tsang' under older systems of Chinese Romanisation.

> touch with his companions, by dropping asleep or for some other reason, and afterwards he wants to rejoin them, then he hears spirits talking in such a way that they seem to be his companions. Sometimes, indeed, they even hail him by name. Often these voices make him stray from the path, so that he never finds it again. And in this way many travellers have been lost and have perished. And sometimes in the night they are conscious of a noise like the clatter of a great cavalcade of riders away from the road; and, believing that these are some of their own company, they go where they hear the noise and, when day breaks, find they are victims of an illusion and in an awkward plight. And there are some who, in crossing this desert, have seen a host of men coming towards them and, suspecting that they were robbers, have taken flight; so, having left the beaten track and not knowing how to return to it, they have gone hopelessly astray. Yes, and even by daylight men hear these spirit voices, and often you fancy you are listening to the strains of many instruments, especially drums, and the clash of arms. For this reason, bands of travellers make a point of keeping very close together. Before they go to sleep, they set up a sign pointing in the direction in which they have to travel. And round the necks of all their beasts they fasten little bells, so that by listening to the sound they may prevent them from straying off the path.[19]

THE HARSHNESS OF THE Taklamakan's interior encouraged silk-road travellers to stick to the two roads looping around the desert's rim: a northern route that passed in the shadow of the Tian Shan Mountains, and a southern road skirting the Kunlun Mountains. The two roads re-converged on the far side of the desert, at the

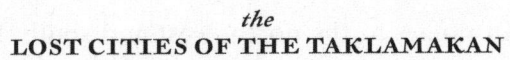

the
LOST CITIES OF THE TAKLAMAKAN

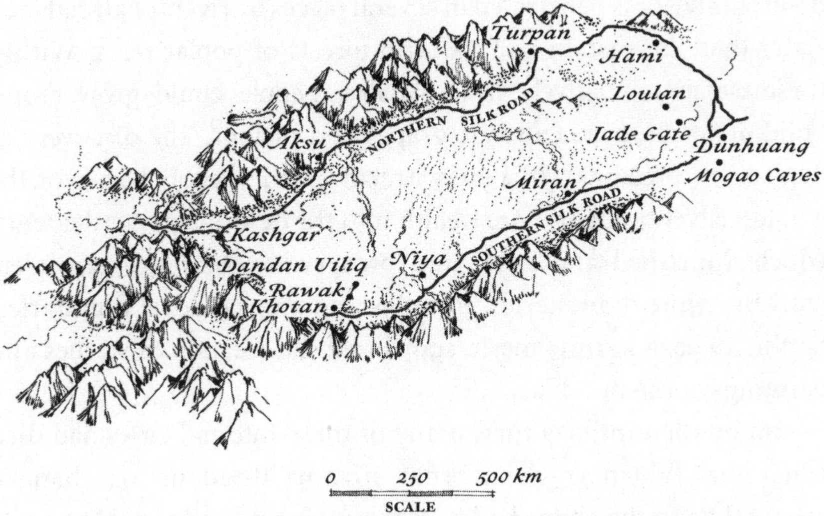

Chinese city of Dunhuang. Kashgar and Dunhuang sit at opposite corners of the eye-shaped Taklamakan.

Stationed along the desert-rim roads was a series of Chinese garrison towns built in the first century B.C.E. by the Emperor Wudi to protect these narrow trade corridors. But in 842, at the time when Sallam's journey was said to have taken place, the garrison soldiers had long since been withdrawn from the area to fight internal revolts in China's heartland. Tibetan soldiers had subsequently poured in to occupy the Taklamakan garrison towns, but Chinese officials continued to administer the districts, and the towns on the Taklamakan's rim roads remained well populated and prosperous. There were no 'ruined cities' there to fit Sallam's description.

The riverine oasis cities *within* the desert, however, were another story. The Taklamakan lies at the base of a deep basin, enclosed by high mountain ranges to the north, west and south. Rain, when it comes, breaks on these mountains and streams down to the edge of the desert, nourishing small fertile pockets here and there. The desert's interior is penetrated in several places by rivers of glacial melt water that can sustain narrow strip forests of poplar trees. Within these isolated, relatively lush patches, people could grow crops, build orchards, even cultivate grapes and melons. The discovery of deposits of precious white jade strewn on the pebbly banks of the Khotan River brought more wealth into the desert basin settlements, which flourished and grew into prosperous oasis towns, replete with Buddhist monasteries, pagodas and stupas. Local dignitaries, hoping to earn karmic merit, sponsored the creation of statues and paintings of the Buddha.

But by the ninth century, many of these internal cities had died when the Taklamakan's internal streams dried up or changed course. Life in the towns had become untenable and the inhabitants had been forced to make new lives elsewhere.[20] Sand blew into the abandoned roads and squares, then onto the rooftops of the houses and temples, caving them in, submerging them under a dry, gritty shroud. At the time of Sallam's journey east, there were perhaps a dozen such eerie 'ruined cities' inside the Taklamakan.

THE TEMPLES OF these empty cities slept for centuries under the silent sun and stars. Empires rose and fell. The Tang Dynasty passed into history. Political disruption killed trade along the overland silk roads, as merchants switched to the less risky maritime routes to China.

After the Muslim conquests of Central Asia, Islam became the predominant religion of Xinjiang and the Taklamakan, and the ancient Buddhist civilisation of the silk roads was forgotten. Rumours of guardian spirits haunting the empty cities kept local people at a distance, and only a few scavengers dared to burrow into the ruins for the gold and silver rumoured to be hidden inside the buried temples.

IN THE 1880s, the Dutch scholar and linguist Michael Jan De Goeje set to work translating a manuscript of Ibn Khordadbeh's *Book of Roads and Kingdoms*. After studying Sallam the Interpreter's report, De Goeje became convinced it was based on historical truth. In 1888, he published a paper titled 'The Wall of Gog and Magog', in which he argued that the caliph's man really had travelled all the way to the far end of the Taklamakan Desert. De Goeje pointed to the city named 'Igu' in the report, the expedition's final stop before reaching the wall: 'Next we reached a city named Igu … It is in this city that the Two-Horned One camped with his army.' De Goeje identified Igu as a garrison town on the eastern fringe of the Taklamakan that was then named 'Iwu' or 'Yizhou'. The town, now known as Hami, still exists in Xinjiang Province.

The link was tenuous, at best, but if true, it placed Alexander's wall somewhere in the vicinity of the eastern Taklamakan. De Goeje pondered where this mighty barrier, three days' march out of Igu, might be located.

An answer, of sorts, was found by a British-Hungarian explorer named Marc Aurel Stein.

The Wonder House

AUREL STEIN WAS DIMINUTIVE and fastidiously groomed, but said to be 'sturdy and tough as nails'.[21] He dedicated his life to the resurrection of the ancient world, an obsession that crowded out almost every other human preoccupation. Stein never married – two biographers looked in vain for evidence of male or female lovers and found nothing – but he kept up a lively and affectionate correspondence with a close circle of friends throughout his life. He seems to have begrudged anything that distracted him from his work, even the need to eat: an old friend complained that Stein could never quite shed the notion that 'time given to such grossness as feeding is time ill-spent'.[22]

Stein's expeditions into Chinese Turkestan, as Xinjiang Province was then called, were hailed in his lifetime as 'the most daring and adventuresome raid upon the ancient world that any archaeologist has attempted',[23] but his discoveries never made him rich; he pursued money only to fund further expeditions. By the standards of the time, Stein was immune to racial prejudice, preferring the company of Chinese and Indian scholars to that of European dullards. But in China he has long been denounced as a thief and a scoundrel.

MARC AUREL STEIN was born in Budapest in 1862 to Hungarian Jewish parents, who had him baptised as a Christian in the hope that it would ease his path through the world. As a boy, Stein became fascinated by the campaigns of Alexander the Great and the Macedonian conqueror would remain his lifelong hero. Educated Europeans had by then put aside the fictional superhero of *The Alexander Romance* and rediscovered the ancient biographies of the historical conqueror penned by Arrian of Nicomedia and Quintus Curtius Rufus, and found them every bit as compelling.

Aurel Stein in Lahore, c. 1900

For Stein, Alexander's brilliant career was a summons to adventure, travel and immortality. He would spend the rest of his life literally following in Alexander's footsteps through Central Asia, looking for traces of the hybrid Hellenic–Buddhist culture catalysed by his conquests in the East.

Stein flung himself into the world as though he didn't have a moment to lose. Having learnt German, English, French and Latin at an early age, he took up Persian and Sanskrit in Germany before pursuing postdoctoral studies at the Oriental Institute in England. It was here that Stein read *Record of the Western Regions*, Xuanzang's seventh-century account of his epic pilgrimage from China through the Taklamakan to India and back. Stein would later name Xuanzang as the patron saint of his expeditions into Chinese Turkestan.

In England, Stein joined the Church of England and took lessons in Punjabi in preparation for service in colonial India, and in 1888, at the age of twenty-five, he took up a position in the city of Lahore as Principal of the Oriental College and Registrar of Punjab University.

IN LAHORE, AUREL STEIN befriended Lockwood Kipling, father of the poet Rudyard. Lockwood was the curator of the Lahore Museum, described by his son as a 'wonder house' of statues and stone slabs 'crowded with figures that had encrusted the brick walls of the Buddhist stupas and viharas of the North Country'.[24]

This was Stein's first encounter with the ancient culture of Gandhara from the Peshawar Valley, a powerful synthesis of Greek and Buddhist influences. He saw that the Buddhist subjects of these statues and paintings had been rendered in ways heavily influenced by the Hellenistic styles introduced to Central Asia by Alexander and his successors. Early forms of Indian Buddhist art had carefully avoided depicting the Buddha in person, representing him instead as a riderless horse, a bodhi tree, or a set of footprints. These forms had predominated until the shock of Hellenistic art came to Asia, with its realistic and sensual depictions of the human form. The Buddha was thereafter presented like a Greek king, swathed in a Mediterranean toga, with classical pouting lips and expressive hands, but also with traditional Asian-style features – fleshy jowls, heavy eyelids and long earlobes.

Stein pondered how it was that Buddhism, which had emerged in northern India around 500 B.C.E., had made its way into China and Central Asia. He concluded that Buddhist ideas must have entered via the silk roads of the Taklamakan Desert.

BY DECEMBER 1897, Stein had conducted several explorations into the mountain passes between northwest India and Afghanistan. In Lahore, he picked up copies of the journal of the Royal Geographical Society, where he found a report by the Swedish explorer Sven Hedin that engrossed him. Hedin, he read, after a disastrous start, had succeeded in leading an expedition across the 'murderous sands' of the Taklamakan, where he'd found several of its lost cities.[25]

Sven Hedin was a romantic who had studied in Berlin, where he became a lifelong admirer of all things German, and he would later count Kaiser Wilhelm II and Adolf Hitler as friends. Hedin's tutor in Berlin was the distinguished Prussian geographer Baron Ferdinand von Richthofen, the uncle of Manfred, the World War I flying ace. Von Richthofen had coined the term 'silk road' (*seidenstrasse*) to describe the ancient trade routes between China and the West. 'Silk road' was a wonderfully evocative term, juxtaposing the very soft with the very hard, but it was somewhat misleading: the 'road' was more like a set of unmarked, unfixed tracks meandering through mountains and deserts, and the caravans that moved along them carried jade, cinnamon, coral, ivory, metals, leather, glass, porcelain and paper as well as silk. But the term caught on and was popularised by Sven Hedin through his heavily publicised exploits in Central Asia.

In December 1895, Hedin had set out along the frozen Khotan River into the Taklamakan Desert, where he'd heard rumours of a buried city. On 24 January 1896, the expedition turned into the dunes, where they came across several rows of bleached posts and wooden walls poking up through the sand. Excavating the site was hard and frustrating work, but the city slowly revealed its secrets.

The timber walls were painted with heavenly paintings of the Buddha seated on lotus leaves, crowned with a halo. In an open temple they uncovered a mural of 'airily-clad' women at prayer, their black hair twisted in a knot on the top of their head. Elsewhere Hedin's workers found painted figures of dogs and horses, and boats rocking on the waves, which Hedin found strangely impressive, given they were in the heart of a desert and so very distant from the sea.

Between the houses, Hedin could make out the outlines of streets lined with the stumps of plum and apricot trees. 'Here I stand,' he scribbled excitedly in his notebook, 'like the prince in the enchanted wood, having wakened to new life the city which has slumbered for a thousand years.'[26]

The buried city, known by local treasure-hunters as Dandan Uiliq, 'The Houses of Ivory', had once been a busy trading post sprawling across four square kilometres. But by the eighth century the glacial streams from the mountains had dried up. Sitting in the silent ruins, Hedin tried to imagine Dandan Uiliq as it had been in its heyday, two thousand years earlier, before the sand had set in:

> Close to the city, and along the banks of the river, luxuriant woods tossed their quivering leaves in the breeze … and in the hot summer days the leafy apricot-trees gave cool shade to the inhabitants. The streams were powerful enough to make millstones revolve. Silk was cultivated, and horticulture and the industries flourished. The people who dwelt there manifestly knew how to decorate their homes with good taste and a sense of artistic fitness.[27]

IN HIS ARTICLE for the Royal Geographical Society's *Geographical Journal*, Hedin made it clear that he thought of himself as an explorer, not an archaeologist, and that the careful excavation and documentation of the site at Dandan Uiliq should be undertaken by someone better qualified than he.

In Lahore, Aurel Stein resolved to do just that: to lead his own expedition into the Taklamakan. His proposal was backed enthusiastically by the new viceroy of India, Lord Curzon, a British imperialist fascinated by time and 'the ineffable pathos of ruin'.[28] Curzon himself had written a book on Central Asia and its strategic significance.

The Taklamakan, in the late nineteenth century, had become a theatre of the Great Game, the contest between the Russian and British Empires for influence in Central Asia. Yet Western maps of Chinese Turkestan were still mostly blank. Military and political missions were sent into the region, followed by explorers armed with modern cartographical equipment, intent on charting its mountain passes and desert roads. With Curzon's help, Stein was able to secure British government funding and a passport from the Chinese capital Peking that permitted him to enter Chinese Turkestan.

STEIN PREPARED FOR the journey into the Taklamakan with typical thoroughness. He set up a base camp in Kashmir, staffed with an experienced Indian cartographer, three servants and a cook.

In August 1900, he arrived at Kashgar, accompanied by his pet terrier Dash. He stayed there for several months at the residence of the local British representative, George Macartney, and his wife Theodora. Kashgar was then divided into an old town populated by Muslim Uighurs, and a Han Chinese new town. Stein hired several translators and attendants, and assembled a caravan of twelve ponies and eight camels. After hours, he lingered in the Macartneys' expansive library, studying translations of the court annals of the Chinese emperors, interludes that would unexpectedly pay huge dividends later.

ON 11 SEPTEMBER, Stein's expedition set out from Kashgar, following the southern silk route towards Khotan. The journey along the dusty road was heavy-going, 'the track marked here and there by the parched carcases and bleached bones of animals that had died on it'. But Stein was buoyed by the certainty that he was trudging along the same road walked by Xuanzang and Marco Polo centuries earlier. For Stein, slow progress through ancient villages by camel and pony was far preferable to the hectic blur of rail travel. 'To peep into every house and hut along the road', he wrote, 'is better than to see towns in electric illumination flit past like fireflies.'[29] The stark silence of the Taklamakan fired his imagination. One night, camping on a ridge outside Khotan, Stein stepped out of his tent to see a full moon illuminating the sparkling peaks of the dunes below:

> It seemed as if I were looking at the lights of a vast city lying below me in the endless plains. Could it really be that terrible desert where there was no life and no hope of human existence? I knew that I should never see it again in this alluring splendour. Its appearance haunted me as I sat shivering in my tent.[30]

IN KHOTAN, STEIN recruited thirty labourers and a guide who said he could lead them out to the ruins of Dandan Uiliq. After eleven days of trudging up and over the cresting dunes they found the site. Stein set up camp with his crew and began excavating houses and temples.

Stein soon realised that the lost city had been filled with beautiful art. At the base of a shrine, he found a set of wooden panels, one depicting saintly Bodhisattvas – enlightened beings who have delayed entering Paradise to help others – seated on lotus flowers; another displayed an image of the Indian elephant god Ganesha;

The Taklamakan Desert
Photographed by Aurel Stein, 1900

a third panel held the image of a dancing woman, with black tresses of hair whirling around her. The panels, Stein thought, were positioned just as they had been when left as votive offerings by the city's last inhabitants.

To his dismay, he saw the site had been damaged in places by looters looking for gold and silver. Here and there he saw Buddhist statues that had been defaced by Muslims offended by the presence of pagan idols in the desert. These acts of desecration convinced Stein that the artefacts should be removed from the site to be conserved and studied. And so, over the course of three weeks, Stein's crew removed dozens of murals and stucco wall reliefs from Dandan Uiliq. Each one was photographed, catalogued and carefully packed into a wooden case with cotton wool and soft paper. The crates were despatched to Kashgar, and from there to the British Museum in London.

AFTER HE HAD FINISHED at Dandan Uiliq, Stein's guides led him on to other buried cities in the desert. In a walled town once known as Niya, Stein and his men excavated an ancient latrine. Over three long days, they choked and gagged as they dug away at this 'consolidated mass of refuse', still somehow pungent after many centuries,[31] but from the waste they extracted a set of documents engraved on wooden tiles, dating all the way back to 105 B.C.E. The text, Stein was overjoyed to see, was recognisably Indian, but the clay seals that held the tiles together were stamped with figures from Greek mythology: Eros, Heracles, and Athena, the goddess of wisdom, clutching a lightning bolt. It was thrilling evidence that a Greek-influenced Indo-European population had existed here before the arrival of the Han Chinese.

Moving on from Niya, they came to yet another site of sand-drowned ruins, gathered around the base of a domed Buddhist shrine that emerged from the desert floor like the conning tower of a submarine. This had once been the city of Rawak, 'High Mansion', abandoned long before Dandan Uiliq. The excavation revealed a stupa, enclosed by a spacious walled quadrangle that was lined with dozens of Buddhas and Bodhisattvas. These stone figures were too huge and brittle to be transported, so after photographing the panels, Stein reluctantly ordered his labourers to carefully refill the excavations to protect the statues from the desert winds. The reburial, he wrote in his memoir, was a melancholy duty; it pained him 'to watch the images I had brought to light vanishing again, one after the other, under the pall of sand which had hidden them for so many centuries'.[32]

STILL, STEIN HAD REASON to be well satisfied with the bounty of his first expedition into the Taklamakan: his excavations had yielded twelve cases of treasure for the British Museum.

On his return to Khotan, Stein called on Pan Zhen, a district magistrate well versed in Chinese history whom he had befriended.

Pan Zhen had been warmly supportive of the expedition, but as Stein presented the ancient wooden documents for his inspection, Pan Zhen became anxious when he realised they were all to be carried away to the West. What would he tell his superiors? Stein brushed aside his concerns, promising to send the governor photographs of the documents.

On 2 July 1901, Stein delivered the trove of documents, paintings and sculptures to the British Museum in Bloomsbury. He spent the following weeks carefully unpacking and labelling the treasures in the museum's basement. Stuck in those gloomy, lightless rooms, he became despondent, and dreamt of returning to the desert and the endless open sky.

STEIN'S DISCOVERIES AT Dandan Uiliq, Niya and Rawak created a sensation among Europe's archaeologists and explorers. In 1904 the Thirteenth International Congress of Orientalists passed a special resolution praising his exceptional work. Stein was credited with having salvaged from the sands a dazzling Buddhist society that until now had been wholly unknown to the Western world. It was obvious that there were more treasures to be found in the Taklamakan, and so other explorers in Berlin, Paris, St Petersburg and Tokyo urged their governments to fund their own expeditions into Chinese Turkestan. Stein realised he was now in a race to get back there ahead of these rivals.

For his next expedition he intended to explore the eastern region of the Taklamakan, the Desert of Lop, where he hoped to investigate another promising lost city called Loulan, spotted by Sven Hedin six years earlier.

Along the way, almost as an afterthought, Stein planned to stop at a network of cave temples outside Dunhuang that were said to house a great treasury of Buddhist art.

Wooden tablets excavated from Niya

Desert Angels

IN EARLY JUNE 1906, Aurel Stein returned to Kashgar, ready to embark on his second expedition into the Taklamakan. Stein was aware that a rival expedition led by the French sinologist Paul Pelliot was on its way into the region, and he was intent on reaching Loulan first.

For the next several months, Stein scrambled to pull together a crew of workers to do the digging, as well as teams of camels and ponies to transport the treasures he expected to find. In the evenings, he worked in the Macartneys' library on proofs of the book of his first expedition, *Ancient Khotan*.

While in Kashgar, Stein secured the services of translator and scholar Jiang Xiaowan. Jiang taught him to speak rudimentary conversational Chinese and the two men became close friends. Stein was appreciative of Jiang's company and his abilities, which would prove far more valuable than he could have imagined at the outset of the expedition.

In December, after carefully preparing for a winter trek, Stein and his crew of local labourers set out from Kashgar for the far side of the Taklamakan. Jiang would catch up with them later. A week after entering the Desert of Lop, Stein's party found their way to the ruins of Loulan using maps and sketches drawn up by Hedin six years earlier. There was no sign of the French expedition; Stein had won the race.

Loulan had once been the capital of an ancient kingdom, mentioned in the Han Dynasty annals, that was established in the second century B.C.E. The town had boasted a post office, a hospital and a school. But Loulan was already a ghost town when Xuanzang came through the Taklamakan, and a long-dead ruin when Marco Polo fought his way through the Desert of Lop in 1224.

Over the next week, battered by numbingly cold desert winds, Stein and his workers dug up ancient spoons, bronze mirrors, pieces of Chinese lacquer-ware, and a tattered remnant from a brightly coloured rug bearing a Buddhist swastika design. Stein was most excited to find well-preserved military correspondence written in Kharoshthi, an ancient Indian script, indicating that people from the Gandhara region might have settled in Loulan in ancient times.

In late January 1907, Stein moved the party south to investigate yet another buried city named Miran, which would yield some of the most spectacular finds of his career. First, he found larger-than-life statues of the seated Buddha. Then, as he brushed away at a timber wall, a painted mural emerged, depicting winged angels with dimpled round faces and pink cheeks. These angels were Gandharvas, flying celestial beings in Buddhist mythology, but they were delineated in an unmistakably Hellenic style. Stein was able to date the mural to the third century C.E.

Other panels showed cherubs cavorting around undulating flowers and wreaths. Stein spotted an inscription, recording the artist's name as 'Tita', a local version of the Roman name Titus. He wondered if the artist had wandered east from Syria or Mesopotamia onto the silk roads, and ended up in this faraway desert city, where he put himself at the service of its Buddhist masters.

A Greco-Buddhist angel in the lost city of Miran

The Blazing Beacon

STEIN WAS FILLED WITH awe and gratitude by these discoveries. With his hands numbed by the cold and chapped by the arid desert air, he removed the fragile wall panels, then had them packed and sent off to Kashgar, and from there to London. It's clear from Stein's memoir, *Ruins of Desert Cathay*, that he believed he was making a gift of them to the world by bringing them into the full light of scholarship in the safe confines of the British Museum. He never gave a moment's thought as to whether this might be an act of vandalism, sacrilege or theft.

Their work complete, Stein and his exhausted crew began the long trek across the saltpan desert towards Dunhuang for supplies. For seventeen days they saw no other human being.

Then, on the evening of 7 March, Stein spotted the ruins of several Chinese towers in the desert. The next morning, he took Jiang and several workers with him to investigate the nearest of these structures, jutting up on the edge of a plateau. Stein saw that it was a square tower, built with sun-dried clay bricks, rising to a height of seven metres. Further along from the tower he saw a long row of stacked tamarisk reeds, built up like a fortification along the ridge. Looking into the distance, he was amazed to see this was just one segment of a continuous line of stacked, bundled reed mats, cropping up here and there in the sand, leading to another ruined tower in the distance. These mysterious fortifications reminded him of Hadrian's Wall in Northern England.

Stein decided to press on because supplies were running low, but he made a mental note to return to this place after his visit to Dunhuang, with enough food and water to allow him to conduct a proper investigation.

In camp that night, Stein lay in his tent, pondering what he'd seen with growing excitement. The towers, the long rows of bundled reed mats, tallied with what he'd read in the Han Chinese court annals in Kashgar.

Stein was convinced he'd located the oldest and westernmost end of the Great Wall of China.

CHINA'S GREAT WALL is not a single barrier, but a series of discontinuous lines of fortification, built under different dynasties for different reasons. The stretch of wall and watchtowers Aurel Stein found outside Dunhuang had been constructed by the Han Dynasty, under orders from the Emperor Wudi (156–87 B.C.E.), to protect the empire from their own 'Gog and Magog': the mounted warriors of the northern Xiongnu people, who periodically descended on the settled Han lands 'like flocks of birds'.[33] The Xiongnu inspired stark terror among the Han Chinese, raiding farms and townships, and murdering or enslaving the inhabitants. Such was the fear and hatred of the Xiongnu that the Han wall was extended to span the whole of China from west to east, all the way from the Taklamakan Desert to the Yalu River on the Korean border. Wudi then attempted to shut the door on the western approaches to his empire, by colonising and fortifying the Taklamakan area with a line of beacon towers along the wall. If an enemy army was spotted from one tower, soldiers lit a relay of signal fires to warn garrisons up and down the line, just like the lights of Gondor in Tolkien's *Lord of the Rings*.

The squat desert walls that Stein found outside Dunhuang are far older and simpler than the stern granite battlements of the Great Wall outside Beijing today. In the Taklamakan, builders were obliged to use local materials, piling up layers of matted luwei weeds and tamarisk twigs, and cementing them in place with gravelly mud. These crude fortifications bear no resemblance to the mountainous iron barrier of Alexander described by Sallam the Interpreter in *The Book of Roads and Kingdoms*. But medieval accounts of true historical events were often spiced with exaggerations and fabrications, slanted to suit the

The Han Great Wall near Dunhuang
Photographed by Aurel Stein, 1907

prejudices of their intended audiences. If we can accept that Sallam's expedition did indeed travel out to Igu/Hami, and from there to the Han Great Wall, Sallam most likely coloured in the picture to make his report more pleasing and reassuring to the caliph.

The Abbasid world had never been the focus of Stein's work, and there's no evidence he had any knowledge of the report of Sallam's journey to discover Alexander's wall. If he had, the connection to his boyhood hero would surely have amused and delighted him no end.

FIVE DAYS LATER, Stein and his crew arrived in Dunhuang with a howling *kara buran* scouring the streets. The city, whose name means 'Blazing Beacon',[34] was the point where the bifurcated northern and southern silk routes re-converged on the eastern edge of the Taklamakan and rolled on through the Gansu Corridor to central China.

Stein paid a visit to the newly appointed Chinese governor of the province, but was baffled by the flustered formality with which he was received. Only later did he discover that China's ministry of foreign affairs had awarded him on his passport the absurd title of 'Da Ying Zongli Jiaoyu Dachen', literally 'Prime Minister of Education of Great Britain'.[35] Stein was full of questions about the chain of towers and walls he'd just seen in the desert. The governor was friendly, but distracted by an uprising of the local peasants, and as a newcomer to the area could offer Stein little help.

WHILE IN DUNHUANG, Stein set aside time for his side trip to a network of grottoes gouged from the side of a cliff, known as the Mogao Caves, or the Thousand Buddha Caves. Western archaeologists were only now becoming aware of the significance of the grottoes and the treasures that lay within them, but Stein's interest was perfunctory. He was not a China specialist; he was going to the Thousand Buddha Caves as a tourist, not in any professional capacity.

But his visit to the caves would change his life utterly, and make him one of the most reviled Westerners in Chinese history.

The Thousand Buddha Caves

DUNHUANG HAD BEEN ESTABLISHED as a forward base in 104 B.C.E. by the Emperor Wudi to secure the heavily contested western border regions. As the population grew, farmers were brought in to work fields within and outside the city; inns and stables catered to passing silk-road traders, and roadside stalls sold melons, pomegranates and peaches. Buddhist pilgrims would stop at Dunhuang on their way to India, to rest and to lay in supplies for the difficult journey ahead.

In 366 C.E., one such pilgrim, named Yuezun, was trekking past a long sandstone cliff outside Dunhuang when he was given a vision of a thousand Buddhas wreathed in light. The awestruck monk dug out a hole in the cliff wall and created a small shrine, where he slept and prayed for a safe return from his pilgrimage.

Over time, other pilgrims passing through the area chiselled out more grottoes from the soft, crumbly sandstone. Travelling merchants and soldiers stopped to pray for protection from ghosts and bandits that might be lurking in the wilderness. The cave shrines became more ornate as artists plastered the cave walls with smooth layers of plant fibre, sand and clay, and painted richly coloured murals depicting stories from the life of the Buddha. Still more caves were excavated to house sculptures of Buddhas and Bodhisattvas. The larger grottoes served as meeting halls, with altars and niches carved from the stone.

The construction of the cave temples, the creation of Buddhist art and the sponsoring of shrines by wealthy donors were all means of creating karmic merit, a moral force that would carry people towards enlightenment. Caught up in this dizzying virtuous circle, art generated karmic merit, which generated more art, until there were 492 cave temples thrumming with riotous arrays of hand-painted sculptures surrounded by mural scenes of Paradise, saviour gods, saints and flying asparas. Multi-tiered pagodas were constructed on the honeycombed cliff face to protect the cave openings. In the course of a thousand years, the network of grottoes at Dunhuang – known as the Mogao ('Peerless' or 'None Higher') Grottoes,[36] became the single biggest treasure house of Buddhist art in the world.

THE GOLDEN AGE of the Mogao Grottoes had come to a close when silk-road traffic dried up in the eleventh century. Ongoing wars and religious upheavals in Xinjiang kept merchants away and encouraged them to use the maritime routes to China's coastal cities instead. Dunhuang's population dwindled, and the caves became derelict.

Then the desert moved in. Sand from the dunes above the cliff wall poured down, scouring the wall paintings in the entranceways. The brittle rock crumbled and sheared away in places, exposing some of the temple interiors to the elements. Imperial China, itself in slow decay, forgot all about them.

IN 1900, A LONE monk from Shanxi Province named Wang Yuanlu came to the cave complex and appointed himself its guardian. He went about restoring the damage here and there as best he could, funding his work by passing a begging bowl throughout Dunhuang.

One afternoon, Wang was sweeping sand from the entrance to Cave 16 when he noticed a long hairline crack in the plaster wall. Running his finger along the edge, Wang realised it was a small, concealed door. He ordered a worker to chip away the plaster.

Behind the door, they discovered a secret chamber.

Stacked up from floor to ceiling, they saw tens of thousands of scrolls and paintings that had been perfectly preserved in the dark, dry desert air. There were documents written in Uighur and Tibetan, and paintings on fine silken banners that had once dangled from the cliffs outside. There were copies of the Buddhist sutras, handwritten in black ink on paper, dating back to the fifth century. The most recent document they found was dated 996 C.E., indicating that the cave had been sealed up a thousand years earlier to protect its contents from the Muslim armies rampaging through the area at that time.

Suspecting the importance of the ancient scrolls in the Library Cave, as it came to be known, Wang brought a sample to the local prefect, hoping to secure funds to support his conservation efforts. The sheaf of manuscripts was passed on to the education commissioner for Gansu Province, who recognised their significance, but had no funds to transport them to the provincial capital for safekeeping. He could come up with no better solution than to order Wang to put the scrolls back in the Library Cave under lock and key.

Abbott Wang Yuanlu, guardian monk of the Mogao Caves, 1907

BY NOW, AT THE dawn of the twentieth century, Western archaeologists were becoming aware of the Mogao Cave temples and the trove of statues and frescoes that lay within. Aurel Stein had heard of them from a Hungarian geographer named Lajos Loczy but had no plans to take or purchase the cave temples' treasures and had no inkling of the existence of the Library Cave.

In Dunhuang, Stein asked around for information about the Mogao Caves without much success. Unlike Kashgar, Dunhuang was still primarily Buddhist, and his inquiries about the cave temples were rebuffed with a polite 'I do not know.' Stein suspected they were trying to protect their holy site from foreign intruders.

Stein turned to Zahid Beg, a Muslim merchant from Urumchi, who had come to Dunhuang to hide out from his Turkish creditors. Zahid told Stein of a rumour he'd heard: that a hoard of ancient manuscripts had been discovered in a sealed-off room at the Thousand Buddha Caves. Highly excited by this information, Stein and his advisor Jiang set off immediately for the caves, some twenty-five kilometres outside of town. But when they got to the cave complex, the door to the Library Cave was locked. They met a young monk, who told them the key was with Wang Yuanlu, the guardian monk, who was away on one of his begging tours of the area to raise funds for his restoration work. Wang, he said, was not expected back for several weeks.

But the young monk was able to show Stein and Jiang a single manuscript retrieved from the cave. It was a well-preserved scroll of paper fourteen metres long, but it was written in a form of Chinese that Jiang couldn't decipher.

Stein wandered through the caves for a while, stunned by the drama and majesty of the frescoes and statues, but concluded it would be too risky to attempt to remove them, given that the site was still used as a sacred place of worship.

Stein and Jiang then told the young monk they'd be back in three weeks, when they hoped Wang Yuanlu would have returned with the key to that intriguing door. In the meantime, Stein decided they would head back out for a closer examination of that line of fortifications he'd seen weeks earlier in the desert.

The Jade Gate

ON 24 MARCH 1907, Stein and Jiang made their way back into the eastern Taklamakan accompanied by a dozen labourers in search of the Han Great Wall. After several days, they came upon a long line of walls and watchtowers, dipping and rising, submerging and re-emerging into the desert, running all the way to the horizon. In a low dune they found a particularly well-preserved segment where the wall was revealed to be two and a half metres thick and two metres high.[37] Stein marvelled at the skill of the ancient Chinese engineers, who had constructed such a resilient barricade from such crude materials; unlike brick, which is hard but brittle, the stacks of bundled reeds had a degree of give and elasticity that had kept them upright for two millennia.

In the base of a watchtower, Stein found scattered Chinese records written on little wooden slats, which Jiang was able to date to the first century C.E. The slats revealed that the soldiers who had dwelt there two thousand years earlier were mainly convicts, sent to the outer provinces to pay their debt to the Han Emperor.

At the base of one tower, they found an enclosure containing a small Buddhist shrine. Stein was puzzled by this, until he realised that this segment of the wall had been a gate for an ancient road, a cart track, leading to Hami, the walled city identified by De Goeje as the place where Sallam the Interpreter had paused before arriving at the wall of Gog and Magog. Stein, unaware of the connection, concluded that Buddhist pilgrims passing along the road would have stopped here for worship on their way to Hami.

AS HE SAT IN the ruins of a tower watch room, where Chinese soldiers had rested two thousand years earlier, Stein was flooded with a delicious sense of being transported to the ancient world. 'No life of the present', he noted with satisfaction, 'was there to distract my thoughts of the past.'[38] He wrote to a friend:

> Two thousand years seems so brief a span when the sweepings from the soldiers' huts still lie practically on the surface in front of the door, or when I see the huge stacks of reed-bundles used for repairing the wall still in situ near the posts, just like stacks of spare sleepers near a railway station.[39]

On 17 April, Stein shifted his camp closer to 'a small but well-preserved fort' he'd seen further down the line of the Han wall. That evening in camp, one of his assistants presented Stein with a parched bundle of papers that had been found wedged between a wall and a watchtower in the fort. Stein carefully unrolled one of the documents and was astonished to see it was a letter written in Soghdian, an ancient Iranian language that neither he nor Jiang could decipher. Later the documents were identified as a bundle of letters from an ancient mailbag that had lost its way between Dunhuang and Samarkand. The letters were from the families of Soghdian merchants living in China, full of news for the folks back home.

One of the letters, written in 313 C.E., came from a woman in Dunhuang named Miwnay, who had written to her deadbeat husband in Samarkand to berate him for stranding her and her mother in a frontier outpost with no money:

> I obeyed your command and came to Dunhuang and did not observe my mother's bidding or that of my brothers. Surely the gods were angry with me on the day when I did your bidding. I would rather be a dog's or a pig's wife than yours![40]

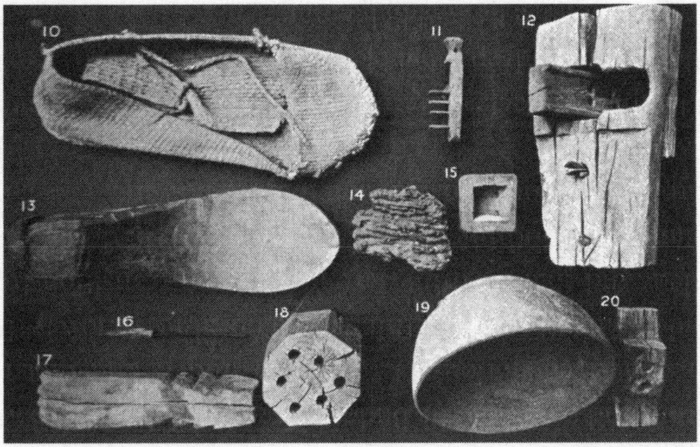

Ancient everyday objects and implements found by Stein's crew in the watchtowers of the Han wall, among them a hemp shoe, a wooden lock and key, and a rice bowl

The following day, Stein realised that the watchtower where the mailbag had been found was part of a larger fortress complex, dominated by a crumbling castle made of compacted earth. After carefully surveying the site, Stein realised he'd stumbled on Yumenguan, 'the Jade Gate', a famous frontier pass of the Great Wall, so named for the countless jade caravans from Khotan that had once passed through it. In its time, the Jade Gate had controlled much of the traffic coming in and out of western China. For returning Chinese travellers, the gate represented the end of the desert and a welcome return to civilisation, with the pears, peaches and melons of Dunhuang waiting for them just down the road. Now the castle stood in isolation, but with its four-and-a-half-metre-thick walls still mostly intact.

Stein had succeeded in tracing a ninety-seven-kilometre stretch of the Great Wall. It would be his greatest archaeological achievement. But the winter cold of the Taklamakan had lifted, unleashing swarms of marsh mosquitos. Many of Stein's exhausted workers drifted back to Dunhuang in search of opium to smoke and comfortable lodgings to sleep in. Stein, preoccupied by thoughts of what he might find in the Library Cave, decided to strike camp and head back to Dunhuang as well.

STEIN RE-ENTERED DUNHUANG on 14 May, relieved to be back in the shady oasis. He pitched his tent in an orchard of pear and peach trees that left a sprinkle of blossoms on the canvas. He was eager to get back to the Mogao Caves, but the following day some ten thousand Buddhists filled the streets of Dunhuang dressed in bright colours for the festival of the annual pilgrimage to the cave shrines. Stein was advised by the local governor that it would not be prudent for foreigners to be present at the Mogao Caves at this time, so instead he and Jiang decided to take some time off to visit the picturesque Crescent Lake, six kilometres south of the city.

The lake, a perfect arc of blue water surrounded by tall sand dunes, was set into the desert like an inlaid jewel. At the edge of the water stood a temple and pagoda decorated with Buddhist and Taoist statues. Stein was so moved by the surreal beauty of the Crescent Lake and its temples, he considered for a moment choosing it as his own burial site. Jiang meanwhile amused himself by trudging down the side of a steep dune in his velvet boots to make the falling sand produce the famous 'singing' effect of the sand hills: a weird, sustained bass note that rumbled like a trombone blast over the empty dunes.

ON 21 MARCH, after the pilgrimage festival was concluded, Stein and Jiang returned to the Thousand Buddha Caves, and were pleased to find that Wang Yuanlu, the guardian monk, had come back from his begging tour. 'He looked a very queer person,' Stein later wrote, 'extremely shy and nervous, with an occasional expression of cunning which was far from encouraging. It was clear from the first that he would be a difficult person to handle.'[41]

In an effort to 'handle' the monk, Stein feigned a complete lack of interest in the Library Cave, and pretended he was more interested in photographing and surveying the other caves. He was very glad to have Jiang at his side as a trusted intermediary. The two men spent days flattering Wang, taking an interest in his piecemeal attempts to renovate the caves and trying not to overplay their hand.

Jiang talked with Wang for hours in the monk's smoke-filled kitchen. He offered, on Stein's behalf, a donation for the temple if the monk would let them examine the contents of the Library Cave, but Wang nervously refused; he was fearful of igniting local indignation, should he be seen to be letting foreigners defile the precious manuscripts. 'To rely on the temptation of money alone as a means of overcoming his scruples'. Stein realised, 'was manifestly useless.'[42] Instead, Stein coyly asked to be shown the restored temple that he knew contained the door to the Library Cave. Looking around the room, he saw the entrance had been freshly bricked up. Wang said it had been done to keep its contents safe from the thousands of curious pilgrims who had been wandering through the caves during the festival.

Stein finally broke through Wang's reserve when he spoke of his reverence for Xuanzang. Wang's face lit up. The great Buddhist pilgrim was his hero too, and he brought Stein to see a newly painted set of frescoes illustrating Xuanzang's adventures on the road. Stein went back to his tent thinking he'd at last established some kind of rapport with Wang.

LATE THAT NIGHT, Jiang came to Stein's tent outside the caves in a state of 'silent elation'. Wang had just furtively handed him a bundle of rolls for him to examine. Jiang stayed up all night studying the documents under his lantern, and in the morning he declared excitedly that the inscriptions on the rolls indicated they were copies of the sutras translated by Xuanzang on his return from India.

Stein and Jiang suggested to Wang that this fortuitous turn of events was proof enough they had Xuanzang's heaven-sent blessing to enter the Library Cave, and with that, Wang relented and unbricked the entrance. Then he opened the ramshackle wooden door.

Stein was wide-eyed with wonder:

> Heaped up in layers, but without perfect order, there appeared in the dim light of the priest's little lamp a solid mass of manuscript bundles rising to a height of nearly ten feet, and filling, as a subsequent measurement showed, close on five-hundred cubic feet.[43]

There was no room to examine the manuscripts inside the cramped cave, so Wang discreetly brought them out a few bundles at a time to an enclosed chapel where Stein and Jiang could peruse them out of sight from passing pilgrims. Over the following days, Wang's reticence fell away. He produced bundle after bundle from the cave, which Stein opened in a state of joyful excitement. There were sheaves of documents written in Chinese, Tibetan, Soghdian, Sanskrit and Uighur and, astonishingly, a tiny eighth-century manuscript in Hebrew containing a prayer for forgiveness, evidence that Jewish traders had passed through the area long ago. Within one canvas parcel, Stein found rolled-up banners of gauze-like silk, painted with fine images of Buddhist divinities, which he guessed had once fluttered outside a temple. He saw that the dark, dry conditions inside the Library Cave had kept their colours in perfect freshness.

The manuscripts were full of insights into how people from long ago had taken their day-to-day pleasures in this lonely outpost. There was a sixth-century manual for Go, the strategic Chinese board game. Another document referred to the singing sand dunes, which had entertained people from Dunhuang a thousand years ago, just as it had Jiang only a few days earlier. Also among the papers was an ancient bureaucratic form letter, drafted by the 'Dunhuang Bureau of Etiquette', to be used when a dinner guest had offended his host:

> Yesterday, having drunk too much, I was so intoxicated as to pass all bounds; but none of the rude and coarse language I used was uttered in a conscious state. The next morning, after hearing others speak on the subject, I realised what had happened, whereupon I was overwhelmed with confusion and ready to sink into the ground with shame. It was due to a vessel of small capacity, on that occasion, being filled too full.[44]

ON 29 MAY, STEIN and Wang reached an agreement: in exchange for a temple donation, Stein would be permitted to take a large portion of the Library Cave's contents with him back to England. Over several nights, sackfuls of manuscripts and silks were brought from the cave to Stein's camp under cover of darkness, so as not to alert the authorities or local worshippers. Stein spent two days carefully packing his precious cargo, which filled twelve cases. In compensation, he handed Wang four silver ingots, which were presented as 'an ample donation for the benefit of the shrine he had laboured to restore to its old glory'.[45] The value of the silver amounted to £130, a sum Stein thought 'would make our friends at the British Museum chuckle'.[46] Stein took his leave of the cave complex on 12 June, believing that he and Wang had parted 'in perfect amity', and that the monk was content to know that the documents would find a good home in England's 'temple of learning'.[47]

But there were more men to come from other far-off temples of learning, all wanting their share of the treasures of the Thousand Buddha Caves.

IN MARCH 1908, nine months after Stein's departure, his rival, French sinologist Paul Pelliot, arrived at the Mogao Caves. As a fluent Chinese-speaker, Pelliot had no trouble in persuading Wang to admit him to the Library Cave, where he crouched throughout the night, sorting the documents by candlelight.

Pelliot was also proficient in written Chinese, enabling him to pick and choose the most valuable of the remaining manuscripts, which he purchased and sent to Paris's Bibliotheque Nationale.

In December 1911, two Japanese agents posing as archaeologists arrived at Dunhuang, hoping to purchase Buddhist manuscripts from the Library Cave. But by now, word had spread to Peking that a priceless part of China's cultural heritage was endangered, and the central government had sent a cohort of troops out to Dunhuang to bring the remaining manuscripts to the capital for safekeeping. But Wang had managed to conceal some of the remaining documents inside a statue, and was able to sell the Japanese agents 600 scrolls of Buddhist sutras.

French sinologist Paul Pelliot in the Library Cave, 1908

THE OUTBREAK OF World War I made further excursions by outsiders to the Mogao Caves almost impossible. But then in 1924, an ambitious American archaeologist named Langdon Warner arrived in Dunhuang. Warner, reputedly one of the inspirations for Steven Spielberg's Indiana Jones, was a specialist in Asian art, and more interested in the frescoes and statues of the cave temples than any Library Cave documents that might still be stashed away.

At first Warner was overcome by the scale and beauty of the work, but on closer examination, he became enraged. The caves had recently been occupied by hundreds of White Russian soldiers on the run from the Bolsheviks. The soldiers had cooked food in the caves, smearing the frescoes with greasy smoke. In their boredom, they had amused themselves by vandalising the images. 'Across some of these lovely faces', Warner wrote in a furious letter to his wife, 'are scribbled the numbers of a Russian regiment, and from the mouth of a Buddha where he sits to deliver the Lotus Law flows some Slav obscenity.'

Warner believed he had to act fast. 'My job', he wrote, 'is to break my neck to rescue and preserve anything and everything I can from this quick ruin.' Any ethical qualms could be quickly brushed aside in pursuit of the greater good: 'As for the morals of such vandalism, I would strip the place bare without a flicker. Who knows when Chinese troops may be quartered here as the Russians were? And, worse still, how long before the Mohameddan rebellion that everyone expects?'[48]

Using a chemical agent, Warner managed to peel off twelve of the Mogao frescoes from the cave walls. The paintings were wrapped in felt and shipped to Harvard University in the United States. He tried and failed to remove several other frescoes from the walls, leaving them in place but badly damaged. Stark white gaps and scars remain on the walls today, which are labelled in English and Chinese as the location of 'Langdon Warner's theft'.

A Lamp, a Cataract, a Star in Space

THE CAPTURE OF THE Library Cave's treasures made Aurel Stein a hero in England. The universities of Oxford and Cambridge rushed to present him with honorary degrees, and the king eventually awarded him a knighthood. But the Chinese authorities, alerted at last to the threat to their cultural heritage, had soured on the foreign archaeologists, and Aurel Stein's reputation there was sinking fast.

On 27 December 1930, while Stein was in Xinjiang preparing for yet another expedition, a newspaper in Tianjin ran a story denouncing him as a thief under the headline: 'Under Pretence of "Travel", Stein Plunders Xinjiang Antiquities'. The editorial demanded he be expelled from Chinese territory for his 'pilfering' of Dunhuang's treasures, a criminal act that it said amounted to an 'enormous loss to our country'.[49] That same year, the Chinese National Commission for the Preservation of Antiquities mourned the loss of the Dunhuang treasures:

> Sir Aurel Stein, taking advantage of the ignorance and cupidity of the priest in charge, persuaded the latter to sell to him at a pittance what he considered the pick of the collection which, needless to say, did not in any way belong to the seller. It would be the same if some Chinese traveller pretending to be merely a student of religious history went to Canterbury and bought valuable relics from the cathedral caretaker. But Sir Aurel Stein, not knowing a word of Chinese, took away what he considered the most valuable, separating many manuscripts which really belonged together, thus destroying the value of the manuscripts themselves. Soon afterwards French and Japanese travellers followed his trail with the result that the unique collection is now divided up and scattered in London, Paris, and Tokyo. In the first two cities at least, the manuscripts lie unstudied for the last twenty years, and their rightful owners, the Chinese, who are the most competent scholars for their study, are deprived of their opportunity as well as their ownership.[50]

Stein defended the removal of the Taklamakan treasures as a rescue mission to conserve 'all those relics of ancient Buddhist literature and art which were otherwise bound to get lost earlier or later through local indifference'.[51] There was some truth to this: Stein had hoped there might one day be a museum in Khotan to safety store the exquisite treasures of Rawak that he'd photographed and carefully reburied, but when he returned to the site years later, he discovered that the fragile statues had been smashed open by local treasure-hunters looking for hidden gold. At the time when Stein removed the Library Cave documents, China was embroiled in a civil war; the officials who had understood the significance of the Library Cave documents lacked the resources to keep them safe from looters, or prevent Wang from handing them out piecemeal as gifts for local dignitaries.

But Stein's claim that the treasures of the Taklamakan were safer in politically stable Europe were undone just over a decade later during World War II, when a Luftwaffe bomb fell on a wing of the British Museum. Fortunately the Dunhuang manuscripts had been temporarily evacuated to a concrete tunnel in Wales. But another trove of silk-road artefacts on display in Berlin's ethnological museum were annihilated when the city was firebombed at the war's end.

After 1949, China's new communist regime ensured that 'foreign devils' were kept well away from Dunhuang and the buried cities of the Taklamakan. But the future of the caves seemed in doubt during the Cultural Revolution of the 1960s, when Mao Zedong exhorted masses of teenagers to go out and destroy the 'Four Olds' – old customs, old culture, old habits and old ideas – which he said were keeping China in a state of backwardness. Temples, churches, statues and paintings were consequently torn down all over China. But Dunhuang never felt the fury of the Red Guards, thanks to its remote location and to Premier Zhou Enlai's decision to quietly despatch cohorts of soldiers and police to protect the Mogao Caves from the students.[52]

TODAY, AUREL STEIN'S trove of manuscripts from the Library Cave are still stored in the British Library. The removal of these treasures from Xinjiang may well have saved some of them from the ravages of the environment, local looting or outraged Muslim piety, but the idea that such precious antiquities were picked up by a British imperialist for a few hundred pounds, at a time when China was vulnerable, is still galling.

Although he doesn't appear to have personally profited from their sale, Wang Yuanlu was made a scapegoat for the loss of the Library Cave's treasures. Today he is denounced in China as a traitor and a criminal. 'His tomb stone and stupa should not be a tourist destination,' declared a Chinese historian, 'but rather be kept standing in front of the Mogao caves as a shame pole.'[53]

A trove of manuscripts might, however, be returned to the place where they were found, and in that sense at least, whatever damage was done by removing them may one day be repaired. The stolen cave paintings are another matter; there is something particularly monstrous about the cack-handed removal of these exquisite works, supposedly in the name of their preservation. The delicate frescoes now on display at Harvard University's Fogg Museum would have been better off taking their chances inside the cave.

SIR MARC AUREL STEIN died in Kabul on 26 October 1943, while preparing an expedition into Afghanistan to follow the trail of Alexander the Great's armies. He was eighty years old.

In 2022, I went to the British Library to see the most precious of the manuscripts Stein had taken from the Library Cave: a copy of *The Diamond Sutra*, acknowledged in the accompanying card as 'the oldest dated complete printed book in the world'. It was commissioned on 11 May 868, six centuries before Gutenberg's Bible, by a man named Wang Jie, on behalf of his parents. The book is thought to have originated in Sichuan Province, and to have been printed with a woodblock cut from a pear tree. How it came to be stashed in the Mogao Caves is not known. Although more than eleven centuries old, the scroll is still in excellent condition.

Ironically, the lesson of the seemingly indestructible *Diamond Sutra* concerns impermanence. In his lecture, using a subtle process of negation and paradox, the Buddha urges his followers to abandon their preconceived notions of reality, to understand that nothing exists independently of other things, that nothing is entirely the thing it is called, and that all things are in constant transition from one state to another. Nothing is fixed or stable. The Buddha concluded his lecture with a poetic instruction to his followers:

> As a lamp, a cataract, a star in space
> an illusion, a dewdrop, a bubble
> a dream, a cloud, a flash of lightening
> view all created things like this.[54]

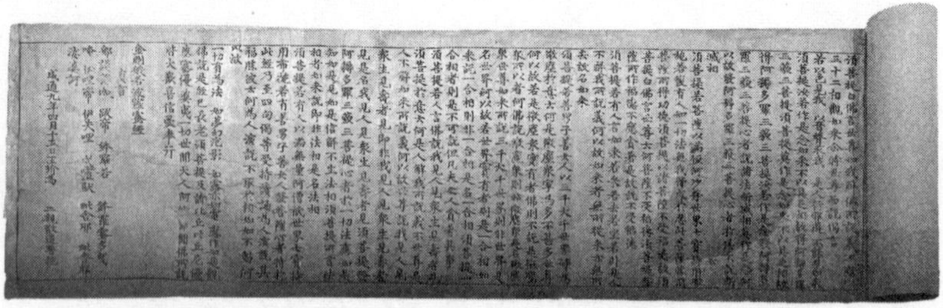

The Diamond Sutra, *on display in the British Library*

Today He Teaches Us Better than Yesterday

SIMILAR THOUGHTS ON THE transitory nature of all things haunted Wathiq throughout his short reign as caliph, from 842 to 847. Although his envoy Sallam had been able to reassure him of the integrity of Alexander's great wall, the Greek conqueror's name was never far from his troubled mind.

Masudi records that one evening at the palace, Wathiq was surrounded by a coterie of scholars debating the principles of medicine. After a while, the caliph became bored and issued the scholars a challenge.

'I want one of you to repeat for me,' he said, 'the most fitting of the words spoken by those who surrounded the sarcophagus of Alexander the Great.'

One of the scholars said that all the words spoken at Alexander's funeral were worthy of admiration, but the most beautiful phrases had been uttered by Diogenes the Greek, who said:

> Yesterday Alexander was less silent than today.
> But today he teaches us better than yesterday.

Hearing this, Wathiq began to cry. Soon everyone in the room was sobbing too. After a while, Wathiq pulled himself together, rose to his feet and quoted a few lines of verse:

> The pleasures of mankind last but a day
> And the life of man is but a borrowed robe.[55]

Wathiq died in 847 from dropsy, the painful accumulation of fluid in the lower parts of the body. Of Sallam the Interpreter's fate following his return from China, nothing is known.

The Bushranger in the Cave

IN JULY 2014, I was in a restaurant in Beijing, at a dinner convened by an Australian writer and academic, David Walker. We were joined by Edmund Capon, who had recently stepped down as Director of the Art Gallery of New South Wales. Edmund had been fascinated by Chinese Buddhist art since his boyhood in England, and the gallery under his leadership had opened a new wing devoted to Chinese art and antiquities.

As the dishes were being spun around the table that night in Beijing, Edmund told us a story about the caves at Dunhuang. He said that in 1978, just before migrating to Australia, he had met the modernist painter Sidney Nolan at a party in London. Nolan had established his name in the international art world decades earlier with his Ned Kelly series, which depicted the armoured Australian bushranger as an assembly of flat black rectangles with a pair of eyes peeking out from his helmet.

At the party, Capon and Nolan realised they shared an obsession with Buddhist art and sculpture. Both were aware of the treasures at the Thousand Buddha Caves, and both longed to visit them. 'And so we made a bet,' Edmund said. 'Whoever got there first would go to Cave 96.' Inside that cave, they knew, was a thirty-five-metre-high statue of a seated Maitreya Buddha, its towering throne mounted on a huge stone plinth about two metres high.

'You can walk right around it,' Edmund said, tracing a circle on the rosewood table with his finger.

He said that he and Nolan agreed that whoever got to Dunhuang first would leave a tiny marker to record their visit, somewhere on this massive stone pedestal.

But this was a difficult proposition in 1978. China was still pulling itself from the wreckage of the Cultural Revolution; travel to such distant regions was arduous, even dangerous, for Westerners, and it wasn't until 1983 that Capon was able to make the long trek out to Dunhuang, and from there to the Thousand Buddha Caves.

To his delight, the authorities gave him permission to enter Cave 96, and there at last Edmund beheld the colossal Buddha in all its majesty. Feeling a surge of triumph, he told himself: *I've beaten Sid! I've beaten Sid!*

Creeping behind the statue, he saw that the back of the stone plinth was covered in graffiti, scrawled by countless Chinese tourists.

'And there it was,' Edmund said. 'In the top right corner. A tiny picture of Ned Kelly.'

A reclining Buddha in the Mogao Caves
Photographed by James and Lucy Ho, 1943

But this was a difficult proposition in 1978 when [illegible] the Cultural Revolution [illegible] dangerous for [illegible] Dunhuang, and [illegible]

[illegible]

[illegible]

[illegible]

BOOK FOUR

South

MUTAWAKKIL ('He Who Relies on God')
Tenth of the Abbasid caliphs

MUHAMMAD ZAYYAT
Mutawakkil's first vizier

Ibn WAHB
Native of Basra and traveller to the Tang court of China

Abu ZAYD
Geographer and compiler of the second book of Accounts of China and India

BIRUNI
Polymath and medieval anthropologist

Ibn ENSHARTOU
A ship's captain

HUANG CHAO
Chinese bandit army leader and instigator of the uprising that bears his name

ISMAILAWAYH
Merchant sailor to East Africa

ALI bin MUHAMMAD
Revolutionary leader of the Zanj Rebellion

MUWAFFAQ
Abbasid general, defeater of the Zanj army

MUTADID ('Seeking Support in God')
Sixteenth of the Abbasid caliphs

the
KINGDOMS TO THE SOUTH
c. 870 C.E.

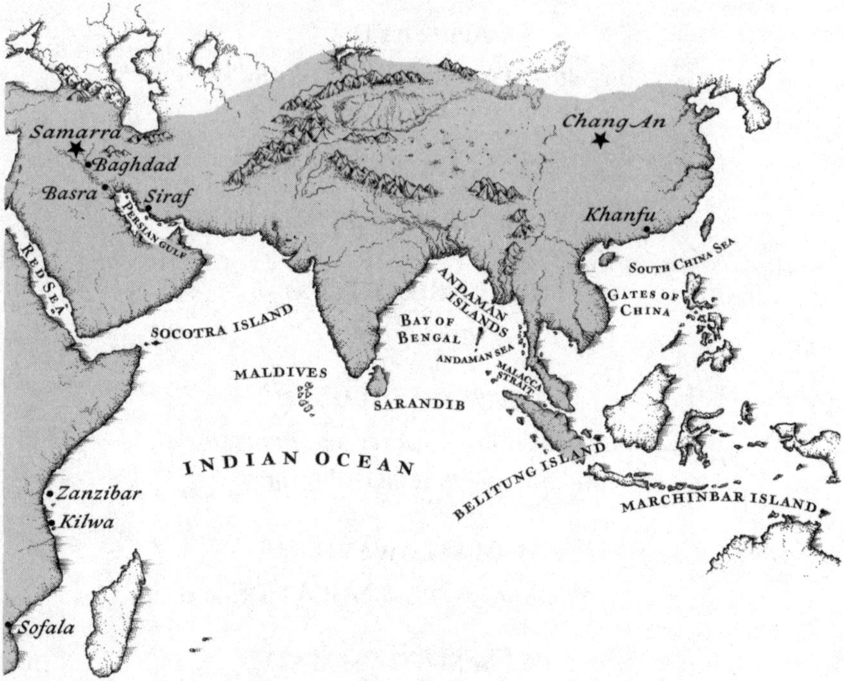

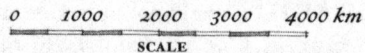

Appointment in Samarra

A MAN WAS walking one morning through the marketplace of Baghdad, looking at this and that, when he saw Death in the crowd, staring at him directly, with a strange expression on her face. Full of fear, the man took a horse and bolted out of Baghdad, fleeing as far as he could.

He arrived that night, exhausted, at the city of Samarra, where he found Death waiting for him.

'I was surprised to see you this morning in Baghdad,' she explained, 'because I knew tonight we had an appointment in Samarra.'

THIS TALE OF DEATH and pre-destination is a very old one that appears in the Babylonian Talmud, and was subsequently retold in different forms in the Muslim world. Although Death is a terrifying figure, she is no more able to shift the time and place of the man's appointment than he is. The moment, set in stone by God, can neither be postponed nor hastened. According to the *hadith*s, there are protective angels who intercede to protect us from dying before that appointed hour:

> Every servant has guardians, who protect him. A wall does not fall down on top of him, he does not fall down a well … until his time has come. The guardians leave him, so that whatever God has willed should hit him, hits him.[1]

Samarra, which lies some 125 kilometres north of Baghdad on the Tigris, met its appointed hour eight centuries ago, but its ruins reveal the outlines of its streets, houses, race courses and palaces. All that's left of its gargantuan Great Mosque, the largest in the world at the time of its construction, is the rectangle of the outer walls, and the adjacent Spiral Minaret that rises up to the Heavens in a conical swirl. The simple dramatic twist of the Spiral Minaret is breathtaking to behold; its helix imbues it with a peculiar sacred energy, both joyful and mysterious, functional and magical.

The Spiral Minaret of the Great Mosque of Samarra

Samarra takes its name from the Arabic phrase *surra man ra'a* – 'a joy to all who see it'. But after the 2003 invasion of Iraq, Samarra became known as '*sa'a man ra'a*' – 'a sorrow for all who see it'. The area became a combat target when American soldiers began to use the Spiral Minaret as a watchtower and a sniper vantage point. And so early on the morning of 1 April 2005, two insurgents climbed the tower and placed a bomb at its summit that blew off the minaret's top tier. In 2007, the mosque was listed as a UNESCO World Heritage site and the slow, halting restoration of the Spiral Minaret could begin.

The Great Mosque and Spiral Minaret were commissioned in 848 by Caliph Wathiq's younger brother and successor, Caliph Mutawakkil, who endowed the city with palaces, hunting parks, polo fields and race courses. During his reign, Samarra began to approach the dignity and grandeur of Baghdad. But its moment of glory would be short-lived. Unlike Baghdad, the city's location was poorly chosen: the water supply was inadequate and the surrounding land was stony and dry. Samarra required heavy investment to keep it going, so when the caliphs abandoned the city in 892, most of the population returned to Baghdad and Samarra rapidly declined into an oversized, underpopulated outpost.

MUTAWAKKIL, WHO CAME to the throne in 847, was a far more energetic and forceful caliph than his older brother. This was not immediately apparent to the cabal of ministers who had engineered his succession, who thought of Mutawakkil as an effete poseur, a long-haired dandy, whom they expected to manage as easily as they had his weak-willed predecessor. But once he'd been universally acknowledged as caliph, Mutawakkil set about destroying these men and taking his revenge against the most senior of his ministers: his vizier Muhammad Zayyat.

Five years earlier, when Mutawakkil was still only a prince, he had come to Zayyat for advice. He'd sensed a growing coldness in his brother's attitude towards him. Perhaps, he wondered, Wathiq was planning to replace him as crown prince with the caliph's son, who was still a boy. But if Mutawakkil was hoping for some kindly compassion from Zayyat he was bound to be disappointed: the vizier was a particularly arrogant and cruel man, who owned an iron maiden – a torture cabinet lined with metal spikes – that he used to extract money and information from his enemies. When

Mutawakkil had come to see him, Zayyat was unable to resist tormenting the anxious prince: he uttered no words of greeting and kept Mutawakkil standing while he silently sorted through his correspondence. When he finally lifted his gaze, Zayyat asked 'in a menacing tone' what it was that the prince wanted.

'I came to see you,' Mutawakkil said, 'so that you might ask the Commander of the Faithful to look more favourably upon me.'

Zayyat snorted with derision. 'Look at this one,' he said to his staff. 'He deliberately annoys his brother, then comes to me to restore him to favour!' He dismissed Mutawakkil with a wave of his hand: 'Go, and if you make amends for your behaviour, then you will be reinstated in your brother's eyes.'

After the mortified prince had made his exit, Zayyat sent a note to the caliph, saying the vain and silly prince had just come to see him, and as usual, 'his style of dress was quite effeminate and his hair was too long'.

Wathiq then summoned Mutawakkil, who arrived wearing a fashionable black robe he hoped would make a good impression. The caliph, angered by this apparent sign of vanity, ordered his page to grab Mutawakkil's hair, shear it off, then strike him in the face with the severed locks. Later, Mutawakkil said he'd never suffered so much distress in his life as he had in that moment of public humiliation: 'I came to him dressed in that black robe to please him, but he had my hair cut upon it.'

AFTER TAKING THE THRONE, Mutawakkil waited a full month to take his revenge. On 22 September 847, he summoned Zayyat to the palace; the vizier obediently rode out from his home but was arrested halfway and imprisoned.

Zayyat, who could have had no illusions about his future, refused to eat and wept continuously in his cell. Each time he tried to sleep, guards pricked him awake with a long needle. Eventually, he was dragged from his cell and placed inside his own iron maiden, where he died four days later in agony.[2] Over the course of that year, Mutawakkil's other ministers were sent into exile or thrown into prison, where they were left to die in ignominy.

For Mutawakkil, the destruction of Zayyat and his cronies served a purpose well beyond petty revenge. The caliph needed these men out of the way to enact some major reforms.

Above all, Mutawakkil wanted to put an end to a debilitating dispute that had wracked the Muslim world over the nature of the Quran. What to modern eyes might seem to be a bafflingly abstract theological argument was actually a struggle to establish who had the ultimate power to interpret it. Conservatives had long upheld the holy book as eternal and 'uncreated', a miraculous text whose message had entered this mortal world from a heavenly realm outside of time. But decades earlier, the Caliph Mamun had been persuaded that this way of thinking was not just misguided, but wicked; that to revere the Quran as magical and eternal was to build it up as a wholly separate deity altogether: a clear violation of Islam's central belief that God is one and indivisible. This stance had proved unpopular, and in response, Mamun had unwisely launched an inquisition to kill or imprison those who refused to recant their belief in the uncreated Quran.

But fifteen years of bloody persecution had failed to silence the dissenters, and the controversy was eroding the spiritual authority of the caliph. Mutawakkil decided to reverse course: he lifted the inquisition and announced that the Quran was henceforth to be regarded as uncreated, and no further discussion on the matter would be permitted.

The door to individual interpretation of the Quran was now closed. From now on, only officially recognised interpretations would be acceptable.

Mutawakkil further improved his standing with religious conservatives by making life more difficult for non-Muslims in the caliphate: Christians and Jews were no longer permitted to serve in any government position where they could exercise authority over Muslims, and were now required to wear a yellow hood and belt in public. Wooden effigies of devils were to be nailed to their front doors to identify their places of residence.[3]

Mutawakkil's decree forcefully settled the fractious dispute over the nature of the holy book, but it also signalled a retreat into dogmatism at the expense of open inquiry. He would later be remembered by Masudi as the caliph who 'ordered the abandonment of investigation and discussion and debate and everything which people had enjoyed in the days of earlier caliphs'.[4] God and his word were one; speculation was heresy. 'That which reason deems to be good' was trumped by 'that which the law and the great mass of people deem to be good'. And then there was no more 'then'.

The Indian Sword

AS CALIPH, MUTAWAKKIL remained a slave to fashion. He wore stylishly cut black robes and adopted the Persian fashion of strapping his sword to his waist, instead of slinging it over the shoulder like a Bedouin.

Indian swords were the most highly prized in the Muslim world. 'No iron', it was said, 'is comparable to the Indian one in sharpness.'[5] The poet Buhtari would recall discussing such swords with Mutawakkil in the palace. One of the caliph's courtiers had mentioned a certain Indian sword he'd heard of in Basra that was known to be the finest in the world. Mutawakkil sent agents to locate the precious sword and buy it, no matter how high the price. The sword was found, purchased for 10,000 dirhams and presented to the caliph in Samarra. Mutawakkil drew the blade slowly from its sheath, closely examining its strength, fineness and sharpness.

The next day, he told Fath, his close friend and advisor, to find a soldier of proven strength and courage to act as a special bodyguard. 'I want to entrust this sword to him,' Mutawakkil said, 'and have him stand behind me, not leaving me for a moment during the day, as long as I am in council.'

Fath came back with a soldier known as Baghir the Turk. 'Baghir's courage and fearlessness are highly praised,' Fath said. 'He is the man the caliph needs.'

Mutawakkil called Baghir forward and handed him the sword. To ensure his loyalty, he promoted Baghir in rank and doubled his allowance.

'And I declare', wrote the poet later, 'that the sword in question never left its sheath from that moment until the night Baghir used it to kill the caliph.'[6]

MUTAWAKKIL HAD FORGOTTEN the painful lesson of his own youthful humiliations. The caliph had let a poisonous suspicion enter his head that his ambitious son Muntasir wanted to overthrow him. Mutawakkil accordingly began to torment Muntasir; he mocked him in public, forced him to get drunk and half-jokingly threatened to kill him.

Terrified for his life, Muntasir conspired with several disgruntled Turkish generals to assassinate his father. Baghir the bodyguard, believing he had a higher loyalty to the generals than to his caliph, agreed to do their bidding.

On the night of 10 December 861, Mutawakkil was having dinner with Fath in his apartments. Both men were very drunk on wine and the caliph kept slumping over.

Ten Turkish soldiers led by Baghir entered the room, all of them veiled and armed with swords that glittered in the candlelight.

Baghir strode forward, unsheathed the Indian sword and slashed Mutawakkil's belly, cutting him open to the waist. Fath threw himself on top of the caliph to protect him from further blows, but then he too was killed.

The killers rolled the bodies into a carpet and dragged them into a corner, where they remained for most of the next day. When Muntasir was confirmed as the new caliph, he ordered the two men to be buried together.

MUTAWAKKIL'S INDIAN SWORD, a two-edged blade if ever there was one, was just one item among the countless goods flowing in and out of the Persian Gulf from the world's richest maritime trade network, which connected the caliphate with the cities of the Indian Ocean rim and southern China. Throughout the ninth century, Arab and Persian seafarers rode the monsoonal trade winds to fetch ivory from East Africa, sapphires from Sri Lanka and nutmeg from the Spice Islands of Southeast Asia. In obedience to the Prophet's commandment to 'seek knowledge, even as far as China', Abbasid sailors pushed on further still, threading their way through the straits of Malacca into the South China Sea. From there they steered their ships up to China's busy coastal ports. Those who survived the return voyage to the Persian Gulf brought with them loads of musk, silk and porcelain, and told stories of the people they met and the wonders they encountered.

China in particular, with its sophisticated, cosmopolitan cities, challenged their own assumptions of cultural supremacy, and the Muslim visitors took note of everything they saw, from the practice of Confucian law to the use of toilet paper. These are the earliest accounts of China written by foreigners in existence.

The Travels of Ibn Wahb the Aristocrat

ONE SUCH ACCOUNT records that in 871 a man named Ibn Wahb decided to leave his home city of Basra, which had fallen into violent chaos, and sailed off to China to pay a visit to the emperor. Ibn Wahb was an Arab aristocrat, a descendant of the Prophet who naturally expected the emperor would grant an audience to such a distinguished guest.

Sailing out of the Persian Gulf, the summer monsoon carried Ibn Wahb's boat down the west coast of India to Sri Lanka. Then, after passing through the Straits of Malacca, Ibn Wahb tacked north, sailing up the coast of Indochina to arrive at the flourishing Chinese port of Guangzhou, a city the Muslims called Khanfu.

Guangzhou's explosive growth was fuelled by foreign trade. According to one account, it was home to some 120,000 foreign merchants at the time of Ibn Wahb's voyage. Muslim traders in Guangzhou were so numerous, and their trade so important, that the Tang Emperor had agreed to let them resolve their legal disputes by referring them to an Islamic judge from their own community.

Some time after arriving in Guangzhou, Ibn Wahb travelled inland to Chang An, the Chinese capital. In the ninth century Chang An was a great metropolis, rivalling Baghdad and Constantinople in population size. The capital was divided by a broad, tree-lined avenue running from north to south. The western side, where most of the inhabitants lived, was filled with markets, houses and manufacturing centres. The eastern side, the imperial district, was dominated by the emperor's palace and the mansions of his high officials.

Ibn Wahb found lodgings near the palace gate, which he approached each day to request an audience with the emperor. Eventually his petitions reached the emperor's courtiers, who arranged for Ibn Wahb to be accommodated in a comfortable guest house inside the palace grounds, where he stayed until they could confirm with the governor in Guangzhou, who kept detailed records of foreign visitors, that Ibn Wahb was indeed, as he claimed, a descendant of the Prophet of the Arabs and a man held in good standing.

With that assurance, Ibn Wahb was granted his audience.

THE TANG EMPEROR Yizong was reputed to be lethargic and fond of strong drink, but Ibn Wahb found him alert and curious. How was it, he asked, that the Arabs had managed to bring down the Sassanid Persians?

'With the help of almighty God,' Ibn Wahb replied. 'The Persians fell because they worshipped fire and bowed to pray to the sun and the moon.'

According to Ibn Wahb's account, the emperor readily acknowledged that the Arabs had indeed established the most magnificent empire.

'They are the richest, most intelligent people in the world,' he said generously. 'Their greatness is known to everyone.'

Then the emperor asked Ibn Wahb, 'How are all the kings of the world ranked by you Arabs?'

The question surprised Ibn Wahb. Not knowing how to answer without causing offence, he said he had no idea.

The emperor then turned to his interpreter and said this:

'Tell him we count five kings as great. There is the ruler of the Romans, whom we call "the King of Men", because there are no other people on Earth who are more beautiful than his people.

'Then above him is the ruler of the Indians, whom we call "the King of Wisdom" because wisdom originates with his people. Then above him is our neighbour, the ruler of the Turks, whom we call "the King of Beasts", because the Turks are the beasts of mankind.

'Then above him is the ruler of this land,' by which he meant himself, 'who is known as "the King of His People", because no other king is more astute nor more in control of his realm, and no other king is more revered by his people.'

'But above all these kings,' admitted the emperor, 'is the ruler of Baghdad. He is the greatest, for he is at the centre of the world and all other kings are ranged around him. We call him "the King of Kings". All the rest are beneath him in rank.'

At the conclusion of their enjoyable conversation, Ibn Wahb said that on his return to Iraq, he would speak highly of China and its emperor. 'I shall recount what I have witnessed of your majesty,' he said, 'and the extent of your country. I will have nothing but good things to say.'

The emperor was very pleased to hear this. He arranged for Ibn Wahb to be presented with fine gifts and to be given every luxury for the duration of his stay in China.[7]

An Insect on a Splinter

THE ACCOUNT OF Ibn Wahb's meeting with the emperor can be found in the pages of a tenth-century Arabic book, *Accounts of China and India*, a compilation of sailors' reports of their voyages into the Indian Ocean and the South China Sea. On the map, this network of trade routes formed a massive arc of maritime silk roads, running from Zanzibar up to Arabia and the Persian Gulf, then down to India, Sri Lanka and the Spice Islands. From there, merchants could sail up to the South China Sea and into the busy port cities of China.

Accounts of China and India is presented in two parts. The author of the first half is unknown, and the first page is missing; the account begins mid-sentence with a sailor's description of a whale on the high seas:

> … like a sail. It often raises its head above the water, and then you can see what an enormous thing it is. It also often blows water from its mouth, and the water spouts up like a great lighthouse. When the sea is calm and the fish shoal together, it gathers them in with its tail then opens its mouth, and the fish can be seen in its gullet, sinking down into its depths as if into a well. The ships that sail this sea are wary of it, and at night the crews bang wooden clappers like those used by the Christians, for fear that one of them will blunder into their ship and capsize it.[8]

Sailors were at times confronted by fantastical scenes on the Indian Ocean. One mariner passing through the Bay of Bengal witnessed a colossal waterspout, a twisting column of wind and water stretching between cloud and sea. This natural phenomenon appeared to him like 'a long thin tongue of vapour' that descended from the sky until it touched the surface of the water, making it 'boil up like a whirlwind'. He warned that 'if this whirlwind makes contact with a ship, it swallows it up. Then the cloud rises, and from it falls rain containing debris from the sea.'[9]

The second part of *Accounts of China and India* was compiled in the 920s by a man named Abu Zayd, who came from the Persian Gulf port of Siraf. Sailors' yarns were notoriously unreliable, so Abu Zayd is at pains to assure his readers that he has chosen to stick to the facts and to keep clear of 'the sort of accounts in which sailors exercise their powers of invention but whose credibility would not stand up to scrutiny in other men's minds'.[10]

And yet Ibn Wahb's report of his conversation with the Chinese Emperor strains credulity; it seems highly unlikely that the Tang Emperor, a man swathed in majesty and attended by armies of deferential eunuchs, would rank himself below the caliph of the Muslims. But the anecdote *does* reflect an underlying reality: the empire of the Arabs had become bigger and richer than Tang China's, and traffic on the Indian Ocean trade routes was now dominated by Muslim ships.

A reconstruction of an early ocean-going dhow, *with a stitched hull and lateen sail*

THE TRADING VESSELS zooming out of the ports in the Persian Gulf were smaller, faster and more agile than the bulky warships Muawiya had sent out to conquer the eastern Mediterranean back in the days of the Umayyad caliphate. The Arab *dhow* was a boat constructed of planks of teak or coconut wood, and stitched together with coir rope that was looped through holes bored into the timber and pulled tight. It's not altogether clear why the Arabs persisted in using rope rather than nails to hold their hulls together; it may have been due to a common belief that there were underwater mountains of magnetic lodestone on the Indian Ocean floor that could drag an iron-fastened boat to its watery doom. Arab merchants did however rig their ships with a lateen sail, one of the major nautical innovations of the age. This triangular sail, running in a fore–aft direction, enabled the *dhow* to tack into the wind, lending it greater speed and manoeuvrability than the old square-sailed ships of antiquity.

ARABS LIVING IN THE coastal settlements of Yemen and Oman had been taking to the sea for centuries, long before the arrival of Islam. But the early caliphs had been men of the Hijaz, the western Arabian Desert, who were suspicious of the sea and sceptical of the value of naval power. That had begun to change when Muawiya was made Governor of Syria and had assumed control of the province's Mediterranean ports. Realising that the conquest of Constantinople and its island colonies was impossible without a navy, Muawiya had begged Caliph Umar to permit him to construct a fleet of transport ships. 'The islands of the Levant', he wrote excitedly to Umar, 'are close to the Syrian shore; you might almost hear the barking of the dogs and cackling of the hens. Give me leave to attack them.' But Muawiya, to his annoyance, had been thwarted by the men of Medina, who dreaded the open sea. 'Trust it little, fear it much,' an advisor had warned the caliph. 'Man at sea is an insect on a splinter.'[11]

When Umar died, Muawiya had tried again; he petitioned his cousin Uthman, and this time the enterprise was given the caliph's blessing. Within two years, Muawiya's Syrian shipyards had constructed a fleet of transports, piloted by experienced Egyptian mariners. In 649, Arab marines landed on the shores of Cyprus, seizing it from the Romans. Four years after that, they took the island of Rhodes. And then in 654, the Arab fleet won a smashing victory against the Roman fleet at the Battle of the Masts, making the caliphate the dominant naval power in the eastern Mediterranean. By the mid-seventh century, the caliph's men, riding their 'camels of the sea', were as much at home on the water as they were in the desert.

JUST AS THE CONQUEST of Syria in 635 had given the Umayyads an opening to the Mediterranean, the shift to Baghdad in 762 had plugged the Abbasid empire into the sprawling trade networks of the Indian Ocean and Southeast Asia.

The main point of embarkation onto these trade routes was the city of Basra, which lay at the head of the Persian Gulf, some 450 kilometres southwest of Baghdad. Basra was an unlikely port city: it was located at a slight remove from both the coast and from the Tigris River. Smaller trading vessels arriving from the Gulf came up to Basra via a network of canals. Larger cargo ships docked instead at the deep-water port of Siraf further down the coast.

Basra had been established in 638 as a military outpost for the further conquest of Sassanid Persia. The site's chief appeal for the men in Medina was that it lay on the borderlands between the northern Arabian semi-desert and the Iraqi floodplains, making it accessible by camel, but even so, finding good drinking water was a constant problem and often had to be fetched from the Tigris. The first houses had to be constructed from rushes, or with baked mud bricks because there were too few stones in the area.

Despite its unpromising location, Basra, like Baghdad, grew rapidly, attracting a mix of Arab, Persian and Indian immigrants, and it soon became a thriving entrepot and manufacturing centre. Basran artisans created a distinctive style of blue and white glazed pottery that would be adopted and perfected by Tang Dynasty craftsmen in China. The goods would be ferried by barge to the port of Siraf, then loaded onto larger ships and sent out to Africa, China and India.

Basra also became a major cultural centre. Its location on the desert fringe brought its urban writers and intellectuals into close contact with Bedouin herdsmen, who periodically rode up from the desert into the city's great open marketplace, the Mirbad, to trade camels and livestock. The illiterate nomads were great repositories of traditional culture, carrying vast memory palaces in their heads filled with poems, songs and stories that had been passed down through the generations. Harun al-Rashid's favourite poet Abu Nuwas, who grew up in Basra, often rose early to come to the Mirbad, and sit with these Bedouin herdsmen, jotting down notes as they told their ancient stories and sang their desert songs.[12]

MARINERS SAILING OUT from the Persian Gulf timed their voyages to catch the seasonal monsoon trade winds blowing around the Indian Ocean rim (the word 'monsoon' is derived from mawsim, Arabic for 'season for sailing').[13]

Although the distances were long, the trade winds were predictable and not particularly fierce, making it possible for sailors to travel as far as Zanzibar or Sri Lanka without too much difficulty. The seasonal nature of the winds required Muslim merchants and seamen to spend several months in their destination ports waiting for the monsoon winds to reverse themselves so they could be carried home. On these extended layovers, they wandered through the streets of the port cities, bought local goods, formed relationships with local families and picked up local customs and languages. When they returned to the caliphate, they brought with them lumps of ambergris from the shores of the Maldives, leopard skins from Ethiopia, porcelain from China, pearls from Sri Lanka, and a whole host of tales of foreign lands that were true, half true, or entirely imaginary.

NO FOREIGN LAND excited the medieval Muslim imagination as much as India, al-Hind, the land of the Hindu people. It was, for them, the home of everything miraculous and strange in the world. They were particularly fixated on the Indian holy men, who were said to 'live on leaves and jungle fruits, and who insert iron rings into the heads of their penises to stop them having sexual intercourse with women'.[14] One traveller told Abu Zayd of a band of ascetics he encountered called the *bikarjis*, who wandered naked from town to town, with only their long hair covering their genitals. 'They let their fingernails grow as long as spearheads,' he observed, 'for they are never clipped.' The *bikarjis*, he noted, carried a human skull suspended by a cord from their neck, which they used to receive donations of rice.[15] Another mariner claimed to have met an Indian holy man clothed in a tiger's pelt who stood all day facing the sun; when the sailor returned to the same place sixteen years later, the holy man was still there, in exactly the same position.

Although Abu Zayd tried to steer clear from fanciful sailors' tales in *Accounts of China and India*, the authors of other travellers' compendiums weren't always so scrupulous. In the mid-tenth century, a mariner named Buzurg ibn Shahriyar produced a book called *The Marvels of India*, which portrayed the subcontinent as a fantastic garden of wonders and terrors. The tales within its pages inspired *The Seven Voyages of Sinbad*, which were later tacked on to editions of *The Thousand and One Nights*.

In *The Marvels of India*, we meet a party of shipwrecked sailors washed ashore on a lonely island, who escape by lashing themselves to the leg of a gigantic bird that flies them back to the Indian mainland. We are told of an elephant sent by its master to the market each morning with a pouch of coins and a shopping list, that will smash a stall to pieces if it believes it has been cheated. We are introduced to an old sailor who is served a bowl of soup with tiny human-like arms and legs bobbing on the surface; the sailor understandably refuses to touch this strange bouillabaisse until he is shown a pool of live fish with these humanoid appendages swimming about in the water.

SOME OF THE TALES in *The Marvels of India* are parables of power. There is a story of a sorcerer from the Indian port city of Serira, who went down to the bay one day with a friend and invited him to take a swim.

When the friend protested that the bay was infested with crocodiles, the sorcerer smiled, then turned to the water and uttered a strange incantation. Turning to his friend, he said, 'The crocodiles are banished. The waters are now safe for you to swim.'

When his friend still refused to enter the water, the sorcerer himself dived in and splashed about. No harm came to him.

When the sorcerer stepped out of the water he lifted the spell.

Moments later, a dog leapt into the bay and was mauled by a thrashing horde of crocodiles.

After this incident, the friend told everyone what had transpired, until word of the sorcerer's abilities reached the ear of the King of Serira, who came to the bay for a demonstration.

'Perform!' the king commanded, and just as before, the sorcerer cast his spell and the waters were becalmed.

The king decided to test the spell: he ordered his soldiers to throw two prisoners into the bay. The crocodiles kept their distance from the terrified men and did not attack.

'Well done! Extraordinary!' cried the king, clapping the sorcerer on the shoulder.

'Thank you, my lord,' he replied.

'And this spell of yours, it encompasses the entire bay?'

The sorcerer confirmed that it did.

And with that, a soldier came forward and chopped off the sorcerer's head.

'It is best to kill such a man,' said the king, 'who could with a few words undo such excellent work.'[16]

The Travels of Ibn Enshartou the Ship's Captain

STORIES OF STRANGE COUPLINGS of land and sea creatures occur repeatedly in *The Marvels of India.* The author records the tale of a sea captain named Ibn Enshartou, whose ship was blown off course to a beautiful island. When the sailors came ashore, they were welcomed by the villagers, who spoke an unknown tongue, but the two groups were able to make themselves understood through signs and gestures.

The sailors indicated they were hungry, and in response, the villagers of the island brought forth rice, chickens, honey, butter and fruit. In return, the sailors gave them gifts of iron, copper-ware, kohl, glass beads and clothing.

'Do you have any other wares to sell?' they asked the islanders.

'Only slaves,' they replied.

When the slaves were brought forth, the sailors were stunned by their beauty and the softness of their skin. The slaves' heads, however, were unusually small, and little wings grew out of their lower legs, like the flippers of a turtle.

'What is that?' the sailors asked, pointing at their legs.

'Oh, don't bother yourself with such things,' the slaves replied cheerfully, pointing to the sky as if to say, *God made us this way.*

The sailors could see that these slaves were an excellent bargain for the price that was being asked for them, and they emptied their ship of their trading stock to make room for them.

As they prepared to leave the next day, Ibn Enshartou and his men agreed that the slaves were a treasure that would enrich their families for generations to come. On their final night, with the slaves on board, the crew took note of the constellation of the stars so they could find their way back to this earthly paradise one day.

THE NEXT MORNING, the ship set out with the newly purchased slaves on board, but when they looked back and saw their island disappearing over the horizon, they became very distressed.

Ibn Enshartou ordered them not to make such a fuss, and the slaves became quiet.

Hours later, a gale blew in and the waves rose up. With the crew distracted, the slaves saw their chance. They leapt from the deck and swam away, far beyond the reach of the ship. Ibn Enshartou saw that although the slaves were in stormy waters, they laughed and sang, and he realised the fish people were as much at home in the sea as they were on land.

But there was one of their number still aboard the ship. A young she-slave was locked in the cabin, frantically trying to tear her way out. Ibn Enshartou ordered her legs and hands to be bound for the rest of the voyage to prevent her from escaping.

THE SHIP SURVIVED THE storm and found its way to India, but with all but one of the slaves gone, the crew had nothing to trade.

As Ibn Enshartou wandered the streets of the port city, he met an old man, who said he was a native of 'the Islands of the Fish', as they are called.

'Long ago,' he explained, 'men coupled there with female fish, while women gave themselves to male creatures of the same kind. Together they created a hybrid people who share the nature of both beings. We are equally of the land and of the sea.'

THE SHE-SLAVE FROM the islands was taken to Ibn Enshartou's home. He kept her tied up in the house for eighteen years and fathered six children upon her, but their children hated him for treating their mother so cruelly. And so, when the captain died, they released their mother from her bonds.

At once, she ran from the house towards the docks.

Her children chased after her but could not keep up.

'Where are you going,' people cried out to her as she ran past them, 'leaving your sons and daughters behind?'

'Enshartou,' she replied, which they took to mean *What have I to do with them?* And she flung herself into the sea.

What becomes of her is not known, for it is God who ordains such things and God alone knows best.[17]

THE MUSLIM WRITER who best understood India as it was, rather than as it was imagined, was Abu Rayhan al-Biruni. Born in 973, Biruni was yet another of those Abbasid-era scholars who was interested in everything and advanced the frontiers of knowledge on several fronts, writing more than a hundred books on astronomy, mathematics and the natural sciences. Biruni loathed dogma and approached every field of inquiry with an open mind. 'In an absolute sense,' he declared, 'science is good in itself ... its lure is everlasting and unbroken.'[18] Although he was raised in the Persian city of Kath, he preferred to write in Arabic. 'I would rather be abused in Arabic', he said, 'than praised in Persian.'[19]

For most of his adult life, Biruni was held in Central Asia as a virtual hostage of a warlord named Mahmud of Ghazni. Mahmud was in the habit of kidnapping scholars from conquered lands and holding them in his court to boost his prestige. In the year 1001, Mahmud invaded northern India, and with each successful campaign, his soldiers sent back groups of Indian intellectuals and craftsmen to his capital. There they were interviewed by Biruni, who became fascinated by Hinduism and learnt Sanskrit to bring himself closer to Indian knowledge and culture.

In 1029, Biruni gathered his findings into a 600-page work, *The Book of India*, in which he explains how the Hindus measure time, how they believe the soul transcends the body and how they record the movement of the planets; he describes their rituals of purity, their festivals and their caste system. Although many Muslims took the view that Hindus were not People of the Book and therefore not entitled to the protections of Islam, Biruni thought that Hinduism was more than idolatry; it was a religion to be respected, one that shared some core values with Islam.

It's not clear whether Biruni actually ventured into Indian territory, but he includes in his book a vivid description of a type of 'unicorn' he calls a *karkadann*, which was almost certainly a single-horned Indian rhinoceros. The accuracy of the description implies that he was able to observe the creature in the wild:

> It is of the build of a buffalo, has a black, scaly skin, a dewlap hanging down under the chin. It has three yellow hooves on each foot, the biggest one forward, the others on both sides. The tail is not long. The eyes lie low, farther down the cheek than is the case with all other animals. On the top of the nose there is a single horn which is bent upwards.[20]

The horn of this 'unicorn' was an exceptionally valuable commodity, but also exceptionally dangerous to procure. One Muslim writer recommends that the best way to hunt the *karkadann* is to shelter behind a broad tree and shout at it; the enraged rhino will then charge at the tree and ram its horn into the trunk, allowing the hunter to spear it to death at his leisure.

Other, more fanciful descriptions of the *karkadann* led Muslim artists to depict the creature as a more conventional unicorn, with a straight horn protruding from its brow instead of its snout. In *Meadows of Gold*, Masudi claims that the unicorn foetus, while gestating, is able to poke its head out of the womb to graze on nearby branches, and then draw back inside its mother. But Masudi was quick to add that no one he'd spoken to who had actually been to India had ever seen such a thing.[21] Another kind of unicorn, the shadhavar, is described by the Muslim cosmographer Qazwini as having a single horn with forty-two holes that play music when a breeze passes through them.

The shadhavar, as illustrated in Qazwini's The Wonders of Creatures and the Marvels of Creation, *c. 1280*

Bilawhar and Budhasaf

IN EUROPE, THE UNICORN symbolised purity and grace; in the Muslim world, where the legend blended into reports of the rhinoceros, the unicorn is presented as a monster and an ambassador of death in a story from eighth-century Baghdad named *The Book of Bilawhar and Budhasaf.*

The tale begins in the court of an Indian king named Janaysar, who immerses himself in the pleasures of the world. He wants for nothing, except the one thing that is most important to him: a son to inherit his throne. One day, the precious son arrives, whom he names Budhasaf. The king's astrologers predict a radiant future for the prince, but one of them foresees that his glory will not be of this world. And so the king orders an entire city to be built for him, where he will be sheltered from all knowledge of human misery.

As a grown man, Budhasaf at last succeeds in escaping from the palace, and for the first time he sees the world as it truly is. He encounters two men, one blind, the other deformed, and from them he learns the realities of human poverty and disease. Then he meets an old man, who makes him aware of decrepitude and death. In his distress, Prince Budhasaf concludes, 'There is no longer any sweetness in this transitory life, now that I have seen these things.'

Then Budhasaf meets a holy man named Bilawhar, who tells him the parable of the unicorn and the pit.

> One day, a man was walking through a forest when he ran into a unicorn. The creature, angered by the man's intrusion into his domain, let out an ear-splitting roar of rage and charged at him. The terrified man ran away as fast as he could, but in his haste he stumbled into a deep pit.
>
> As he fell, he just managed to grab onto a branch and secure a foothold on a stone projecting from the pit wall. But when he looked up, he saw two mice, one white, the other black, gnawing through the branch. Then looking down below his feet, he saw a fire-breathing dragon at the bottom of the pit with its jaws wide open, ready to swallow him. On the ledge where he placed his feet, he saw the heads of four deadly serpents protruding from several holes.
>
> Looking up again at the branch, which would soon snap and send him plummeting to his death, he noticed a few drops of honey trickling down its surface. And even though there was a unicorn above waiting to destroy him, and even though there was a dragon below waiting to devour him, and snakes poised

to poison him, all he could think about was how to get to the sweet honey.[22]

Bilawhar explains the meaning of the tale to Prince Budhasaf: 'The unicorn is death, ever in pursuit of us. The pit is the world, full of dangers. The black and white mice chewing at the branch are the nights and days that eat away the branch of life. The serpents are the four elements of the human body, which, when disordered, bring about death. The mouth of the dragon is the maw of hell, reserved for those who hunger for present joys rather than future blessings. And the trickle of honey represents the sweet delights of the world that distract us from our urgent need for salvation.'

Prince Budhasaf is convinced of the vanity of seeking fame and earthly gratification. He decides to walk away from the pleasures of fine food, drink and sex, and to become an ascetic like Bilawhar.

His father, the king, is appalled by Budhasaf's conversion, but after debating with a holy man he too is won over. Budhasaf renounces his crown, becomes a missionary and after many adventures comes to Kashmir, where he passes on the new way to his disciples and dies.

BILAWHAR AND BUDHASAF speaks vaguely of a supreme deity and of the immortality of the human soul, but the tale's message is not particularly Islamic. Although fasting is required in daylight hours during Ramadan, the monastic way of life was specifically forbidden to Muslims. It was said that when one of the Prophet's close friends proposed to devote himself to constant fasting, prayer and chastity, Muhammad rebuked him and told him to live in the world and go back to his wife.[23]

Far from coming from Muslim tradition, *Bilawhar and Budhasaf* can be easily recognised as a reworking of the story of Gautama

Buddha, who lived and died more than a thousand years before the arrival of Islam. The legend of the Buddha probably entered the Abbasid Empire from Central Asia. When it came to Baghdad the original Sanskrit version was translated into Arabic – Budhasaf, is an Arabicised version of 'Bodhisattva'. The Arabic version was then translated into Georgian, Greek and Latin. In Europe, it became known as the tale of Barlaam and Josaphat, in which the hermit converts the prince to the Christian religion.

The enlightened prince became so popular in medieval Europe that he was venerated as a saint; his feast day is 27 November. In Palermo, the Church of St Giosafat is named in his honour. In this roundabout way, medieval Europeans, by way of Islam, unwittingly brought the Buddha into the company of Christian saints.

The Island of the First Man

SAILORS VENTURING BEYOND the southern tip of India would inevitably arrive at Sri Lanka, which the Muslims knew as the island paradise of Sarandib.

According to *Accounts of China and India*, Sarandib in the tenth century was ruled by two kings, one for the Sinhalese people and one for the Tamils. When one of the kings dies, his people perform a kind of public *memento mori* with his body:

> His corpse is paraded on a low-bedded cart, lying on its back with its head dangling off the rear of the cart, so that the hair drags up dust from the ground. And all the while a woman with a broom sweeps more dust on to the corpse's head and cries out, 'O you people, behold your king! Only yesterday he reigned over you, and you obeyed his every word. See now to what he is come

and the manner of his going from this world. For the angel of death has taken his soul!'

When the dead king is cremated on a pyre, the author notes, 'his womenfolk enter the fire too and are burned alive along with him. But if they wish, they do not do so.'[24]

Mostly, though, the sailors' reports present Sarandib as an island of treasures, a happy land where pearls might be easily plucked from the sea. Precious gems were said to tumble down the sides of a high mountain known by the Arabs as al-Rahun, 'Adam's Peak', where Adam, the first man, descended onto the Earth, leaving his footprint in the rock.[25]

THE ISLAND OF SARANDIB, like India, was imagined as an enchanted wonderland, a place of adventure where sudden changes of fortune were possible.

In 1302, a poet named Amir Khusrau wrote a collection of stories titled *Eight Paradises*, which included a tale, 'The Three Princes of Sarandib', that might be considered the world's first work of detective fiction, preceding the stories of Edgar Alan Poe and Arthur Conan Doyle by several centuries.

The story begins with the King of Sarandib and his three sons, who are clever, but still too unworldly to become good rulers, and so the king sends them out into foreign lands to gain experience.

The three princes wander into Persia, where they meet a herdsman who is very upset because he has lost one of his camels. The herdsman asks the young men if they've seen it.

'Was your camel blind in one eye?' asks the first prince.

The driver says it was.

'Does your camel have a missing tooth?' asks the second.

The driver says it does.

'Is the camel lame in one leg?' asks the third.

'Yes, yes!' agreed the driver.

The young men are then able to trace the path this particular missing camel has taken.

The first prince studies the road and says, 'Your camel carried a load of butter on one side and of honey on the other.'

The second says that the camel was carrying a woman, and the third prince adds that she is pregnant.

The herdsman, convinced that anyone this well informed must have stolen the camel, has the princes jailed as thieves, but when the camel is later found, the princes are released.

The confused camel driver asks them, 'How did you know so much about my camel without having seen it?'

'Well, we realised the camel was blind in the right eye, because only the grass along the left side of the trail was eaten. We guessed the camel lacked a tooth because of the gaps in the way the grass cuds were chewed. We knew it was lame when we saw one of the footprints dragging in the dust.'

'But how did you guess the rest?' asks the astonished herdsman.

'We knew the camel had a load of butter on one side because there were many ants on that side of the road. The flies gathered on the other side told us it was also carrying honey. We guessed the camel had been carrying a woman because we saw a female footprint and found some urine near where the camel had knelt. And we discovered the woman was pregnant by dipping a finger in her urine and tasting it.'

IN THE MID-SIXTEENTH century, a travelling merchant known as Cristoforo the Armenian picked up a copy of *Eight Paradises* and brought it to Venice, where, in 1557, he published an Italian translation of the story of the three princes, titled *Peregrinaggio di Tre Giovani Figliuoli del Re di Serendippo*. The book was subsequently translated and printed all over Europe. In England, *The Three Princes of Serendip* found a wide readership, which included the witty English writer, politician and art historian Horace Walpole.

In 1754, Walpole wrote a chatty letter to an old friend in Florence, in which he mentioned making a happy discovery about a painting he'd just bought. The insight came to him, he wrote, thanks to a moment of accidental good fortune that he called 'serendipity', which was, he thought, 'a very expressive word'. Walpole then explained to his correspondent how he came up with it: 'I once read a silly fairy tale, called *The Three Princes of Serendip*: as their Highnesses travelled, they were always making discoveries, by accidents and sagacity, of things which they were not in quest of.'

Walpole stipulated that the information had to arrive by pure coincidence: '*No* discovery of a thing you *are* looking for comes under this description.'[26]

He had coined the term 'serendipity' as a bit of whimsy to fill a letter that was otherwise devoid of news, but the word was stickier than he anticipated: he had put a name to that happy moment of discovery that briefly makes us feel clever and lucky, and so 'serendipity', a word that rolls so pleasurably off the tongue, caught on in the drawing rooms of England and entered the lexicon.

A Borderless World

FROM SRI LANKA, mariners bound for China would loop around the Bay of Bengal, which the Arabs called the Sea of Harkand, and then tack southwards towards the Spice Islands of Malaya. The bewildering array of islands, the temperamental weather and the presence of pirates sometimes pushed merchant ships off the regular trade routes and left them stranded in *terra incognita*.

In 1998, a crew of Indonesian fishermen were diving for sea cucumber in the shallow waters of the Java Sea near the island of Belitung when they discovered an 1100-year-old shipwreck. The planks on the hull were stitched together, strongly suggesting the ship had been built in Arabia.

The hull was too fragile and barnacled to be properly salvaged, but its full cargo was still in place: 60,000 tightly nested Changsha bowls from Hunan, 1500 ornate pouring jugs adorned with motifs of animals and monsters, thirty gold and silver trinkets, and bronze mirrors.

There were also some personal items found in the wreck that hinted at the ways the passengers passed the time together on the voyage: a die and ivory pieces from a board game, a Chinese lantern and oil lamp, a tiny glass bottle, tweezers, a needle, a cymbal, cooking utensils, and a consignment of star anise – an aromatic seed pod used in Chinese cooking.

Inscriptions on these items indicated that the ship's final, disastrous voyage took place between 820 and 850 C.E.[27] But there remained the mystery of the wreck's location, which was well off course from the maritime trade routes described in *Accounts of China and India*. Perhaps, it was thought, a fierce storm had dragged the ship off course towards Sumatra before it sank in the Java Sea.

THEN IN 2003, a larger wreck was found very close to the Belitung ship, near Cirebon in West Java. This vessel, originating in Southeast Asia, was, at thirty-six metres in length, far bigger than the ships used by Columbus in his Atlantic crossing. The Cirebon wreck, dated to around 970, was found with a cargo of 400,000 Chinese bowls, glassware, glazed turquoise pottery and jewellery from the Abbasid Empire.

These finds and others have led archaeologists to step back from the individual discoveries and draw a bigger picture of the web of connections between the medieval port cities of the Indian Ocean rim. The globalising trade network in the ninth and tenth centuries was more extensive than anyone had thought, with the Abbasid port cities at the centre of this borderless world.

The Bandit Rebellion

THE FAR-OFF CHINESE city of Khanfu (Guangzhou) was the richest destination port for merchants of the caliphate until the late ninth century. After 878, Muslim trading ships stopped coming to Guangzhou because the great port city was in ruins and foreigners were no longer welcome. The two halves of *Accounts of China and India*, written some seven decades apart, present two vivid images of a city on either side of a cataclysm. The first book delivers a detailed description of Guangzhou in happier days as a thriving emporium crammed with timber and bamboo houses, markets, warehouses, temples, churches and mosques. The book describes the mix of people and faiths that were to be found in the city:

> There were three Hindu monasteries where Brahmans resided … On the river, there were merchants' ships of the Indians, the Arabs, the Malays, and others, in numbers that are hard to determine. All of them were loaded with incense, herbs, jewels, and other precious goods. Their merchandise was piled up like a hill.[28]

The customs of the Chinese people often seemed upside down to Muslim sailors and merchants at this time. In Guangzhou it was the men who covered their heads, while the women exposed their hair. Wine was made from rice instead of grapes. The hours of the day were not marked by the call to prayer, but by the public water-clocks of the city. It was observed with some regret that the Chinese used paper to clean themselves after defecating, instead of water, as Muslims do, but overall, it was concluded, China was a healthy country with good-looking people, whose style of clothing was not dissimilar to that of the Arabs.

The author of that first book, compiled before the disaster, was most impressed by the fairness and rigour of China's justice system, and the good order in which foreign trade was managed in Guangzhou. Tang officials recognised how unwise it would be to scare off merchants by squeezing the foreigners too hard. 'The foreign merchants who come to our lands are seeking virtuous enlightenment,' proclaimed one Tang official. 'They should be accorded generous treatment while here.'[29]

Trade was closely supervised by powerful Chinese customs officials, who were typically eunuchs. Foreign merchants could nonetheless petition the imperial government against corrupt behaviour from these officials. *Accounts of China and India* mentions the case of a merchant from Khorasan who had brought in a large shipment of African ivory goods, but on arrival in Guangzhou, the local customs officer apparently took a dislike to him and confiscated his merchandise without recompense.

The outraged merchant travelled north to Chang An, where he asked the emperor's court to hear his grievance against the larcenous eunuch. The merchant was at once put in detention for two months, and then brought to the chancellor and warned of the risk of making a complaint to the emperor. 'If it is decided that you have been lying,' the chancellor said, 'or if your complaint is not serious enough to be worthy of the emperor's time, then the outcome will be nothing less than your death. We do this to deter people from making frivolous or false complaints. If you now withdraw your complaint, then you will be dealt fifty blows with a wooden plank and sent back to your country. If you choose to proceed, you will be admitted to the emperor's presence.'

The Khorasani said he would persist with his complaint, and was thus granted an audience.

Through an interpreter, the merchant explained how the customs official had mistreated him and stolen his goods. The emperor considered this, then ordered the merchant to be detained again and provided with food and drink while his advisors, governors and military officers investigated the complaint. At the same time, other reports of the eunuch's corrupt behaviour reached the emperor's ear, and so he had both the merchant and the miscreant brought before him.

'You deserve to be put to death,' the emperor told the eunuch, 'because you have exposed me to the risk of losing face in the lands bordering my kingdom. This merchant came here in pursuit of honourable gain, and now you want him to return to the lands of the Arabs and the Indians, telling everyone, "I was treated unjustly in China, and my property was seized by force!" But I am loath to shed your blood, if only because you have served me for so long. Instead, I shall appoint you the manager of the dead, because you have failed so badly at your management of the living.'

And so the eunuch was made guard and supervisor of the imperial cemeteries.[30]

BUT BY THE TIME Abu Zayd sat down to compile the second part of *Accounts of China and India*, this era of justice and good government had gone up in smoke. Something terrible had happened to China in the interregnum. Guangzhou had been razed and the roaring maritime trade with the Abbasid Empire had been almost extinguished. Tang China had been dealt a lethal blow, and Abu Zayd was able to name the culprit: 'The reason for the deterioration of law and order in China, and for the end of the China trading voyages from Siraf, was an uprising led by a rebel from outside the ruling dynasty known as Huang Chao.' As a result, he wrote, 'the country itself was ruined, leaving all traces of its greatness gone'.[31]

The troubles in China had begun when the empire's richest farmlands along the Yellow River were devastated first by floods in 858, then by drought in 862, followed by a plague of locusts. The terrible hardships had led to several mutinies among garrison troops in the provinces, which compelled the central government to raise taxes to fund the southern armies, creating yet more hardship and discontent. Peasants were forced into drastic measures to meet payments, some going as far as to sell their children into slavery.

By the 870s, many hungry and angry peasants had abandoned their farms to join bandit gangs in the countryside. The gangs were made up of former farmers and mutineers, as well as members of China's underclasses who had never found a place in society – vagrants, petty criminals and squatters. These bandit tribes soon coalesced into powerful, marauding armies led by charismatic warlords. The most powerful of the bandit generals was Huang Chao, the son of salt smugglers.

In 878, Huang led his men on a long, arduous march through the Fukien Mountains, and then south towards Guangzhou. As his forces neared the city, he sent an emissary to demand he be appointed Governor of Guangdong Province, but instead the officials insulted him by offering him a minor staff position in the Imperial Guard. A furious Huang then set his army loose on the city. Abu Zayd describes what happened when the warlord's soldiers fell upon the foreign merchants of Guangzhou:

> The number of Muslims, Jews, Christians, and Zoroastrians massacred by him, quite apart from the native Chinese, was 120,000; all of them had gone to settle in this city and become merchants there … Huang Chao also cut down all the trees in Guangzhou, including all the mulberry trees … owing to the destruction of the trees, the silkworms perished, and this, in turn, caused silk, in particular, to disappear from Arab lands.[32]

The growing bandit army now presented an existential threat to the central government, and on 5 December 880, they stormed into Chang An. Huang Chao, now known as 'the Heaven Storming General', entered the city in a golden carriage, while his men looted the capital, killing people indiscriminately in the streets. Eight days later, Huang Chao seated himself on the throne in the Tang palace, where he proclaimed himself the founder of a new dynasty, the Qi, and appointed his chief lieutenants as his chancellors. But, having smashed the machinery of the Tang state, Huang had no idea how to reassemble it, let alone make it function, and tried to rule through terror instead. A pall of fear settled on the imperial capital and Huang became a detested and isolated ruler.

Chang An changed hands again several times; it was retaken, lost and retaken again by the Imperial Army. Huang and his men retreated to Henan Province, where the bandit king was hunted down and killed while trying to cross the Yellow River.

THE HUANG CHAO REBELLION had fatally weakened the authority of the Tang regime and left its biggest port a burnt-out husk. Military governors felt free to ignore imperial decrees, while new rebel warlords carved out independent fiefdoms, raiding towns and cities, ravaging farms and villages. After further attacks on foreign merchants in Guangzhou, the maritime trade routes into coastal China withered away, and forced seafaring merchants to look to other destinations in Asia, India and Africa. Abu Zayd wrote sadly:

> Because of this, God withdrew His blessings altogether from the Chinese, the sea itself became uncooperative, and ruin befell the ships' masters and pilots of Siraf and Oman, as ordained, in the course of events, by God the Ruler, may His name be blessed.[33]

IN THE EARLY 1940s, an Australian airman named Morry Isenberg was posted to Marchinbar Island, a narrow strip of land off the coast of Arnhem Land in Northern Australia. Morry had been posted there to man a radar station, one of several Australian Air Force outposts set up to track hostile Japanese aircraft.

One day, while fishing on one of the island's beaches, Morry found a handful of weather-beaten, wafer-thin copper coins in the sand. Thinking perhaps of Treasure Island, he marked the spot where he'd found them on a map, put the coins in a tin, brought them home in his kit bag at the end of the war and then forgot about them.

In 1979, Morry rediscovered the little tin and took the coins to a dealer, who told him they were worthless. Still thinking something might come from their discovery, he took them to a museum in Sydney. Four were identified as having been minted by the Dutch East India Company in the seventeenth and eighteenth centuries, but the remaining five were much older and had Arabic inscriptions. Careful examination revealed that these coins were from Kilwa, a medieval Islamic sultanate founded on the East African coast that existed centuries before European mariners caught sight of the Australian mainland. They are, to date, the oldest foreign objects ever found in Australia.[34]

In 2013, an archaeological expedition set out to unravel the mystery of how the Kilwa coins had fetched up in faraway Northern Australia. Coins from Kilwa might have been passed on many times before arriving on the island. But who might have brought them there? And when? As part of their research, they consulted elders of the Yolngu people of Northeast Arnhem Land, whose oral traditions include stories of foreign visitors and traders from the Spice Islands of Southeast Asia.[35] Yolngu cave art murals on Marchinbar depict visitors on sailing ships wearing hats and yellow trousers.

The researchers, led by Australian anthropologist Ian S. McIntosh, advanced several theories as to how the Kilwa coins had come to Marchinbar, none of them conclusive. The presence of the Dutch East India Company coins in close proximity to the Kilwa coins suggests they might have been left by a Macassan sailor from Ambon or Banda, trading with the local Indigenous people.

Perhaps the true significance of the find is that it finally puts to bed the hoary myth that Australia existed in splendid isolation from the outside world until its 'discovery' by European explorers in the seventeenth century. The Kilwa coins are part of a growing body of evidence that Aboriginal people were themselves participants in the Maritime Silk Roads, trading iron ore and trepang, 'sea cucumber', with Macassan sailors, who dried or smoked its flesh, then took it to China, where it was sold as an expensive aphrodisiac.[36]

Two of the Marchinbar Island coins from Kilwa

THE ISLAND OF Kilwa Kisiwani is only a few kilometres long and it lies just off the coast of modern-day Tanzania. A thousand years ago, it was the capital of a fabulously rich sultanate, the greatest of the Islamic trading states along the Swahili Coast. East Africa was known by the Arabs as the land of the Zanj, 'the Dark-Skinned People', whose ports attracted merchants looking to purchase slaves, ivory and ambergris. Chinese scholars knew it as Po-pa-li, a land of ostriches, giraffes and zebras.[37]

Archaeologists had once assumed that Kilwa and the other Swahili cities had been set up as overseas colonial ports of the Abbasid Empire: the medieval equivalents of Hong King and Singapore. But more recent digs have revealed that these cities existed as fishing and trading ports well before the arrival of Muslim traders in the ninth century. Arabic and Persian culture, it seems, was gradually adopted by Swahili people from their contacts with the wider world, not imposed from the outside.[38]

Abu Zayd praised the quality of the African leopards sold in these ports: 'They are notable for their reddish colour and excellent breeding, as well as for their ample size.' Arab traders were welcomed in the Zanj port cities, he claimed, because the Zanj were addicted to the sweet date syrup the Arabs brought to Africa. 'If they catch sight of an Arab,' he wrote, 'they prostrate themselves before him and say, "This is a man from a kingdom where the date tree grows!"'[39]

Kilwa, however, drew most of its wealth from the gold that was mined from the Zimbabwe Plateau then carried on foot to the Mozambique coast. Gold made the sultans of Kilwa rich enough to mint their own coins, several of which somehow fetched up many centuries later on faraway Marchinbar Island.

Kilwa boasted a palace complex with a sunken reception hall, elaborate gardens and a swimming pool overlooking the Indian Ocean. The walls of its mosque, one of the largest and earliest in East Africa, were clad with fine Chinese ceramics, imported from the other distant terminus of the Maritime Silk Road.

The Island Abode of Bliss

THE VOYAGE FROM the Persian Gulf to the Zanj coast was, like the cruise to India, a relatively easy operation, supported by the seasonal monsoonal winds. The most dangerous stretch of the journey lay between Arabia and the Horn of Africa, where merchant ships might run into wild conditions on the high seas. Masudi, who made his last voyage through this stretch of water in 917, claimed the waves there were 'mad', rising up like mountains and sinking down like valleys.[40]

Merchant ships crossing these waters had to be particularly wary of the island of Socotra, which sat like a sentinel between the southern Arabian coast and the Horn of Africa. Socotra – 'Island Abode of Bliss' – whose name was taken from the Sanskrit *dvipa-sakhadara*,[41] was renowned as an island of otherworldly beauty and danger. 'Socotra', it was said, 'rises like a tower in the dark sea; it is a refuge for the pirates who are the terror of sailing ships in these parts.'[42]

ABU ZAYD CLAIMS (quite erroneously) that Socotra was first settled by Greeks, sent there by Alexander the Great.[43] Merchants and slaves who were kidnapped and dragged off to the island found themselves in a bizarre landscape, one of the strangest on Earth. Socotra is home to 700 endemic species. Bulbous bottle trees sprout from the sides of cliffs. Weird dragon trees poke up from the ground like umbrellas. Clustered together, they look like an assembly of curious extra-terrestrials. A local legend claims the tree was formed from the blood of a dragon that was gored by an elephant. Its bright red sap, known as dragon's blood, was used in medieval times as a lacquer, a nail polish, and a salve to staunch bleeding.

Marco Polo claimed that the Socotrans were 'the most expert enchanters in the world'. It was these vengeful sorcerers, he said, who were responsible for the treacherous seas in the area. 'If a pirate ship has done some damage to the islanders,' he wrote, 'she cannot sail from the island without first making amends for the damage done. She may set sail before a favouring breeze and make some headway on her course; but they will conjure up a headwind and force her to turn back.'[44]

Dragon's blood trees on the island of Socotra

The Travels of Ismailawayh the Liar

IN 922, ACCORDING TO *The Marvels of India*, a merchant named Ismailawayh made a voyage to East Africa. He and his crew were intending to go to the African port of Kanbalu, but a storm drove them further south down the Zanj coast, to the kingdom of Sofala in Mozambique. As their ship came in to shore, they were surrounded by African men in canoes, which terrified the Arab crew, who believed they were among cannibals and that they would soon be killed and eaten.

Their fears were groundless. Instead of being devoured, they were brought before the King of the Zanj who was a strong, young man. The King asked the strangers who they were and where they were going. When Ismailawayh replied that this land was actually their intended destination, the king said, 'You lie. It was the winds alone that brought you here. But you have nothing to fear from us. Bring your goods ashore.'

The trading was very satisfactory for the merchants. They presented the king with many gifts and he reciprocated with presents of even greater value.

When it was time to leave, the king accompanied them to the shore to bid them farewell. He even came aboard the ship and, in the friendliest possible manner, invited them to return some day.

BUT EVEN AS HE spoke, the crew were hauling up the anchor and spreading the sails. And when the king tried to disembark, the crew told him he would have to stay with them. 'We are taking you to our home,' they said cheerfully, 'where we will repay you for your kindnesses.'

'Strangers,' said the king, 'when you came into my lands, it was I who protected you. I asked nothing of you. I came aboard your ship as a token of my good will. You must now treat me as justice demands and let me return to my kingdom.'

But Ismailawayh ignored him, and as the coastline disappeared, the crew sent the king down into the hold, where he was chained up with the slaves.

Of this betrayal, the Zanj King said nothing, and thereafter, the crew and the king acted as though they were strangers to each other.

Once the ship pulled into Oman, the crew sold the king and the other slaves. The king, who was young and strong, fetched an excellent price.

SOME YEARS LATER, Ismailawayh and his crew were again blown off course to the coast of Sofala. Again, as the canoes once more surrounded their boat, they readied themselves for death at the hands of the Zanj, this time for the crime of stealing their king.

The sailors were brought into the palace of Sofala, where they were astonished to see the same king they'd sold at the slave market, sitting on his throne, as though nothing had happened. The men trembled in fear and shame.

'Aha!' said the king scornfully. 'My old friends. Lift up your heads.' But the men could hardly look at him.

'I will be merciful,' the king promised. 'Go about your business of buying and selling as you did before. You are under my protection, just as you were last time you came here.'

The crew were still fearful, suspecting a trick, but they were allowed to offload and sell their cargo without any trouble. This time, however, when they offered the king a gift, he refused to accept it.

'You are not worthy for me to accept a present from you,' he said. 'I will not sully my property with anything that comes from you.'

AS THE VISITORS prepared to leave, Ismailawayh felt compelled to ask the king what had happened after they had sold him at the slave markets of Oman.

'My new master took me with him to Basra,' he explained. 'There I was taught to pray, to fast and to read the Quran. Then my master sold me to another man, who brought me to Baghdad. There I glimpsed the caliph himself and prayed in the Great Mosque.'

Then one day, he explained, he observed a group of pilgrims mounted on camels. Mixing in with them, he succeeded in escaping his master and joining the *hajj* to Mecca.

After completing the pilgrimage, he dared not go back to his master in Baghdad, so he joined another caravan that took him to Egypt. In Cairo, he saw the Nile River flowing through the city and was told it originated in the land of the Zanj. Following its banks, he arrived on the borders of his own lands, where he paused for a moment to think.

Surely another man has replaced me as king, he told himself. *If I make myself known, he will want to kill me.*

And so the king took care to disguise himself before entering his kingdom. But along the road he met a woman who told him they had no king but God. She said their king had long ago been carried off, and they had agreed not to have another one before they had definite news of the last king, for their oracles had told them he was still alive and in the land of the Arabs.

The king then threw off his disguise. He was welcomed back in his city by his family with overwhelming joy, and his kingdom was restored to him. He was astonished to discover that his people, like him, had become Muslims.

All this had happened only a month before the return of Ismailawayh and his sailors.

The Zanj King now told Ismailawayh that he would pardon him, but only because it was his abduction that had brought to him the blessings of Islam.

'But there is still something on my conscience,' the king admitted to Ismailawayh. 'I stole myself from my master without his leave, and without recompense. Now, if you were an honest man, I would give you the money to hand over to him, a sum ten times the amount he paid for me, but you and your crew are no better than traitors and thieves. Go now, and if you come back, you will receive the best possible treatment, for you and I are fellow believers.

'But,' he added, woundingly, 'I will not accompany you to your ship this time. I'm sure you understand why.'

And with that, they parted.

What became of the Zanj King after that is not known, for it is God who ordains such things and God alone knows best.[45]

The Zanj Slave Revolt

THE ZANJ CITIES of the Swahili Coast had become rich selling ambergris and ivory to China; weightier goods such as slaves and timber were sold to the larger merchant ships of the Abbasid Empire.[46]

Slavery existed throughout the medieval world, but it was an institution in slow decline. Mass slavery had provided most of the workforce in mining and agriculture in the ancient Roman world, but was becoming increasingly rare in the Later Roman Empire, where slaves were given legal rights, protecting them from abuse by their masters. In China, male slaves made up little more than one per cent of the population, although the vast majority of the peasantry laboured under conditions akin to semi-slavery.[47]

Slavery was permitted in the caliphate, but Islamic doctrine encouraged Muslims to grant freedom to talented slaves and to be generous with them.[48] Manumission was also recommended as a way of making amends for excessive cruelty to a slave. Islamic law accepted that a Muslim might be kept in a state of enslavement, but could not legally be *reduced* to slavery, and infidels were absolutely not permitted to keep Muslim slaves. The prostitution of a female slave was likewise prohibited; it was stipulated that only her master or husband might 'lawfully enjoy her'.[49]

Male slaves could serve as personal bodyguards or secretaries to their masters, or be inducted into the army, where they might rise to become powerful figures. In Bahrain, slave boys were used as pearl divers. Those who developed the ability to dive deep onto the sea bed were highly prized; others drowned from shock or fright.

But the Islamic world generally refrained from exploiting battalions of slaves for large-scale enterprises. The exception to this was the Zanj slave labour force sent to work in the salt marshes near Basra.

BASRA'S POPULATION HAD swollen dramatically within a generation of its founding, creating a demand for food that could not be sustained by the surrounding countryside. To the southwest of Basra lay the arid desert, to the northeast an unpromising swathe of swampy marshlands choked by dense clusters of reeds and rushes. The water there was brackish, and much of the area could only be penetrated in a flat-bottomed barge. The farmers in the area lived in fear of wolves lurking in the thickets, while swarms of malaria-carrying mosquitos drove many people to simply walk away from the marshlands and try their luck in Basra or Kufa instead. Just as forbiddingly, frequent flooding silted up the land with a crust of salt that had to be scraped away by an army of people to make the soil agriculturally viable.

To solve the problem, the Abbasid government gave permission for rich landowners to bring in thousands of African slaves to clear the land and farm it for sugarcane. Forced by their masters into gangs ranging from 500 to 5000 men, the Zanj slaves were assigned back-breaking work, clad in scraps of cloth and fed on a subsistence diet. Even after many of the slaves adopted Islam, their conditions did not improve, exposing their masters as grasping hypocrites. The Abbasid state had become dangerously indifferent to the suffering of its seething underclasses.

It was these conditions that primed the Zanj workers for the Muslim world's first great slave revolt. All they needed was a Spartacus to lead them.

IN 869, A CHARISMATIC revolutionary named Ali bin Muhammad began haunting the Zanj slave camps around Basra. Ali was a well-educated man, a poet who was said to be well versed in the occult sciences.[50] He was, in some ways, an avatar of the twentieth-century revolutionaries who came from bourgeois families like Lenin, Mao and Castro.

As a young man, Ali bin Muhammad moved from Rayy to the temporary capital of Samarra, where he became politicised after observing the huge disparities in wealth within the city. From there he migrated to Bahrain on the Arabian coast and took up the slogans of the radical Kharijites, who proclaimed that the best man should rule, 'even if he is an Abyssinian slave'.[51] After his attempts to lead an uprising in Bahrain failed, Ali wandered into southern Iraq. In Basra, he tried preaching rebellion in the mosque, but was expelled from the city as a troublemaker. When he saw the wretched conditions of the Zanj plantation slaves labouring outside the city, he instantly grasped their potential as a revolutionary army.

Posing as an agent of one of the caliph's sons, Ali entered the Zanj camps, and on 9 September 869, he met secretly with the slaves. The historian Tabari, who lived through the Zanj Rebellion, records that Ali came to one plantation and addressed the slaves, 'raising their spirits by promising to lead and command them and to give them possession of property. He swore a solemn oath to them that he would neither deceive nor betray them and that they would experience only kind treatment from him.'[52]

Ali gave orders for the overseers to be arrested and manacled. Then the masters were seized and brought before him. 'I wanted to behead you all for the way you have treated these slaves,' he told them. 'But my companions have spoken to me about you, and now I have decided to set you free.'[53]

The masters, thinking they were off the hook, then made the mistake of trying to strike a cynical deal with Ali. They told him that his newfound followers were habitual runaways, who would desert him at the first opportunity. Rather than lose out, the masters suggested he should give the slaves back; in return, Ali would be duly compensated.

In response, the incensed Ali ordered the masters to be pinned to the ground and lashed with palm branches. After their chastisement, he released the masters and sent them back to Basra.[54] For the Zanj, it was a stunning spectacle, a radical inversion of power that bound them to Ali's cause.

Like China's Huang Chao Rebellion, the Zanj Rebellion erupted with astonishing speed, attracting disaffected peasants, craftsmen and Bedouin tribesmen as well as African and European slaves and semi-slaves.[55] The tall reeds and rushes of the salt marshes were an ideal base for such an insurgency, allowing rebels to move without being seen and to ambush the passing river traffic. The Abbasid army, made up primarily of Turkish cavalry, was unable to penetrate this marshy and dangerous zone.

THE CALIPHATE WAS IN a poor position to launch a coherent response to the Zanj threat. The assassination of Mutawakkil in 861 had triggered a period of violent disorder, later dubbed 'the Anarchy at Samarra'. One caliph after another had been murdered, mostly by their Turkish bodyguards, who demanded more and more donative payments from a bankrupt treasury. The caliphs, by placing themselves on a throne inside a barracks, had made themselves captives of their own army.

The Anarchy in Samarra had emboldened whole provinces to break away and become autonomous. The Governor of Egypt, Ibn Tulun, evicted the caliphate's agent and founded a dynasty of his own. In eastern Iran the Saffarid family set up another breakaway dynasty that invaded Khorasan in 870. These renegade provinces remained Muslim, but no longer accepted the political authority of the Commander of the Faithful, whoever that happened to be with each passing week.

After nine ruinous years, a new caliph, Mutamid ('Dependent on God'), took the throne as a figurehead. Mutamid presided over a shrunken empire, with only central Iraq, parts of Syria and western Persia still under the caliphate's control.

Under these chaotic conditions, Ali and his Zanj army could roam across southern Iraq almost unchallenged. They built a capital city of their own named Mukhtara near the entrance to the Gulf, and captured the port of Uballa which gave Ali a chokehold on the flow of goods into the Tigris and Euphrates. Ali minted his own coins and proclaimed himself Mahdi, a divinely guided saviour who would bring justice to the Muslim world.

ON 4 SEPTEMBER 871 there was a lunar eclipse. During his prayers that night, Ali claimed he'd heard a voice telling him that Basra 'was but a loaf of bread, which one could nibble around the edges'. When half the loaf had been devoured, he was told, Basra would be destroyed.[56] On Friday 7 September, after two days of bloody fighting, the victorious Ali entered Basra and his army fell upon the empire's second-biggest city and its inhabitants. 'Killing and burning continued through the day and into the evening and throughout all of Saturday as well', wrote Tabari, who condemned Ali as 'the abominable one'.[57] 'Some managed to escape,' recorded Masudi, 'others were drowned or massacred. A large number of them hid among the houses and in the wells. They appeared only at night and hunted dogs, rats and cats, which they killed for food; but soon this supply was exhausted and they found nothing left to eat.'

The victorious Zanj troops took pleasure in enslaving women taken from the Arab aristocracy. The Zanj auctioneer called out their lines of descent as he sold them. According to Masudi, each of the Zanj took ten to thirty women as concubines and house maids.[58]

The auction of the women made it clear that the Zanj rebellion was a revolt against unspeakable living and working conditions, not an ideological campaign against slavery as an institution. Ali had not promised to abolish human enslavement, a concept that would have seemed bizarre in medieval times, but to overturn the social order and grant the rebels slaves of their own – a promise he now was able to fulfill.

BASRA NEVER FULLY recovered from the retribution of the Zanj. Whole neighbourhoods had been ransacked and burnt to the ground, along with the main mosque, the bridges and the wharves along the canals. It was the Zanj destruction of Basra that drove the high born Ibn Wahb to leave the city in 871 and sail off to faraway China to meet the Tang Emperor.

Ali and his Zanj army now controlled all of southern Iraq. In 879, his rebels advanced north through the central marshlands and took the garrison city of Wasit, granting them another trove of gold, arms and slaves, and putting them within striking distance of Baghdad. The very survival of the Abbasid caliphate was now at stake.

IN 879, TEN YEARS into the Zanj Rebellion, the Abbasid forces were finally ready to launch a sustained and systematic campaign to take back southern Iraq. The Abbasid attacks were led by the caliph's brother Muwaffaq and his son, Abu al-Abbas, who put the rebel capital Mukhtara under siege for thirty gruelling months.

Unable to break through, the Abbasid army set about steadily demolishing the rebel city's infrastructure. Muwaffaq ordered a large ship to be fitted with a tall mast, then had it filled with reeds doused in flammable naphtha oil. His men pushed the ship into Mukhtara's central canal and set fire to it. The blazing vessel drifted up to the city's main bridge, where the tall mast stopped it from passing under, allowing the flames to ignite the bridge and burn it down. With one part of the Zanj city now cut off from its army, Muwaffaq's troops were able to invade the rebels' shipyards and to destroy their barges and galleys.

Ali the Messiah was now exposed as fallible, and his senior men and soldiers began to desert him. As government troops pushed forward, setting fire to buildings as they advanced, Ali and the last of his men fell back to the western side of the city where they made their last stand.

On 1 August 883, after a three-hour battle, the last of the Zanj rebels broke and ran. In Ali's mansion, government soldiers found some of the Basran women the rebel leader had taken as slaves. Ali was tracked down and killed; his head was delivered to Muwaffaq, who fell to his knees and thanked God for the victory.

The Abbasid Recovery

MUWAFFAQ'S SON ABU AL-ABBAS was given the honour of parading Ali's head at the end of a lance through the cheering streets of Baghdad. The warrior prince's willingness to expose himself to enemy arrow fire and his concern for his soldiers' welfare had won him the respect of the Abbasid military, and in 892 he succeeded his deceased uncle as caliph, taking the regnal name Mutadid, 'Seeking Support in God'.

DURING MUTADID'S NINE-YEAR reign, the long decline of the caliphate was checked and reversed. Civilian control was reasserted over the military, and the empire's finances were carefully repaired. 'When the caliphate came to Mutadid,' wrote Masudi, 'discord ceased, the provinces once again became obedient, war stopped, prices fell and turmoil simmered down.'[59] The caliphate no longer controlled as many lands as it had in the golden age of Harun al-Rashid, but it unquestionably remained the strongest Muslim power in the world. Baghdad was still the world's most populous city.

In another sign of a return to greatness, Mutadid moved the capital back to the City of Peace. He spent lavishly on restoring Baghdad to its full imperial glory, after it had been allowed to become run-down in the decades when the caliphs had ruled from Samarra. Mutadid built new mosques on the east bank of the Tigris, and a palace complex named The Pleiades, after the constellation.

CALIPH MUTADID, PROBABLY the most capable Abbasid ruler since Mansur, was skilful in diplomacy and ruthless towards his enemies. 'He was not a man much touched by pity,' admits Masudi, 'and his character was both energetic and bloody.'[60]

As always, however, the shadow of a potential succession crisis lingered over the caliphate. Mutadid had three sons, and he took care to prepare Ali, the eldest, to succeed him. But the gentle character of his second son Jafar filled him with apprehension.

The chatty jurist Tanukhi relates a piece of palace gossip about Jafar, passed on to him by one of Mutadid's eunuchs. One day, it was said, Mutadid came to the private apartments of the boy's mother, a former Roman slave named Shaghab. The caliph spotted the five-year-old Jafar playing with his friends and happily sharing his grapes with them. Mutadid gloomily told the eunuch that if the boy should ever become caliph, he would squander his inheritance.

'He will distribute the money that I have collected, just as he distributed the grapes,' he predicted. 'Were it not for hell-fire and shame, I should slay that child today, for his death would be a blessing to the community.'[61]

BOOK FIVE

North

MUQTADIR ('Mighty in God')
Eighteenth of the Abbasid caliphs

SHAGHAB
Queen mother and ruler of the Abbasid harem

Ibn al-FURAT
Vizier to the caliph

ALMISH
King of the Bulgars

Ibn FADLAN
Envoy of the caliph

The ANGEL of DEATH
Viking witch-woman

ZEKI VELIDI TOGAN
Bashkir scholar and revolutionary

Abu TAHIR
Qarmatian warlord

QAHIR ('Victorious by the Will of God')
Brother of Muqtadir and nineteenth of the Abbasid caliphs

the
KINGDOMS TO THE NORTH
c. 924 C.E.

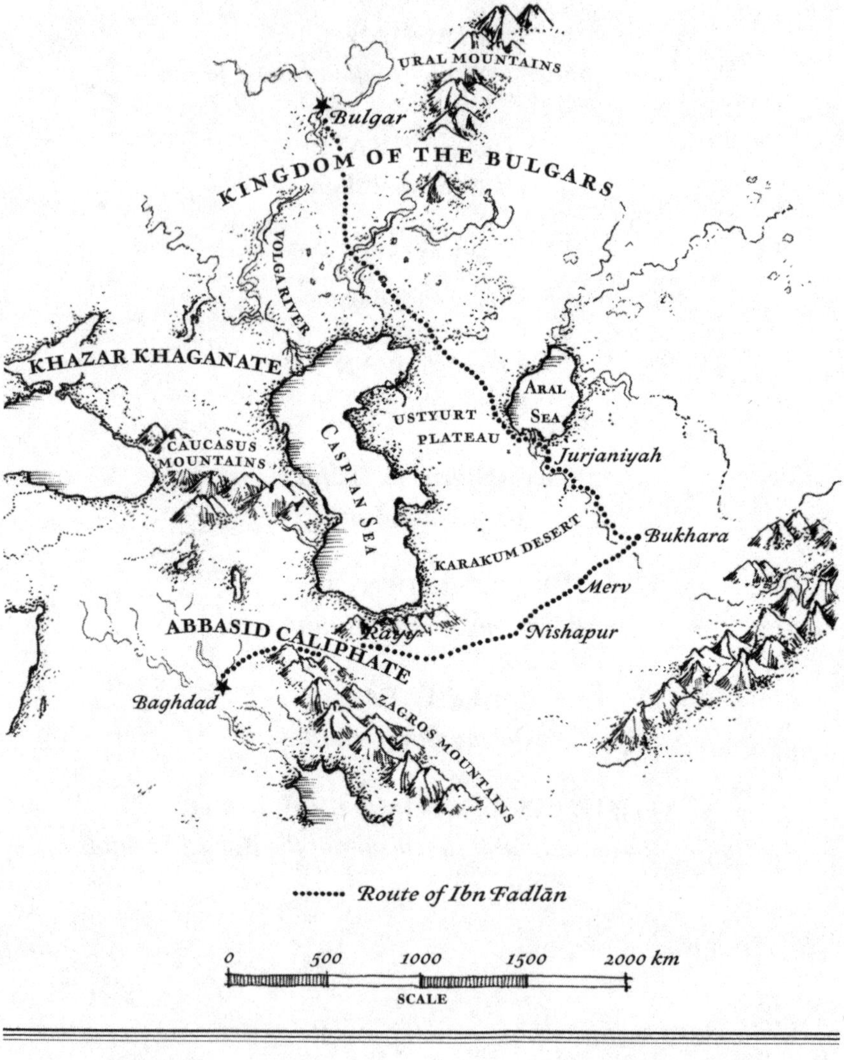

Trouble in Paradise

IN THE YEAR 917 C.E., two envoys from Constantinople sailed down the Euphrates River to Baghdad. John Radinos and Michael Toxaras had been sent by the Emperor of the Romans to propose a truce with the Abbasid Empire. On their arrival, they were given lodgings in a mansion on the east bank of the Tigris, and an invitation to the mansion of the caliph's vizier, a man named Ibn al-Furat.

Crossing the Tigris, the visitors were escorted into the mansion's garden wing, where they found Furat sitting on an intricately woven prayer carpet, attended by officials and servants. Through an interpreter, the ambassadors put forward their emperor's proposal for a truce and an exchange of prisoners of war. They asked for an audience with the caliph, and the vizier said he'd see what he could do.

The envoys were sent out of town to Tikrit so that elaborate preparations could be made in the capital for their meeting with the Commander of the Faithful.

Two months later, everything was in readiness, and Radinos and Toxaras were summoned back to Baghdad. As they rode from the capital's outskirts to the palace, they saw the entire city had come out to witness their progress. Baghdadis crammed into the streets and onto balconies and rooftops to catch a glimpse of the Christian foreigners as they trotted past thousands of mounted cavalrymen in full dress armour lining the route.

WITH THE EYES of Baghdad upon them, the ambassadors arrived at the public gate of the palace. The original caliphal residence, the Palace of the Golden Gate, had long ago been superseded by a far larger complex of mansions, gardens and mosques on the other side of the Tigris that was similar in scale to Beijing's Forbidden City. Its main structure, the Palace of the Crown, was capped by a dome known as the Cupola of the Ass, so named for its spiral stairs, which allowed the caliph to ride comfortably to the top on a donkey, to take in the view of the river traffic, the suburbs and the rich lands beyond.

After the envoys dismounted, they were guided through a maze of passageways and vestibules and then led into the caliphal stables, where they passed hundreds of mares with brocaded saddles standing under marble colonnades, each one attended by a uniformed groom.

Then there were more corridors and halls before they emerged into the caliph's private zoo. In the elephant enclosure they saw four elephants draped in peacock-coloured silk brocade, mounted by riders brandishing flaming javelins. Then it was on to the lion house, where dozens of big cats lounged about, restrained by iron collars and chains.

ON AND ON the envoys were guided, through carpeted corridors and quadrangles, each space crowded with retainers and servants. Serried ranks of Slavic and African slaves stood by, offering juice, beer, and water chilled with lumps of snow.[1]

They passed from garden to garden, past trees bearing dates and citrus fruits, before entering the most enchanting mansion in the complex, the Palace of the Tree. Inside, they were amazed by the sight of a silver tree with branches of gold and silver rising up from a pool of water. On each branch, mechanical clockwork birds, also of silver and gold, seemed to fill the room with artificial birdsong. As they warbled, painted leaves rustled on the branches, as if touched by a passing breeze. This magical tree was guarded on either side by fifteen clockwork knights on horseback, which operated their lances robotically.

AT LAST, THE FOOTSORE and overwhelmed envoys staggered into the Qasr al-Taj, the Palace of the Crown, where they found Muqtadir, the caliph, seated on an ebony throne, surrounded by his sons. Above their heads, chains of precious gems caught the sun's rays, refracting beams of coloured light throughout the throne room. The caliph, they saw, was a young man of middling height, with fair hair and a beard, a round face and small, dark eyes.[2]

The ambassadors kissed the ground, keeping at a good distance from the throne as required by protocol, then read out a letter proposing the prisoner exchange. Answering on the caliph's behalf, Furat said their request would be accepted, 'out of compassion for the Muslims and a desire to set them free'.[3]

The audience was over. The envoys were led out through a private gate to a boat waiting on the Tigris.

THE VISIT OF THE Roman ambassadors in 917 was recorded by chroniclers who no doubt exaggerated the wonders of the palace complex, but the story the envoys brought back home clearly had some effect: Constantinople, the self-proclaimed Queen of Cities, could not possibly suffer itself to be overshadowed by the Muslim capital, and so, before too long, visitors to the Emperor Constantine VII would report encountering a similar mechanical singing tree in his throne room.[4]

The elaborate show in Baghdad had augmented its reputation as a city of marvels, but it was all an illusion, contrived to conceal weakness and disorder. Under Muqtadir, the former Prince Jafar, the caliphate was flaking away at the edges and shrivelling at the centre.

MUQTADIR HAD INHERITED an empire on the road to recovery, thanks to the energetic stewardship of his father Mutadid and older brother Muktafi (Ali). But under the hapless Muqtadir, caliphal power was disintegrating again. Since coming to the throne at the age of thirteen, Muqtadir had been dominated by a council of regents, made up of his mother and his principal advisors, which was supposed to step aside when Muqtadir was old enough to rule in his own right. But the day never came. As a sheltered princeling in a world of ruthless adults, the caliph was happy to float above the hard and boring work of administration, leaving all that unpleasantness to his courtiers, his generals and his mother.

Within the frictionless world of the palace, Muqtadir grew up without any sense of financial limitations; he spent lavishly on his entertainments, and handed out precious gems that had once belonged to the shahanshahs of ancient Persia. A ring featuring an ancient ruby known as 'the Mountain', said to be large and bright enough to light up a room like a lamp, disappeared from the treasury during Muqtadir's reign.[5] A famous gigantic pearl, known as al-Yatimah – 'the Non-Pareil' – was awarded to one of his concubines.[6]

'People reflect their times more than they resemble their fathers,' was a proverb attributed to Ali, son-in-law of the Prophet, and that quip surely applied to Muqtadir.[7] Whereas his father, the Caliph Mutadid, was a respected figure who dominated his government, Muqtadir divided his time between bouts of pleasure and penitence. A coin struck at the time shows him on one face clutching a vial of wine, and playing a lute on the other – but when sober, he would give himself over to fasting and praying. He was far from a cruel man, and when he did intervene in court politics, it was often in response to his compassionate nature.[8] His chamberlain once remarked that although Muqtadir's character and instincts were honourable, he was too easily thwarted from acting on them. The caliph was, he explained, 'not used to presiding over an assembly, or dealing with the state affairs, administering its small details so as to judge its big questions; nor has he read the biographies and the chronicles. Except for this, he has the best intentions, the noblest conscience, and is the most pious of people.'[9]

IN THE COURSE OF Muqtadir's long reign, civilian control of the empire was slowly lost to a military that bullied him and his regime. Muqtadir's successors would reign as mere ornaments of an army dictatorship.

The Abbasid chroniclers were quick to hold Muqtadir responsible for this unhappy state of affairs, pointing to his youth and fecklessness. But it was these very qualities that had encouraged cynical palace courtiers to install him on the throne in the first place.

When his brother, the Caliph Muktafi, took to his deathbed in August 908, there was no clear consensus on who should succeed, and no legal mechanism to smoothly engineer it. Senior bureaucrats wanted an experienced, competent prince like Abd Allah, son of the former Caliph Mutazz, but Furat, then acting as deputy to the vizier, disagreed, saying: 'For God's sake do not appoint to the post a man who knows the house of one, the fortune of another, the gardens of a third, the slave girls of a fourth, the estate of a fifth and the horse of a sixth; nor one who has mixed with the people, has had experience of affairs, has gone through his apprenticeship and made calculations of people's fortunes.'

Instead, Furat nominated the dead caliph's young brother, Jafar, who had given away his grapes so freely as a small child. When the vizier objected that Jafar was still a boy, Furat retorted, 'Why should you appoint a caliph who will govern? Wouldn't it be better to choose someone who will leave all that to his advisors?'[10]

On reflection, the vizier agreed. The army commanders wanted the throne to remain within the royal family, and so the thirteen-year-old Jafar was proclaimed by a court riven with tension and intrigue. He was awarded the regnal name of al-Muqtadir – 'Mighty in God'.

FURAT'S EXPECTATION THAT Muqtadir would be pliable was correct, but his plan backfired: the boy-caliph was still living inside the confines of the harem, and was easily dominated by his powerful mother, Shaghab. Muqtadir spent most of his time immersed in the luxuries of this sanctum, a private space that no vizier or male courtier could enter. Anyone wanting the caliph's ear therefore had to approach the office of the queen mother, or form alliances with powerful members of her entourage.

Shaghab, whose name means 'Trouble' or 'Turbulence',* had amassed a huge fortune and was possibly the richest single individual in the world, unlike her son, who was always spending more than he had. She used the revenue from her extensive agricultural holdings to build her own patronage networks, and burnished her name by donating millions of gold dinars towards improvements along the pilgrimage route to Mecca, and to pay for defensive walls along the Roman frontier.

Shaghab's power base was the harem, which lay deep within the palace complex. It was a city within a city, populated by the caliph's

* Beautiful slave girls were often given ugly names, perhaps ironically, or to ward off the evil eye.

female relatives, his concubines and children, as well as thousands of eunuchs, slave girls and chamber servants.[11] Under Shaghab, the harem became a parallel court, supported by its own *diwan* and her personal staff of stewardesses, eunuchs and factotums.

THE TENSIONS IN THE court boiled over just months into Muqtadir's reign, when a cabal of bureaucrats and soldiers launched a coup attempt. On 16 December 908, Muqtadir's first vizier, al-Abbas ibn al-Hasan, was ambushed and murdered while riding out of the city. The conspirators nominated Prince Abd Allah as the new caliph, but they had not yet arrested Muqtadir, who was on the polo field when he was told of the plot. He fled at once to the protection of the palace, while Shaghab sent orders for Munis, the army chief, to come to their aid. Munis in turn sent members of the palace guard on a barge up the Tigris to arrest the coup leaders. The plotters lost their nerve, and either fled or defected back to Muqtadir, claiming they'd been forced into the whole thing. Muqtadir awarded an extra donative to the troops and the remaining insurgents were executed. Prince Abd Allah, who had reigned for a single day and night, was hunted down and strangled. The devious but capable Furat was appointed as Muqtadir's new vizier.

AS THINGS SETTLED DOWN, Muqtadir returned to the comforts of the harem, and was happy to let Shaghab appoint and remove his advisors as she saw fit. The queen mother took care not to let any one of them predominate; when Furat attempted to sideline the court chamberlain and his senior general, she warned her son to rein him in. 'On whom, I should like to know,' she asked tartly, 'will you call for aid if he means mischief and plots your dethronement?'[12]

Furat's first term as vizier lasted two years, before he was arrested for corruption in 912. But his overall administrative competence could not be overlooked, and in 917, he was recalled for a second term, during which he engineered the lavish reception of the Roman ambassadors. Within a year he was arrested again on suspicion of treason and his wealth was confiscated by the state.

Fourteen viziers would come and go during Muqtadir's long, sorry reign. The most upright of these advisors, Ali ibn Isa, was repeatedly appointed and dismissed, while less capable viziers were content to let matters drift as the regime sank deeper into financial crisis.

The chronicler Miskawayh captured the unhurried management style of a particularly inert bureaucrat named al-Khasibi:

> Throughout his tenure of office Khasibi drank wine all night and slept during the day. When he woke he was fuddled, and had no energy left for work. So he assigned responsibility for the opening and reading of letters from the ministers of public security to an assistant, who also had to make notes on them and forward them to the various government departments … For important documents, either arriving or leaving, the assistant would make brief summaries, which he showed to the vizier when he woke, and the vizier sometimes read them and sometimes he did not. In the latter case they would be read by another assistant who would make such notes upon them as he chose. The summaries were written out by a third assistant, and at times would remain for days in the vizier's presence. And when they accumulated, the vizier would order them to be read out, and have comments as he thought proper entered under each paragraph. The summary would then be handed out to the first assistant, with whom it would

> remain for a day or two. It would then be delivered to the chief of the various departments, who would read it and enter such comments as he thought fit. Then an answer would be composed in the office, which would go first to the chief of the office, who would read it and mark it. Before the reply could be despatched, canals would have burst, breaches in the irrigation system would have widened, the Bedouin would have carried off the crops, or some other catastrophe would have happened which rendered the reply useless.[13]

THE BLAME FOR THIS absence of drive and confusion was laid at the feet of the caliph. Muqtadir's soft-heartedness, his ruinous love of luxury, his tolerance of corruption were, it was widely believed, symptoms of a far more serious problem: that he had allowed himself to become ensnared by the world of women. 'He avoided male companions – even minstrels,' Miskawayh wrote incredulously, 'and consorted with women so that slaves and women became supreme in the empire.'[14] 'Those who had power were women, servants and others,' wrote another, 'and this faulty leadership, which befell the empire, swept away whatever wealth or provisions were in the treasuries of the caliphate.'[15]

Modern historians look askance at such complaints. Nadia El Cheikh makes the point that, far from being a disruptive influence, Shaghab was more often a stabilising force in the palace who gave sound advice to her son, supported talented courtiers, and was quick to offer her personal riches for the defence of the state.[16] The instinctive chauvinism of the chroniclers may have obscured their ability to discern where the problem really lay: in the caliphate's dangerously overgrown, over-indulged army.

'BE HARMONIOUS, ENRICH the soldiers, and scorn all other men' was the deathbed advice given centuries earlier by the Roman Emperor Septimius Severus to his sons. The Roman military in Severus's time had cut itself loose from civilian control; emperors came and went at the pleasure of the legions, which demanded constant donatives to keep them at bay from the palace, or to fight on any emperor's – or would-be emperor's – behalf. So it was in the later Abbasid era: the army of the caliphate operated a vast protection racket, less interested in defending the empire of the Muslims than it was in squeezing money and privileges from its treasury. Opinion was divided on whether the army was a tool of the state, or the state was a tool of the army.

Muqtadir's Abbasid army was radically different from the armies of the early Muslim conquerors: the ranks of Arab and Persian warriors had been almost entirely displaced by Turkish slave soldiers. These troops, known as *ghilman* – 'serving lads' – had been captured or bought during boyhood from slave markets in Central Asia, then raised and educated in the house of the caliph. Trained as highly skilled horse archers, the *ghilman* knew no other life than that of the army and they formed a distinct community in Muslim society. The intent had been to create an elite force of outsiders, hardened to harsh conditions and committed only to the welfare of the caliph, but their deeper loyalties were to each other and their father-figure commanders.

Lacking a strong caliph to direct them, the army lost interest in safeguarding the empire and became preoccupied with extortion and intrigue, demanding regular pay rises and donatives at sword-point. State expenditure on the 40,000-man force ballooned to the point where it exceeded the entire revenue of the treasury year after year, bogging the empire in a state of continual crisis and a frantic search for revenue.

At the same time, tax revenue from the great *sawad* of Iraq, the black-soiled agricultural lands that ran down to the Persian Gulf, had shrunk dramatically. The complex irrigation systems that sustained these highly productive lands had broken down, ruined by floods, the Zanj Rebellion and neglect.[17] Desperate for income, viziers resorted to shaking down their disgraced predecessors, confiscating their wealth and property and tipping the funds into the army.

The Mission to the North

BURDENED BY A BLOATED, parasitic military, a demoralised bureaucracy, a bankrupt treasury and an indifferent caliph, Baghdad had steadily lost its grip on its empire. The administration gave little thought to extending its reach, concerned only with holding on to its existing domains – until, in 921, another envoy arrived in Baghdad with a proposition for the caliph.

The message was from Almish, King of the Bulgars, a people dwelling in the cold lands far to the north of the empire's borders, on the banks of the Volga River in modern-day Russia.

In his letter, King Almish declared his sincere desire to become a Muslim. He asked the caliph to send him someone to instruct him in the faith and teach his people the laws of Islam. He also requested money so that he could build a mosque and a stone fortress to protect his people against their mutual enemy, the neighbouring Khazars, who oppressed the Bulgars and forced them to pay tribute.

Despite the enormous distance between Almish's kingdom and Baghdad, this was a proposition that offered potential rewards to both parties: the Volga River had become a major trade artery, along which slaves, furs, amber and honey were carried from the Baltic down to the Caspian Sea, and from there to Baghdad, Constantinople and the cities of Central Asia. An alliance with Almish might allow the caliphate to capture a large part of that trade at the expense of the Khazar Khaganate. For his part, Almish would bring his people into the *ummah*, the community of Muslims, and make them all subject to the caliph. Almish was, in essence, asking for the tools to perform a kind of civilisational upgrade of his people; to be given the law, language, religion and settled stone buildings that would bring his kingdom of yurt-dwelling nomads into tenth-century modernity.

Almish's request was approved, and a special embassy recruited to travel to the Bulgar lands. Once there, the caliph's envoys were to accept the king's allegiance, give him the money for his mosque and fort, and teach the Bulgar people the laws of Islam. The mission would be a dangerous one, passing through hostile territory and bleak terrain.

The party was to be led by a special envoy, who would be accompanied by several jurists, teachers, guards and retainers. Two slave soldiers, Tikin the Turk and Bars the Slav, were included because of their familiarity with the languages and customs of the area. Also among the party was a court official named Ahmad ibn Fadlan.

WE KNOW NOTHING OF Ibn Fadlan's background, other than what can be gleaned from his writing. He seems to have been a well-educated bureaucrat, honourable and upright, a man well versed in the Quran and Islamic law and a somewhat prissy urbanite. It was he who would write the account of this strange mission to the north.*

* This account of Ibn Fadlan's journey is drawn from *Ibn Fadlan and the Land of Darkness: Arab Travellers in the Far North*, trans. P. Lunde & C. Stone, Penguin, 2012; and *Mission to the Volga*, trans. James Montgomery, New York University Press, 2017.

The eyewitness report he compiled of the mission to the Bulgars is categorised as a *risala*, a genre of Arabic literature defined as 'a piece of writing on a particular topic … composed in a literary style that excites the feelings of the readers'.[18] Ibn Fadlan would take care to be precise and factual in his observations, but there would be moments over the coming months when he would fear he was losing his mind.

The Travels of Ibn Fadlan the Diplomat

IBN FADLAN AND HIS companions joined a caravan that set out from the City of Peace on 21 June 921 in the midsummer heat. Following the old Khorasan silk road, the train of camels and horses filed out of the lush Tigris valley and onto the Iranian plateau. They stopped at several caravanserais to rest and feed their pack animals, and then passed through the Persian city of Rayy, keeping an eye out for bands of religious fanatics, which had become more predatory in recent years. The party headed east to Nishapur and then tacked north to Merv, where they rested for three days and purchased fresh camels for the seventy-five kilometre desert trek to the Amu Darya River. Crossing the river, they followed the silk road up to Bukhara.

THE THOUSAND-YEAR-OLD CITY of Bukhara was an assembly of creamy stone and brick buildings that turned golden in the afternoon light. After passing through the city gates, Ibn Fadlan and his associates were welcomed and given comfortable lodgings. Two days later they were granted an audience with the local emir, Nasr ibn Ahmad, who was fifteen years old. Nasr was a vassal of the caliph in name only, but he welcomed the envoys warmly and politely inquired after the wellbeing of Muqtadir.

Ibn Fadlan read Nasr an official letter from Baghdad, commanding his loyal emir to offer every assistance to the envoys. He was to provide them with several letters of passage for the road ahead, and to assist them in procuring 4000 dinars to be paid to the King of the Bulgars.

This was an awkward moment. The caliph hadn't actually provided his envoys with gold from the treasury – there was none; instead, he had decreed that the money was to be seized from an estate on the emir's lands that belonged to the disgraced Furat, the former vizier, who had again been jailed for corruption. The visitors explained that the money from Furat's estate was to be picked up by another emissary from Baghdad, a man named Ahmad ibn Musa, who would in turn bring it to the Bulgar King.

Nasr readily agreed to help collect the money. 'But where', he asked, 'is this Ahmad ibn Musa?'

The visitors were forced to admit that Ibn Musa was not yet with them. For reasons unknown, the money man had elected to leave four days after the main party had set out from Baghdad, but they expected him to join them any day now.

IBN FADLAN AND HIS companions lingered anxiously in Bukhara, waiting for their man to show up. Weeks passed and the weather cooled; still there was no sign of Ibn Musa. After waiting a whole month, members of the party began to fret about the onset of winter and the dangers of delaying their journey any longer. Ibn Musa would just have to catch up with them further down the road.

So they left Bukhara without him, and without the 4000 dinars promised to King Almish in the letter they were carrying.

IT WAS ONLY MUCH later that they learnt what had become of the luckless Ibn Musa: somehow, Furat's loyal property manager had got wind of the plan to seize the estate, and had sent letters to his soldiers and spies, ordering them to search every caravanserai and lookout post for the envoy. They eventually found Ibn Musa in Merv, and put him in chains.

The money, so critical to Ibn Fadlan's mission, would not be forthcoming.

HEADING OUT OF BUKHARA, the travellers returned to the Amu Darya River and hired boats, which ferried them 965 kilometres north, towards the province of Khwarezm in modern-day Uzbekistan.

Ibn Fadlan noticed their progress was slowing, as the days grew shorter and colder. He began to feel like a stranger in a strange land. To him, the Khwarezmi people sounded like birds twittering. In another village, he thought the locals spoke like croaking frogs.

In the Khwarezmian city of Kath, the envoys were given accommodation and then brought before the local Muslim shah. He gave the party a hearty welcome, but after hearing of their mission he said he could not possibly allow them to proceed; it was simply too dangerous. 'There are a thousand infidel tribes in your path,' he warned. 'The caliph has been seriously misled in this. I will write to the emir in Bukhara, so he in turn can write to the caliph and consult with him. In the meantime, you must wait here until we receive an answer.'

Ibn Fadlan and his companions groaned inwardly at the prospect of being stuck in Khwarezm while the agonisingly slow exchange of letters played out over weeks and months. It was clearly a ploy to thwart the alliance with the Bulgars. When the envoys returned to the shah several days later, they begged him to let them continue. 'We have the caliph's orders clearly stated in this letter,' Ibn Fadlan said. 'So why do you need to consult him again on this?'

With that, the shah agreed to let them move on.

BY NOW THE Amu Darya River had frozen over with a thick crust of ice, firm enough to bear the weight of their carts, camels and horses. The icy weather, Ibn Fadlan wrote, was like 'the burning cold of hell'. Howling blizzards blasted their faces as they advanced still further into the north.

Arriving at the city of Jurjaniyah, at the entrance to the bleak isthmus between the Caspian and Aral Seas, the expedition decided to hibernate for three months to wait out the worst of the winter.

Ibn Fadlan was touched by the Jurjanis' hospitality; even strangers and beggars could simply walk into a house, warm themselves by the fire and be given bread. But it was still impossible for him to get warm. At night, he would wrap himself in cloaks and pelts, and then creep inside his tent, a Turkish yurt covered in animal skins that was enclosed within another tent. Even so, he sometimes woke in the morning with his cheek frozen to the pillow. Returning from the bathhouse one day, he noticed his beard had become a solid block of ice that he had to thaw in front of the fire.

Outside, the bleak weather had emptied the streets of Jurjaniyah. Tall trees cracked and split open with the cold. Ibn Fadlan was told by the Jurjanis that two men had gone out recently with their camels to gather firewood, but had forgotten to take a flint and tinderbox.

In the morning, they and their camels had been found icy and rigid in the snow.

IN LATE FEBRUARY, the weather warmed slightly and the Amu Darya thawed into an icy slush. The members of the expedition packed collapsible boats made of camel hide and wicker for the river crossings that lay ahead. But not everyone would be continuing with them. As they prepared to leave, a jurist, a teacher and several retainers admitted they'd had enough; they were too frightened to enter the lands of the Turks and would be turning back.

Ibn Fadlan had also by now resigned any hope that Ibn Musa would show up with the money for Almish. He fretted over what would happen when he arrived in the Bulgar kingdom without the 4000 dinars promised to the king.

'He will demand this money,' Ibn Fadlan told his companions.

'He won't ask us for it,' they replied. 'Don't worry so much.'

'I *know* he will demand it.'

ON 4 MARCH 922, the expedition, somewhat reduced in numbers, hired a local guide and joined another caravan heading north. The Jurjanis had warned them of the harrowing cold they were riding into, but Ibn Fadlan found the conditions even worse than they'd described. To protect themselves against the biting wind, each member of the party wore a kaftan and padded pants, covered by a sheepskin cloak and then another hooded cloak made of animal felt that covered everything except the eyes. Perched on top of a camel, the thickly swaddled Ibn Fadlan found he could barely move, but there was nothing for it. 'We put our trust in almighty God,' he wrote, 'and placed our fate in His hands.'

The party passed through the final outpost of the Muslim lands, the Gate of the Turks, without incident. The road led them up onto the Ustyurt Plateau, a frozen desert of rocky clay valleys framed by low, wind-blasted, limestone cliffs. In the warmer months, the area resembles Monument Valley in the southwest United States, with its reddish stone pinnacles and flat-topped mesas. It was once the basin of a prehistoric sea that had dried up eons earlier, leaving traces of sharks' teeth and ammonite sea shells in the rock,[19] which might have brought to mind the flood of Noah, had the travellers been able to see them through the snowstorm.

The party saw no other soul for days on end. 'Compared to this,' Ibn Fadlan recorded, 'the days of cold in Khwarezm were like summer.' The snow-blind party lost all sense of time and space in the shapeless white void: 'We forgot all that had happened to us in the past and almost perished.'

Ibn Fadlan saw Tikin the slave soldier talking with a fellow Turk and laughing. Then Tikin trotted alongside Ibn Fadlan and said, 'This Turk wants me to ask you: "What does God want of us? He is killing us with this cold. If we knew what He wanted, we could just give it to Him."'

'Tell him that what God wants of you is this: that you should say, "There is no god but God."'

Tikin laughed and said, 'Well, if we knew Him, then we'd do it.'

THE CARAVAN PRESSED ON until they came to the edge of a forest where they could gather dried branches to make a fire. At last the miserable travellers were able to strip off and dry their snow-drenched clothes.

The expedition adopted a new routine: striking camp at midnight, then setting out until the midday or afternoon prayer, when they would stop and rest. After fifteen days of this, they came to the foot of a huge rocky mountain, with rivulets of spring water running down into a lake. Crossing the mountain, they came upon a camp of Oghuz Turks, a semi-nomadic tribe dwelling in animal-hair tents, spaced out on the lonely plain and interspersed with herds of sheep that milled around, scratching away at the snowy ground to find the little thatches of pasture underneath.

The Oghuz were a pragmatic people, proficient in a range of skills that sustained them in an unforgiving landscape, but these qualities were lost on Ibn Fadlan and his companions. The Oghuz would have had far more in common with the visitors' Bedouin ancestors than with the shivering Baghdadis who had wandered into their camp. The tribespeople nonetheless extended their unstinting hospitality to the visitors, providing them with several yurts and a live sheep, so they might slaughter it in accordance with the dictates of Islam.

But Ibn Fadlan could find nothing good to say about his hosts. Like nomadic peoples the world over, the Oghuz practised an egalitarian form of politics, deciding matters by absolute consensus: a procedure that Ibn Fadlan scorned as a recipe for group paralysis. He was horrified by their 'wretched lives'. The Oghuz, he said, were like 'asses gone astray': unenlightened and without recourse to reason. To make a good impression they might declare, 'There is no god but God, and Muhammad is his Messenger', but when something went wrong, they would raise their heads to the Heavens and shout, 'Bir Tengri!', a cry to the pagan sky-god worshipped by herders of the Great Eurasian Steppe, the open pastural plains running across Northern and Central Asia.

Despite the bitter cold, Ibn Fadlan diligently performed his ritual ablutions before prayer, a practice integral to maintaining his sense of himself as a civilised man in the badlands of the north. He was disgusted by the Oghuz's aversion to cleanliness. 'They do not wash themselves when they defecate and urinate,' he noted, 'and do not clean themselves when intercourse puts them in a state of impurity.' He seemed unaware of their need to conserve water in such an arid environment. For their part, the Oghuz distrusted the Muslims' ritual cleansing, suspecting them of performing some kind of sinister magic spell upon the water.

But nothing appalled Ibn Fadlan so much as the immodesty of the Oghuz women, who refused to veil their faces, or any other part of their bodies if it suited them. One afternoon, while sitting in the tent of an Oghuz husband and wife, Ibn Fadlan was horrified to see the wife pull aside her clothes and openly scratch at her crotch.

'God forgive me,' Ibn Fadlan muttered, while burying his face in his hands. 'God forgive me.'

The husband burst out laughing and told the interpreter, 'Tell him this: my wife uncovers her private parts in your presence, and you see them, but she allows no one near them. This is better than covering them up and letting you get at them!'

And indeed, Ibn Fadlan noted, adultery was almost unknown among the Oghuz. If they found someone guilty of this crime, they told him they would place the culprit between two trees, bend down a strong branch from each, and tie it to an arm. Then they would simply let the branches spring back, tearing the man in two.

BEFORE IBN FADLAN and his companions could move on, they had to receive permission for their passage from an Oghuz chieftain, a man named Yinal the Younger. Yinal was friendly, but obstructive. He told them he couldn't possibly permit the caliph's expedition to continue through these dangerous lands. It was unheard of, unthinkable. But when presented with a Jurjani kaftan, along with some bread, raisins and nuts, Yinal relented and allowed them to move on.

The next morning the caravan was held up on the road by a single unkempt Turkish soldier who stood in the rain and ordered them to halt. 'Not one of you will pass,' he said.

'But we are friends of Yinal, your chieftain,' they objected.

The soldier laughed. 'What is this chieftain?' he said. 'I shit on the chieftain's beard!' Then he laughed again and demanded they give him some flatbread. They did this and he waved them on.

'Pass,' he said. 'I have taken pity on you.'

FURTHER ALONG THE ROAD, they entered a camp of Oghuz horse archers. The commander, Atrak, assigned them several yurts for shelter and treated them to a great feast. Ibn Fadlan was impressed by Atrak and observed him closely; he saw that the commander had plucked every hair from his lip and chin, making him look like a hairless eunuch. The visitors presented Atrak with silver coins, three portions of musk, some fine cloth from Merv, leather slippers, silk garments and a brocade robe. There was also a veil and a ring for Atrak's wife, who had previously been married to Atrak's recently deceased father. Ibn Fadlan watched as she picked up a bundle of the gifts, took them outside, then buried them in a hole, saying, 'This is a gift for Qataghan, the father of Atrak. The Arabs offer this to him.'

That night, Ibn Fadlan and his interpreter were granted an audience with Atrak in his tent, where he read the commander a letter from Baghdad, urging him to embrace Islam. Atrak said he would think about it, and let them know his decision on their return. In the meantime, he was eager to try on the brocaded coat the Arabs had given him. When he stripped off his old coat, Ibn Fadlan saw that the tunic underneath was a filthy rag; it was the Oghuz's custom, he said, never to wash or remove an item of clothing until it had fallen to pieces.

Ibn Fadlan was nonetheless impressed by the charismatic warrior, who was said to be the most skilful of all the Turkish horsemen. One day, while riding with him, Ibn Fadlan saw a goose fly overhead. He turned to see Atrak string his bow, ride up under the goose, and shoot it down from the sky.

DESPITE THE EVIDENT good will between Atrak and the visitors, his senior men were suspicious of the interlopers from Baghdad and unsure what to do with them. Atrak summoned his four best men and asked them for advice on this.

The first to speak was the most eminent among them, who was blind and lame and had a withered hand. 'This is something new for us,' he said. 'Never in our lives has an envoy of the caliph come into our lands. I can only think this is some trick; their true mission is to the kingdom of the Khazars, where they will mobilise an army against us.' There really was no choice, he said: they must chop the envoys in half and seize all their possessions.

Atrak's second advisor adopted a more reasonable tone; he said they should refrain from dismembering their guests, but they should indeed take their goods and clothes, then send them back the way they had come, naked.

The third advisor had another idea: he said they should hold the envoys captive and ransom them in a prisoner exchange with the Khazars.

The debate continued for days, while the visitors waited to learn their fate. Then on the seventh day, Atrak blandly announced they were all free to go. A relieved Ibn Fadlan presented him with another robe of honour, along with coats for his disgruntled advisors, and the party moved on.

THE CALIPH'S MEN rode further north, past the Caspian Sea. At the Yaghindi River, they assembled their camel-skin boats, placed their goods on board, and paddled furiously to the other side, fighting the current. They crossed another three mighty rivers in the same way, keeping a nervous eye out for bandits.

At the Ural River, the largest and swiftest they'd encountered so far, Ibn Fadlan watched in anguish from a distance as one of the camel-skin boats, laden with people and goods, got caught in a cross-current. The boat flipped over, tossing those on board into the rapids, where they drowned. Horses and camels were also lost midstream.

The survivors who assembled on the far side found themselves in the lands of the Bashkirs, another tribe of nomads whom Ibn Fadlan describes as 'the wickedest, filthiest and most ferocious of the Turks'. The Bashkir warriors, he saw, wore carved wooden phalluses around their necks, which they kissed and prayed to before going into battle. Ibn Fadlan asked one of them why he worshipped such an idol. 'Because', he said, 'I came from such a thing and I cannot imagine anything else to be my creator.'

Like those of the Oghuz, the personal habits of the Bashkirs made Ibn Fadlan's head swim. He looked on in horror one day as a Bashkir riding alongside their party extricated a louse from his clothes, popped it between his fingers and then shoved it in his mouth. 'Delicious!' the Bashkir said, clearly enjoying Ibn Fadlan's discomfort.

The Kingdom of the Bulgars

THERE WERE MORE RIVERS to cross, and then, after a journey of 4800 kilometres, the expedition at last entered the country of the Bulgars, an expanse of flat grassy plains, intercut with winding watercourses feeding into the river system.

On the road they were met by the king's brothers and sons, who formally escorted them to the capital, Bulgar, which lay at the confluence of the Upper Volga and Kama Rivers, close to the modern-day Russian city of Kazan.

King Almish welcomed the expedition with great fanfare and full honours, going as far as to dismount from his horse and prostrate himself, giving thanks to God. Almish then produced handfuls of silver coins from his sleeve and showered them onto the caliph's men. The honoured guests were led to their tents to relax and recover from their long journey. It was now mid-May; they had been travelling for almost an entire year.

FOUR DAYS LATER, the king's commanders and subjects from near and far assembled in the royal tent for the reading of the caliph's letter. The tent was enormous, sheltering a huge mass of people, and the ground was carpeted with Armenian rugs that led up to the thrones of the king and queen, brocaded in colourful Byzantine silk.

The envoys unfurled the caliphal banners and approached the throne to ceremonially dress Almish in a black robe and turban. The donning of such a robe was an act rich in symbolism: it signified both the bestowing of a mantle of honour, and an acceptance of the donor's sovereignty.

Ibn Fadlan, acting as spokesman, then came forward holding the caliph's message and announced that all were required to stand for the reading. The king obligingly rose to his feet, as did everyone else. Ibn Fadlan read out the caliph's words, pausing occasionally to prompt the correct responses from the crowd. At the conclusion, the assembly cried out thunderously, 'Allahu akbar!' – 'God is great!'

Ibn Fadlan read out several more letters from lesser officials, and then brought forward gifts for the queen – perfume, fine clothes, a string of pearls and a robe of honour, which she received while her attendants sprinkled coins over her. The ceremony was now complete, and the envoys could return to their tents well satisfied. It was all going so well.

That night, they returned to the king's tent for a formal dinner. Almish, who was stout and broad, made for an impressive sight in his new ceremonial robes, surrounded by his sons and chieftains. A table of roasted meat was brought to the king; he sliced off several choice cuts and ate them, then sliced off more pieces for his guests.

After the meal, they were served a honeyed wine called *suju*. Almish drained his cup and toasted the caliph: 'Such is my joy in my patron, the Commander of the Faithful. May God grant him long life!' He did this three times and the party broke up in good spirits.

THE FOLLOWING DAY, the king approached Ibn Fadlan for advice; he said he was now uneasy about having his name proclaimed from the pulpit during the Friday oration, because he still carried the name of his late father, an unbeliever. Almish humbly asked if it would be appropriate to adopt the name of the caliph, his new lord and protector, as his father. Ibn Fadlan assured him this would be most acceptable.

Almish had fully embraced the faith and the caliph. Despite the terrible hardships of the journey, the mission appeared to have been a total success.

TWO DAYS LATER, the king summoned Ibn Fadlan to his tent and told him to sit down. Then he threw the caliph's letter at him. 'Who brought me this letter?' he asked.

Ibn Fadlan admitted that he had done so.

'And this one?' he said, throwing the vizier's letter at him.

'I did.'

'Then what have you done with the money mentioned in these letters?' roared the king, whose voice seemed to come from inside a barrel.

Ibn Fadlan explained that another man had been sent to collect the king's money and bring it to him, but they had not seen him since they left Baghdad.

'But you have all arrived,' said the king. 'My patron the caliph has entrusted you with this money so I may build a fortress to protect me against the Khazars, who have tried to make me their slave!'

'We did our best,' Ibn Fadlan replied, feebly.

Almish then told Ibn Fadlan that he did not hold any other of the caliph's men responsible for the missing money. Only him.

'I do not expect to receive one single dirham from anyone but you,' he said. 'Produce the money. This would be the best thing for you to do.'

IBN FADLAN NOW FELT himself to be in great danger. The king regarded him as a thief. 'I warned you about this,' Ibn Fadlan told his companions. Without the money, their mission was going to fail and their long journey would be rendered pointless.

No longer honoured guests, the caliph's men were effectively Almish's prisoners, forbidden to leave his lands. And they would have to eat the local foods, which they found repugnant. 'Everything was unwholesome and greasy,' Ibn Fadlan moaned. The meat was often rancid; the local apples were tart and acidic. Worst of all, everything was cooked not in the fine olive oil the Arabs were accustomed to, but in foul-smelling fish oil. Fortunately there were jugs of honeyed wine at hand to wash it all down, and delicious berries could be found in the thickets. And there was a certain kind of tall tree in the forest which, when tapped, oozed out a sweet, syrupy sap that the Arabs found more intoxicating than wine.

AS THE WEEKS went by, Ibn Fadlan tried to make up for the missing money by freely offering his services as a religious advisor. He corrected the king's *muezzin*, who had been doubling the lines of the call to prayer.

'These phrases are sung only once in the realm of the caliph,' he advised Almish.

The king accordingly instructed the *muezzin*, 'Do this as he tells you.'

Meanwhile, Ibn Fadlan encouraged the king to forgive the missing money, deftly using his knowledge of law and moral argument. Then the king quietly ordered the *muezzin* to go back to doubling the phrases of the call to prayer. When Ibn Fadlan heard this, he marched out of his tent and shouted at the *muezzin* to be silent.

Almish immediately summoned the Arab to him. He turned to his interpreter and said, 'Ask Ibn Fadlan if the single call to prayer is permissible or impermissible.'

'It is permissible,' Ibn Fadlan replied through the interpreter.

'There is no disagreement on this?'

'There is not.'

'Now ask him if it is permissible in the laws of Islam to steal money intended for a group of people who are weak, beset by troubles and on the verge of slavery.'

'It is impermissible,' Ibn Fadlan replied.

'There is no disagreement on this?' the king asked.

'There is not.'

Almish then asked if there was any reason why he and his people should fear invasion from the armies of the caliph, or from the Emir of Khorasan.

'No, there is not,' Ibn Fadlan admitted.

'Is it because of the great distance, and the many infidel tribes between us?'

"Of course,' he answered.

'So,' the king said, 'here we are now in this far-off land, you and I, and yet I still fear my patron, the Commander of the Faithful. I fear his curse. If he should learn something about me to displease him, I think I would die on the spot, despite the vast distance between my kingdom and his.'

The king turned his gaze on Ibn Fadlan.

'And yet you who eat his bread, wear his fine clothes, and look to him every day, you have betrayed him in this mission he has entrusted to you, a mission to a needy people. And you have betrayed all Muslims. I will accept no instructions from you in matters of religion, until an honest, learned man comes to me. When such a man comes, I will accept what he says.'

Ibn Fadlan found himself defeated by the king's legal argument. He could think of nothing to say, and shuffled out of the king's tent.

DESPITE THIS DRESSING DOWN, Almish soon resumed friendly relations with the miserable Ibn Fadlan, while ignoring the other members of the mission. Almish may well have enjoyed conversing and jousting with an educated man, but there was an edge of menace to the banter. The Bulgars joked that when they encountered a learned man, their custom was to say, 'This man deserves to serve our Lord.' Then they would take a rope and hang him so they could despatch the clever man to God straight away.

After a while, Ibn Fadlan felt emboldened to ask Almish, 'O king, your kingdom is vast, your wealth is great, the taxes you raise are considerable. Why then did you ask the caliph to pay for a fortress?'

The king smiled. 'Yes,' he said, 'I could easily have built a fortress with my own silver and gold, but I know the empire of Islam is rich beyond belief, and I wanted the blessings that would come from the money of the Commander of the Faithful. That is why I sent the petition to him.'

THE STRANGENESS OF THIS land, so far from the comforts and warmth of Baghdad, began to overwhelm Ibn Fadlan. In the northern summer, the days grew so long and the nights so short that he confused the times of the call to prayer. 'In this country,' he wrote, 'I saw uncounted marvels.' He'd never seen so much lightning in the sky. And he noted that when a bolt struck someone's tent, the Bulgars would not go near it, understanding it to be a tent upon which the wrath of God had fallen; they would simply leave the yurt as it was, with everything and everyone still smouldering inside.

One day in the forest, as Ibn Fadlan approached a fallen tree trunk, it suddenly twisted and writhed, and then slithered into the undergrowth. He'd never seen a snake so large. When he asked the king about it, Almish reassured him, 'Have no fear. It can do you no harm.' When he asked the king about rumours that a rhinoceros lived nearby, Almish showed him three large bowls that he claimed had been carved from the animal's horn.

THERE WERE MORE oversized creatures to reckon with. Tikin the Turkish slave soldier had told him that a giant had once lived in these lands. The existence of giants was commonly acknowledged among medieval Arab people. They had only to inspect the Pyramids of Giza, or the ruins of ancient Ctesiphon, just thirty kilometres south of Baghdad, with its gigantic archway still intact, the largest of its kind in the world. Who else but an army of giants could have built such colossal things?

When Ibn Fadlan asked Almish if a giant really had once dwelt among them, Almish said it was true, but he was dead now. He said that when the Volga burst its banks some years ago, some merchants reported they'd seen a terrifying giant swimming down the river. Almish insisted the merchants take him to see this awesome creature. 'He was twelve cubits tall,' Almish told Ibn Fadlan. 'His head was as big as a cooking pot. His eyes were huge, and his nose was more than a span long.' Almish had tried to speak with the giant, but the creature merely gazed at him in silence.

The king had brought the giant back to the capital and put him up in his own home, but he worried about the creature's origins. He wrote a letter to the people of Wisu in the far north, who warned him that the giant was a creature of Gog and Magog, who had somehow slipped out from behind Alexander's wall.

The giant soon became a malignant presence among Almish's people. Children would drop dead when they saw him. Pregnant women miscarried. And so, Almish said, he had ordered the giant to be killed, and they hanged him from a high tree in the forest.

'If you want to see his bones,' Almish told Ibn Fadlan, 'I will gladly take you.'

And so they rode out to a high tree in the forest, where Ibn Fadlan saw a heap of oversized bones lying at its base. He was frightened, but Almish shoved him forward to inspect the remains. The skull, he saw, was as big as a beehive; the ribs, arms and legs were like the branches of a tree. The skeletal remains, possibly those of a bear or some other creature, discombobulated him. 'I departed', he wrote, 'filled with wonder.'

BUT NOTHING ASTONISHED Ibn Fadlan as much as the visions in the sky. Late one afternoon, he saw a bright red smear of light across the horizon, and a great roaring din rose up from all around. Above his heads he saw a cloud swirling in a fiery red mist, and from it emerged the shapes of ghostly cavalrymen on horseback with swords and spears. Then from a similar cloud, another army of spectres on horseback charged forward and crashed into the first group. The clash of the celestial armies continued for an hour, while Ibn Fadlan and his companions fell to their knees and begged for God's protection.

The Bulgar people were unperturbed by the spectacle, which was most likely an aurora borealis. 'They are the believing and the unbelieving *jinn*,' explained the king. 'They fight every evening and have done so since for as long as anyone can remember.'

Ibn Fadlan was already feeling a million miles from the light and learning of the City of Peace when a large party of Vikings arrived on the Volga.

The Angel of Death

IN THE AGE OF VIKING expansion, Norse raiders had set out in all directions from their Scandinavian homelands: some groups sailed west to Iceland and Greenland; others went south to Britain and France; while other Viking parties from Sweden travelled east across the Baltic Sea into the forests and rivers of modern-day Russia. Sometime in the eighth century, these Vikings reached Lake Ladoga, near modern-day St Petersburg. There they forged alliances with the eastern Slavs, building the trading posts that became the cities of Kiev and Novgorod.

In the early spring, Viking traders would carve out their flat-hulled longboats from hollowed tree trunks. When the winter ice melted, they would sail with their cargoes of furs, wax, honey, walrus ivory, swords and slaves along Russia's fast-flowing river systems, down to the Caspian and Black Seas. Wherever there were dangerous rapids, the men would disembark and haul their boats across the terrain with their hands.

It was one such party of Viking traders that arrived in the Bulgar capital on that day in 922. Ibn Fadlan looked on in fascination as the tall painted pagans moored their longboats, and brought their slaves and other trading goods ashore. Then they set to work, assembling a campsite of timber huts on the river's edge.

IT'S UNCLEAR WHETHER these Volga Vikings were primarily Norse or Slavic, but most likely they were a mix of the two. Ibn Fadlan identified them as the Rusiyyah, antecedents of today's Russians. He was, at first, excited by their physical beauty: 'I have never seen bodies more perfect than theirs,' he wrote. 'They are as tall as palm trees, fair and reddish.' The men, he saw, had dark green painted tattoos snaking all the way up from their toes to their necks; each of them wore a cloak draped over one shoulder, and carried an axe, a knife and a broad sword. The women wore gold and silver torques ringed around their arms and necks, and strings of dark ceramic beads. Their woollen tunics were fastened by a brooch pin, with a ring and a knife dangling from it.

The pious Ibn Fadlan was both appalled and intrigued by their pagan rites. He observed a Viking trader make an offering to his gods by jamming a block of wood etched with a human face into the ground, then encircling it with little figurines. Having laid food and drink in front of the idol, the trader begged the gods to send him a wealthy merchant who would buy all his goods and not haggle over the price. When his business went slowly, he brought more gifts for the little figurines and asked for their intercession. Once he had sold all his goods, he thanked his gods by slaughtering some cows and sheep. Some of the meat he set down in front of the idol. At nightfall, after the dogs had eaten up the sacrifice, he declared, 'My Lord is pleased with me and has eaten my offering.'

The fastidious Ibn Fadlan reeled at the Vikings' daily ablutions. He deplored their willingness to shit in the open, with no regard for squeamish onlookers. Each morning, a slave girl would come around with a large basin of fresh water for her master, who would wash his face and hands, then wet his hair from the bowl and comb it out. Then, after blowing his nose into the basin and spitting into it, he would pass the basin on to the next man, who also washed, spat and blew his nose into it. This ritual was repeated with the same bowl by every man in the house.

The flagrant cruelty of the men distressed him. 'They have intercourse with their female slaves in full view of their companions,' he wrote. 'Sometimes, they do this as a group in front of each other. If a merchant comes to buy the slave girl while her master is having intercourse with her, he does not get off her until he has satisfied his urge.'

IBN FADLAN WAS TOLD one day that a chieftain among the Volga Vikings had died. After the chieftain's wealth was divided, his family temporarily interred his body in an open grave covered by timber.

Then they summoned the chieftain's young slaves and asked, 'Who will die with him?'

One of the slave girls said, 'I will.'

Once these words were spoken, Ibn Fadlan was told, they could not be undone.

The unnamed slave girl's decision made her, for a short while, a bride to her dead master. Two handmaidens were appointed to attend to her; each day they would exalt her, give her wine and wash her feet with their hands. They gave her bracelets, anklets and combs for her hair.

WHILE THE SLAVE GIRL and her attendants drank and sang, the men constructed a wooden platform on the shore. They hauled the chieftain's longboat onto it and built a tent with a bed inside the hull. Ibn Fadlan saw people going back and forth, muttering phrases he did not understand.

Then a witch-woman they called 'the Angel of Death' came forward. The sight of this large, sinister woman chilled Ibn Fadlan. She stepped onto the funeral boat, entered the tent, and scattered quilts and silk cushions across the bed.

The body of the chieftain was then brought up from his temporary grave. Ibn Fadlan saw that his skin had blackened from the cold. The dead man was dressed in trousers, boots and a fine kaftan with gold buttons; on his head was fixed a brocade and sable cap. The corpse in all its finery was then lifted onto the boat, brought into the tent and propped up on the bed with the cushions. Fine foods, wine and weaponry were arrayed around him.

Ibn Fadlan saw the Viking men seize a dog, cleave it in half, then throw the pieces into the boat. They cut up horses, cows and chickens with swords, and their meat was also thrown into the boat.

While this was taking place, the sacrificial slave girl went in and out of the tents of the senior men. Ibn Fadlan records that 'the master of each pavilion had intercourse with her, saying: "Tell your master that I only did this out of love for you."'

IN THE LATE AFTERNOON, the slave girl was led to an upright rectangular structure resembling a doorframe. Then she placed her feet into the hands of two men, who hoisted her up so she could peer over this frame.

'Look!' she said. 'I can see my dead mother and father.'

The second time they brought her up she said, 'Look! I can see my dead kinfolk sitting there.'

The third time she said, 'Look! I can see my dead master. Paradise is green and beautiful. There are people with him and he is calling for me.'

They put her feet back down on the grass.

'Take me to him,' she said.

THE MEN BROUGHT HER to the funeral boat, where she removed the two bracelets from her wrists and handed them to the Angel of Death. Then she removed her anklets and gave them to the young girls who had been serving her; these were the daughters of the Angel of Death.

Men came forward and lifted her onto the deck of the boat. More men came with shields and sticks and handed her a cup of wine. She sang an incantation over the cup and then drained it. Ibn Fadlan's interpreter whispered to him: 'Now she is bidding her female friends goodbye.'

The slave girl drank another cup of wine. She sang and drank some more. The witch-woman passed her cup after cup.

THEN THE ANGEL of Death invited the slave girl to enter the tent and join her master. But by now she was very groggy, and she stumbled, catching her head between the tent and the boat. The old woman grabbed her head and pushed her inside the tent. Outside, the men bashed their sticks on their shields so no one could hear the slave girl's cries.

'Six men followed her into the tent,' Ibn Fadlan recorded. 'They all had intercourse with her, one after the other, then they laid her beside her master.'

Her hands and feet were pinned down. A rope was looped around her neck. Two men pulled on the rope, strangling her, as the Angel of Death stepped forward with a dagger and stabbed her between her ribs until she was dead.

AFTER THE LIVING stepped off the funeral boat, a naked man came forward, a close relative of the dead chieftain. He took a stick of wood and lit the end of it on a bonfire. He then walked backwards towards the boat – one hand holding the fire stick, the other covering his behind – and ignited the wood that had been stacked and bundled underneath. More men came forward with burning sticks and logs and tossed them into the pyre.

The wind picked up. The flames roared up and engulfed the wood, the boat and then the tent and everything in it.

IBN FADLAN MUST have looked shocked, because one of the Viking men muttered something about him to the interpreter. Ibn Fadlan asked the interpreter what he had said.

'He told me, "You Arabs are fools."'

'Why is that?'

'Because,' he said, 'you put your best men into the earth, where worms and insects gnaw at them. We burn them at once, so they enter Paradise instantly.'

And indeed, within an hour, the ship, the wood, the master and the slave girl had disintegrated into a heap of fine ash.

IBN FADLAN'S REPORT is the only eyewitness report we have of a Viking ship cremation and human sacrifice. Medieval accounts of Viking atrocities were often luridly exaggerated, but Ibn Fadlan's meticulously detailed account rings true, and there is archaeological evidence that Norse peoples did at times sacrifice slaves to their dead masters. In some Viking burial sites extra bodies have been unearthed lying next to the honoured dead. In Birka, Sweden, the bones of an elderly man were found laid out with elk antlers behind his head, and the skeleton of a decapitated younger man draped on top of him.[20] Another burial site uncovered in Gerdrup, Denmark, contained the skeleton of a middle-aged noblewoman accompanied by her grave goods – an iron knife, a lance and a needle – and the remains of a man with bound feet and a twisted, broken neck.[21]

In the *Poetic Edda*, one of the main texts of Norse mythology, such sacrifices are presented as the price of occult knowledge. Odin, chief of the gods, chooses to pierce himself with a spear, then suspend himself upside down from the world-tree, Yggdrasil, for nine days, until the secret knowledge of runes is revealed to him. He does this willingly, he says, as a sacrifice *of* himself *to* himself.[22]

MUSLIMS AND CHRISTIANS who survived their encounters with the Norsemen were often left traumatised or in a state of furious awe. But the language in Ibn Fadlan's account of the Viking funeral is curiously spare; the horror is embedded in the bare bones of his narrative. Although he stresses the voluntary nature of the slave girl's decision to die, we can only guess at her reasons. Perhaps it was the only escape she could think of from the miseries of sexual slavery, and her decision did grant her a few days as an honoured bride for the dead chieftain. Peering over the doorframe, it seems she was convinced she was racing towards a joyful afterlife.

But perhaps all that was a lie, and the slave girl was coerced into that tent, delivered into the hands of the Angel of Death and her accomplices as they revelled in a kind of homicidal ecstasy. We don't know. But we can at least be certain that the ordeal of the Viking slave girl, a rite steeped in blood, sex and magic, carried her, and the ceremony's participants, right out to the furthest edge of human experience.

AFTER THE VIKING FUNERAL, Ibn Fadlan's narrative runs on a little longer, then abruptly breaks off. The pages relating his journey back home are missing. We can only assume that Almish gave up on getting his money and released Ibn Fadlan and his compatriots, and that he returned to Baghdad or perhaps Bukhara, where he penned the story of the expedition to the north in comfortable and familiar surroundings, but we know nothing more of Ibn Fadlan's fate. His account, it seems, was copied out, deposited here and there, and then forgotten.

SOME THREE HUNDRED years went by. Then, in 1219, a Muslim scholar, Yaqut al-Rumi, came across a copy of Ibn Fadlan's report in a library in Merv. He took some quotes from it for his compendious *Dictionary of Places*, and for the next seven centuries, these scattered quotes appeared to be all that was left of Ibn Fadlan's account.

Then, in 1923, a man named Zeki Velidi Togan happened to be searching through an ancient library attached to a shrine in the Iranian city of Mashhad. In a sheaf of old documents, Togan found a complete copy of Ibn Fadlan's manuscript (minus the missing pages at the end). Togan was himself a remarkable man, a Bashkir nationalist leader and historian. At the outset of the 1917 Russian Revolution, Togan had allied himself with the Bolsheviks, but when Moscow refused to grant autonomy to his native Bashkortostan in the Volga region, he led an uprising against Lenin and Stalin, who was then the Bolshevik Commissar of Nationalities. The revolt was quashed and Togan was forced to flee into Iran, where he serendipitously stumbled upon Ibn Fadlan's manuscript.

Zeki Velidi Togan, c. 1917

Togan published a German translation in 1939, but it was only in 1979 that the account was translated into English. Author Michael Crichton incorporated parts of the story, including the Viking funeral, into his novel *Eaters of the Dead*, which was subsequently adapted into a movie, *The 13th Warrior*, starring Antonio Banderas as Ibn Fadlan. The raising up of the slave girl above the doorframe appears in the Robert Eggers film, *The Northman*.

He Creates Mankind and I Destroy It

THE CALIPHATE THAT Ibn Fadlan returned to after his years in the north had become further ensnared in lethargy and confusion. The slow bleeding of the treasury's finances, the unceasing demands of the army, the constant arrest and reinstatement of senior officials, and the enervation of the Caliph Muqtadir in the face of these troubles, had paralysed the administration of his empire. The peace concluded in 917 with Constantinople was soon broken, and in 926, Roman armies retook parts of Anatolia and Armenia.

At the same time, a lethal revolutionary force had resurfaced within the caliphate. Muqtadir's predecessors had been tormented by the Qarmatians, an apocalyptic Shia cult that had emerged from the deserts of Syria and Arabia. Although small in number, bands of Qarmatian raiders were able to launch lightning raids on Abbasid cities and trade routes, then slip back into the desert, just as the first Muslim warriors had attacked the cities of the failing Sassanid empire with impunity centuries earlier.

By the early tenth century, the Qarmatians had built their own stronghold in Bahrain on the Arabian coast. Their capital, al-Ahsa, operated on utopian, communal principles for their followers, but was sustained by the labour of thousands of Ethiopian slaves. The Qarmatians were at once fervidly religious and savagely amoral in pursuit of their ideals; like many of the Christian cults that would later emerge in Europe, they were willing to cleanse the earth with blood to prepare the way for their messiah, the Mahdi, who would bring down God's judgement and set in train the End of Days.

IN 923, A QARMATIAN warlord named Abu Tahir al-Jannabi led a series of devastating raids on several Abbasid cities. In 924, he and his followers fell on the already badly ravaged city of Basra, massacring its inhabitants. By the time the caliph's troops arrived, the Qarmatians had already looted everything they could carry, burnt down everything they couldn't, and disappeared back into the desert.

The climate of dread intensified when Qarmatian raiders attacked the *hajj* caravan from Iraq that same year, as it made its way towards Mecca. Male pilgrims who resisted were slaughtered and their bodies dumped on the road; women and children were carried off as slaves. The rest were left behind in the desert with no transport, no food, no water and no clothes.

The news of this outrage, when it arrived in Baghdad, induced a kind of 'fear-psychosis' and furious recriminations.[23] Furat, now in his third term as vizier, became a figure of hate on the streets. Furious Baghdadis accused him of being a Qarmatian agent and threw rocks at his barge as it passed down the Tigris. Furat tried to bribe his way out of trouble, but it was no good; Muqtadir was obliged to dismiss him once more. He intended to spare Furat's life, but Munis, his chief military commander, threatened mutiny if Furat and his son were not executed, and Muqtadir bowed to his demands.

The following morning, a servant entered Furat's room and laid the severed head of his son Muhassin at his feet. Then two African executioners came in and Furat too was decapitated. The two heads were shown to Muqtadir, then placed in a sack filled with sand and thrown into the river.

IN 926, THE cultists again attacked the *hajj* caravan, then rode on to sack the city of Kufa, and once more, the Abbasid army arrived on the scene too late, long after the raiders had fled back into the desert with their slaves and booty.

During Ramadan the following year, the Qarmatians reappeared in Kufa, then prepared to attack Baghdad itself, only 170 kilometres away. Traumatised refugees staggered into Baghdad with stories of Qarmatian atrocities. Panic broke out, shops shut down and people prepared to get out while they could.

Muqtadir looked to his army, but despite their overwhelming numerical superiority and the existential nature of the threat to the caliphate, Muqtadir was told he could not rely on his men to fight unless they were paid to their satisfaction. The city's boatmen would not even ferry the soldiers across the Tigris to face the enemy unless they too were paid off. The treasury, however, was empty.

Muqtadir's latest vizier, Ali ibn Isa, asked him to appeal to his mother for money to pay the troops. He told Muqtadir that the hour was late; if the queen mother had been keeping any funds aside to deal with critical threats to the empire and her family, now was the time to bring them out. Otherwise, he said, it would be best for the caliph to drop everything and escape Baghdad at once. Shaghab accordingly gave over half a million gold coins to pay the military to defend their own capital against the hated Qarmatians.

The defence was led by Munis, the army chief, who ordered the bridges on the Tigris to be torn down and the canal embankments to be opened, flooding the approaches to the city. The Qarmatian forces, frustrated and water-logged, slunk off in search of smaller, less well defended towns to attack.

When the threat had passed, Muqtadir's soldiers demanded a pay rise as the reward for their 'victory' over the Qarmatian forces, even though they'd done no actual fighting. The caliph, cornered by his own military, agreed to pay each soldier an extra gold dinar.

THE WARLORD ABU TAHIR was not done yet. In January 929, the Qarmatians committed a shocking, unthinkable act of desecration. That year, the *hajj* caravan had arrived at the outskirts of Mecca without incident, only to be massacred near the city gates by Abu Tahir and a force of 1500 Qarmatian raiders. Entering the Holy City, they dumped the corpses of their victims in the sacred well of Zamzam. Believing that veneration of holy shrines was a form of idolatry, the Qarmatian rebels contemptuously smashed down the door to the Kaaba, ripped up its ceremonial covering and threw away its holy relics. Next they prised the Black Stone – the precious relic believed to have been placed there at the direction of Muhammad himself – from the wall of the Kaaba, and carried it off to the Qarmatian citadel in Bahrain, where it would remain for the next twenty years.

Mecca was awash in blood. As he departed the ravaged Holy City, Abu Tahir proclaimed, in a howl of triumph:

> I am God's agent, and the agent of God is myself;
> He creates mankind, and I destroy it![24]

MUQTADIR, THE COMMANDER of the Faithful, had been exposed as contemptibly weak, incapable of fulfilling his primary duty to protect Muslims in the observance of their religion. Within weeks, feuding broke out among the Abbasid military. A palace guard revolt in Baghdad briefly deposed Muqtadir and installed his half-brother Qahir. But two days later, when Qahir was unable to come up with the funds for a fresh donative, the military restored Muqtadir to the throne. The shaky caliph survived at the whim of the troops that had looted his palace and now lolled around its corridors. The provinces, hearing of the chaos in the capital, ignored Baghdad's demands to forward their tax revenues. Food supplies in the capital began to run dangerously low.

THE FINAL PROP HOLDING up Muqtadir's reign was kicked away when Munis, his last loyal army commander, turned against him. The general, who had been away fighting on the Syrian border, marched back to Baghdad at the head of his army. Muqtadir's vizier frantically attempted to build up the city's defences at the Shammasiyyah Gate, on the northeastern periphery of the city.

Muqtadir was advised that his soldiers would need to be paid off once more to ensure their loyalty. Again, he went to his mother, but Shaghab ruefully told him she had already given up the last of her gold. That night, Muqtadir contemplated fleeing, but then resolved to stay and fight.

THE NEXT MORNING, 30 October 932, the caliph rose, prayed for a while in his throne room, and then said farewell to his mother. Muqtadir, who had never led an army into battle, adorned himself in the full regalia of the Deputy of the Prophet. He donned a black turban and a glittering silver kaftan, and draped the cloak of Muhammad over his shoulder; at his waist was strapped the Prophet's sword. In his right hand he held Muhammad's seal and staff. Armoured with these holy talismans, Muqtadir rode out to the Shammasiyyah Gate accompanied by his son and his nervous courtiers, bearing black and white banners.

The battle was already underway. Muqtadir held back, watching the fighting from a high vantage point. Then, just as Munis's rebel forces looked like they would prevail, Muqtadir strode into the fray, holding aloft a copy of the Quran.

The sudden appearance of the caliph shamed some of Munis's soldiers, who asked for his forgiveness and blessing. There was a moment of uncertainty until a group of Berber horsemen rode forward. One of them struck Muqtadir on the shoulder with a scimitar and another yanked the cloak of the Prophet from his back.

'Take care!' he cried out. 'I am the caliph!'

'Then it's you we're looking for,' the Berber replied.

Muqtadir tried to fend off their swords with his hand, and his thumb was sliced off. He fell to the ground. Then one came forward and stabbed him in the throat. They cut off his head and hoisted it on a spear, crying victory.

When the head was brought to the formerly loyal Munis, the general burst into tears.

THAT EVENING, A WORKER rode through the quietened battlefield on a donkey, pulling a cart that bore a load of thorns. Among the scattered dead he identified Muqtadir's headless body. Feeling pity, and not wanting it to be devoured by wild animals, he pulled it into his cart and brought it inside the city, where a few pious citizens set up a small shrine to the dead caliph.

MUQTADIR'S DEATH PUT his half-brother Qahir back on the throne. He too was required to come up with money for the army, so he summoned Shaghab and demanded she surrender what was left of her treasures. The former queen mother, ill and bent with grief over her son's death, denied she had anything more than a few boxes filled with trinkets and perfume.

'You must have some riches hidden away in the city,' Qahir insisted.

'Had I possessed any money,' she said sadly, 'I should not have delivered my son to his death.'

Qahir struck her and confined her to the palace, where she died seven months later on 3 June 933.

The power of the parallel court died with her. 'It was the end of an era,' wrote Abbasid historian Hugh Kennedy, 'the last of the great women of the Abbasid house had perished in poverty and disgrace. There were to be no more like her.'[25]

A donative coin from the reign of Muqtadir

Asabiyya

IN WESTERN ALGERIA, on the edge of the Sahara Desert, lie the ruins of an ancient clifftop castle named the Banu Salama, with grottoes and monumental stone tombs going back to pre-Islamic times.

In the year 1375, a man named Ibn Khaldun rode into this wilderness. He was then forty-five years old. For several decades, Ibn Khaldun had served and schemed against various Muslim rulers in North Africa and Spain, and was now weary of politics. With the permission of the local Berber people, he stayed in the castle for three years.

Looking out from his window in the quiet of that semi-desert, he watched the Berber herdsmen passing by, moving their sheep from summer to winter grazing grounds, and was filled with admiration for the simplicity of their lives and their upright bearing, which seemed uncorrupted by the greed and softness of urban life. Suddenly his mind was ablaze with ideas, and he began to write, he said, 'with words and ideas pouring into my head like cream into a churn, until the finished product was ready'.[26] The completed book was nothing less than an explanation of all of human history.

The dizzy optimism of the early years of Islam, when the easy conquests of the caliphate seemed to promise that the whole world would soon fall under its dominion, had long since dissipated. Baghdad was, by then, a ghost of its former self. The caliphate had fractured into more than a dozen individual principalities that were often at war with each other. Cordoba, the former capital of Muslim Spain, had fallen to the Christians. The ancient Roman ruins that lay near Ibn Khaldun's retreat offered a stern rebuke to foolish notions of imperial permanence. 'This entire world is trifling and futile,' he wrote grimly. 'It ends in death and annihilation.'[27]

As he pored over the work of earlier historians, he came to admire Masudi the most. He praised the breadth and scale of Masudi's vision, and for his willingness to go out and see the world for himself. But Ibn Khaldun took issue with Masudi for his willingness to give credence to some old tales that were clearly, to his mind, absurd. He thought Masudi had been foolish to recount the story taken from *The Alexander Romance* of the conqueror's voyage to the bottom of the sea to sketch monsters from inside a glass diving bell. The sceptical Ibn Khaldun scoffed at this tale as 'a long story, made up of nonsensical elements'. No great king, he thought, would be permitted to risk his own life in such a cavalier manner. And in any case, 'were one to go down deep into the water, even in a box, one would have too little air for natural breathing'.[28]

Masudi was enchanted by the world; Ibn Khaldun was decidedly disenchanted. Too much had happened in the four centuries that separated the two historians. At Banu Salama, he meditated on Islam's lost golden age and the crumbling Roman pillars nearby.

Ibn Khaldun did not see the world as a magical carpet rolled out before him. As a child, he had lost his parents, teachers and friends to the Black Death, the most fatal pandemic in human history, and he preferred to confront hard truths unflinchingly. There was no chance he would give his great work a delightful title like *Meadows of Gold and Mines of Gems*, or *Tales of the Marvellous, News of the Strange*.

Other medieval scholars had seen the rise and fall of empires as bewildering events best explained by the unknowable will of God. But holed up in his African castle, Ibn Khaldun began to perceive an underlying human mechanism at work, a hidden machine of history that could bring up an obscure people to greatness and then cast them down again.

THE INTRODUCTION TO Ibn Khaldun's history, known as the *Muqaddimah* or 'Prologue', is widely regarded today as a work of preternatural genius, a brilliant fusion of politics, history, economics, religion and the natural sciences. When the *Muqaddimah* was eventually translated into English in 1958, it was praised by historian Arnold Toynbee as 'undoubtedly the greatest work of its kind that has ever been created by any mind in any time or place'.[29] The *Muqaddimah* would inspire (via Toynbee) Isaac Asimov's *Foundation* series, Frank Herbert's *Dune* and Bruce Chatwin's *Songlines*.[30]

Ibn Khaldun's most powerful idea was the concept of *asabiyya* – an Arabic word meaning 'group feeling'. It was, he said, the presence or absence of such a feeling that determined the rise and fall of civilisations. Living among the Berbers, he saw how the harshness of desert life could forge strong bonds of solidarity within a tribe. This form of *asabiyya* was powerful, he noted, but did not extend to members of other tribes, putting these tribes into a state of ongoing competition and conflict. However, he saw that when a large, holistic belief system like Islam came along, the fellow feeling could extend much further.

For the Arabs of the Hijaz, Islam was the galvanising shock that had brought the squabbling tribes together. Muhammad's vision had unlocked enormous latent energies that had empowered the Arabs to conquer famous cities and build a great empire of their own. But that was all done now. The *asabiyya* was gone.

This was how it would go with all great empires, Ibn Khaldun thought. The process was inevitable. Dynasties would arise. Royal authority would exert, for a while, its own form of group feeling, but eventually the *asabiyya* would seep away, the people would lose 'the old desert toughness'.[31] The leaders would become softened by luxury. No longer able to rely on fierce Bedouin warriors for defence, the regime would be forced to raise taxes to pay for mercenaries, who would eventually bankrupt the state. Then new desert armies would arrive and pull the old empire down.

Ibn Khaldun, writing after the fall of Baghdad, concluded that 'something of the sort happened to the Abbasids … The group feeling of the Arabs had been destroyed … The influence of the dynasty grew smaller, and no longer extended beyond the environs of Baghdad.'

'Finally,' he recorded ominously, 'the Tatars closed in' – the descendants of the Mongol ruler Genghis Khan.

BOOK SIX

The Summit of the Sky

NASIR
Thirty-fourth of the Abbasid caliphs

Ibn JUBAYR
Arab traveller and geographer

GENGHIS KHAN
Universal ruler and founder of the Mongol Empire

MUHAMMAD II
Shah of the Khwarezmian Empire

TERKEN QATUN
Queen mother of the Khwarezmian Shah

HULAGU
Mongol conqueror and grandson of Genghis Khan

JUVAYNI
Persian historian and aide-de-camp to Hulagu

RUKN al-DIN
Grandmaster of the Order of Assassins

MUSTASIM
Thirty-seventh, and last, of the Abbasid caliphs

TUFAH al-KULUB
Slave singer and concubine of Harun al-Rashid

the
MONGOL INVASIONS
c. 1219–1258 C.E.

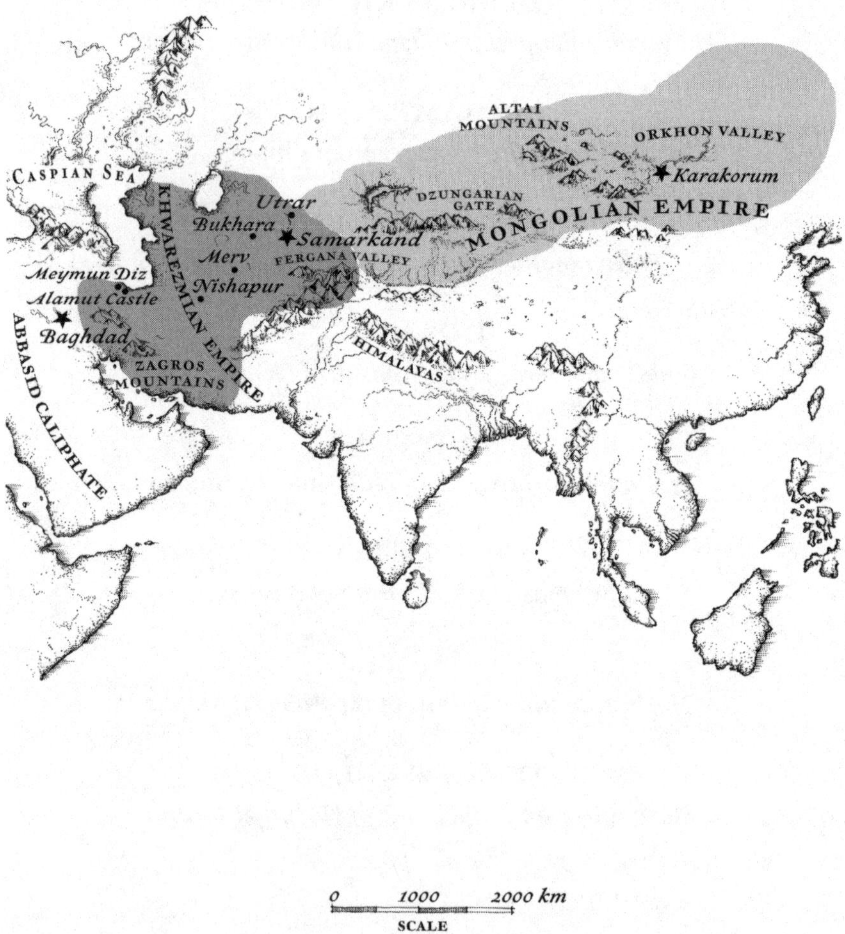

Baghdad, you know, is a house of calamity.
May God save us from this very prison.
Anonymous poet[1]

The Statue of a Ghost

IN FEBRUARY 1183, an Arab traveller and geographer named Ibn Jubayr left his home in Cordoba and set out on a pilgrimage to Mecca. From the Spanish coast, Ibn Jubayr sailed across the Mediterranean to Alexandria, where another boat ferried him down the Nile. After crossing the Red Sea to Arabia, he joined the merging multitudes on the pilgrims' road through the desert. Along the way, he stopped at the way-stations and the roadside pools established centuries earlier by Zubaydah, wife of Harun al-Rashid, which he noted gratefully were 'filled with sweet and limpid water'.[2]

Having discharged his pilgrim's duties in Mecca and Medina, where he prayed at the Prophet's tomb, Ibn Jubayr decided to take the long way home through Mesopotamia, and in May 1184, he came to the outskirts of Baghdad.

Passing through the city's famous gates, bathed in the golden late-afternoon sun, he said he felt aroused by 'a call to happiness'. But as he surveyed the state of Baghdad, his spirits fell. Like fourth-century Rome, the great metropolis had sunk into a kind of torpor, living off its famous name and faded grandeur. Ibn Jubayr thought it was like 'the statue of a ghost'.

Two and a half centuries had passed since Caliph Muqtadir had been cut down at the Shammasiyyah Gate, clutching at the cloak of the Prophet. Mansur's original Round City was ruined. The pontoon bridges had been destroyed by floods, so people had returned to using boats to cross the Tigris. The inhabitants, once so outward-looking and curious, had, in Ibn Jubayr's opinion, become small-minded and unfriendly. He felt Baghdadis wore a mask of pious humility, but inwardly were vain and disdainful of outsiders. 'The stranger with them is without fellowship,' he wrote, 'his expenses are doubled, and he will find amongst them none who do not practise hypocrisy with him or make merry with him only for some profit or benefit.' Baghdad, he said, was still a great city. 'But ah, what is she to what she was! Today we may apply to her the saying of the lover: *You are not you, and the houses are not those I knew.*'[3]

Still, he sighed, the Tigris shone for him 'like a string of pearls between two breasts'. Baghdad's hospital still ministered to the sick. The city's great mosques were in good order, and Ibn Jubayr was impressed by their preachers, who could arouse powerful emotions in their congregations. There was one *imam* he saw whose intoxicating sermon made the souls of the worshippers rise like clouds, 'and from their tears there poured a heavy shower of rain'. By the end, everyone, including the *imam*, was weeping.

And there were some tentative, hopeful signs of renewal. The current caliph, Nasir, was the most energetic and capable leader in many generations. Lacking a large army, Nasir tried to use the prestige of his title to claw back some of the political power that his predecessors had once enjoyed.

Nasir took care to limit his public appearances before the people of Baghdad in order to enhance his mystique. Nonetheless, Ibn Jubayr spotted him one day descending the steps of his summer palace to board the royal barge on the Tigris, wearing a Turkish-style cap in an attempt to go about incognito. Ibn Jubayr liked what he saw: the caliph, he noted, was a young man, 'with a fair beard that is short but full, is of handsome shape and good to look on, of fair skin, medium stature, and comely aspect'.[4]

THE CALIPH WAS still widely acknowledged by Muslims as Commander of the Faithful, a figure of immense spiritual authority, but his role was now more like that of an influential pope than a mighty emperor. Nasir's predecessors had been powerless to prevent Christian Crusaders from Europe invading the Holy Land. Muslims now looked instead to the powerful Kurdish general Saladin to expel the hated infidels from Jerusalem.

The provinces of the caliphate had long since broken away politically, and the sliver of land Nasir still controlled in Mesopotamia was now surrounded by a patchwork of unstable Muslim powers, jostling for supremacy. Cairo had risen to rival Baghdad as the world's greatest Muslim city, and was now the seat of Saladin's Ayyubid Sultanate, which ruled over Egypt, Syria and the holy cities of western Arabia and northern Iraq.

The overbearing Seljuk sultans had assumed the role of 'protector' of the caliphate, in much the same way as the armies of a German king might seek to protect the papacy in Rome, but as Seljuk power waned, Nasir saw his chance to reclaim some of the traditional lands of the caliphate, and he formed an alliance with the new rising power in Central Asia, the Khwarezmian Empire, which controlled parts of Iran and Transoxiana, the lands beyond the Amu Darya.

In 1194, Nasir sent his army to assist the forces of Tekish, the Khwarezmian Shah, in his clash with the Seljuks near the Caspian Sea. Toghrul II, the last Seljuk sultan of Persia, was killed and his severed head was sent back to Tekish as a war trophy. Victory over the Seljuks made the Khwarezmian Empire the most powerful Muslim state east of Cairo.

In the warm afterglow of their shared triumph, Nasir expected Tekish to award Iraq to the caliphate. But Tekish simply acted as though supreme secular power in the region had passed on from the defeated Seljuks to him. A frustrated Nasir sent an envoy to complain to the shah, but Tekish was irked by the envoy's pompous attitude, and the caliph's man was forced to make a quick escape back to Baghdad, rather than lose his head in a practical demonstration of where power in the region *really* lay. Nasir's attempt to bluff Tekish into concessions had failed, and there was little he could do about it other than bide his time and wait for an opening.

Fire in His Eyes, Light in His Face

TEKISH DIED from a tonsillar infection in 1200. His son and successor Shah Muhammad II had even less patience with Nasir's pretensions to great power status, particularly after a round of fresh conquests expanded the Khwarezmians' domain even further. By 1218, Shah Muhammad's empire encompassed the rich silk-road cities of Bukhara, Nishapur, Balkh and Merv, and he could claim the famous city of Samarkand as his capital.

But Muhammad was not entirely the master of his own domain. He had to share control of the empire with his mother, the formidable Terken Qatun, who maintained a separate court in Khorasan. Mother and son issued separate decrees that often countermanded each other. Terrified Khwarezmian officials eventually settled on the tactic of obeying the most recently issued order and hoping for the best.

Shah Muhammad was, if anything, even more bellicose and essive than his father, but he could not afford to break entirely his mother. Terken Qatun was a daughter of the Qipchaq people of the steppe, and the highest posts in the Khwarezmian army were occupied by her kinsmen, effectively giving her personal control of the empire's military.

Despite (or perhaps because of) these constraints, Muhammad awarded himself the grand title of 'the Second Alexander',[5] and demanded that Caliph Nasir acknowledge him as the Sultan of Baghdad. When Nasir refused, Muhammad set out with an army to bring the caliph to heel, but the Khwarezmians were held at bay by snowstorms in the Zagros Mountains and forced to head back.

Several medieval chroniclers record that at this point, a desperate Nasir sent a letter asking for assistance against the Khwarezmians from the most dangerous man in the world: the Mongol ruler Genghis Khan.

GENGHIS KHAN (ALSO spelt 'Chinggis' or 'Chingiz' Khan) was born in 1162, in Mongolia's Orkhon River Valley. Legend has it he emerged from the womb clutching a blood clot the size of a knucklebone, a sign that he was destined for greatness.[6] He was given the name Temujin, and a Mongol source records that as small child, 'there was fire in his eyes and light in his face'.[7] After a turbulent early life, and a youth spent building alliances and eliminating rivals, Temujin succeeded in uniting the nomadic clans of Northeast Asia under his personal authority, and was awarded the title Genghis Khan, meaning 'Fierce' or 'Hard' Ruler.*

In 1206, in an unconscious imitation of the strategy of the first caliph, the great khan gathered up the feuding energies of his tribes and directed them outwards towards the settled societies

* Other interpretations suggest the title should be translated as 'Oceanic' or 'Universal' Ruler.

beyond the steppe. And like the early Muslims, they met with more success than they could have dared imagine. No other conqueror in history, not even Alexander, had ever seized so much territory, nor left such an indelible scar on the face of humanity. Admirers of the Mongol expansion likened the conquests to a forest fire that burnt away endless medieval deadwood and allowed new growth to emerge.[8]

Under Mongol rule, Europe and China were able to make proper contact with each other for the first time in history. Genghis Khan's successors opened up the Eurasian continent, introducing a new era of stability and commerce, a 'Pax Mongolica' along the silk roads that enabled the safe passage of travellers and traders like Marco Polo.

But the Pax Mongolica was, in so many places and for so many people, the peace of the graveyard. Genghis Khan's conquest of northern China, beginning in 1211, was a campaign of unprecedented mass murder. Chinese census reports before and after the Mongol invasions indicate a drastic population collapse from fifty million to eight and a half million people.[9] The loss of life was so great that enormous swathes of cultivated land were abandoned and retaken by the forest, resulting in a measurable drop in global carbon dioxide levels.[10] The effects of plague, floods and other natural disasters were no doubt contributing factors, but responsibility for the largest part of the stupefying death toll can be laid at the feet of Genghis Khan and the policy of 'surrender or die' that he deployed against all those who stood against Mongol power.

Although he regarded settled societies with the predator's contempt for its prey, Genghis Khan seems to have seen himself as a moderate. To his mind, it was the Jin rulers of China, softened and corrupted by luxury, who were the true moral reprobates. His thinking was captured in a letter sent to a Chinese alchemist he hoped to lure to his court:

> Heaven has grown weary of the excessive pride and extravagant luxury in China and has abandoned her . . . But I, living in the barbaric north in the wilderness, have no inordinate passions . . . I wear the same clothes and eat the same food as the cowherds and horse-herders. We make the same sacrifices and we share the same riches. I look upon the nation as a newborn child and I care for my soldiers as if they were my brothers.[11]

A finely painted silk portrait presents Genghis as an avuncular figure, with a thin beard, a simple leather cap and a pleasant expression on his face. In keeping with Mongol tradition, the great khan lived simply and took care to share the mountains of looted treasure equitably among his followers. He refused to discriminate on the ground of birth or religion, and appointed his senior men on the basis of merit.

THE GREAT KHAN was prone to outbursts of hysterical, purple-faced rage, yet he chose his targets coolly and deliberately. Although sometimes caricatured as a bloodthirsty maniac, he was in fact a strategist of genius, able to coordinate his horse archers, engineers and infantry with extraordinary dexterity. The key to the speed and scale of his victories was his mastery of logistics; he planned the route ahead of his armies with meticulous care to ensure there was adequate pasturage, wells and waterholes for his horses and for the oxen teams that pulled his colossal wagon trains over vast distances. While his men were on the move, engineering units were sent ahead to prepare for river crossings by assembling broad timber bridges that could bear the load of the Mongol transport wagons.

Mongol horsemen were astonishingly skillful in battle, trained from an early age to ride at speed and shoot at a gallop. Their saddles were fitted with short stirrups padded with felt, enabling them to stand while riding in a semi-erect position and fire arrows from a range of angles, all the while directing their horses by swerving their waist and hips.

Each soldier was responsible for as many as five horses, and he changed them regularly to avoid tiring them out. This allowed Mongol soldiers to move in great bursts of speed when necessary, to scout terrain, to gather intelligence and to pass messages between commanders. The Mongols had sprinting horses for urgent missions, horses with stamina for long-distance messaging, pack horses for pulling heavy carts and war horses trained to withstand the stress of battle. Horses were an endlessly exploitable resource for the Mongol army, providing not only transport, but also hair for their bows and ropes, and dried dung for their campfires. Mare's milk was fermented into a slightly sour, mildly alcoholic beverage called *airag*, which kept up the men's spirits while on the march. As a last resort, when milk and food were in short supply, the men would carefully open a vein and drink their horses' blood. When a horse died, its meat would be quickly consumed.

TEMUJIN'S ROCKET-LIKE ASCENDANCY from obscurity to greatness convinced him he had been entrusted by Tenggri, the Mongol god of the eternal blue sky, with a divine mission to rule the world. His followers proclaimed that he had been granted dominion over 'all the face of the Earth, from the going up of the sun to its going down'.[12] Resistance to Genghis Khan was therefore an act of sacrilege, an affront to the will of Heaven, that justified the unleashing of genocidal violence.

The performance of conspicuous cruelty was also, to Genghis's mind, a military necessity. The Mongol army, while highly skilled and disciplined, was initially relatively small. Conquest by capitulation was speedier, and preferable to frittering away his forces in long, grinding campaigns. Cities and villages that offered immediate surrender and tribute were therefore left largely unmolested, while those that chose to resist were razed and their inhabitants exterminated so as to encourage the next city to open its gates quickly and without a fight.

Intimidation through terror went hand in hand with the use of deception and disinformation, psychological weapons that hobbled Genghis's enemies before any of his warriors had lifted their bows. His spies, carefully placed within the enemy's camp, provided him with intelligence on their vulnerabilities, while other agents disseminated false rumours and counterfeit orders that demoralised and baffled their generals.[13]

Portrait of Genghis Khan

The Sovereign of the Sunrise and the Sunset

BUT IF CALIPH NASIR had ever sent that letter to Genghis Khan proposing an alliance against the Khwarezmians it would have been to no avail. In 1218, Genghis Khan wanted no war with Shah Muhammad. There were no serious border issues, at this stage, between the Mongols and the Khwarezmians. The two empires were well spaced apart and separated by geographical obstacles that formed a natural border between them, and the khan needed Shah Muhammad's goodwill to allow Mongol traders to pass along the silk roads to the West. In any case, Genghis Khan's primary goal that year was the completion of his conquest of Jin China; war with the Khwarezmians would be a pointless distraction.

But the great khan hadn't counted on the wounded pride of Muhammad II. Despite the enormous distances between their domains, the shah had once entertained fantasies of conquering China himself, and he resented Genghis Khan for beating him to it.[14] And so he kept poking the Mongol bear again and again until it turned around and devoured him.

In 1218, a Mongol force strayed into Khwarezmian territory and ran into Muhammad's army at the Irghiz River. The Mongols, who were heavily outnumbered, asked for safe passage but were refused by the Khwarezmians, who accused them of trespassing. Despite the numeric mismatch, the subsequent battle was inconclusive. Unwilling to engage in a pointless fight without authorisation from the great khan, the Mongols escaped the battlefield that night under cover of darkness.

Rather than declare war on Muhammad for this provocation, Genghis uncharacteristically waved the offence away. He sent a placatory message to the shah, proposing a diplomatic exchange to settle their borders and avoid any further misunderstandings.

Seeing no harm in this, Muhammad sent a party of envoys east to parley with the khan.

The Mongols were intent on making a powerful impression on the shah's men. Approaching the Mongol encampment at the end of their long journey, the Khwarezmian envoys saw in the distance what first appeared to be a gleaming pyramid of snow. But as they came closer, they realised it was in fact a tower of bleached human bones. Inside the camp, they noticed, the ground was slippery with human fat.

When the rattled envoys entered the great khan's ceremonial tent they were welcomed graciously and presented with lavish gifts for Shah Muhammad, including a massive gold nugget, 'as big as a camel's neck', that required its own cart to haul it back to Samarkand. In his personal letter to the shah, Genghis Khan passed on his warmest wishes and expressed his hopes for free trade between them:

> I am the sovereign of the sunrise, and you are the sovereign of the sunset. Let there be between us a firm treaty of friendship, amity, and peace, and let traders on both sides come and go, and let the precious products and commodities which may be in my territory be conveyed by them into yours, and those of yours, in the same manner, let them bring into mine.[15]

To initiate this new era of peaceful commerce, the returning envoys were to be accompanied by a Mongol trade caravan carrying gold, silver, silks and sable furs, fitted out and paid for by Genghis Khan himself. But when the caravan entered Khwarezmian territory, it was held up at the border city of Utrar. The local governor Inalchuq angrily accused the merchants of being Mongol spies, which was an odd accusation, given that espionage and trade typically went hand in hand along the silk roads. Then, acting with or without the shah's authority, Inalchuq had the Mongol merchants executed and their goods confiscated.

This was an offence that Genghis Khan could hardly let stand, but he remained unwilling to be diverted from his plans for China, and so he smothered his rage and made one last attempt to keep the peace with Muhammad. A three-man delegation was sent to Samarkand, which told the shah that the great khan was prepared to accept that the slaughter of the merchants and the theft of the goods had taken place without his knowledge or consent, and that relations between them could be repaired. But this was only possible, they said, if the shah handed over Inalchuq to the Mongols for punishment. Muhammad's son Jalal al-Din advised his father to comply with the demand, but instead, an indignant Muhammad had the leader of the Mongol delegation executed; the other two envoys' heads and beards were shaven and they were sent back home to report on their treatment.

And with that, Genghis Khan finally ran out of patience with the Khwarezmian Shah.

'He is no king, he is a bandit,' he told his staff.[16]

The final conquest of China would have to be postponed. The Mongols instead prepared for an invasion of the lands to the West, setting in train a series of events that would eventually tear down the Abbasid Caliphate.

The Punishment of God

WHILE GENGHIS KHAN gathered his forces, he discovered from his spies in Samarkand that Muhammad's court astrologers had foretold doom for the shah's cause. Knowing that Muhammad would likely be unsettled by the forecast, the khan rattled him further by tripping up his war preparations with disinformation: Mongol agents counterfeited separate decrees from Muhammad and Terken Qatun countermanding each other, then circulated poisonous rumours that the queen mother was making plans to defect to the Mongols, all of which left the Khwarezmians anxious and demoralised as they awaited the inevitable arrival of the great khan's army.

Genghis then distracted Shah Muhammad by sending a diversionary force, led by his eldest son Jochi and his general Jebe, over the steep, snow-blanketed Pamir Mountains into the Fergana Valley, an extraordinary military feat that has been likened to Hannibal's crossing of the Alps.[17]

The sudden arrival of Jochi and Jebe's army came as a total shock to Muhammad. Unwilling to cede the resource-rich valley, he sent the larger part of his army to hunt them down. Meanwhile, the main Mongol force led by Genghis Khan streamed uncontested through the Dzungarian Gate, following the trail along the northern foothills of the Tian Shan ranges. In October 1219, they arrived at the walls of Utrar.

Shah Muhammad had expected Utrar and its governor to be a primary target for Genghis's wrath, and had sent 60,000 soldiers to reinforce the city's garrison. But rather than expend his men in a grinding siege, the khan sealed off the city and camped outside its walls for two months, hoping to lure Muhammad into sending a relief expedition that he could fight on open ground. When he realised Muhammad wouldn't fall into that trap, Genghis tried to terrorise Utrar's civilians into offering their surrender.[18]

As they charged around the walls, the Mongol horsemen howled and bashed pots, pans and bells, creating an awful, ear-splitting racket. A Russian chronicler described the effect when a Mongol army stormed the walls of Kyiv:

> The rattling of their innumerable carts, the bellowing of camels and cattle, the neighing of horses, and the wild battlecry, were so overwhelming as to render inaudible the conversation of the people inside the city.[19]

The garrison in Utrar, knowing the fate that awaited them if they surrendered, held out for five gruelling months, until starving civilians decided to open the gates and the Mongol warriors poured into the outer city. Inalchuq, the governor who had killed the merchants and stolen the khan's goods, retreated to the city's fortified citadel with several thousand troops, then retreated again to the roof of the citadel tower, where he and his last loyalists defended themselves by throwing bricks onto the enemy. As they made their last stand, Mongol sappers dug cavities under the citadel and the tower collapsed. Inalchuq was pulled from the rubble, still alive.

The citadel and its walls were levelled, the remaining soldiers were slaughtered, and Inalchuq was dragged before Genghis Khan in chains. One chronicler records that the great khan took his revenge by having molten metal poured into the governor's eyes, ears and mouth.[20]

NOW THAT UTRAR HAD been reduced to a heap of rubble, Muhammad's capital Samarkand, some 450 kilometres away, was the next obvious target. Inside the city, Shah Muhammad's soldiers dug in and braced themselves for the imminent Mongol attack. But then the invading army seemed to simply disappear. The road to Samarkand was empty.

A month later, Muhammad received the shocking news that Genghis Khan had arrived, not at Samarkand, but at the gates of Bukhara. In a strategic masterstroke, he had led his army through the red sands of the Kizil Kum Desert, then looped around to the west, deep behind enemy lines, thus encircling Bukhara and isolating Samarkand.

Bukhara had not expected the Mongol army to arrive so soon, but the city could take some comfort from its impressive fortifications. The outer city was protected by high walls, and its inner citadel, known as the Ark, was enclosed by thick, sloping mud battlements.

The walls of Bukhara's citadel, the Ark

Genghis spent a day riding around the city, inspecting its defences. Then he ordered his catapults to commence an assault on the weakest points in the outer walls. After two days of relentless pounding and psychological pressure, Bukhara's garrison troops lost their nerve and attempted to escape the city in the dead of night, but were chased down by the Mongol cavalry and slaughtered.

In the morning, the now defenceless inhabitants opened the gates to the invaders. Genghis Khan rode into the city and occupied the great mosque, where he demanded that the Bukharans signal their submission by providing fodder for his horses. He summoned the city's richest men and presented himself to them as an instrument of divine vengeance. 'I am the punishment of God,' he told the trembling merchants. 'If you had not committed great sins, God would not have sent a punishment like me upon you.'[21]

But Bukhara was not yet completely subdued: 400 of Shah Muhammad's loyalists were holed up inside the Ark, still willing to fight to the death. The great khan ordered his battalions of captured prisoners to fill in the moat around the citadel walls with corpses, earth and timber. Then he brought up his siege engines to fire flaming projectiles at the citadel's battlements. The defenders held out for another ten desperate days until the Ark was made uninhabitable by the relentless, scorching bombardment.

For the crime of resistance, Genghis Khan decided to single out Bukhara for exceptionally harsh treatment. The entire population was ordered to walk out of the city taking nothing with them other than the clothes they wore, so that the Mongol army could plunder Bukhara at its leisure. Artisans were separated from the other civilians so they could be sent to work in Mongolia. The rich were tortured to reveal their hidden treasures. The women of Bukhara were handed out among the soldiers; terrible scenes of mass rape played out in front of the city walls. Some men fought their captors to the death rather than helplessly observe the assault on their daughters, wives and sisters. The remaining male prisoners were conscripted into a Mongol shock battalion, to be used as 'arrow fodder' in the coming attack on the next Mongol target: Bukhara's sister city, Samarkand.

SHAH MUHAMMAD HAD expected he would be able to call upon his garrison at Bukhara to help defend his capital. But now that Bukhara was gone, Samarkand was isolated, 'like a tent whose ropes have been cut'.[22] In February 1220, the defenders on Samarkand's walls observed the approaching mass of Mongol soldiers. A suicidally brave contingent of citizens rushed out to engage the first wave of the invaders but were encircled and cut to pieces. Shah Muhammad, however, accompanied by thousands of horsemen, broke through the siege lines and managed to bolt away, leaving his capital to fend for itself.

As in Bukhara, the garrison troops in Samarkand's citadel were ground down by the Mongol attack, and were massacred when they eventually surrendered. Again, the remaining inhabitants were rounded up outside the gates; craftsmen were set aside to be sent to Mongolia, the younger women were handed out to the soldiers and the men were enlisted as suicide troops for the next stage of the campaign, while the city was plundered and devastated. All this was accomplished by the middle of March 1220.

At this time, Genghis sent a message to Muhammad's mother Terken Qatun, who was in Khiva; he told her his quarrel was with her son, not her, and that if she surrendered her army, there could be peace between the Khwarezmians and the Mongols. The defiant Terken Qatun replied to his message by drowning every one of her Mongol hostages in a river. She then fled with her courtiers to a castle near the Caspian Sea, but after several months their supplies of fresh water ran dry and she surrendered to the Mongols. The sources record that the proud Terken Qatun was dragged off to Mongolia, where she lived out the rest of her days in poverty and degradation.

STILL THE SHAH of Khwarezm eluded the great khan. He sent Jochi and Jebe to track Muhammad down wherever he was hiding, 'even if he has climbed up to the sky'.[23] Distrusting his advisors and unable to settle on any strategy, the panic-stricken Shah Muhammad fled from place to place, telling his remaining commanders that all was lost and they should run for their lives.[24]

In October 1220, with more and more of his territory falling to the advancing Mongols, the shah sailed out to an island in the Caspian Sea, hoping to elude the khan's horsemen who had an aversion to crossing bodies of water. Dressed in rags and wracked with pneumonia, Muhammad died of an attack of pleurisy on 10 January 1221 and was buried on the island.

WITH HIS ENEMY DEAD and his need for vengeance satisfied, Genghis Khan could now return to the East to resume his invasion of China. Before leaving, he entrusted his youngest son Tolui with the task of subduing all of Khorasan and capturing the great city of Merv. Once again, the city's garrison refused to surrender, but the civilian leaders, torn by dissension, buckled under the pressure and opened the city's gates.

Bukhara and Samarkand would one day recover from the Mongol assaults, but Tolui ensured that Merv never would. Seated in a golden chair outside the city, he ordered every last inhabitant to leave the city and then looked on impassively as almost every one of them was slaughtered. Historians place the city's population at the time at 200,000.[25] The killing took four days and nights to complete.

Merv, now emptied of its population, was sacked and its complex irrigation system wrecked. The gleaming mausoleum of the Sultan Sunjar, capped with a glazed turquoise dome, was ransacked and demolished in the search for treasure. Three weeks after the massacre, thousands of people who had been hiding in boltholes and cellars emerged from the rubble, but were picked off by Mongol patrols kept behind for this purpose. Afterwards, Mongol soldiers built towering pyramids with the skulls of the dead.[26]

HAVING WON CONTROL of these emptied cities, the Mongols would here and there attempt to rebuild and repopulate them. But Merv, a metropolis once renowned for its orchards, gardens, mosques and palaces, was too far gone. Today the site of what was briefly one of the world's biggest cities, is a forgotten, silent ruin in modern-day Turkmenistan. Mammoth brickworks poke up from the arid ground like broken teeth. The Arab chronicler Ibn al-Athir, who observed the disaster from a distance, struggled to bring himself to write about the fall of Merv:

> For several years I continued to avoid mention of this disaster as it horrified me and I was unwilling to recount it. I was taking one step towards it and then another back … History books do not contain anything similar or anything that comes close to it.[27]

IN 1226, WITH his health failing, Genghis called a *kurultai*, a meeting of the Mongol chiefs and clan leaders, to decide on the succession. He decreed that his empire was to be divided after his death between his sons and grandsons. The fierce, unresolvable antagonism between his eldest two sons Jochi and Chagatai led him to name his third son Ogodei as his successor, an arrangement everyone could at least tolerate.

The following year, while on campaign, Genghis Khan came down with a fever and summoned his sons to his bed. 'Life is short,' he told them. 'I could not conquer all the world. You will have to do it.'[28] He died on 18 August 1227.

UNDER OGODEI KHAN, the pace of Mongol expansion picked up even greater speed. In 1240, the army of Genghis's grandson Batu sacked and burnt Kyiv. In 1241, Mongol armies entered Poland and Hungary, defeating and destroying some of the largest coalition armies ever assembled in Europe. A stunned Templar knight advised the King of France that there was nothing that could now stop the Mongols from reaching the Atlantic. But Europe was given a reprieve when Ogodei Khan suddenly died in 1242 after a long drinking bout.

With the death of the great khan, the machinery of Mongol conquest suddenly seized up, as every Mongol prince and commander across the empire was required to rush to a new *kurultai* to elect a new leader. But the succession was stalled, when Batu tried to thwart the ascent of his hated rival Guyuk by refusing to attend the assembly, which under Mongol law could not proceed without him. In the meantime, Ogodei's widow Toregene acted as regent and ran a caretaker administration. After four years of delay and inertia, Batu was told the *kurultai* was going to proceed with or without him, and Guyuk was elected as the new great khan at Karakorum, the new Mongol capital.

AMONG THE OBSERVERS at the inauguration ceremonies was a small delegation of Christian clerics. Friar John of Plano Carpini and his colleagues had been sent all the way to Karakorum by Pope Innocent IV on a difficult and dangerous mission. The pope had picked up a tantalising rumour that Guyuk had accepted baptism from the Nestorian priests in his court. If it were true, it would have fulfilled one of the Church's most cherished hopes, that a great Christian power might arise somewhere in the Far East, which would enable both Western and Eastern Christendom to crush Islam from both sides like a vice. Pope Innocent told the priests to reprimand the great khan for his incursions into Europe, and then to follow this rebuke with an invitation to Christian fellowship.

The journey to Karakorum had taken them almost a year. The sixty-five-year-old priest and his fellow friars received a warm welcome from the Mongols and the khan's Nestorian priests, but they soon discovered Guyuk's interest in Christianity was purely superficial. The khans were unfussed when it came to the great universal religions, and took care not to offend any of their gods as a means of hedging their bets in the afterlife.

Friar John soon realised there had been a terrible misunderstanding. The Mongols had welcomed them under the assumption that they had come to Karakorum to offer the pope's submission. Instead, in his lengthy, cantankerous letter to Guyuk, Pope Innocent IV attempted to lecture him on the divinity of Christ, and ordered him to desist from attacking the Christian lands. He concluded by asking him to accept baptism and demanding that he 'make fully known to us what moved you to destroy other nations and what your intentions are for the future'.

Guyuk read the translated letter with mounting anger and incredulity. His written reply to the pope was succinct and ominous. He mocked the Holy Father's claim to speak on God's behalf: 'How do you know who it is that God forgives, and whom God speaks to? It is God who has given all the lands to us. We hold them. Except by the will of God, how can anyone do anything?'

Guyuk concluded with a blunt threat:

> You must come at once with all your princes and pay homage to us, and say: 'We shall become your subjects. We shall give you our strength.' We shall then recognise your submission.

> If you do not accept God's command and act contrary to our command, then we shall regard you as enemies.[29]

FRIAR JOHN AND his companions returned to Europe to give the pope the worrying news that the great khan was planning a fresh invasion of Poland and Hungary, which was to be followed by an attack on Germany and Italy.

Guyuk, however, did not live long enough to bring these plans to fruition. The sickly khan died in 1248 after just two years on the throne, and again the Mongol machinery of conquest seized up. After another three years of infighting and stalling, another *kurultai* was called to elect his successor.

A city under Mongol siege

The Travels of Juvayni the Historian

AMONG THE PRINCES and commanders summoned to attend the assembly was Arghun Aqa, the Mongol Viceroy of Persia. In August 1251, he duly set out on the long journey to Karakorum, accompanied by his most senior advisor, a Persian bureaucrat named Baha-ad-Din, and Baha's twenty-year-old son, Ala-ad-Din.

The father and son were known by the family name of Juvayni, taken from their ancestral home of Juvayn in Khorasan. The Juvaynis were descended from a long line of distinguished government advisors who had served in the courts of various Muslim rulers. Juvayni the elder had acted as advisor to Muhammad II, and on the shah's death, had passed into the service of the Mongol viceroy.

On the road to Karakorum, the party received the news that Mongke, a grandson of Genghis, had already been elected as the new great khan. Despite the onset of winter snow, the governor and the Juvaynis pressed on to pay their respects to Mongke, and arrived in the Mongol capital on 2 May 1252.

KARAKORUM CONTAINED A mix of peoples of different religious faiths who could attend any one of the city's many temples, mosques and churches. There was a Muslim quarter with a marketplace and a Chinatown crowded with workshops. There were thousands of Hungarian, Georgian and Armenian artisans captured from the conquered territories, busily manufacturing saddles, harnesses, stirrups, horseshoes, bows and arrows and felt tents for the khan's army.[30] On the eastern bank of the river stood the Palace of Ten Thousand Tranquilities, where the world-emperor held court on a high throne approached by two stairways. At its entrance stood an artificial silver tree, not unlike the mechanical devices seen in the palaces of imperial Baghdad and Constantinople, that had been fashioned for the khan by a Parisian silversmith. At the base of the tree sat four silver lions; when the clockwork angel at the top of the tree blew its horn, four different kinds of drink poured out of the lions' mouths for the great khan and his guests: clarified mare's milk, rice mead, honey mead and red wine.[31]

JUVAYNI THE ELDER was detained in Karakorum for several months, advising Mongke on various administrative issues. Meanwhile, Juvayni the younger decided to make use of his spare time by taking on a major challenge: to write a history of the Mongol conquests, a task that would occupy him for the next decade or so.

In the introduction to his work, *The History of the World Conqueror*, Juvayni takes care to acknowledge his benefactor, the great and powerful Mongke Khan: 'the World-Emperor, the Commander of the Earth and the Age, the source of the blessings of peace and security ... may his august shadow extend over all mankind!'[32] But underneath that outward deference, Juvayni the sincere Muslim had to struggle to make sense of the crisis inflicted by the Mongols on the House of Islam.

Juvayni writes unsparingly of the devastation of Bukhara, Samarkand and Merv, but he can only humbly accept these atrocities as some unknowable form of divine retributive justice, as the fulfilment of an ancient *hadith* that prophesied that God would send horsemen to punish the rebellious and the wicked.[33] It is in the pages of Juvayni's history that we hear Genghis Khan identify himself as an instrument of the divine will to the merchants of Bukhara: 'I am the punishment of God. If you had not committed great sins, God would not have sent a punishment like me upon you.'[34] Juvayni even tries to find solace in the thought that the innocent victims of the khans are now at peace in Paradise, a claim that led his translator to condemn him for his willingness to 'produce facts to show it was for the good of the Muslims that the Mongols came to slaughter them'.[35] But Juvayni had to find some way to accommodate himself to the stark new reality in which he and the rest of the Muslim world now found themselves.

IN KARAKORUM, WHILE Juvayni was beginning his *History of the World Conqueror*, the grandsons of Genghis Khan – Mongke, Kublai and Hulagu – were convening in the great khan's tent to plot the next phase of their conquests. Kublai was sent to conquer China, while Hulagu was ordered to subdue or destroy the remaining Muslim states to the southwest, including the caliphate of Baghdad, if need be.

Hulagu had been raised as a Mongol prince and blooded within the traditional culture of the steppe. At the age of nine, he was sent on his first hunt with Kublai, who had returned with a hare; Hulagu had somehow managed to kill a deer. The boys had presented their catches to their grandfather Genghis, who was very pleased and gave them the 'baptism of the chase' by anointing their middle bowstring fingers with the flesh and fat of their game.[36]

To ensure the success of Hulagu's mission, Mongke placed a fifth of the entire Mongol army at his command. On their long march from Karakorum, the immense procession of Mongol warriors was joined by detachments of Christian Armenians, as well as a thousand Chinese artillery specialists and their families.

Hulagu's 150,000-strong army moved westward over the mountain passes and through the western grasslands and river valleys of modern-day Mongolia and Kazakhstan. The journey took more than two years. The pace of the Mongol advance was slowed by their convoys of oxen-drawn supply carriages, packed with tents, tools and weaponry.

Like his grandfather Genghis, Hulagu planned his advance meticulously, sending scouts sprinting ahead to clear away every herd that stood in his army's path, so that the army's horses would have adequate pasturage to sustain them. Corps of engineers were also sent ahead to build bridges over rivers and streams.

SOMEWHERE IN THE MIDST of this vast trundling procession was Juvayni the younger, who had been transferred into Hulagu's service. Writing on the fly whenever the expedition came to rest, he marvelled at the sea of busy soldiers around him, a force, 'of such great numbers that Gog and Magog themselves would have been destroyed by the waves of its battalions'.[37]

IN 1255, HULAGU'S ARMY passed into the mountain pastures around Almaliq, where they paused for the summer. In September, they arrived at Samarkand, now a Mongol outpost, and set up camp in the meadows just outside the city. For forty days and nights, Hulagu and his commanders gave themselves over to bouts of drinking and lavish banquets under an enormous white tent. Meanwhile, messages were sent out to local rulers, inviting them to contribute to the Mongol campaign, on the implicit understanding that refusal would mean their destruction. Within a month Hulagu's forces were joined by detachments from Azerbaijan, Fars and Georgia.

But Hulagu couldn't fail to note that the current ruler of Baghdad, Caliph Mustasim, had conspicuously failed to send any troops. Hulagu's 'request' had thrown the caliph's court into a panicked dispute over how they should respond. Eventually, Mustasim accepted the advice of his ministers who argued the letter was a ploy designed to weaken his defences. The caliph, they said, should hold his precious troops close to him in Baghdad in readiness for any Mongol attack. Knowing that a failure to respond to the message would likely incur offence, Mustasim contemplated sending a delegation with valuable gifts to Hulagu, but then decided to send a smaller group with goods of minor value instead. In Hulagu's eyes, this shabby response rendered the caliph's vague assurances of friendship worthless.

But for the moment, the submission of the caliphate would have to wait. Hulagu's immediate objective was to root out and destroy an Ismaili sect known as the Order of Assassins.

THE ASSASSINS WERE FEARED and detested by every other Muslim regime in the region. Juvayni called the sect a 'disorder of the Faith'.[38] Rather than maintain a standing army, the order sent teams of *fedayin* – 'self-sacrificers' – on suicide missions against their enemies. Disguised as beggars or monks, the Assassins would attack their targets with daggers in crowded public places, stabbing them to death to instil maximal shock and terror. Operating from their castle strongholds in northern Iran, the Assassins had murdered caliphs, sultans, viziers and Christian Crusaders, and had made two attempts on the life of Saladin.

It was Marco Polo who later associated 'assassin' (*hashashin*) with the use of hashish, which he claimed was fed to the order's recruits to delude them into thinking they had entered the Garden of Paradise.[39] Another, less colourful interpretation of the name links it to the word for 'fodder' – implying that the recruits were worthless herbage to be sacrificed by the Assassins' ruthless grandmaster.[40]

The Assassins had established good, if uneasy, terms with Genghis Khan during the Mongols' sweep through Khorasan three decades earlier, but relations had collapsed after the Assassins murdered a senior Mongol general. Hulagu's first order of business was to flush out these fanatics from their Iranian fortresses.

ON 1 JANUARY 1256, Hulagu's army crossed the Amu Darya, and in the spring they besieged and destroyed an Assassin stronghold in eastern Iran. Hulagu then moved on to the grasslands near the Caspian Sea, where he called a halt to let the ponies graze and fatten up during the summer in readiness for the next phase of the campaign.

On 7 November, Hulagu's forces closed in on Maymun Diz, the headquarters of the Assassins' grandmaster. Maymun Diz was a heavily defended castle, built on top of a lofty rocky outcrop with battlements and a tall central tower. Hulagu's army set up camp at the base of the fortress, while his Chinese artillerymen climbed to the top of an adjoining hill overlooking the castle. There they assembled their powerful trebuchets so as to bombard the castle from a commanding height.

Hulagu then sent a message to the Assassins' grandmaster, Rukn al-Din, ordering him to come out and surrender. The grandmaster played for time by sending out his brother, who told Hulagu that the grandmaster wasn't actually at home, and they couldn't surrender without his permission: an excuse that generated laughter in the Mongol camp. Then Rukn al-Din tried to open negotiations by sending his seven-year-old son as a hostage, but Hulagu sent the boy back.

On 13 November, his patience exhausted, Hulagu ordered his artillery to open fire on Maymun Diz. Some sixty-five Chinese trebuchets pounded the walls with boulders doused in burning naphtha. Flaming javelins were fired from super-sized crossbows mounted on stands. From the Mongol camp, Juvayni witnessed 'the devil-like heretics' on the walls catch fire, hit by the meteoric shafts.[41]

After a day of this punishment, Rukn al-Din sent a message to Hulagu admitting he had been present all along and promising to come out within the next few days. But opinion was split inside the Assassins' castle between those who wanted to stand and fight, and those who, like Rukn al-Din, argued they would have to make an accommodation with the Mongols. At this point, the court astronomer Nasir al-Din Tusi interceded and said that the stars were inauspicious and that the grandmaster should give himself over to Hulagu. Instead, Rukn al-Din remained inside the castle and sent Tusi out to negotiate the surrender. There were more delays and excuses before the grandmaster lost all hope, and on 20 November, he emerged at last from the fortress and made his way to the Mongol camp, bringing valuable gifts as a token of his submission to the khanate.

Despite his petty deceptions, the grandmaster was received warmly by Hulagu, who declared that he should be given every comfort he might ask for. On Rukn al-Din's command, Maymun Diz was evacuated the next day. The Mongols then entered the fortress and pulled down its walls and buildings.

In the following weeks, Rukn al-Din accompanied Hulagu to the remaining Assassin fortresses and ordered them to surrender. The garrison at Alamut, the strongest of the castles, defied Rukn al-Din's call to lay down their arms. They fended off the Mongol attack for several days, but then sued for peace.

As Hulagu's men charged through Alamut's corridors in the hunt for treasure, Juvayni was given permission by Hulagu to enter the castle's famous library to retrieve rare and precious books, while soldiers made a bonfire of heretical works that he thought were 'neither founded on tradition nor supported by reason'.[42]

AFTER THE DESTRUCTION of the last of the Assassins' strongholds, Hulagu concluded that Rukn al-Din was of no further use to him and cut him loose. The grandmaster journeyed all the way to Karakorum to ask to be admitted to the court of the great khan, but Mongke refused to see him. On the road back to Iran, Rukn al-Din was ambushed and murdered. 'He and his followers were kicked to a pulp and then put to the sword,' wrote Juvayni with satisfaction, 'and of him and his stock no trace was left, and he and his kindred became but a tale on men's lips and a tradition in the world.'[43]

Tusi, the Assassins' astronomer, was placed into Hulagu's service, and they struck up an unlikely friendship. Hulagu bluntly asked Tusi what the point of astrology was, since everything it ordained was inevitable anyway. Tusi replied that it was better to be warned about the future, even if there was nothing that could be done to avert it.[44]

The Death of the City of Peace

HAVING DEALT WITH the Assassins, Hulagu sent an envoy over the Zagros Mountains into Iraq in March 1257 with a blunt message for the caliph in Baghdad. Hulagu had not forgotten Mustasim's failure to send troops to aid his campaign against the Assassins, and so he wrote:

> We have warned you already and we say to you today: rid yourself of feelings of hatred and hostility, don't struggle against our standard, because you will be wasting your time. Therefore, without revisiting the past, let the caliph agree to dismantle the city's defences and fill up the moats, let him hand over the administration to his son and come in person to us in good time … If he obeys our orders, it will be unworthy of us to demonstrate any hatred towards him and he will remain in possession of his states, his troops and his subjects. But if he refuses to listen to our advice and prefers to follow the path of opposition and war, deploying his forces and naming the battlefield, we are committed and ready to fight him. And once

> I lead my forces to Baghdad in righteous anger, while you are hiding, from the highest heavens to the depths of earth,
>
> I will bring you crashing down from the summit of the sky,
> Like a lion I will throw you down to the lowest depths.
> I will not leave a single person alive in your country,
> I will turn your city, lands and empire into flames.

MUSTASIM, THE LAST of the Abbasid caliphs, was forty-five years old. Now, in the fifteenth year of his reign, he faced the greatest crisis in Baghdad's long and storied history, but the caliph was unequal to the task. The sources portray him as a feckless pleasure-seeker, a man of weak resolve and poor judgement. Mustasim had nonetheless convinced himself he would prevail against the Mongol juggernaut. His confidence had been bolstered by his court astrologer, who reassured him the stars had decreed that all those who attacked the Abbasid caliphs were doomed to die a miserable death. The astrologer was so sure of Mustasim's safety that he offered to give up his own life if his forecasts turned out to be mistaken.

Mustasim imagined he could summon loyalists across the Muslim world to pick up the sword and rally to his defence, but in truth he was bereft of allies and unable to command much loyalty even within his own capital. The city was riven by entrenched hatreds between its religious and political factions. Mustasim was also being undermined by his own vizier, Ibn al-Alkami, who was secretly sending intelligence to the Mongol camp, advising Hulagu that Mustasim had neglected to reinforce the city's walls, that the army was ill equipped and poorly trained, and that the caliph was widely hated in the city.

Unaware of his vizier's treachery, the caliph responded to Hulagu's menacing letter with airy bluster:

> Oh, young man, barely started on your career, who shows such little desire to live, who, drunk with the happiness and riches of ten days, believes you are greater than the whole world, who thinks your orders have the irresistible force of destiny, why do you ask of me what you have not the slightest chance of obtaining?
>
> Do you believe with your greatest efforts, the strength of your armies and your bravery, you can bring a star tumbling down into your chains?
>
> The prince forgets that from the east to the west all the worshippers of Allah, whether kings or beggars, young or old, are slaves of this court and make up my armies. The moment I give the order to these defenders of my realm to come together, I will begin by finishing the business of Iran, after which I will continue my march to Turan and will put everyone where he belongs. Certainly the face of the earth will be covered with troubles and disorder but I am neither eager for vengeance nor hungry for the consideration of men … I do not want my subjects to be the victims of passing armies, above all when I and Hulagu Khan have but one heart and one language. If, like me, you have sown the seed of friendship, why do you talk of dismantling defences and ramparts? Follow the path of wellbeing and return to Khorasan.
>
> If, however, you want war, do not hesitate and do not have any excuses. If you have decided to fight, I have millions of cavalry and infantry, all ready for war, who, when the moment of vengeance arrives, will dissolve the waters of the sea.

The final letter from Hulagu came quickly:

> The love of great things, riches, pride, the illusions of fleeting happiness have so completely seduced you that the words of well-intentioned men make no impression upon you, and your ears are closed to the advice and warnings of those who are closest to you. You have completely abandoned the path followed by your father and your ancestors. Now all you can do is prepare for war because I am going to march against Baghdad at the head of an army as numerous as ants and grasshoppers.[45]

HULAGU NOW SPLIT his forces into three separate divisions that converged on the outer suburbs of Baghdad from different directions. On 11 January 1258, one Mongol division crossed the Tigris and advanced along its banks towards the city's crumbling western defences. Mustasim sent out 20,000 cavalry, who fought fiercely and succeeded in driving the invaders back, until Mongol engineers opened the dykes of the dams along the Tigris, flooding the caliph's army. Those soldiers who did not drown were pulled out of the water and slaughtered.

Groups of Mongol soldiers now pushed into Baghdad's western suburbs, while others gathered up bricks from ruined buildings to construct tall siege towers. Meanwhile, on the eastern wall, the caliph's well-trained slave soldiers took their posts on the battlements, standing shoulder to shoulder alongside terrified civilians armed with whatever weapons they could lay their hands on. Within the city, gates were sealed up, streets were barricaded. Mustasim, fretting inside the palace, now realised that no one was coming to rescue him. He sent a delegation to the Mongol camp, offering to negotiate a surrender, but Hulagu, knowing he had the upper hand, refused to see them.

On 29 January, the Mongol artillery began a steady bombardment of the eastern walls. Heavy boulders were in short supply in the area, so the Mongols chopped down tall date palms nearby, doused the logs in flaming naphtha and hurled them over the battlements, sending them crashing into mosques, palaces and houses. The Chinese artillerymen fired primitive bombs – cases packed with shrapnel and gunpowder designed to explode on impact – that terrified the residents. Mongol archers fired arrows into the streets carrying messages promising safety to those who laid down their arms and surrendered.

ON THE FIFTH DAY of the bombardment, a breach opened near a corner tower. Mongol soldiers charged in, and by the following morning, they had possession of the entire wall.

The caliph's treacherous vizier, who had earlier advised him not to escape, now recommended he should surrender unconditionally. And so on 10 February, Mustasim, his three sons and his retinue came out of the city and put themselves at Hulagu's mercy.

HULAGU RECEIVED THEM with great courtesy, but he demanded that Mustasim's court astrologer be given over to him. Aware the astrologer had sworn on his life to the caliph that the Mongols would be defeated, Hulagu taunted him for a while then had him executed. Hulagu told Mustasim that he must now order his remaining troops to lay down their arms. After receiving assurances of clemency, the garrison surrendered and came out of the city. But Hulagu reneged on his promise and had all of them killed.

With the city now completely defenceless, the Mongol army entered Baghdad on 13 February. On Hulagu's advice, the city's Christians, who had been feeding him a stream of intelligence, found sanctuary inside the city's Nestorian church, while the rest of the City of Peace was dragged into a vortex of looting, rape, murder and destruction.

Among the most enthusiastic participants were the Mongols' Christian allies from Armenia and Georgia, who rejoiced in pulling down the palaces of their Muslim overlords. 'Five hundred and fifteen years have passed since the founding of the city,' wrote a gleeful Armenian chronicler. 'Throughout its supremacy, like an insatiable leech Baghdad had swallowed up the entire world. Now it restored all that it had taken.'[46]

WITHIN SEVEN DAYS of Baghdad's surrender almost every last inhabitant of the city had been killed. The accounts differ widely concerning the death toll, but the figure most likely exceeded 100,000.[47]

After every bit of loot had been discovered and removed, the invaders set alight the mosques and palaces. The tombs of the Abbasid caliphs were raided and desecrated. According to one of the Persian sources, the House of Wisdom, the world's largest library, was ransacked and destroyed; books of astronomy, medicine, zoology and geography were hurled into the river. The Tigris was said to have run red with the blood of its scholars, and black with the ink of their literature.[48]

THROUGHOUT THIS WEEK, Hulagu entertained Mustasim in mock formality in his camp outside the city. Halugu acted as though the caliph were his gracious host who had invited him to come to Baghdad. As the looted treasure piled up in great heaps outside

Hulagu's tent, he jokingly asked Mustasim why he hadn't spent some of his riches buying more troops to defend his city.

'And why did you not make your doors into arrowheads? And why did you not come to the river and try to stop me crossing?' he asked.

'That was God's will,' the caliph replied.

Hulagu said, 'What will now happen to you is also God's will.'[49]

Mustasim was no longer of any use to him, but Hulagu still hesitated to have him executed. There was a longstanding Mongol taboo against the shedding of royal blood; it was said that if a single drop fell on the ground, it would generate earthquakes.

Hulagu resolved the dilemma by having Mustasim rolled into a carpet and trampled to death by horses.

And with that, the 508-year-long reign of the Abbasid caliphs of Baghdad was finally extinguished.

NEWS OF THE FALL of Baghdad left the Muslim world numb with shock. A poet mourned the death of the City of Peace:

> Oh grief, what a loss for the kingdom, for true religion,
> what a loss – Baghdad struck with misery.
> Death is touching me;
> death is doing what it wants.
> It is a dark cruel catastrophe
> which turns a child's hair and liver white.[50]

Juvayni, who had witnessed the devastation of Baghdad from the Mongol camp, was appointed to take over as the city's new governor, a post he held for the next twenty years. It was there, in the ruins of the City of Peace, that he completed his *History of the World Conqueror*, which he dedicated to his benefactor Hulagu. But his account comes discreetly to a close just before the start of Hulagu's Baghdad campaign. Perhaps he felt unable to deliver an honest account while in the service of the Mongols, or perhaps the fall of the city and the murder of the Commander of the Faithful left him too heartbroken to lift up his pen.

UNDER MONGOL RULE, Baghdad shrank into a mere provincial capital. New people were brought in from the countryside to repopulate the empty streets, but they lacked an ancestral connection to the city. Baghdad became a stranger to itself. The destruction of Baghdad's libraries would later be blamed for the centuries of Arab technological and political stagnation that followed.[51] It wasn't until the twentieth century that the city's population returned to the levels of the pre-Mongol era.

The name of Genghis Khan became a byword for genocidal conquest, whereas his grandson Kublai is remembered, thanks to Marco Polo and Samuel Taylor Coleridge, as a cultured ruler, the builder of Xanadu.

Hulagu has been forgotten in the West, but not in the Arab world. In November 2002, Osama bin Laden released a recorded message to the world, in which he denounced US Vice President Dick Cheney and Secretary of State Colin Powell as men who had 'killed and destroyed in Baghdad more than Hulagu of the Mongols'.[52] The obscure reference sent Western analysts scurrying for their history books.

THE ARRIVAL OF JUVAYNI in Baghdad as governor marked a return of sorts for the Juvayni clan. His distant ancestor, Rabi ibn Yunus, had served there centuries earlier as an advisor to Caliph Mansur, the city's founder, and had supervised the construction of the Palace of the Golden Gate.

For Juvayni, then, overseeing the slow reconstruction of the broken city must have been a melancholy duty. But in these years and decades, imperial Baghdad underwent a more profound restoration in the bookshops of the Arab world. It was in the thirteenth and fourteenth centuries that *The Thousand and One Nights* crystallised into its current form. Medieval Baghdad on the Tigris was no more, but *The Thousand and One Nights* transfigured it for all time, like the lost city of Byzantium, into an immortal city of the imagination, as a dream-like labyrinth filled with bold thieves and bottled *jinn*, giant birds and talking fish, with princes and princely doppelgangers, with hidden gardens and houses inhabited by strange and dangerous women – the whole scene presided over by Harun al-Rashid, whose presence in the pages of the *Nights* evoked deep nostalgia in its readers for their lost Abbasid golden age.

TOWARDS THE END of the endless *Nights*, Shahrazad the storyteller brings in Juvayni's ancestor, the courtier, Rabi ibn Yunus for a walk-on role. He appears within the tale of the last of our travellers: Tufah the slave singer, the female Orpheus who brings heavenly music to the monsters of the underworld.*

* The following tale is taken from several translations of the same tale from *The Thousand and One Nights*, which appears under the title 'The Tale of the Girl Heart's-Miracle, Lieutenant of the Birds', or 'The Tale of the Damsel Tufah al-Kulub and the Caliph Harun al-Rashid'. Tufah appears to be loosely based on Harun's real-life paramour, Dananir the slave singer.

The Travels of Tufah the Slave Singer

And when the 996th night had come, Shahrazad said:

I AM TOLD, O king, that one night in Baghdad, the home of pleasure and the garden of wit, the Caliph Harun al-Rashid summoned his friends: Jafar the Barmakid and his brother Fadl, Ishaq his court musician, Masrur the sword-bearer of his vengeance, and Yunus the scribe. They found the Commander of the Faithful dressed as an ordinary citizen.

'I'm bored,' he said. 'Let us go out together in disguise and explore the city at night.'

Doing as they were bidden, the five men donned plain clothes and together they stepped down from the Palace of Eternity into a waiting boat on the Tigris. In the cool of the night, a slave rowed them to a busy marketplace, where they walked through the streets, laughing and talking, until they ran into an old man with a white beard. Ishaq recognised him as a procurer of talented singing slaves for his music school.

'How happy I am to run into you, Master Ishaq,' said the old man (who did not recognise the caliph), 'for I was just on my way to the palace to tell you something. I have at my house an exceptionally talented slave. Perhaps you and your friends might like to hear her sing tonight. She would make a fine addition to your school. If she pleases you, I will send her to your mansions. If not, I will sell her to some rich merchant.'

Ishaq glanced at Harun, who subtly gave his assent, and they all followed the old man to his house. He brought them into a large hall, where they sat on a bench until their host led the veiled singing girl into the room. Seating herself on an embroidered chair, she gently gathered up the *oud* into her arms, just as a sister might embrace a little brother. She tuned its strings, then began to sing:

My desire is stronger and climbs above
The difficult mountains, but, until I cross,
My feet are wounded on the diamond steep.
Also, my soul couched in its jewelled loss
Has taught my eyelids to forget their sleep.

Harun al-Rashid was deeply moved by the music, but wishing to remain incognito, he kept his peace. Ishaq opened his mouth to bestow his compliments, but before he could do so, the girl ran to him and said urgently, 'O great master! Only you, master, can lift the veil of my need. May we speak in private?'

The bewildered Ishaq followed her into the next room. She raised her veil. Her black side locks curled in trails from her temples; her dark eyes shone from under darker brows. She was as lovely as the moon.

'Who are you,' he asked, 'and what is this great need you speak of?'

'O lord,' she said, 'the name of your music school has spread far and wide, even to the distant plains of my homeland. Throughout these last five months, I have deliberately withheld myself from sale at every auction, in the hope that you may purchase me and take me as your pupil.'

Ishaq called for the slave master and asked for her name and her price.

'Her name is Tufah,' he said, 'and her price is 10,000 dinars.

I must tell you that all kinds of rich men have expressed an interest in her, but each time they came to auction, she made pointed remarks about their appearances, and they shied away from bidding for fear of her tongue. Therefore I cannot ask for more than 10,000 for her, even though such an amount will barely cover my expenses.'

'Double that amount,' said Ishaq, 'and we will pretend we have reached her true value. If Tufah consents, send her to my house.'

Then Ishaq returned to Harun and the others in the hall, and the friends went on their way.

THAT NIGHT, THE OLD man brought Tufah to Ishaq's mansion, where she bathed in a scented *hammam*. As Ishaq's slaves dressed her, each of them gave her an item of jewellery. When Ishaq came home, he saw her adorned in rings, bracelets, anklets, silks and a gold-embroidered veil, and he told himself, *After a few months of instruction in playing and singing, she will become the conquering star in the caliph's harem.*

OVER THE FOLLOWING WEEKS, Tufah followed her lessons diligently, along with her fellow students. One day, while the others were in the garden, Tufah wandered into an empty room, picked up an *oud* and began to sing. When Ishaq came in from the garden and heard the heavenly music, he had to sit down on the floor.

I do not think Tufah is altogether mortal, he said to himself.

Tufah saw his confusion and rushed to his aid. He tried to kiss her hand, as an act of obeisance, but Tufah instantly withdrew it.

'Oh, my lord,' she said, 'please do not do that! It's not correct for an artist to kiss the hand of a slave.'

'It is not so, Tufah,' he replied shaking his head. 'It is not so. Ishaq has found his master. I will take you to the caliph at once.'

At this point the light of dawn crept into the room and Shahrazad fell silent. But when the 997th night had come, she said:

ISHAQ'S SLAVES DRESSED Tufah in seven swathes of fine Nishapur silk, then he led her to the Palace of Eternity, with one slave holding the long train of her robe, and a child slave carrying her *oud*. He left her waiting in an anteroom while he begged for admittance to the caliph's chambers. He found Harun there with Jafar the Barmakid.

'I have brought you a stray from Paradise,' Ishaq said earnestly. 'Her name is Tufah. She is my teacher and not my pupil.'

Harun al-Rashid smiled and asked, 'Is this the same girl we saw at the slave house?'

'She is, my lord. She is brighter than the morning and more musical to the ear than the song of water over pebbles.'

'Then let the morning in!' Harun decreed.

WHILE ISHAQ WENT TO fetch Tufah, the caliph laughed and turned to Jafar and said, 'Is it not a miracle to hear Ishaq praising someone else? I must confess I am curious to see this woman.'

Tufah entered the room, carrying her *oud*, with her silks flowing behind her. She kissed the ground before the caliph and said, 'Greetings, O auspicious blood of our Lord Muhammad (on whom be prayer and peace). Greetings, O fold and shelter of the righteous, O upright judge of the Three Worlds.'

'The blessing of Allah be upon you,' Harun replied. 'Your coming has lighted this room. May we now hear the music that has entered with you?'

Tufah sat down with her *oud* and began to play, performing complex modes and scales, all the while improvising poetic couplets as she sang.

Harun and Jafar were moved and unsettled. They had never heard music like this before.

'She is a thief of souls,' Jafar said quietly.

When she finished her song, Harun arose from his couch and sat down on the carpet next to her and looked at Tufah closely. Then he gently let down the silk veil over her face, to signify that she now belonged to his harem.

That night Harun al-Rashid stayed with Tufah in her room, and every night thereafter, and he fell deeply in love with her. He bestowed every kind of luxury upon her and consulted her on the affairs of his realm. Fearful of losing her, Harun carried away the key to her chamber whenever he left her. One day, as she sang for him, he told her: 'You are my sole queen now. You are more to me than Zubaydah, my cousin and my wife.'

THE NEXT DAY, while Harun rode out to hunt, Tufah sat alone in her room, reading a book by candlelight. Suddenly, a musk-apple fell into her lap. Looking up, she saw the Lady Zubaydah standing in front of her. Tufah sprang up at once, and begged her forgiveness for not yet coming to visit her. 'If I had been free in my movement,' Tufah said, 'I would have come to you every day to offer you my service.'

Zubaydah sighed, sat on the edge of Tufah's bed and patted her gently on the leg.

'I knew you had a good heart, Tufah,' she said, 'and I am not surprised by your kind words. Generosity is your native garment. Now, I swear that it is not my habit to pay visits to all my husband's favourites. Yet I have come to you, because I think that you should hear of the humiliation that has been put upon me ever since you came here. The Commander of the Faithful no longer comes to see me, nor does he ask after me. I am cast aside, I am relegated to the importance of a barren concubine.'

Zubaydah's face crumpled and she began to weep.

'I have come to ask you to give him back to me, for just one night a month. One night only. So that I may not seem altogether a slave. This is all I ask of you.'

Tufah wept also, kissed her hand and said, 'I promise you I will do what I can.'

At this moment, they could hear noises in the hall, indicating that the caliph had returned from his hunt and was approaching Tufah's chamber. Zubaydah slipped out into the hall unnoticed.

Harun al-Rashid entered Tufah's room and smiled. They ate and drank together, then removed each other's clothes. Only then, when they were both naked, did Tufah beg him to think of Zubaydah and to go to her that night.

'But why did you wait until we were naked before you asked this of me?'

'I remembered the words of the poet,' she said.

If you would beg, plain nakedness is best,
A leg's a better beggar than all complaining.

Hearing this, Harun laughed and embraced her. Then did as he was bidden and left the room to go to Zubaydah, taking care to lock the door behind him.

At this point the light of dawn crept into the room and Shahrazad fell silent. But when the 998th night had come, she said:

AFTER HARUN AL-RASHID left her room, Tufah returned to her book. She read for another hour or so in solitude, then she idly picked up her *oud* and began to play. The music was so exquisite that the walls came in closer to listen.

Then, beyond the little orb of candlelight, in a dim corner of the room, she saw a figure writhing in the darkness.

Straining with her eyes, she realised it was an old man, dancing to her music in ecstasy. Tufah suddenly grew cold with fear, for all the windows were locked and eunuchs stood guard outside her door. How had this thing entered her room?

Uttering a silent prayer, she tried to ignore it.

She played on, forcing her fingers to the notes, while the figure continued to dance.

After an hour, he came forward into the candlelight and showed his face to her.

'O Tufah, do you not know me?' he asked.

'By God, I do not know you,' she said, 'but I fear you are a *jinn*, a demon of smokeless flame.'

'That's right,' he replied with a sly smile. 'I am a *jinn*. From the lands of Jinnistan. My name is Iblis and I am the lord of that place.'

Before Tufah could cry out for protection, Iblis kissed her hand and told her she had nothing to fear. She was under his protection.

Tufah asked him why he had come to her.

'I am here to tell you that Kamariyah, the queen of the *jinn*, wants you badly,' Iblis said. 'For many weeks we have watched you in this room while you slept. Kamariyah loves you madly, fiercely. She aches for you. Please, let me take you to our lands, where you will be our most honoured guest. Come with me. Feast with us. You will stay as long as you like, queening it over the hearts of the *jinn*. Then, upon my sacred oath, I shall return you at the first moment you ask me to do so.'

Tufah thought for a moment, bowed her head, then said, '*Bismillah*. Let us go.'

At this point the light of dawn crept into the room and Shahrazad fell silent. But when the 999th night had come, she said:

IBLIS PICKED UP her *oud* and then led her through locked doors into the palace's smallest room, the Chapel of Ease – the privy. Through the disgusting hole, she saw a stairway descending into darkness. Tufah thought she was going mad, but Iblis explained that it is only through such filthy portals that the *jinn* are permitted to travel (which is why no one should enter a privy without first invoking the name of Allah).

The terrified Tufah permitted herself to be led down into the privy. They passed through a vaulted hallway and emerged into a gloomy landscape, where a horse was waiting for her. Iblis lifted her into the saddle.

'*Bismillah*,' he said, blasphemously. 'Let us go.'

At once, the horse rose up underneath Tufah with the force of a wave. She felt the cold wind in her face and heard the slow thump of great wings beating against the air. Through the murky clouds, she saw Iblis flying beside her. Below her she saw a vast meadowland carpeted with dark, shimmering flowers. The horse flew on towards a castle ringed with towers and copper doors and then brought Tufah down to its threshold. The castle gates opened and the lords of the *jinn* emerged, clapping their hands and crying out, 'Tufah has come! Tufah has come!' The *jinn* lords lifted her off her horse and carried her inside, into a hall so large and lavishly decorated that the tongue of a man would grow hair before he could tell of it.

They set Tufah down on a red-gold throne and arrayed themselves subserviently at her feet. As she studied the *jinn* lords, she noticed that all of them had taken on a human aspect except for two, who had single eyes twisted into their foreheads and tusks projecting from their cheeks.

When they had settled into their places, Kamariyah, the queen of the *jinn*, swept into the hall accompanied by her three sisters. Tufah thought she was strikingly beautiful. Kamariyah grasped her, pressed her close and kissed her for a very long while upon the cheeks and mouth.

Watching this, Iblis smirked and said, 'Be kind and take me between you!' Laughter rippled through the hall and Kamariyah said, 'I love you, dear sister. I loved you even before I saw you.'

'And you are very dear to me, Lady Kamariyah,' she replied. 'I became your slave as soon as I laid eyes upon your face.'

The queen kissed Tufah again, and then introduced her to her three sisters, Gamra, Sharara and Wakhimah. And then slaves suddenly appeared with trays of food and wine, and the five women sat down to eat, drink and talk.

Tufah was enjoying herself very much until she glanced at the two ugly one-eyed *jinn* with the tusks.

'I am very frightened by them,' she told Kamariyah. 'Who are they?'

Kamariyah said, 'Oh that is my father, Shisban, and his swordbearer, Maymun. In reality, everyone else here looks just like them, but on your account they are wearing glamours so as not to alarm you. Those two are too arrogant to do so.'

Hearing this, both of the ugly *jinn* began to laugh and bray like mules.

When the feast came to an end, Iblis presented Tufah with her *oud* and said, 'Now that you have enjoyed our hospitality, will you sing for us? There are only a few hours of night left to us.'

At this point the light of dawn crept into the room and Shahrazad fell silent. But when the 1000th night had come, she said:

TUFAH PLUCKED THE STRINGS, opened her voice and sang 'The Song of the Rose'. The music came from her like a great intoxicating wave that rolled over the *jinn* in the cavernous hall.

My visit is shorter than a ghost's,
Between winter, it is, and summer.
Hasten to play with me, play with me.
Time is a sword.
I balm my breath,
I am the colour of love,
I tingle in the hand of the girl who takes me.
I am your guest,
Hope not to keep me long,
The nightingale loves me.

The lords of the *jinn* began to sway with pleasure. Maymun the hideous swordbearer leapt about the hall with his finger in his arse, yelping, 'The joy is too much. It stops my blood, it hurts my breathing!'

At the end of the song, Queen Kamariyah rose, kissed Tufah between the eyes and said, 'Heart of my heart, cool of my soul, I beg you to sing again.'

And so Tufah played another song and then another. She sang of the flowers in the field and the birds of the forest, and after twenty such songs she lay down her *oud*, exhausted.

Iblis kissed her feet with gratitude. The queen embraced her and gave her another long, slow kiss. Meanwhile, the assembled *jinn* jumped up and down in their seats, kicking their legs in the air as a sign of their appreciation. Maymun, still with his finger in his arse, cried out, 'I marvel! I marvel!'

Tufah was greatly moved by this ovation, and said that if she were not so weary, she would play more songs for them, but now it was time for her to leave.

'Will you not stay a little while longer?' begged Iblis. 'We have only just sipped the wine, and now you want to snatch it from our lips!'

'I must return to Baghdad,' she said, 'to the palace of my master. He will be greatly upset by my disappearance. Surely you will not keep me here against my will?'

'Certainly not,' replied Iblis. 'But you must not depart empty-handed. Come now, before you go, I will teach you a new form of music that will make you famous throughout the world and increase the caliph's love for you.'

With that, Iblis snatched Tufah's *oud* and played a tune with a strange new mode and scale, finding queer notes between the tones that made Tufah shiver.

When he finished, Tufah took the *oud* back and repeated it note for note.

'Excellent! Excellent!' Iblis said. 'You have reached the very pinnacle of this art!' He called for some parchment and wrote a formal inscription, stating that Tufah had been appointed on his authority: *Queen of All Earthly Lute Players and Lieutenant of the Birds.* He placed his seal on the parchment, put it inside a small gold box and handed it ceremoniously to Tufah, who raised it to her brow as a sign of thanks.

Then, with a gesture from Queen Kamariyah, twelve slaves entered the hall carrying twelve cupboards on their backs, stuffed with gold, silks, musical instruments, scented oils, jewels and carpets of more beauty and majesty than any Caesar or Khusrau had ever possessed.

Kamariyah said, 'Although you are leaving us, dear sister, I hope you will let us come to watch over you in your chamber sometimes. If you wish, I shall not be invisible next time. If you wish, I shall assume the form of a little human girl, and wake you with my breath.'

'Please do so,' answered Tufah. 'I will rejoice to wake under your breath and feel you lying against me.' And they kissed for one last time.

Iblis crouched down and Tufah climbed onto his neck. Then he flew up into the air and returned her to her bed at the palace.

At this point the light of dawn crept into the room and Shahrazad fell silent. But when the 1001st night had come, she said:

TUFAH BLINKED SEVERAL TIMES into the pearlescent light coming through her window and it seemed that the events of this long night had never happened. So she picked up her *oud* and played upon it the strange tune Iblis had taught her, improvising new couplets of poetry as she sang.

The music wafted outside the room into the hall where her loyal eunuch still stood guard. On hearing her voice, the startled eunuch ran across the palace to the caliph's bedchamber. He was a heavy man, and when he reached the door he fell panting at the feet of Masrur, the caliph's bodyguard.

'My lord, my lord,' he gasped, 'wake the Commander of the Faithful, for I bring astonishing news!'

Masrur cursed him, saying, 'You must be mad if you think I dare wake the caliph at such an hour.'

But the eunuch made such a racket that Harun al-Rashid woke, and cried out from his bed, 'What on Earth is going on?'

The eunuch shouted through the door, 'I tell you, O Commander of the Faithful, that Tufah has returned. She is playing and singing in her bedroom!'

Harun leapt from his bed, pulled on the first garment that came to hand and flung open the door.

'What are you saying? How dare you say that to me! No one who is abducted by the *jinn* can ever return! You know this! What maggot of a dream has entered your head that you should disturb me in this way?'

'But this was no maggot of a dream!' the eunuch cried. 'I have not even been to bed! I tell you Tufah is not dead!'

'If you are telling the truth,' Harun said, 'I will make your fortune; I will free you and give you 1000 dinars. But if you have been dreaming, I will have you crucified.'

The trembling eunuch led the caliph to Tufah's door, all the while whispering a prayer, 'O Allah, O Protector, O Master of Salvation, grant that it was no maggot of a dream.'

Then Harun heard Tufah's distinctive voice floating towards him. His shaking hands fumbled with the key for half a minute before he could open the door.

And there she was, seated with her *oud*. Her return was like a miracle. Although she had spent a single night in Jinnistan, she had been missing from Baghdad for an entire month.

Harun stood in the middle of the room in disbelief, and his tears fell through his beard to the floor. Tufah held him and told him the whole story: the appearance of Iblis, the journey through the privy, the night flight on horseback, the performance for the queen of the *jinn*, the special music lesson, and the special commission awarded to her as Queen of All Earthly Lute Players and Lieutenant of the Birds.

Harun heard all this in joyous amazement.

Then Tufah showed him the twelve closets of gold, silk and jewels from Queen Kamariyah lined up against the wall of her room, which became the foundation of the treasure of the Abbasids.

TUFAH'S SAFE RETURN filled Harun al-Rashid with so much joy that he had the city of Baghdad lit up with fireworks and gave feasts to the poor.

He and Tufah remained together for many, many years, until they were visited by the Inexorable, the Tomb Filler, the Parter of Companions.

An image from a nineteenth-century Ottoman manuscript of The Thousand and One Nights

ACKNOWLEDGEMENTS

AS ALWAYS, I WOULD like to express my most urgent feelings of gratitude to the magnificent trio of Brigitta Doyle, Lachlan McLaine and Elizabeth Troyeur for their support, insight and encouragement; and to the gifted Yehrin Tong and Mark Campbell for turning a few crudely sketched cover ideas into an explosive psychedelic lovebomb of sacred geometry. If a space telescope ever takes a picture of the mind of God or the birth of the universe, it will almost certainly look something like this. I am also very thankful to Alex Hotchin, whose international cycling adventures have given her first-hand experience of so many of the far-off places she has delineated in her distractingly beautiful maps.

Emma Dowden, my editor, was wonderful; her discerning eye helped raise the shipwrecked *dhow* of the first draft from the sea bed and bring its cargo to the surface. I am very thankful for the advice I received from Kári Gíslason, Viking Prince of the Antipodes, and from Kim Traill who shared with me her first-hand knowledge of the back roads of Central Asia and the Taklamakan Desert. Thanks are also due to Hugh Riminton for directing my attention to a beautiful scrap of Arabic poetry.

My love and grateful thanks go to my wife Khym, whose research skills were able to gather gold from some of the dustiest corners of the internet.

And finally, thanks and praise are due to the shades of those great storytellers of the lost caliphate who provided me with such excellent company during the long months of COVID-induced home detention: al-Kindī, al-Ṭabarī, Ibn Hawqal, Abū Zayd al-Sīrāfī, Ibn Miskawayh, al-Tanūkhi, Ahmad ibn Fadlān, Ibn Jubayr, Ibn Khaldūn, Atâ-Malek Juvayni, and above all, to al-Masʿūdī and the unseen voices behind the mask of Shahrazad. To you all, a thousand blessings, in whichever realm of heaven you might be

ENDNOTES

Please refer to the Bibliography for full details of many of the books and articles cited here.

EOI = *Encyclopaedia of Islam*.

INTRODUCTION

1 Langermann, pp. 169–178.
2 Masudi, 1841, p. 4.
3 Freya Stark, 'The Valley of the Assassins to the Caspian Sea', *Scottish Geographical Magazine*, 53:3, p. 156.
4 Masudi, 1989, p. 3.
5 Gudrid's story is recounted in my earlier book, co-authored with Kári Gíslason, *Saga Land*, HarperCollins, 2017.
6 Mehdi Golshani, 'Seek Knowledge Even if It Is in China', *Islam & Science*, 13 September 2013: islam-science.net/seek-knowledge-even-if-it-is-in-china-1260/.
7 Quoted in Hermes, pp. 22–23.
8 *Accounts of China and India*, 2.4.2.
9 Rudyard Kipling, 'The White Man's Burden', 1897.
10 Quran 71:19–20.

BOOK ONE: THE CROSSROADS OF THE UNIVERSE

1 EOI, Vol. 1, p. 894.
2 A. de Jong, '*Sub Specie Maiestatis*', in Stausberg, pp. 356–357.
3 Ibn al-Balkhi, *Fars-nama* ('The Book of Fars'), quoted in Canepa, p. 143.
4 Brown, 1971, p. 163.

5 Cassius Dio, *Roman History*, 68:29.
6 Heather, p. 60.
7 Frankopan, p. 33.
8 Theophylact, 4:11:2.
9 Procopius, 'The Wars of Justinian', 2:19.
10 Mackintosh-Smith, p. 116.
11 Irwin, 2000, p. 221.
12 *The Enactments of Justinian*, 'The Code', First Preface.
13 Procopius, 'History of the Wars', 4:14.
14 Ann Gibbons, 'Why 536 Was "The Worst Year to Be Alive"', *Science*, 15 November 2018: www.science.org/content/article/why-536-was-worst-year-be-alive.
15 Pseudo-Dionysius, p. 103.
16 Agathius, pp. 4–5.
17 Theophilus of Edessa, p. 92.
18 Ernest Renan, quoted in Bernard Lewis, 2002, p. 32.
19 Crone, pp. 3–4.
20 *Ibid.*, pp. 6–7.
21 Bowersock, p. 12.
22 Quoted in Mackintosh-Smith, p. 155.
23 Quoted in introduction of Penguin edition of *The Koran*, p. 9.
24 Quran 73:4 & 69:40–42.
25 *Ibid.*, 33:38.
26 *Ibid.*, 54:1.
27 *Ibid.*, 3:113.
28 Kennedy, 2004, p. 51.
29 W. Montgomery Watt, 'Muhammad', in Holt *et al.*, p. 54.
30 Baladhuri, Vol. 1, p. 210.
31 Hoyland, 1997, p. 69.
32 Kennedy, 2007, p. 93.
33 Theophilus of Edessa, p. 114.
34 Quran 2:216.
35 Peter Brown, 'The Great Transition', *New York Review of Books*, 10 May 2012: www.nybooks.com/articles/2012/05/10/byzantium-islam-great-transition/.
36 Baladhuri, Vol. 1, p. 403, & Tabari, Vol. 11, p. 188.
37 Tabari, Vol. 13, p. 24.
38 *Ibid.*, p. 33.

39 Sizgorich, 2009, p. 902.
40 Tabari, Vol. 14, pp. 89–90.
41 EOI, Vol. 10, p. 946.
42 Sharon, p. 40.
43 Tabari, Vol. 15, pp. 182–185.
44 Ibn Ishaq, p. 496.
45 *Ibid.*, pp. 493–497.
46 Madelung, p. 211.
47 *Ibid.*, p. 238.
48 Laura Veccia Vaglieri, 'The Patriarchal and Umayyad Caliphates', in Holt *et al.*, p. 71.
49 Madelung, p. 254.
50 Humphreys, pp. 3, 9.
51 Quoted in Kennedy, 2007, p. 214.
52 Hoyland, 2015, p. 103.
53 Letter from Thomas the Patriarch to the Pope, 678 C.E., quoted in Hoyland, 2015, p. 109.
54 Donner, p. 180.
55 Baladhuri, Vol. 1, p. 75.
56 Robinson, Ch. 3.
57 *Ibid.*, p. 85.
58 Baladhuri, Vol. 1, p. 301.
59 Berkey, p. 74.
60 EOI, Vol. 5, p. 298.
61 *Ibid.*, p. 82.
62 Tabari, Vol. 23, p. 127.
63 Narshakhi, p. 45, & Tabari, Vol. 23, p. 137.
64 Kennedy, 2007, p. 298.
65 *Ibid.*, p. 220.
66 EOI, Vol. 4, p. 422.
67 Tabari, Vol. 24, p. 41.
68 Theophanes, p. 399.
69 Quoted in Hoyland, 2015, p. 163.
70 Wickham, p. 294.
71 Mackintosh-Smith, p. 256.
72 Sharon, p. 203.
73 Tabari, Vol. 27, pp. 154–155.

74 Masudi, *Meadows of Gold*, III, quoted in Mackintosh-Smith, p. 259.
75 Mackintosh-Smith, p. 260.
76 Hoyland, 1997, p. 245.
77 *On the Knowledge Possessed by the Ancient Chinese of the Arabs and Arabian Countries*, p. 8.
78 Quoted in Bloom, p. 42.
79 *Ibid.*, p. 9.
80 Bowersock, p. 12.
81 Tabari, Vol. 29, p. 115.
82 *Ibid.*, Vol. 28, pp. 34–35.
83 Wiet, pp. 10–11.
84 Tabari, Vol. 28, pp. 240–241.
85 Le Strange, 1900, p. 27.
86 Lassner, p. 56.
87 Tabari, Vol. 28, p. 238.
88 Masudi, 1989, p. 33.
89 Tabari, Vol. 29, pp. 152–153.

BOOK TWO: WEST

1 Einhard & Notker the Stammerer, p. 77.
2 *Ibid.*, p. 76.
3 Edward Gibbon, *The History of the Decline and Fall of the Roman Empire*, Strahan & Cadell, 1776–1789, 52:16.
4 Brown, 2013, p. 433.
5 Einhard & Notker the Stammerer, pp. 61–62.
6 Becher, p. 60.
7 Moss, p. 227.
8 Einhard & Notker the Stammerer, p. 67.
9 *Ibid.*
10 *The Capitulare de Villis.*
11 Catherine Donnelly (ed.), *The Oxford Companion to Cheese*, Oxford University Press, 2016, p. 293.
12 Kempf, pp. 82–83.
13 Fichtenau, p. 87.
14 Letter from Alcuin to Charlemagne, 796 C.E., quoted in Colby, p. 18.
15 Brown, 2013, p. 444.
16 Quoted in *ibid.*, p. 439.

17 Becher, pp. 93–94.
18 Einhard & Notker the Stammerer, pp. 52, 63.
19 Heck, Appendix H.
20 *Carolingian Chronicles: Royal Frankish Annals and Nithard's Histories*, p. 87.
21 Ibn Yaqub, in Jan Bažant, *et al*, *The Czech Reader: History, Culture, Politics*, Duke University Press, 2002, p. 14.
22 B. Lewis, 2001, p. 204.
23 Masudi, T*he Book of Notification and Verification*, quoted in Tolan *et al*., pp. 15–16.
24 Ibn al-Faqih, *The Book of Countries*: sites.google.com/site/historyofeastafrica/ibn-al-fakih-al-hamadhani-2.
25 Tabari, Vol. 38, p. 58.
26 Masudi, 1989, p. 67.
27 *Book of Gifts and Rarities*, p. 111.
28 Masudi, 1989, p. 389.
29 Tertius Chandler, *Four Thousand Years of Urban Growth: An Historical Census*, St David's University Press, 1987.
30 Tabari, Vol. 29, p. 228.
31 Borges & Weinberger, p. 566.
32 *Ibid*., p. 574.
33 Clot, p. 45.
34 Tabari, Vol. 29, p. 212.
35 *Ibid*., p. 243.
36 *Ibid*., Vol. 30, p. 58.
37 *Ibid*., p. 44.
38 *Ibid*., p. 47.
39 *Ibid*., p. 44.
40 *Ibid*., pp. 94–95.
41 Masudi, 1989, p. 67.
42 *Ibid*., p. 67.
43 *Ibid*., p. 105–106.
44 Jahiz, pp. 15, 31–32.
45 Masudi, 1989, pp. 109–113.
46 Le Strange, 1900, pp. 114–115.
47 Milwright, p. 163.
48 Abbott, pp. 139–147.
49 Masudi, 1989, pp. 89–90.

50 Davila, p. 134.

51 Catlos, pp. 95–97.

52 Quoted in El Cheikh, *Byzantium Viewed by the Arabs*, p. 204.

53 Fidler, *Ghost Empire*, pp. 15–16.

54 Ibn Hayyan, *Al-Muqtabis fi Tarikh al-Andalus*, quoted in El Cheikh, *Byzantium Viewed by the Arabs*, pp. 159–160; & Jesus Cano & Louis Werner, 'Travelers of Al-Andalus, Part IV: Al-Ghazal: From Constantinople to the Land of the Vikings', *AramcoWorld*, July/August 2015: www.aramcoworld.com/Articles/July-2015/Travelers-of-Al-Andalus-Part-IV-al-Ghazal-From

55 Egil Mikkelsen, 'The Vikings and Islam', in Brink & Price, p. 546.

56 *Ibid.*, p. 21.

57 *Ibid.*, pp. 24–25.

58 Tabari, Vol. 30, p. 240.

59 Masudi, 1989, p. 87.

60 *Ibid.*, pp. 133–134.

61 Tabari, Vol. 30, pp. 217–218, & Kennedy, *When Baghdad Ruled the Muslim World*, pp. 71–72.

62 Tabari, Vol. 30, p. 322.

63 Masudi, 1989, p. 160.

64 *Ibid.*, pp. 158–159.

65 Tabari, Vol. 31, pp. 193–194.

66 Masudi, 1989, p. 174.

67 Cooperson, 2005, p. 72.

68 Abbott, p. 229.

69 From the *Anwar of al-Idrisi*, quoted in Cooperson, 2005, p. 3.

70 Quoted in Mackintosh-Smith, p. 271.

71 Malise Ruthven, 'The Otherworldliness of Ibn Khaldun', *New York Review of Books*, 7 February 2009.

72 Mackintosh-Smith, p. 238.

73 Ahmad, p. 48.

74 Quoted in Adamson & Pormann, p. xx.

75 Ibn Abi Usaybia, *Sources of Information About the Classes of Physicians*, quoted in *ibid.*, p. lxvii.

76 Ibn Khallikan, *Ibn Khallikan's Biographical Dictionary*, trans. William MacGuckin, Baron de Slane, 4 vols, Oriental Translation Fund of Great Britain and Ireland, 1842–1871, quoted in Kennedy, *When Baghdad Ruled the Muslim World: The Rise and Fall of Islam's Greatest Dynasty*, pp. 258–259.

77 'Ibn Hawqal in Sicily', pp. 94–99.
78 See Rapoport, pp. 44–45, & Savage-Smith, pp. 109–127.
79 Caroline Williams, 'Maps Have "North" at the Top, But It Could've Been Different', *BBC Future*, 15 June 2016: www.bbc.com/future/article/20160614-maps-have-north-at-the-top-but-it-couldve-been-different.
80 Joshua C. Birk, *Norman Kings of Sicily and the Rise of the Anti-Islamic Critique*, Springer, 2017, p. 3.
81 Revelation 20:7–10.

BOOK THREE: EAST

1 Tabari, Vol. 34, p. 52.
2 Quran 70:8–9.
3 Ezekiel 38, Revelation 20:7–10, Quran 18:83–98 & 21:95–96.
4 Van Donzel & Schmidt, pp. 66–67.
5 *Ibid.*, p. 71.
6 Quran 18:90–108.
7 Quintus Curtius Rufus, 5:21–22.
8 Byron, p. 187.
9 Plutarch, *Life of Caesar*, 11:6.
10 Quran 18:83–86.
11 Brook, p. 80.
12 Van Donzel & Schmidt, p. 158.
13 Quoted in Zadeh, p. 166.
14 Van Donzel & Schmidt, p. 192.
15 Sykes & Sykes, p. 54.
16 Golden, p. 16.
17 Le Coq, p. 36.
18 Huili, p. 18.
19 Polo, 1:39.
20 Steffen Mischke *et al.*, 'The World's Earliest Aral-Sea Type Disaster: The Decline of the Loulan Kingdom in the Tarim Basin', *Nature*, 27 February 2017: www.nature.com/articles/srep43102.pdf.
21 Morgan & Walters, p. 240.
22 Mirsky, p. 14.
23 *Ibid.*, p. ix.
24 Rudyard Kipling, *Kim*, Doubleday, 1901, p. 10.
25 Hedin, 1898, p. 792.

26 Hedin, 1926, p. 158.
27 Hedin, 1898, p. 798.
28 Curzon, Vol. 2, pp. 195–196.
29 Stein, 1904, p. 172.
30 *Ibid.*, p. 221.
31 *Ibid.*, p. 368.
32 *Ibid.*, p. 446.
33 Sima Qian, 2.194.
34 Whitfield, Whitfield & Agnew, p. 11.
35 Wang Jiqing, 'Aurel Stein's Dealings with Wang Yuanlu and Chinese Officials in Dunhuang in 1907', in Wang, p. 1.
36 Whitfield, Whitfield & Agnew, p. 55.
37 Stein, 1964, p. 150.
38 *Ibid.*, p. 162.
39 Mirsky, p. 263.
40 'Ancient Letters', *The Sogdians: Influencers on the Silk Roads*: sogdians.si.edu/ancient-letters/.
41 Mirsky, p. 266.
42 Stein, 1912, Vol. 2, p. 167.
43 Mirsky, p. 269.
44 'Model Letters – An Apology for Getting Drunk', British Library, SRE catalogue nos 172, 856, *International Dunhuang Project*: idp.bl.uk/4DCGI/education/dialogue/letter.html.
45 Stein, 1912, Vol. 2, p. 180.
46 Walker, p. 170.
47 Stein, 1912, Vol. 2, p. 194.
48 Hopkirk, pp. 219–220.
49 Jacobs, 2010, p. 65.
50 Meyer & Brysac, p. 374
51 Stein, 1964, p. 183.
52 Denyer, Simon, 'China's Ancient Buddhist Grottoes Face a New Threat – Tourists', *Washington Post*, 16 May 2016: washingtonpost.com/world/asia_pacific/chinas-ancient-buddhist-grottoes-face-a-new-threat--tourists/2016/05/16/4f31b68e-184e-11e6-8329-f3767b06317f_story.html.
53 Rong Xinjiang, p. 107.
54 *The Diamond Sutra*, trans. Red Pine, Counterpoint, 2001, Ch. 32.
55 Masudi, 1989, pp. 236–237.

BOOK FOUR: SOUTH

1 Quoted in Burge, p. 79.
2 Tabari, Vol. 34, pp. 65–71.
3 *Ibid.*, p. 90.
4 Masudi, 1989, p. 239.
5 Quoted in Alexander, p. 204.
6 Masudi, 1989, pp. 258–259.
7 *Accounts of China and India,* 2.4.1–6.
8 *Ibid.*, 1.1.1.
9 *Ibid.*, 1.2.7.
10 *Ibid.*, 2.19.1.
11 G. Hourani., pp. 54–55.
12 Irwin, 2010, p. 92.
13 Mackintosh-Smith, p. 29.
14 *Accounts of China and India*, 1.9.3.
15 *Ibid.*, 2.12.13.
16 *The Marvels of India*, pp. 135–137.
17 *Ibid.*, pp. 25–30.
18 Quoted in Wain & Kamali, p. 119.
19 Von Grunebaum, p. 129.
20 Ettinghausen, p. 12.
21 Masudi, 1841, p. 392.
22 EOI, Vol. 1, pp. 1215–1217, & Siegfried Schultz, 'Two Christian Saints? The Barlaam and Josaphat Legend', *India International Centre Quarterly*, Vol. 8, No. 2, June 1981.
23 Mutahhari, p. 5.
24 *Accounts of China and India*, 1.9.2.
25 *Ibid.*, 1.2.2.
26 Merton & Barber, pp. 1–2.
27 George, pp. 582–583.
28 *Ibid.*, pp. 594–595.
29 *Ibid.*, p. 596.
30 *Accounts of China and India*, 2.9.1.
31 *Ibid.*, 2.2.1.
32 *Ibid.*, 2.2.1.
33 *Ibid.*, 2.2.3.
34 McIntosh, p. 116.

35 *Ibid.*, p. 115.
36 *Ibid.*
37 EOI, Vol. 9, p. 715.
38 Horton, p. 90.
39 *Accounts of China and India*, 2.13.1.
40 G. Hourani, p. 81.
41 *The Periplus of the Erythraean Sea*, p. 103.
42 Muqaddasi, p. 21.
43 *Accounts of China and India*, 2.14.1.
44 Polo, Ch. 8.
45 *The Marvels of India*, pp. 44–52.
46 Horton, p. 89.
47 Perry *et al.*, p. 453, p. 271.
48 Quran 24:33.
49 EOI, Vol. 1, p. 25.
50 EOI, Vol. 11, p. 446.
51 Talhami, p. 455.
52 Tabari, Vol. 36, p. 36.
53 *Ibid.*, p. 37
54 *Ibid.*, pp. 36–37.
55 *Ibid.*, p. 457.
56 Tabari, Vol. 36, p. 126.
57 *Ibid.*, p. 127.
58 Masudi, 1989, pp. 317–318.
59 *Ibid.*, p. 329.
60 *Ibid.*, p. 181.
61 Tanukhi, pp. 152–153.

BOOK FIVE: NORTH

1 Le Strange, 1897, pp. 42–43.
2 Bowen, p. 102.
3 Miskawayh, Vol. 1, p. 55.
4 Liutprand of Cremona, pp. 207–208.
5 Masudi, 1989, p. 295.
6 Bowen, pp. 100–101.
7 Al-Qadi al-Qudai, p. 223.
8 Bowen, p. 101.

9 Letizia Osti, 'The Caliph', in Van Berkel *et al.*, p. 60.
10 Miskawayh, Vol. 1, p. 3.
11 El Cheikh, 'Servants at the Gate: Eunuchs at the Court of Al-Muqtadir', p. 236.
12 Miskawayh, Vol. 1, p. 117.
13 *Ibid.*, pp. 143–44.
14 *Ibid.*, p. 13.
15 Osti, *op. cit.*, p. 51.
16 See Nadia Maria El Cheikh, 'The Harem', in Van Berkel *et al.*, pp. 165–186, & El Cheikh, 2004.
17 Kennedy, *The Prophet and the Age of the Caliphates*, p. 187.
18 Abed, p. 165.
19 Matthew Traver, 'The Mystery of Central Asia's "Desert Kites"', *BBC Travel*, 7 September 2020: www.bbc.com/travel.
20 Neil Price, 'Dying and the Dead: Viking Age Mortuary Behaviour', in Brink & Price, p. 266.
21 *Vikingeskibsmuseet* ('Viking Ship Museum'): www.vikingeskibsmuseet.dk/en/.
22 *Poetic Edda*, 'Sayings of the High One', v. 38.
23 D. Sourdel, 'The Abbasid Caliphate', in Holt *et al.*, p. 136.
24 Bosworth, p. 229.
25 Kennedy, *When Baghdad Ruled the Muslim World: The Rise and Fall of Islam's Greatest Dynasty*, p. 197.
26 Irwin, 2018, p. 40.
27 Ibn Khaldun, pp. 251–252.
28 *Ibid.*, p. 91.
29 Arnold Toynbee, *A Study of History*, Vol. 3, Oxford University Press, 1934, p. 322.
30 Irwin, 2018, pp. 9, 231.
31 Ibn Khaldun, p. 281.

BOOK SIX: THE SUMMIT OF THE SKY

1 *Baghdad: The City in Verse*, trans. Reuven Snir, Harvard University Press, 2013, p. 57.
2 Ibn Jubayr, p. 236.
3 *Ibid.*, pp. 253–259.
4 *Ibid.*, p. 257.
5 EOI, Vol. 7, p. 997.
6 *The Secret History of the Mongols*, 1.59.

7 *Ibid.*, 1.62.
8 Juvayni, Vol. 1, p. 4.
9 McLynn, pp. 498–499.
10 'War, Plague No Match for Deforestation in Driving CO2 Buildup', *Carnegie Science*, 20 January 2011: carnegiescience.edu/news/war-plague-no-match-deforestation-driving-co2-buildup.
11 McLynn, p. 350.
12 Juvayni, Vol. 1, p. 145.
13 Juvayni, Vol. 1, p. 145
14 Minhaj-i-Siraj Juzjani, Vol. 2, p. 963.
15 *Ibid.*
16 Ratchnevsky, p. 123.
17 McLynn, p. 265.
18 McLynn, p. 265.
19 *Complete Collection of Russian Chronicles, Volume 7*: Annals of Voskresensk List, quoted in E. Bretschneider, 'Notices of the Mediæval Geography and History of Central and Western Asia', *Journal of the North-China Branch of the Royal Asiatic Society*, No. 10, 1876, p. 158.
20 Peter Jackson, *The Mongols and the Islamic World*, Yale University Press, 2017, p. 78.
21 Juvayni, Vol. 1, p. 105.
22 *Ibid.*, p. 124.
23 Ibn al-Athir, p. 210.
24 Minhaj-i-Siraj Juzjani, Vol. 1, p. 274.
25 Tertius Chandler & Gerald Fox, *3000 Years of Urban Growth*, Academic Press, 1974, p. 232.
26 McLynn, p. 302.
27 Ibn al-Athir, p. 202.
28 *The Secret History of the Mongols*, p. 15.
29 Ratchnevsky, p. 159.
30 William of Rubruck, p. 221.
31 *Ibid.*, p. 209.
32 Juvayni, Vol. 1, p. 4.
33 *Ibid.*, p. 24.
34 *Ibid.*, p. 105.
35 *Ibid.*, p. xxxiv.
36 Minhaj-i-Siraj Juzjani, Vol. 2, p. 1084.

37 Juvayni, Vol. 2, p. 625.
38 *Ibid.*, p. 725.
39 Polo, pp. 71–73.
40 Benjamin T. Acosta, 'Assassins', in Andrea L. Stanton (ed.), *Cultural Sociology of the Middle East, Asia, & Africa: An Encyclopedia*, 1. Middle East, SAGE Publications, 2012, p. 21.
41 Juvayni, Vol. 2, p. 631.
42 *Ibid.*, p. 719.
43 *Ibid.*, pp. 724–725.
44 George Saliba, 'Horoscopes and Planetary Theory: Ilkhanate Patronage of Astronomers', in Komaroff (ed.), *Beyond the Legacy of Genghis Khan*, Brill, 2019, p. 361.
45 Rashid al-Din Hamadani, *Compendium of Chronicles*, quoted in Marozzi, pp. 135–140.
46 Grigor of Akanc, *History of the Nation of the Archers*, quoted in Jack Weatherford, *Genghis Khan and the Making of the Modern World*, Random House, 2005, p. 184.
47 EOI, Vol. 1, p. 902.
48 McLynn, p. xxx.iv.
49 James Chambers, *The Devil's Horsemen*, Book Club Associates, 1979, p. 145.
50 Al-Majd al-Nashabi, quoted in *Baghdad: The City in Verse*, op. cit., p. 27.
51 *Ibid.*, p. 28.
52 'Full Text: "Bin Laden's Message"', *BBC News*, 12 November 2002: news.bbc.co.uk/2/hi/middle_east/2455845.stm.

BIBLIOGRAPHY

Ancient and Medieval Sources

Accounts of China and India, trans. Tim Mackintosh-Smith, New York University Press, 2017.

Adam of Bremen, *History of the Archbishops of Hamburg-Bremen*, trans. Francis J. Tschan, Columbia University Press, 2002.

Agathius, *The Histories*, trans. J.D.C. Frendo, De Gruyter, 2011.

Al-Qadi al-Qudai, *A Treasury of Virtues: Sayings, Sermons, and Teachings of Ali, with the One Hundred Proverbs Attributed to al-Jahiz*, trans. Tahera Qutbuddin, New York University Press, 2013.

The Annotated Arabian Nights: Tales from 1001 Nights, trans. Yasmine Seale, W.W. Norton, 2021.

The Arabian Nights: Tales of 1001 Nights, trans. Malcolm & Ursula Lyons, 3 vols, Penguin, 2010.

Arrian, *The Campaigns of Alexander*, trans. Aubrey de Sélincourt, Penguin, 1971.

Baladhuri, *The Origins of the Islamic State*, trans. Philip Hitti, 2 vols, Columbia University Press, 1916.

Book of Gifts and Rarities, trans. Ghadah Hijjawi Qaddumi, Harvard University Press, 1996.

Buzurg ibn Shahriyar, *The Book of the Marvels of India*, trans. L. Marcel Devic & Peter Quennell, George Routledge & Sons, 1928.

The Capitulare de Villis: www.le.ac.uk/hi/polyptyques/capitulare/trans.html.

Carolingian Chronicles: Royal Frankish Annals and Nithard's Histories, trans. Bernhard Walter Scholz with Barbara Rogers, University of Michigan Press, 1970.

Cassius Dio, *Roman History (Books 61–70)*, trans. Earnest Cary, Loeb Classical Library, Heinemann, 1925.

Colby, C.W. (ed.), *Selections from the Sources of English History*, Longmans, 1899.

Constantine VII Porphyrogenitus, *De Administrando Imperio*, trans. R.J.H. Jenkins, Dumbarton Oaks, 1967.

Einhard & Notker the Stammerer, *Two Lives of Charlemagne*, trans. Lewis Thorpe, Penguin, 1969.

Fakhri, *On the Systems of Government and the Moslem Dynasties*, trans. C.E.J. Whitting, Luzac & Co., 1947.

Freeman-Grenville, G.S.P., *The East African Coast: Select Documents from the First to the Earlier Nineteenth Century*, Rex Collings, 1975.

The Greek Alexander Romance, trans. R. Stoneman, Penguin, 1991.

Huili, *The Life of Hsuan Tsang: The Tripitaka-Master of the Great Tzu En Monastery*, trans. Li Yung-hsi, Chinese Buddhist Association, 1959.

Ibn al-Athir, *The Chronicle of Ibn al-Athir*, Vol. 3, trans. D.S. Richards, Routledge, 2008.

Ibn Fadlan, *Ibn Fadlan and the Land of Darkness: Arab Travellers in the Far North*, trans. P. Lunde & C. Stone, Penguin, 2012.

— *Mission to the Volga*, trans. James Montgomery, New York University Press, 2017.

Ibn Hawqal, 'Ibn Hawqal in Sicily', trans. William Granara, *Alif: Journal of Comparative Poetics* Vol. 3, 1983, pp. 94–99.

Ibn Ishaq, *Sirat Rasul Allah: The Life of Muhammad*, trans. A. Guillaume, Oxford University Press, 1955.

Ibn Jubayr, *The Travels of Ibn Jubayr: A Medieval Journey from Cordoba to Jerusalem*, trans. R. Broadhurst, I.B. Tauris, 2020.

Ibn Khaldun, *Muqaddimah*, trans. F. Rosenthal, Princeton Classics, 2005.

Jahiz, *The Epistle on Singing Girls*, trans. A. Beeston, Aris & Phillips, 1980.

Jayyusi, S.K. (ed.), *Classical Arabic Stories: An Anthology*, Columbia University Press, 2012.

Justinian, *The Civil Law* trans. S.P. Scott, 1932, constitution.org/2-Authors/sps/sps01.htm

Juvayni, Ala-ad-Din Ata-Malik, *The History of the World Conqueror*, trans. John Andrew Boyle, 2 vols, Harvard University Press, 1958.

Kindi, *Al-Kindi's Metaphysics: A Translation of Yaqub ibn Ishaq al-Kindi's Treatise 'On First Philosophy'*, State University of New York Press, 1974.

The Koran, trans. N.J. Dawood, Penguin, 2006.

Liudprand of Cremona, *The Works of Liudprand of Cremona*, trans. F.A. Wright, E.P. Dutton, 1930.

Masudi, *Meadows of Gold and Mines of Gems*, trans. Aloys Sprenger, Oriental Translation Fund of Great Britain & Ireland, 1841.

— *The Meadows of Gold: The Abbasids*, trans. P. Lunde & C. Stone, Routledge, 1989.

Minhaj-i-Siraj Juzjani, *Tabakat-i-Nasiri*, trans. H.G. Raverty, 2 vols, Gilbert & Rivington, 1881.

Miskawayh, *The Eclipse of the Abbasid Caliphate*, trans. D.S. Margoliouth, 7 vols, Oxford, 1921.

Muqaddasi, *The Best Divisions of Knowledge in the Regions*, trans. B. Collins, Asiatic Society of Bengal, 1897.

Narshakhi, *The History of Bukhara*, trans. Richard N. Frye, Medieval Academy of America, 1954.

On the Knowledge Possessed by the Ancient Chinese of the Arabs and Arabian Countries, And Other Western Countries, Mentioned in Chinese Books, trans. E. Bretschneider, Trubner & Co., 1871.

The Periplus of the Erythraean Sea, trans. G.W.B. Huntingdon, Hakluyt Society, 1976.

The Poetic Edda, trans. Carolynne Larrington, Oxford University Press, 2014.

Polo, Marco, *The Travels*, trans. Ronald Latham, Penguin Classics, 1958.

Procopius, *The Complete Works of Procopius of Caesarea*, trans. H.B. Dewing, Delphi Classics, 2016.

Pseudo-Dionysius of Tel-Mahre, *Chronicle*, Pt III, trans. Witold Witakowski, Liverpool University Press, 1996.

Quintus Curtius Rufus, *The History of Alexander*, trans. John Yardley, Penguin, 1984.

The Russian Primary Chronicles (or *Tales of Times Gone By*): pages.uoregon.edu/kimball/chronicle.htm.

The Secret History of the Mongols, trans. Igor de Rachewiltz, Australian National University, 2015.

A Source Book for Medieval History: Documents Illustrative of European Life and Institutions from the German Invasions to the Renaissance, trans. F.F. Ogg, American Book Company, 1908.

Sima Qian, *Records of the Grand Historian of China*, trans. Burton Watson, Vol. II, Columbia University Press, 1993.

Tabari, *The History of al-Tabari*, ed. Ehsan Yarshater, 39 vols, State University of New York Press, 1985–1999.

Tanuhki, *Table Talk of a Mesopotamian Judge*, trans. D.S. Margoliouth, Royal Asiatic Society, 1922.

Theophanes, *The Chronicle of Theophanes Confessor*, trans. C. Mango & R. Scott, Clarendon Press, 1997.

Theophilus of Edessa, *Theophilus of Edessa's Chronicle and the Circulation of Historical Knowledge in Late Antiquity and Early Islam*, trans. R. Hoyland, Liverpool University Press, 2011.

Theophylact, *The History of Theophylact Simocatta*, trans. M. & M. Whitby, Oxford University Press, 1986.

Warraq, *Annals of the Caliphs' Kitchens: Ibn Sayyār al-Warrāq's Tenth-Century Baghdadi Cookbook*, trans. Nawal Nasrallah, Brill, 2007.

William of Rubruck, *The Mission of Friar William of Rubruck: His Journey to the Court of the Great Khan Mongke 1253–1255*, ed. Peter Jackson, Hakluyt Society, 1990.

Modern Sources

Abbott, Nadia, *Two Queens of Baghdad*, University of Chicago Press, 1946.

Abed, Sally, 'Water Rituals and the Preservation of Identity in Ibn Fadlan's

Risala', in *Time, Space, and Identity in the Middle Ages and the Early Modern Age*, ed. Albrecht Classen, De Gruyter, 2018.

Adamson, Peter, & Pormann, Peter E., *The Philosophical Works of Al-Kindi*, Oxford University Press, 2012.

Ahmad, N., *Muslim Contributions to Geography*, Muhammad Ashraf, 1947.

Alexander, David, 'Swords and Sabers During the Early Islamic Period', *Gladius*, Vol. 21 (2001), pp. 193–220.

Al-Khalili, Jim, *Pathfinders: The Golden Age of Arabic Science*, Penguin, 2010.

Becher, Matthias, *Charlemagne*, Yale University Press, 2003.

Bennison, Amira K., *The Great Caliphs: The Golden Age of the Abbasid Empire*, Yale University Press, 2009.

Berger, Albrecht, 'Imperial and Ecclesiastical Processions in Constantinople', in *Byzantine Constantinople: Monuments, Topography and Everyday Life*, ed. Nevra Necipoglu, Brill Leiden, 2001.

Bergwik, Staffan, 'Elevation and Emotion: Sven Hedin's Mountain Expedition to Transhimalaya, 1906–1908', *Centaurus*, Vol. 62, No. 4 (2020), pp. 647–669.

Berkey, Jonathon, *The Formation of Islam: Religion and Society in the Near East, 600–1800*, Cambridge University Press, 2003.

Bloom, Jonathon M., *Paper Before Print: The History and Impact of Paper in the Islamic World*, Yale University Press, 2001.

Borges, Jorge Luis, & Weinberger, Eliot, '*The Thousand and One Nights*', *The Georgia Review*, Vol. 38, No. 3 (1984), pp. 564–574.

Bosworth, C.E. 'Sanawbari's Elegy on the Pilgrims Slain in the Carmathian Attack on Mecca (317/930): A Literary-Historical Study', *Arabica*, Vol. 19, No. 3 (1972), pp. 222–239.

Bosworth, C.E., *et al.*, *Encyclopaedia of Islam*, 2nd edition, 12 vols, Brill, 1960–2005.

Bosworth, C.E., *et al.*, *Historic Cities of the Muslim World*, Brill, 2007.

Bowen, H., *The Life and Times of Alí ibn 'Isà*, Cambridge University Press, 1928.

Bower, Hamilton, 'A Trip to Turkestan', *The Geographical Journal*, Vol. 5 (1895), pp. 241–257.

Brink, Stefan, & Price, Neil (eds), *The Viking World*, Routledge, 2008.

Brook, Kevin Alan, *The Jews of Khazaria*, Rowman & Littlefield, 2006.

Brown, Peter, *The World of Late Antiquity*, Thames & Hudson, 1971.

— *The Rise of Western Christendom*, Wiley-Blackwell, 2013.

Brunner, Jean-Claude, 'Charlemagne Versus the Avars: A Reign at an End', *Medieval Warfare*, Vol. 5, No. 2 (2015), pp. 27–34.

Burge, Stephen, *Angels in Islam: Jalal Al-Din Al-Suyuti's Al-Haba'ik Fi Akhbar Al-mala'ik*, Taylor & Francis, 2015.

Burns, Ross, *Damascus: A History*, Routledge, 2019.

Byron, Robert, *The Road to Oxiana*, Macmillan, 1937.

Cammann, Schuyler V.R., 'Christopher the Armenian and the Three Princes of Serendip', *Comparative Literature Studies*, Vol. 4, No. 3 (1967), pp. 229–258.

Campbell, Darryl, 'The *Capitulare de Villis*, the *Brevium Exempla*, and the Carolingian Court at Aachen', *Early Medieval Europe*, Vol. 18, No. 3 (2010), pp. 243–264.

Canepa, Matthew P., *The Two Eyes of the Earth*, University of California Press, 2009.

Catlos, Brian, *Kingdoms of Faith*, Hachette, 2018.

Chejne, Anwar G., *The Arabic Language: Its Role in History*, University of Minnesota Press, 1968.

Chin, Tamara, 'The Invention of the Silk Road, 1877', *Critical Inquiry*, Vol. 40, No. 1 (2013), pp. 194–219.

Clot, André, *Harun al-Rashid and the World of The Thousand and One Nights*, trans. John Howe, Saqi Books, 2005.

Cooperson, Michael, 'al-Ma'mun, the Pyramids and the Hieroglyphs', *Papers from the Seventh Conference of the School of Abbasid Studies*, 2004.

— *Al-Ma'mun*, One World, 2005.

Crone, Patricia, & Cook, Michael, *Hagarism: The Making of the Islamic World*, Cambridge University Press, 1977.

Crone, Patricia, & Hinds, Martin, *God's Caliph: Religious Authority in the First Centuries of Islam*, Cambridge University Press, 2003.

Curzon, George N., 1st Marquess Curzon of Kedleston, *Persia and the Persian Question*, 2 vols, Longmans, Green & Co, 1892.

Danielsson, Sarah K., *The Explorer's Roadmap to National-Socialism: Sven Hedin, Geography and the Path to Genocide*, City University of New York, 2012.

Davila, Carl, 'Fixing a Misbegotten Biography: Ziryab in the Mediterranean World', *Al-Masaq*, Vol. 21, No. 2, August 2009.

De Goeje, Michael Jan, 'De Muur van Gog en Magog', *Verslagen en Mededeelingen der Koninklijke Akademie van Wetenschappen*, Series 3, Vol. 5 (1888).

Diamond, Sarah, *Spiritual Warfare: The Politics of the Christian Right*, Black Rose Books, 1989.

Donner, Fred, *Muhammad and the Believers*, Harvard University Press, 2010.

Dunlop, D.M., *The History of the Jewish Khazars*, Schocken, 1967.

El Cheikh, Nadia Maria, *Byzantium Viewed by the Arabs*, Harvard University Press, 2004.

— 'Gender and Politics in the Harem of al-Muqtadir', in *Gender in the Early Medieval World: East and West, 300–900*, ed. Leslie Brubaker & Julia Smith, Cambridge University Press, 2004.

— 'Revisiting the Abbasid Harems', *Journal of Middle East Women's Studies*, Vol. 1, No. 3 (2005), pp. 1–19.

— 'Servants at the Gate: Eunuchs at the Court of al-Muqtadir', *Journal of the Economic and Social History of the Orient*, Vol. 48, No. 2 (2005), pp. 234–252.

El-Hibri, Tayeb, *Reinterpreting Islamic Historiography: Harun al-Rashid and the Narrative of the Abbasid Caliphate*, Cambridge University Press, 1999.

— *The Abbasid Caliphate: A History*, Cambridge University Press, 2021.

Ettinghausen, Richard, 'Studies in Muslim Iconography: I. The Unicorn', *Freer Gallery of Art Occasional Papers*, Vol. 1, No. 3 (1950).

Fichtenau, Heinrich, *The Carolingian Empire: The Age of Charlemagne*, trans. Peter Munz, Harper & Row, 1964.

Fidler, Richard, *Ghost Empire*, HarperCollins, 2016.

Frankopan, Peter, *The Silk Roads: A New History of the World*, Bloomsbury, 2015.
Fried, Johannes, *Charlemagne*, Harvard University Press, 2016.
George, Alain, 'Direct Sea Trade Between Early Islamic Iraq and Tang China: From the Exchange of Goods to the Transmission of Ideas', *Journal of the Royal Asiatic Society*, Series 3, Vol. 25, No. 4 (2015), pp. 579–624.
Giles, Lionel, *Six Centuries at Tunhuang*, The China Society, 1944.
Golden, Peter B., *Central Asia in World History*, Oxford University Press, 2011.
Gordon, Murray, *Slavery in the Arab World*, New Amsterdam, 1987.
Hadley, J., & Singmaster, D., 'Problems to Sharpen the Young', *The Mathematical Gazette*, Vol. 76, No. 475 (1992), pp. 102–126.
Harley, J.B., & Woodward, David (eds), *The History of Cartography, Volume Two, Book One: Cartography in the Traditional Islamic and South Asian Societies*, University of Chicago Press, 1992.
Hawting, Gerald, *The First Dynasty of Islam*, Routledge, 2000.
Heather, Peter, *The Fall of the Roman Empire*, Oxford University Press, 2006.
Heck, Gene W., *Charlemagne, Muhammad, and the Arab Roots of Capitalism*, Walter de Gruyter, 2006.
Hedin, Sven, *Through Asia*, Vol. 2, Methuen, 1898.
— *My Life as an Explorer*, Cassel & Co., 1926.
Hermes, Nizar F., *The [European] Other in Medieval Arabic Literature and Culture: Ninth–Twelfth Century AD*, Palgrave Macmillan, 2012.
Hitti, Phillip K., *History of the Arabs*, Macmillan, 1970.
Holland, Tom, *In the Shadow of the Sword*, Little, Brown, 2012.
Holt, P.M., *et al.* (eds), *The Cambridge History of Islam*, Vol. 1A, Cambridge University Press, 1984.
Hopkirk, Peter, *Foreign Devils on the Silk Road: The Search for Lost Cities and Treasures of Chinese Central Asia*, John Murray, 1980.
Horton, Mark, 'The Swahili Corridor', *Scientific American*, Vol. 257, No. 3 (1987), pp. 86–93.

Hourani, Albert, *A History of the Arab People*, Faber & Faber, 1991.

Hourani, George, *Arab Seafaring in the Indian Ocean in Ancient and Early Medieval Times*, Octagon, 1975.

Hoyland, Robert G., *Seeing Islam as Others Saw It*, Darwin Press, 1997.

— *In God's Path: The Arab Conquests and the Creation of an Islamic Empire*, Oxford University Press, 2015.

Humphreys, R. Stephen, *Mu'awiya ibn Abi Sufyan: From Arabia to Empire*, One World, 2006.

Irwin, Robert, *Camel*, Reaktion, 2010.

— *Ibn Khaldun: An Intellectual Biography*, Princeton University Press, 2018.

Irwin, Robert (ed.), *Night & Horses & the Desert: An Anthology of Classical Arabic Literature*, Overlook Press, 2000.

Jacobs, Justin M., 'Confronting Indiana Jones: Chinese Nationalism, Historical Imperialism, and the Criminalisation of Aurel Stein and the Raiders of Dunhuang, 1899–1944', in *China on the Margins*, ed. Sherman Cochran & Paul G. Pickowicz, Cornell University Press, 2010.

— 'Langon Warner at Dunhuang: What Really Happened?', *The Silk Road*, Vol. 11 (2013), pp. 1–11.

Johns, Jeremy, & Savage-Smith, Emilie, '*The Book of Curiosities*: A Newly Discovered Series of Islamic Maps', *Imago Mundi*, Vol. 55 (2003), pp. 7–24.

Kempf, Damien, 'Paul the Deacon's *Liber de Episcopis Mettensibus* and the Role of Metz in the Carolingian Realm', *Journal of Medieval History*, Vol. 30, No. 3 (2004), pp. 279–299.

Kennedy, Hugh, *The Prophet and the Age of the Caliphates*, Pearson Longman, 2004.

— *When Baghdad Ruled the Muslim World: The Rise and Fall of Islam's Greatest Dynasty*, Da Capo Press, 2004.

— *The Great Arab Conquests*, Da Capo Press, 2007.

Koetsier, Teun, 'On the Prehistory of Programmable Machines: Musical Automata, Looms, Calculators', *Mechanism and Machine Theory*, Vol. 36, No. 5 (2001), pp. 589–603.

Krahl, Regina, *et al.* (eds), *Shipwrecked: Tang Treasures and Monsoon Winds*, Smithsonian Books, 2011.

Langermann, Y. Tzvi, 'From My Notebooks: *Materia Medica et Magica* from Animals, Including a Long, Unknown Passage from al-Masʿūdī', *Aleph*, Vol. 11, No. 1 (2011), pp. 169–178.

Lassner, Jacob, *The Topography of Baghdad in the Early Middle Ages*, Wayne State University Press, 1970.

Lavers, Chris, *The Natural History Of Unicorns*, Granta, 2014.

Le Coq, Albert von, *Buried Treasures of Chinese Turkestan*, George Allen & Unwin, 1928.

Le Strange, Guy, 'A Greek Embassy to Baghdad in 1917 A.D.', *Journal of the Royal Asiatic Society of Great Britain & Ireland*, Vol. 29, No. 1 (1897), pp. 35–45.

— *Baghdad During the Abbasid Caliphate*, Oxford University Press, 1900.

Lewis, Bernard, *The Middle East: A Brief History of the Last 2000 Years*, Scribner, 1995.

— *The Muslim Discovery of Europe*, W.W. Norton, 2001.

—*The Arabs in History*, Oxford University Press, 2002.

Lewis, David L., *God's Crucible: Islam and the Making of Europe, 570 to 1215*, W.W. Norton, 2008.

Lindesay, William, *The Great Wall Revisited: From the Jade Gate to Old Dragon's Head*, Harvard University Press, 2008.

McIntosh, Ian S., 'Australia's Kilwa Coins Conundrum', in *Early Maritime Cultures in East Africa and the Western Indian Ocean*, ed. A. Sarathi, Archaeopress, 2018.

Mackintosh-Smith, Tim, *Arabs: A 3,000-Year History of Peoples, Tribes and Empires*, Yale University Press, 2019.

McLynn, Frank, *Genghis Khan: His Conquests, His Empire, His Legacy*, Da Capo Press, 2015.

Madelung, W., *The Succession to Muhammad*, Cambridge University Press, 1997.

Marozzi, Justin, *Baghdad: City of Peace, City of Blood*, Penguin, 2014.

Merton, Robert K., & Barber, Elinor, *The Travels and Adventures of Serendipity: A Study in Sociological Semantics and the Sociology of Science*, Princeton University Press, 2011.

Meyer, Karl E., & Brysac, Shareen Blair, *Tournament of Shadows: The Great Game and the Race for Empire in Central Asia*, Basic Books, 2006.

Milwright, Marcus, *An Introduction to Islamic Archaeology*, Edinburgh University Press, 2010.

Mirsky, Jeanette, *Sir Aurel Stein: Archaeological Explorer*, University of Chicago Press, 1977.

Morgan, Joyce, & Walters, Conrad, *Journeys on the Silk Road*, Lyons Press, 2011.

Moss, H. St L.B., *The Birth of the Middle Ages*, Oxford University Press, 1935.

Mutahhari, Murtada, *Sexual Ethics in Islam and in the Western World*, trans. Muhammad Khurshid Ali, Islamic Centre of England, 2011.

Norwich, John Julius, *Byzantium: The Early Centuries*, Penguin, 1990.

Perry, C., *et al.* (eds), *The Cambridge World History of Slavery*, Vol. 2, Cambridge University Press, 2021.

Popovic, Alexandre, *The Revolt of the African Slaves in Iraq in the 3rd/9th Century*, Marcus Weiner Publishers, 1999.

Rapoport, Yossef, *Islamic Maps*, Bodleian Library, 2020.

Rapoport, Yossef, & Savage-Smith, Emilie, *An Eleventh-Century Egyptian Guide to the Universe: The Book of Curiosities*, Brill, 2014.

Ratchnevsky, Paul, *Genghis Khan: His Life and Legacy*, trans. Thomas Haining, Blackwell, 1991.

Richards, Anne. R., & Iraj Omidvar (eds), *Historic Engagements with Occidental Cultures, Religions, Powers*, Palgrave Macmillan, 2014.

Robinson, Chase, *Abd al-Malik*, One World, 2005.

Rodinson, Maxime, *Mohammed*, Penguin, 1971.

Rong Xinjiang, *Eighteen Lectures on Dunhuang*, trans. Imre Galambos, Brill, 2013.

Savage-Smith, Emilie, 'Memory and Maps', in *Culture and Memory in Medieval Islam: Essays in Honour of Wilferd Madelung*, ed. Farhad Daftary & Josef W. Meri, I.B. Tauris, 2003.

Shahid, Irfan, *Byzantium and the Arabs in the Fourth Century*, Dumbarton Oaks, 2006.

Sharon, Moshe, *Black Banners from the East: The Establishment of the Abbasid State –Incubation of a Revolt*, Hebrew University, 1983.

Shboul, Ahmad M.H., *Al-Mas'ūdī and His World: A Muslim Humanist and His Interest in Non-Muslims*, Ithaca Press, 1979.

Shehadi, Fadlou, *Philosophies of Music in Medieval Islam*, Brill, 1995.

Silverstein, Adam, 'Enclosed Beyond Alexander's Barrier: On the Comparative Study of 'Abbāsid Culture', *Journal of the American Oriental Society*, Vol. 134, No. 2 (2014), pp. 287–306.

Sizgorich, Thomas, '"Do Prophets Come With a Sword?" Conquest, Empire, and Historical Narrative in the Early Islamic World', *The American Historical Review*, Vol. 112, No. 4 (2007), pp. 993–1015.

— 'Sanctified Violence: Monotheist Militancy as the Tie That Bound Christian Rome and Islam', *Journal of the American Academy of Religion*, Vol. 77, No. 4 (2009), pp. 895–921.

Stausberg, Michael (ed.), *Zoroastrian Rituals in Context*, Brill, 2004.

Stein, Aurel, *Sand-Buried Ruins of Khotan*, Hurst & Blackett, 1904.

— *Ruins of Desert Cathay*, 2 vols, Macmillan, 1912.

— *On Ancient Central Asian Tracks*, Pantheon, 1964.

Sykes, Ella, & Sykes, Percy, *Through Deserts and Oases of Central Asia*, Macmillan, 1920.

Talhami, Ghada Hashem, 'The Zanj Rebellion Reconsidered', *International Journal of African Historical Studies*, Vol. 10, No. 3 (1977), pp. 443–461.

Tolan, John, *et al.*, *Europe and the Islamic World: A History*, Princeton University Press, 2013.

Touati, H., & Cochrane, L., *Islam and Travel in the Middle Ages*, University of Chicago Press, 2010.

Toueir, Kassem, 'Heraqlah: A Unique Victory Monument of Harun ar-Rashid', *World Archaeology*, Vol. 14, No. 3 (1983), pp. 296–304.

Treadgold, Warren, *A History of the Byzantine State and Society*, Stanford University Press, 1997.

Truitt, E.R., *Medieval Robots: Mechanism, Magic, Nature, and Art*, University of Pennsylvania Press, 2015.

Twitchett, D., & Fairbank, J.K. (eds), *The Cambridge History of China*, Vol. 3., Cambridge University Press, 2007.

Van Berkel, M., 'The Young Caliph and His Wicked Advisors: Women and Power Politics Under Caliph Al-Muqtadir (r. 295–320/908–932)', *Al-Masāq: Islam and the Medieval Mediterranean*, Vol. 19, No. 1 (2007), pp. 3–15.

Van Berkel, M., *et al.*, *Crisis and Continuity at the Abbasid Court: Formal and Informal Politics in the Caliphate of al-Muqtadir (295–320/908–32)*, Brill, 2013.

Van Donzel, Emeri, & Schmidt, Andrea, *Gog and Magog in Early Eastern Christian and Islamic Sources*, Brill, 2009.

Von Grunebaum, G.E., *Classical Islam: A History, 600 AD to 1258 AD*, Transaction, 1970.

Wain, Alexander, & Kamali, Mohammad Hashim (eds), *The Architects of Islamic Civilization*, International Institute of Advanced Islamic Studies Malaysia, 2019.

Walker, Annabel, *Aurel Stein: Pioneer of the Silk Road*, John Murray, 1995.

Wang, Helen (ed.), *Sir Aurel Stein, Colleagues and Collections*, British Museum Research Publication 184, 2012.

Whitfield, Roderick, Whitfield, Susan, & Agnew, Neville, *Cave Temples of Mogao at Dunhuang*, Getty Conservation Institute, 2015.

Whitfield, Susan, *Life Along the Silk Road*, University of California Press, 2015.

Wickham, Chris, *The Inheritance of Rome: A History of Europe from 400 to 1000*, Viking Penguin, 2009.

Wiet, Gaston, *Baghdad: Metropolis of the Abbasid Caliphate*, University of Oklahoma Press, 1971.

Zadeh, Travis, *Mapping Frontiers Across Medieval Islam*, Bloomsbury, 2017.

IMAGE CREDITS

Maps by Alex Hotchin

6 Wikimedia Commons; **55** Wikimedia Commons; **73** Guy Le Strange, *Baghdad During the Abbasid Caliphate;* **92** Wikimedia Commons; **95** Wikimedia Commons; **99** William Muir, *The Caliphate: Its Rise, Decline, and Fall*, John Grant, 1924: Wikimedia Commons; **118** Wikimedia Commons; **124** James Ford Bell Library, University of Minnesota; **143** Wikimedia Commons; **147** Ibn Hawqal, *The Face of the Earth*, **977**: Wikimedia Commons; **151** Idrisi, *Book of Pleasant Journeys into Faraway Lands*, 1154: Wikimedia Commons; **162** Wikimedia Commons; **167** Idrisi, *Book of Pleasant Journeys into Faraway Lands*, 1154: Wikimedia Commons; **177** Smithsonian sogdians.si.edu/sidebars/marc-aurel-stein; **183** Aurel Stein, *Ruins of Desert Cathay*, Vol. 2; **186** Aurel Stein, *Ruins of Desert Cathay*, Vol. 2; **188** Wikimedia Commons; **191** Wikimedia Commons; **195** Wikimedia Commons; **199** Aurel Stein, *Ruins of Desert Cathay*, Vol. 2; **205** Wikimedia Commons; **210** Richard Fidler; **213** James and Lucy Ho; **220** Wikimedia Commons; **231** Nabataea.net; **242** Wikimedia Commons; **257** Powerhouse Museum, Sydney; **260** Rod Waddington, Wikimedia Commons; **315** Wikimedia Commons; **322** Numista.com; **339** National Palace Museum, Taipei: Wikimedia Commons; **345** Wikimedia Commons; **352** Rashid ad-Din, *Jami al-Tawarikh*: Wikimedia Commons; **383** Public Domain

INDEX

Note: Page numbers in *italics* refer to illustrations.